*PROUST AND RILKE*

# Proust and Rilke

## The Literature
## of Expanded Consciousness

### E. F. N. JEPHCOTT

BARNES & NOBLE BOOKS · NEW YORK
(a division of Harper & Row Publishers, Inc.)

Published in the U.S.A. 1972 by
HARPER & ROW PUBLISHERS, INC.
BARNES & NOBLE IMPORT DIVISION

ISBN 06 4933156

© E. F. N. Jephcott 1972

Printed in Great Britain

TO
PAUL ROUBICZEK

# CONTENTS

# Foreword

THIS book is addressed to two kinds of reader. It is intended, of course, for those for whom the value of literature and its study is self-evident, and it is my hope that specialised students of Proust and Rilke will find something of interest in these pages. But although this is a detailed treatment of two writers, it is written also for those for whom literature and literary criticism are by no means self-explanatory or self-justifying phenomena. In a world in which the study of man, the traditional preserve of the humanities, is becoming more and more the concern of positive sciences, of psychology, sociology and linguistics, literature is beginning to appear to many as an archaism, irrelevant to our vital concerns, at best a luxury. How can an approach to reality through the individual imagination be anything other than subjective, unreliable, lacking in rigour?

In a situation where such questions can – and should – be asked, there is a need not only for books which continue the work of scrutiny and evaluation within the established boundaries of literary criticism. There is a need also to re-examine the scope and foundations of the discipline, to raise the questions: what is literature, what is it for, why is it written? It is to readers who have these questions – unformulated, perhaps, but persistent – in their minds that this book may, I hope, have something to say. For it will argue that literature is indeed relevant to our most vital interests, since it concerns itself with the most immediate level of our experience, our consciousness; and that an imaginative work is the most rigorous possible means of approaching the reality with which it is concerned, since the laws it embodies, which can be objectively explored, necessarily reproduce those governing the quality and structure of our consciousness.

The purpose of this study, then, is to explore and reveal these laws, and in so doing to show how literature can not only elucidate, but also enhance, the nature of our consciousness. A book of this kind must clearly try to achieve a rigour adequate to that of its subject. It must proceed by logical argument rather than by rhetoric, and its author must remain aware that literary works are made up, not of ideas or intentions, but of words, so that his argument must be supported at all points by the actual words of the writers under discussion. Since their works are to be studied here primarily in translation, this presents a particular difficulty. The existing translations of Proust and Rilke in English, notably those by C. K. Scott-Moncrieff and J. B. Leishman

A*

respectively, are rightly regarded as classics. They can be read as literary creations of a high order in their own right. But to achieve this effect in the different language the translators have had necessarily to depart in places from the literal wording of the original. For this reason their translations are not suited to the entirely different purpose of this book, which is to derive an argument from the exact words of the writers, generally using very short quotations.

I have had, then, to make my own translations, in which I have tried to convey the literal sense of the original as exactly as possible without entirely forfeiting its literary quality. In poetry translations I have reproduced what I could of the rhythm and 'colour' of Rilke's language. When quoting longer passages of poetry, I thought it indispensable to give them in the original language, for the 'look' of the words on the page, even for those whose knowledge of German is imperfect, plays an important part in conveying their meaning. In these cases I have accompanied the text with an English transliteration.

My particular thanks are due, therefore, to the publishers who have granted me permission to make these translations: to Éditions Gallimard and Insel Verlag, the publishers of Proust and Rilke, and to Chatto and Windus and the Hogarth Press, who publish the English translations. I am also indebted to Weidenfeld and Nicolson and Dobson Books for permission to publish my translations from *Jean Santeuil* and *Les Plaisirs et les Jours* respectively, and to Éditions Gallimard for permission to quote a short extract in French from *Jean Santeuil* (© Éditions Gallimard 1952).

The incalculable help and encouragement which I have received in preparing this book are acknowledged in the dedication.

E. J.

# Introduction

THERE are moments when consciousness seems to expand – when the mind takes in the world with a rare and strange intensity. Such moments – so this book will attempt to show – are the source of the impulse to create a work of art. We are concerned, then, with the fundamental question why men create art. But the broader and more general the question, the more precise and particular – though comprehensive – must be the evidence on which an answer is based. The method adopted here is therefore not that of a wide-ranging survey, but of a close study in depth of two major writers in a specific period. The conclusions flowing from this detailed study are, however, far-reaching. For it will be argued that the phenomenon of 'expanded consciousness' is centrally important not only for the understanding of art, but for that of human experience in general.

Despite this importance, the moment of expanded consciousness has received little attention from critics. Exact terminology for describing it has not yet been invented. The term 'expanded consciousness' itself can do no more than point to a general area of subject matter; in the course of our study a more specific vocabulary will have to be developed. The term which will be used here to denote the experience in question is the 'privileged moment'. There are others which might have been chosen: 'epiphanies', 'visionary moments', 'timeless moments', and so on. Perhaps we should now add the 'psychedelic moment'. But the shortcoming of all these is that, where they are not distorted by controversy, they are too narrow. They concentrate on this or that aspect of the experience and, in so doing, pre-judge our interpretation of it. The 'privileged moment' – certainly the most colourless of the possible terms, is just for this reason the best for our purposes: if we leave aside as irrelevant the social connotations attaching to the term, it is ideally pale and neutral. It will accept without resistance the comprehensive meaning which is needed for our study, and which will be built up from an examination of concrete examples of the experience.

Kenneth Clark, in a lecture on the subject of these experiences, has called them by yet another name: 'moments of vision'. But, as he acknowledges, this term is limited in its application to visual perception and painting. We cannot use it here; but his description of the experience itself will serve well as a preliminary definition of the privileged moment:

We can all remember those flashes when the object at which we are gazing seems to detach itself from the habitual flux of impressions and
becomes intensely clear and important for us. We may not experience
these illuminations very often in our busy adult lives, but they were
common in our childhood, and given half a chance we could achieve
them still.[1]

The relevance of such moments to painting is, perhaps, evident. But
their application to literature, though less obvious, is not for that
reason less deep and pervasive. In discussing literature from the point
of view of these moments, however, we shall be concerned also with its
relation to the other arts.

The reasons for taking Proust and Rilke as subjects for this study are
several. In the first place, they are both writers of unquestioned stature,
on whose work reliable and widely-acceptable conclusions can be
based. Secondly, in their work the implications of the privileged
moment appear with particular clarity. Thirdly, in comparing them it
can be shown that the importance of the privileged moment is not confined to any single literary *genre*, and, at the same time, that writers
can have specifically literary qualities in common which are more
fundamental than the *genre* in which they write. Finally, there are two
main reasons for choosing to discuss two writers rather than one:
not only because a comparative study might give wider application to
the conclusions drawn, but because more light can be thrown on individual writers by this means than if they are studied separately. This
second reason is, of course, the only final justification of the comparative method.

Before enlarging on what the subject of this book is, it will perhaps
be as well to say what it is not. It is not a study of the influence of one
writer on the other, or of contacts between them. On the contrary, a
further main reason for choosing these two writers is that such contacts
and influences were at a minimum. In their absence the common
features resulting from the influence of the privileged moment can be
more clearly seen. Fundamental to this approach is the belief that a
writer does not derive his work from other writers, but from his own
experience. It will be seen repeatedly in this study that there is only
one way in which a writer can 'influence' another who is genuinely
creative: by showing him by example how to achieve something which
is already latent in his work. The 'influence' acts as a catalyst in the
reaction between the writer's experience and his creative impulse, but
is in no way present as a constituent in the final product. Within these
limits 'influences' can, of course, serve a useful if minor purpose in
making it easier for the critic, as for the writer himself, to 'read off' the
tendencies inherent in his work.

The reaction just mentioned – between the writer's experience and his creative impulse – is the subject of this book. We shall be involved, therefore, in a discussion both of the writer's life and of his work, but of his life only in so far as it is seen passing directly into his work. This book might be called a comparative 'creative biography', or 'inner biography', of the two writers. It concentrates on the area of their lives in which their experience came under the influence of their creative impulse and was transformed into art. It argues that this area can only be located by reference to the privileged moment, and indeed that the creative impulse might be defined as the attempt to impose on experience the qualities of the privileged moment. The evolution of the reaction between the writers' experience and the creative impulse is traced throughout their development. For this purpose, the comparative method is particularly suitable. It is able, through its 'binocular vision', to focus more accurately and more consistently on the required area of experience than would be possible by other means.

This study therefore takes the form of a parallel, chronological analysis of the creative development of two writers. But for the general conclusions drawn from it to be valid, the privileged moment must be shown to be not merely a peculiarity of Proust and Rilke, but a phenomenon occurring widely in human experience, or at least in that of artists. How far it is also open to others will be left to the reader to decide. In the opening chapter, therefore, a general definition of the privileged moment is derived from descriptions of the experience given by a number of writers who lived in broadly the same period as Proust and Rilke.

How far would the two writers themselves have approved of the treatment to which we are about to subject their work? We shall never know; but though Proust expressed horror at the thought of scholars dissecting his manuscripts and drawing conclusions from them that would invariably be wrong, he did also write this about the primary function of the critic:

> He would try to reconstruct the singular spiritual life of a writer haunted by such special realities, whose inspiration was the measure in which he was granted the vision of these realities, his talent the measure in which he was able to recreate them in his work, his morality, finally, the instinct which ... impelled him to sacrifice to the need to perceive and reproduce them, so that a clear and lasting vision of them might be assured, all his pleasures, all his duties and even his life.[2]

It is hoped that the following chapters will go some way towards satisfying Proust's requirements, and will show in so doing that the 'realities' he speaks of are indeed those revealed by the privileged moment.

# CHAPTER ONE
## *Privileged Moments in Literature*

WHAT is a 'privileged moment'? Before the study of Proust and Rilke can begin, an answer must be given to this question. The privileged moment is particularly difficult to define; it is an experience which, by its nature, can scarcely be described in abstract terms or at second hand. It will therefore be necessary in this chapter to quote extensively from descriptions of privileged moments by a number of writers who are qualified to give a reliable account of their experience. From their descriptions a generalised conception of the experience will be drawn, and at the same time an explanation will be offered for a number of its principal characteristics.

A starting-point for this study is to be found in Baudelaire's introduction to the privileged moment in his essay 'The Poem of Hashish'. There are days, he writes, when we wake up with 'a young and vigorous genius'. We have hardly opened our eyes when we are impressed by the strong relief, precise outlines and rich colours in the world around us. The moral world too seems full of new illuminations. Compared to the 'heavy shadows of common everyday existence', such states can justly be called paradisiac, Baudelaire asserts, but they are rare and fleeting. And their most curious feature is that they occur without any visible or definable cause.

Baudelaire has no hesitation in saying that man has always held this exceptional 'enthusiasm of the senses and the mind' to be his 'highest good'.[1] This statement may seem extreme, but it is supported in the writings of other artists. In Flaubert's correspondence, for example, we find the following: 'I have sometimes glimpsed (in my great days of sunlight), by the glow of an enthusiasm which made my skin tingle from my heels to the roots of my hair, a state of the soul thus superior to life, for which fame would be nothing, and happiness itself useless.' Such emotions are experienced unexpectedly without any external cause and are even, Flaubert emphasises, 'independent of all personal factors and all human relationships'.[2]

Such is the case, too, with the 'joyous and revivifying moments' experienced by Hofmannsthal's Lord Chandos – whose 'Letter to Francis Bacon'* is essentially a transposition of Hofmannsthal's own situation – moments, in an otherwise barren existence, when 'something nameless and almost unnamable' reveals itself to him. An object in his everyday surroundings is suddenly filled like a vessel with 'an overflowing flood

* See p. 300 for conversion-table giving original titles.

of higher life'.[3] At the same time, a subtle emotion fills Chandos 'from the roots of the hair to the marrow of the heels' – the repetition here of the words used by Flaubert to describe this sensation is worth noting. But for Hofmannsthal too this is a rare and unpredictable occurrence, totally unrelated to common feeling or to 'comprehensible human thought processes'.[4]

Paul Valéry describes certain moments distinguished from ordinary existence by a 'superior emotion'. He calls these moments 'the purest states of the self'[5] and sees them as basic to the poet's experience. But, like the privileged moments described by Baudelaire, Flaubert and Hofmannsthal, 'this "poetic state" is perfectly irregular, inconstant, involuntary, fragile, and we lose it, as we obtain it, by accident'.[6]

The privileged moment is a central theme of Sartre's novel *Nausea*. Antoine Roquentin's existence is even more arid and monotonous than that of Lord Chandos, but it is illuminated at rare intervals by moments of inexplicable abundance: 'for me there is neither Monday nor Sunday, there is a disorderly jumble of days and then, suddenly, an illumination like this'.[7] Roquentin has his own term for these experiences: he calls them 'adventures'. One such experience described at length consists of walking down a street across a square to a café window. Outwardly, this hardly seems an adventure, but it is Roquentin's inner state that justifies his use of the term: 'I seem to have reached the summit of my happiness. In Marseilles, Shanghai, Meknès, what didn't I do to get a feeling as intense as this? Today I no longer expect anything, I'm on my way home at the end of an empty Sunday: it's there.'[8]

These introductory descriptions give some indication why the experiences in question have been called 'privileged' moments. They occur without warning or apparent cause, as a kind of arbitrary gift of grace; and they involve a state of being which, according to those who experience it, is immeasurably superior to everyday life.

If the privileged moments described by these five writers are now compared in more detail, further common features emerge. In the first place, all the experiences begin in a similar way – with a change in visual perception. In the passage already referred to, Baudelaire pointed to the 'admirably strong reliefs, precise outlines and rich colours' which we see around us. The act of seeing is not only more intense than usual, but also more pleasurable. The case is similar with Flaubert's accounts of the experience: 'Often, catching sight of something or other – a drop of water, a shell, a hair – you stopped and stood quite still, your gaze transfixed, your heart opened.'[9] A visual impression strikes the onlooker with such force that he is momentarily dispossessed of all his everyday purposes and faculties; such, too, is an experience described by Valéry. Crossing London Bridge he paused to look at the swirling water: 'My eyes stopped me short; I leant on the balustrade, as if compelled by a vice. The voluptuous pleasure of seeing held me like a thirst, drinking in the rich, delightfully composed light, of which I could not have enough.'[10] A visual object – this time a white-painted post ahead of him as he walks – exerts a similar fascination over Roquentin at the beginning of his 'adventure': 'That dark shape, slowly growing brighter, makes an extraordinary impression on me: when it's quite bright, quite white, I shall stop, just beside it, and then the adventure will begin.'[11] Likewise for Hofmannsthal a heightened visual awareness of an everyday object – a watering-can, a harrow left behind in a field, a dog in the sun – marks the beginning of a privileged moment:

> Any one of these objects, and the thousands of others like them which the eye normally takes for granted and passes over with indifference, can suddenly, in a moment which I am quite powerless to call up at will, take on for me a sublime and moving aspect that all words seem too poor to express.[12]

In all these experiences an everyday object is seen to detach itself from the background of awareness where it normally passes unnoticed, and to begin to exist intensely in its own right. It is not only experienced more vividly in terms of sensation: it also seems to 'mean' more. Its meaning, which is now out of all proportion to its everyday function, can no longer, as Hofmannsthal indicates in the passage just quoted, be expressed by conventional language. Baudelaire experiences this heightening of meaning during privileged moments so intensely that 'the whole depth of life is revealed in the spectacle, however ordinary it may be, that meets one's gaze'.[13]

Paul Valéry gives valuable insight into the nature of this heightened sense of meaning. For him the privileged moment is a state of 'absence', in that the man enjoying it no longer exists in the world where things have their normal meanings: 'He falls abruptly out of a world made up almost entirely of *signs*, into another world almost entirely formed of *significances*'. By signs, Valéry means the abstract concepts which in normal life enable us to recognise objects, and thereby to orientate ourselves in a known reality. In a privileged moment these concepts disappear: 'Everything suddenly ceases to have its ordinary effect, and what we guide ourselves by tends to vanish. There are no longer any abbreviations and practically no names on things.'

For Valéry there is a direct connection between the reduction in the conceptual knowledge present in consciousness and the increase in the intensity of sensation: 'the power of our senses gets the better of what we know. Knowledge is dispersed like a dream.'[14] By following up the

implications of this and other observations of Valéry's, we can take
the analysis of the privileged moment some stages further.

Recognition involves abstract thought. When an object is recognised, it is grouped by the mind in a general category of similar objects.
The knowledge of its name and function makes it unnecessary to give
the object itself, as a particular thing, further attention; it recedes
into the neutral background of everyday awareness. Valéry calls this
faculty whereby objects are identified and then expelled from awareness 'our great power of ordered forgetting'.[15]

The recognition of objects, though normally almost instantaneous,
is a creative process. The mind, or imagination, combines the sensations it receives until is has built up a recognisable whole. As an object
is perceived, Valéry notes, 'everything moves from one degree to the
next, in the imagination'. Awareness is progressively heightened – that
is, sensations are intensified and impressions take on increasing interest
and importance – until they are recognised as 'meaning' something: an
object, a movement.

At this point the creative activity of the mind comes to an end. Once
it is recognised, an object can be named and, if necessary, used for a
practical purpose. Direct perception gives way to abstract thought
and action. A 'significance' becomes a 'sign', in the terms used by
Valéry in 'London Bridge'. In this way recognition limits the intensity
of perception.

But if the power of recognising and naming things, that is, the
faculty of conceptual thought, were suspended, the creative activity of
the mind during perception would continue indefinitely. The intensity
of awareness, the degree of significance seen in objects, would be
limited only by the power of the imagination itself. Valéry describes
what would then be experienced, for example, in contemplating the
things in a room:

> the objects are *active* like the flame of the lamp: the armchair consumes
> itself where it stands, the table describes itself so quickly that it remains
> motionless, the curtains flow without end, continuously.[16]

The existence of objects is seen no longer as a state, but as a process
having the intensity of combustion; despite their stillness, they seem to
exist actively, dynamically. To describe them, words expressing static
posture are replaced by those expressing movement: in Valéry's description, curtains no longer hang, they flow. Baudelaire, in a prose-
poem entitled 'The Double Room', uses similar terms to describe the
heightened awareness of hanging drapery: 'Muslin pours down in front
of the windows and the bed; it gushes in snowy cascades.'[17]

The intense activity of the mind, unchecked by recognition, produces a constant heightening of awareness; this is the characteristic

experience of the privileged moment. Sensations are taken in more and more avidly, objects seem constantly to outgrow themselves in intensity and significance:

> Things seem to shine more and more brightly in an ever-growing light; it is as if the excited flowers, in the intensity of their colours, are burning with the desire to rival the blue of the sky, and the scents, made visible by the heat, are rising to the heavens like smoke.[18]

This is taken from another of Baudelaire's prose-poems. Flaubert, at the beginning of a privileged moment, describes a similar intensification: 'It was the hour when shadows are long. The rocks seemed bigger, the waves greener. The sky seemed to be expanding and the whole face of nature changing.'[19]

Of course, in these descriptions, which represent only the initial phase of the privileged moment, objects are still recognised and named. But their names seem less important than their individual quality of being as they are, their 'essence'. All general notions seem inadequate to express the particular sense of joy and meaning they convey. 'Certain men,' Valéry observes, 'feel a special, voluptuous delight in the *individuality* of things. They have a predilection, in each object, for this quality of being unique.'[20]

As general notions vanish and each object begins to appear unique, so too that object appears more interesting, more valuable. The paradoxical truth emerges that things seem to have more meaning, not less, when they cannot be recognised.

But the intensification of sense-impressions is not the only way in which the privileged moment differs from normal experience. The change in consciousness affects not only the way objects are perceived, but the way they are related together.

In normal life the things surrounding us are related to us and to each other by the use we can make of them in our immediate projects. During a privileged moment these everyday functional relationships disappear, and are replaced by a far more complex and intense system of analogies not normally perceived. Now all parts of the visual field are seen to form a pattern, and in addition there are 'correspondences', to use Baudelaire's term, between impressions taken in by different senses. Baudelaire treats these analogies as an integral part of the privileged moment: 'who has not known those admirable hours, ... when the senses, more attentive, perceive more reverberant sensations ... when sounds have a musical timbre, when colours speak, and perfumes tell of worlds of ideas?'[21]

This network of analogies gives to awareness during a privileged moment a far greater unity than it has in normal life. Each part of a scene seems necessary to all the others. Roquentin, during his 'adventure', remarks: 'I don't know whether the world has suddenly drawn more tightly together or whether such an intense unity between sounds and shapes is put there by me: I can't even imagine any of the things around me being other than it is.'[22] Valéry expresses the same experience in somewhat different terms: the privileged moment involves the perception of a 'world, or complete system of relationships', in which objects, while remaining themselves, enter a new relation to the laws of our sensibility. They seem, he says, to change value: 'They call one another, they are associated quite differently than under normal conditions. They become ... "musicalised", commensurable, resonant with one another.'[23]

In talking of a 'musical' quality in the experience, Valéry introduces an important new concept into this discussion. The interrelatedness of all parts of awareness during a privileged moment gives a sense of musical harmony, and this harmony not only involves the relations perceived in the outside world: it extends to include the relation between the inner and outer worlds. The self becomes immersed and lost in the scene contemplated, as in Baudelaire's prose-poem 'The Artist's Confiteor': 'All these things' – the sea, the sky, a distant sail, the sound of the waves – 'are thinking through me or I through them (for in the vastness of reverie the "self" is quickly lost); they are thinking, I say, but musically, picturesquely, without quibbles, syllogisms or deductions.'[24]

Baudelaire here associates the musical quality of the experience with the absence of logical thought processes. Whereas the rational mind breaks the world down into its elements, here reality is experienced, like music, as a harmonious totality. The initial intensity of sensation and meaning communicated by a single object is now diffused and muted by the expansion of awareness to embrace a universal harmony covering the whole spectacle of existence.

Heightened awareness suffused with a rich musical harmony: this is the characteristic tonality of the privileged moment. In 'The Double Room' Baudelaire defines this dual quality of consciousness as follows: 'Here everything has the sufficient clarity and the delightful obscurity of harmony'.[25] There is a similar formulation in 'The Artist's Confiteor': sensations have 'a vagueness which does not exclude intensity'.

There may seem to be a paradox in this coupling of intensity with a dreamy vagueness; in fact, however, both qualities spring from the same source: the absence from the mind of precise intellectual notions. We have already seen how this intensifies sensation, and it is self-evident that it should produce also a feeling of vagueness and disorientation.

In Hofmannsthal's poetry, too the intensification of awareness is accompanied by a sense of 'dream': for the man experiencing a privileged moment 'gulfs of infinite dream noiselessly open between two glances'.[26] Valéry's term 'absence' has similar implications. It does not mean absent-mindedness or vague day-dreaming; the poetic 'reverie' involves an expansion and intensification, not a relaxation, of consciousness. As one critic writes: 'Valéry's word "absence" can be replaced by terms such as "sleep", "reverie", but also by "extreme concentration".'[27]

Two distinct qualities have now emerged as principal characteristics of the privileged moment. The first is the intensification of sensation, the second the unification of awareness. Both these phenomena have been seen to be related to the absence of abstract thought from consciousness. Abstract thought appears from the passages studied to be that which limits the intensity and unity of consciousness by interpreting impressions in terms of concepts serving the needs of practical life. But this conceptualising faculty does not seem, from the descriptions discussed here, to be the only, or the first, of the mechanisms by which the mind gives order and unity to experience. In the absence of rational thought another, apparently autonomous, faculty is still active, and indeed its degree of activity seems to be in inverse proportion to that of the conceptualising faculty. Baudelaire calls the former power 'imagination', and sees it as a capacity, not for fantasy, but for analysis and synthesis.[28] This faculty, working autonomously, appears to be capable of producing in awareness a degree of unity and intensity far in excess of the needs of practical life.

In discussing the unity experienced during a privileged moment, we have so far been mainly concerned with visual, spatial unity. This is no doubt because visual impressions are the most prominent aspect of the world of the senses. But other orders of sensation were also involved. Roquentin felt a unity existing between sounds as well as forms, Baudelaire wrote that 'sounds have a musical timbre', and Valéry too stressed the musical quality of the experience. The analogy with music indicates unity in time as well as in space. In heightened awareness moments of time follow one another with the same necessity and reciprocal significance as the notes of a melody.

This is the aspect of the experience which is primarily implied by Roquentin's term 'adventure'. During a privileged moment, as during an adventure, intervals of time and events, even if these events, in Roquentin's case, are only brief impressions received while walking in a town, are connected by the sense that 'something is happening', that one moment leads on inevitably to the next in a chain of evolving significance. During his 'adventure' Roquentin says 'I am as happy as the hero of a novel'. Like the hero, or rather, like the hero as he appears to the reader, Roquentin knows that 'there is something waiting for me' – 'something which needs me in order to take place'.[29] The moment in which he exists is linked to those which will follow it, like an episode in a novel or a note in a piece of music, by a chain of necessity.

Roquentin sums up this experience by saying: 'The sense of adventure is, quite simply, the feeling of the irreversibility of time.' For him this feeling that a certain order of moments is necessary and irreversible is normally lacking in experience. The future is apprehended vaguely as absence and possibility, not as a necessity growing constantly and dynamically out of the present. 'All in all,' he observes, 'the passing of time is something we talk a lot about but hardly ever see. We see a woman, we think that she will be old, only we do not *see* her growing older. But, at some moments, we seem to *see* her growing older and to feel ourselves ageing with her: that is the feeling of adventure.'[30]

During such moments, the sense of passing time becomes almost palpable. Georges Poulet, analysing a privileged moment which occurs in *Madame Bovary*, writes of a 'dilated duration', in which the *tempo* of things seems to have become slower and therefore more perceptible. Time can be felt passing like a breeze; 'there is nothing but a general moving onwards, both of things and of the sentient being, with the sense of an absolute homogeneity between the different elements composing the moment'.[31] In other words, the awareness of moments in time is heightened like that of objects in space. And in the case of time as in that of space this heightening of awareness can be explained with reference to the reduced rôle of abstract thought in consciousness.

A moment of time cannot be experienced in isolation: it must be recognised in relation to other moments as an object is recognised in relation to other objects. The recognition of moments, like that of objects, is a creative act of the mind. But this creative act ceases as soon as a unifying notion has been discovered and the moment identified. As with objects, the unifying notions most readily found are the most familiar, the most practical, the most abstract. A walk in familiar surroundings demands less conscious attention than one in unfamiliar surroundings. A walk to a known destination is less vividly experienced than one without destination. The knowledge: 'I am walking in a certain street to a certain place for a certain purpose', is sufficient to give the moments of the walk coherence; no further creative act of the mind is necessary.

But if this knowledge were taken away, the connection between moments would no longer be taken for granted; it would have to be created by the mind. No longer the continuity of a simple practical purpose, but that of a complex physical environment, embracing both the inner and outer worlds as in Poulet's description, would be needed to establish the union of one moment with the next. No sensation which unites these moments could now be ignored; nothing is irrelevant, attention is heightened, awareness is dilated. Each moment is experienced to the full as an abundance of sensations constantly issuing from and giving birth to an abundance of sensations:

> I am born of each moment for each moment ... I BREATHE ... Each time, always for the first time, I open those inner wings which beat true time. They carry him who is from him who was to him who will be.[32]

In these terms Valéry describes a privileged moment in *My Faust*. Baudelaire experiences time with the same intensity in 'The Double Room', where he writes of 'this supreme life that I know now, that I am savouring minute by minute, second by second'.

But such abstract notions as minutes and seconds, with their implications of succession and separation, are inadequate and foreign to this concrete experience of time. As the past, the present and the future merge into a single evolving totality, the intervals of time disappear altogether: 'No! there are no more minutes, there are no more seconds! Time has disappeared; Eternity is reigning, an eternity of bliss!'[33] Likewise in the poem of Hofmannsthal's already referred to, the short space of time the privileged moment lasted 'seemed eternal time'.

It may seem inconsistent that the heightened awareness of time should lead to the disappearance of time and a state of 'eternity'. We find a similar apparent contradiction when Flaubert writes of the soul's desire during a privileged moment 'to transform itself endlessly under the sun of eternity.'[34] Transformation implies movement and time, whereas eternity implies their absence. Likewise in the passage of *My Faust* just quoted, each breath seems to be the first, as if the past, and therefore time, did not exist. But at the same time the lungs 'beat true time' and 'carry him who is from him who was to him who will be'.

These contradictions are resolved if it is realised that the word time is being used to describe two different experiences: everyday time, and the 'true time' of the privileged moment. In everyday life, as we saw, moments are related to one another abstractly, in terms of practical objectives and preoccupations. Awareness constantly gravitates away from the impressions of the 'here and now' towards a practical goal in the future, or to other moments implied by these preoccupations. Time experienced in this way necessarily impoverishes the awareness of the present.

But in a privileged moment, where practical preoccupations are absent, this impoverished awareness of time disappears; in this sense the experience is timeless. But this 'timelessness' is really another, less abstract, way of experiencing time. The present moment is now connected to other moments concretely, in particular through analogies or continuities of sensation. Past and future are no longer experienced as absent and separate from the present, but as an integral part of it.

These connecting sensations are most likely to exist between consecutive moments. But they could relate the present to a moment in the more distant past, if the past moment happened to present analogies of sensation more striking than those offered by the immediately contiguous moments. The concretely experienced present might, therefore, include a sense of the depth of the past, also experienced concretely through sensation. Such a sense of the past plays a part in hashish-dreams described by Baudelaire, who, incidentally, treats drug-induced states and 'natural' privileged moments as virtually identical as far as the sensations involved are concerned. But this study is not concerned with drug experiences as such, except where they illuminate aspects of the privileged moment, as they do in this case. Baudelaire's hashish-dreamer has the sense of the past discussed above: he experiences 'time grown to monstrous proportions ... with a certain melancholy delight he looks into the depths of the years, launching himself boldly into infinite perspectives.'[35]

Such perspectives of the past are not common, however, in the privileged moments described by the five writers under discussion in this chapter. More generally, their experiences involve the union of consecutive moments through sensations continued or repeated from one moment to the next. In this connection it is significant that the experience of 'true time' in Valéry's My Faust is bound up with the act of breathing, and that Roquentin experiences the 'irreversibility of time' while walking. Breathing and walking both involve regularly repeated organic sensations. These sensations are not normally noticed, but during a privileged moment when the mind is searching for sense-impressions identical in one moment and the next, such regular and therefore predictable sensations take on a new significance. They provide a ready-made temporal structure, a system of relationships which the mind can isolate more easily than those between sensations occurring irregularly.

Breathing and walking and similar organic functions can therefore give unity to awareness in a privileged moment as rhythm does while one is listening to music. And in certain forms of the privileged moment the unity produced by organic rhythms can be so highly developed that all other sensations are disregarded. Valéry describes an experience of this kind; walking in Paris, he was suddenly 'seized' by a rhythm which 'imposed itself' on him. It was soon joined by a second rhythm, and between the two a complex interplay was set up: 'This combined the movements of my legs as I walked with some song or other I was murmuring, or rather, which was being murmured *through me*.' This experience occurred like other privileged moments without any apparent cause, and while it lasted Valéry was 'absent', that is, unaware of the everyday world: 'After about twenty minutes the spell broke abruptly, leaving me walking beside the Seine ...'[36]

This is not a typical privileged moment because it involves no visual impressions; it is concerned with time rather than with space. Even here, however, the spatial aspect is not entirely excluded. For even a structure created purely in time, by rhythm or music, suggests a spatial dimension, a geometry of related points perceived simultaneously by the mind. As Baudelaire observes: 'Music gives the idea of space.'[37] Time and space are both involved inseparably in the privileged moment, and in the statement which may be taken as Baudelaire's definition of the experience, both are mentioned equally: 'There are moments of existence when time and space are deepened, and the feeling of existence immensely augmented.'[38]

In addition to the changed perception of time and space, Baudelaire's definition draws attention to another major feature of the privileged moment: the change in the feeling of existence. Normally the fact that one exists is taken for granted and remains little more than an abstract notion. But now it becomes intensely important in its own right, as in the privileged moment described by Valéry's Faust:

> This is a supreme state, in which everything is summed up by living, and which, by the smile it brings to my lips, refuses all questions and all answers ... LIVING! ... I am feeling, breathing my masterpiece.[39]

Life as experienced during such moments is quite different from what is normally meant by the abstractions 'life' or 'existence': 'What is generally called life, even at its happiest and most exhilarating, has nothing in common with this supreme life that I know now.'[40] These words are from Baudelaire's 'Double Room'; Roquentin, too, has an intensified feeling of his own existence: 'at last I am having an adventure and when I ask myself about it I see that what is happening is that I am myself and that I am here; it is I who am cleaving the night'.

This heightened feeling of existence does not, however, involve a greater awareness of the self as a separate individuality. For the notion of a self – of a separate subjective identity – is an abstract concept like any other, which is indispensable in practical life but is absent from awareness during a privileged moment. Like other concepts, the notion of a particular individuality limits awareness. As Roquentin's feeling

of existence reaches its height, it overflows the limits of his individuality: 'I am walking alone, but I am like a horde descending on a town.'[41]
Like Baudelaire's hashish-dreamer, he lives 'several men's lives in the
space of an hour'.[42]

As the notion of a separate self disappears, consciousness expands to
embrace external things in the same way as it does the inner content of
the mind. The physical and mental spheres are perceived as identical
or at least inseparable. Valéry's Faust affirms during his privileged
moment: 'the slightest glance, the least sensation, the smallest acts and
functions of life have for me now the same dignity as the plans and
inner voices of my thoughts'. This equal awareness of the inner and
outer worlds can extend even to things outside the direct compass of
the senses: to see truly one part of existence is to see any other part,
even to see the whole of existence. 'TO SEE', Faust realises, 'therefore
means to see something else as well; to see what is means to see what is
possible ...'[43] Roquentin, during his 'adventure', also sees 'something
else as well':

> There are, at this moment, ships blaring music at sea; lights going on in
> all the cities of Europe; communists and Nazis shooting at each other in
> Berlin streets, there are men without work on the streets of New York,
> women in hot rooms are at their dressing-tables putting mascara on
> their eyelashes.

Roquentin might at any other time have known theoretically that
innumerable events of this kind are happening together in a given
moment. But they only really 'exist' for him when he becomes aware
of them in terms of his own existence. At this moment, each of the
actions listed above 'answers each step I take, each beat of my heart'.[44]

This almost cosmic apprehension of existence is an extreme development of the privileged moment. But it is shared by Lord
Chandos, for whom not only objects visibly present, but absent,
imagined realities, could be invaded by the 'flood of divine feeling'
referred to earlier. The thought of exterminating a colony of rats on
his estate fills him suddenly with the panic of dying creatures, the
sharp smell of poison in the musty cellar; and also with the feelings of
the inhabitants of Alba Longa, in the last hours before the destruction
of the town, as described in a passage of Livy: 'this I bore within me,
and at the same time Carthage in flames; but it was more, it was more
godlike, more animal; and it was the present, the fullest, most sublime
present'.[45]

Words such as 'the present' and 'existence', like the ideas 'time' and
'self', are abstract and problematical terms; to establish their meaning
philosophical discussion is necessary and not always sufficient. But

during a privileged moment what they mean becomes simple and indeed self-evident. Abstract discussion is no longer necessary; the meanings of the terms are given by a single concrete experience. The awareness of the present is now the awareness of time and of existence; the awareness of the self is the awareness of all that is: 'Everything, everything there is, everything I remember, everything my most confused thoughts touch, appears to me to be something.'[46] 'To be', in this context means far more than in everyday expressions such as: 'there is'. Everyday language and syntax are indeed incapable of expressing this meaning. It is as if the term 'I' subsumes no longer merely the meagre content of normal self-consciousness, but the whole of existence. Chandos experiences external reality as much as a part of himself as his most intimate thoughts, and because of this the monotony and poverty of his inner life give way to a feeling of universal participation:

> My own heaviness too, my brain's habitual torpor, appears to me as something; I feel an exquisite, infinite interplay in me and about me, and among the counterpoised substances there is not one that I could not flow over into.

As this quotation shows, the heightened feeling of existence is coupled with a sense of participation in the outside world. The distinction between subject and object is blurred, and so too is that between things directly perceived and those remembered or imagined. For Lord Chandos, Carthage and Alba Longa, evoked by his imagination, were as intensely present as his immediate surroundings, and the case was similar with Roquentin. The converse is also true: the world perceived by the senses takes on the quality of an inner state, or of an imagined world. In Hofmannsthal's poem 'The Message', the landscape is changed into 'a realm of the soul';[74] in 'The Double Room', Baudelaire experiences the room he is in as if it were absent and were being imagined – it is 'a room resembling a reverie, a truly *spiritual* room'.[48]

In this 'spiritualised' awareness, the world is transfigured by a quality of the mind or imagination projected on to external objects: 'the mind ... casts a magic, supernatural light on the natural obscurity of things'.[49] It is worth noting that the word 'supernatural', as used here by Baudelaire, has no religious, transcendental connotations. It refers to the heightened quality of sensations experienced during a privileged moment: 'intensity, sonority, limpidity, vibrancy, depth and resonance in space and time'.[50]

A further consequence of the suspension of the subject-object relationship is that the outer world appears to manifest the qualities of the inner life – feeling, consciousness, knowledge. The landscape seems to live as a part of the contemplator, it becomes like a mood or a thought, as in 'The Message'. Inanimate things seem to possess know-ledge – a deep secret normally concealed from human consciousness – as in another of Hofmannsthal's poems: 'There is something the deep well seems to know,/ Something that all knew long ago,/ Now it's a dream flitting to and fro.'[51] But even during a privileged moment this secret knowledge is not clearly revealed; it remains an enigmatic half-consciousness, a kind of day-dreaming of the physical world. Flaubert's Saint Anthony also has impressions of this kind: 'Are there not inani-mate existences, inert things that seem animal, vegetative spirits, statues that dream and landscapes that think?'[52] In Baudelaire's poem 'Correspondences' objects observe the observer 'with familiar glances', and in 'The Double Room' there is an intense feeling of the 'still-life' of things in a secluded interior:

> The furniture has lounging, prostrate, langorous forms. It seems to be dreaming, as if, like things in the vegetable and mineral worlds, it were endowed with a somnambulistic life. The cloth is speaking a silent language. [53]

In this state of participation the nature of knowledge undergoes a profound change. There is no longer a subject which knows and an object which is known. Knowledge now becomes an intuitive, unitive act which, as mentioned earlier, appears to reveal the 'essence' of things, or the essence of life itself contained in things. It is this kind of knowledge that Lord Chandos achieves at rare moments: 'an im-mense participation, a flowing-over into those creatures or a feeling that a fluid of life and death, of dreaming and waking has for a moment flowed over into them'.[54] It is significant that Chandos's capacity for this kind of knowledge makes him quite incapable of thinking or talking in the manner demanded by everyday life.

The feeling of participation may finally become one of complete identification with the thing contemplated. A privileged moment described by Flaubert culminates in 'union with nature': 'by imbuing ourselves with it, by getting inside it, we became nature'.[55] Valéry, on London Bridge, announces: 'I am what I am, I am what I see.'[56] In the case of Baudelaire's hashish-smoker this phenomenon is taken to a bizarre extreme: 'You are sitting smoking; you think you are sitting in your pipe and that your pipe is smoking you; you are exhaling yourself in the form of blue-tinged clouds.'

'This piece of imagining', Baudelaire adds, 'lasts an eternity'.[57] The disappearance of the separate individuality coincides with the sus-pension of everyday time. This marks the culmination of the privileged moment. With the notions of space, time and individuality, all the conditions and limitations of ordinary life are suspended together;

eternity and infinity become a physical experience. This climactic moment, however widely individual descriptions of it may differ, is in all cases, in terms of the changed awareness of time, space and individuality, essentially the same experience. These are the descriptions of the climax of the privileged moment given by Flaubert, Valéry and Sartre:

> in the sympathy of that contemplative effusion, we would have liked our souls to spread their light everywhere and to go and inhabit all that life, taking on all its forms, lasting like them, and, changing constantly, to undergo endless metamorphoses beneath the sun of eternity. [58]

> Then, for a length of time which has boundaries but no measure, (for what was, what will be, what must be, are no more than futile signs), *I am what I am, I am what I see*, present and absent on London Bridge. [59]

> From the depths of the café something moves backwards over the disconnected moments of this Sunday and welds them together, gives them meaning: I have come all through the day to finish here, with my forehead pressed on this window, contemplating that delicate face blooming against a deep red curtain. Everything has stopped; my life has stopped: this big window, the heavy air, as blue as water, that succulent white plant at the bottom of the water, and myself – we form a whole, motionless and abundant: I am happy. [60]

The privileged moment, as it has emerged from this introductory study, has two essential characteristics: both the quality and the structure of awareness are changed. The qualitative change involves a heightening of sensations and of the apparent meaning they convey. The structural change involves a unification of all parts of awareness to form a total system. In embracing this unified system, the field of consciousness expands far beyond its normal limits. These and all the other characteristics of the experience have been shown to be related to a reduced participation of abstract thought in consciousness, which in turn can be seen as an increased participation of a faculty which may be called imagination. Above all, the privileged moment is characterised by an intense feeling of joy and liberation which is not given by any other experience.

Within the scope of the generalised notion now established, individual privileged moments may of course vary widely. In the intensification of awareness different orders of sensation may predominate; in the merging of self and world, the self may seem to expand to embrace the whole world, or to disappear into a particular object. These moments should be seen, therefore, not as identical, but as a group of related experiences; and when the general term 'the privileged moment' is used in this study, it is always subject to this restriction.

It would nevertheless be wrong to stress only the differences between particular privileged moments. They are united, as we have seen throughout this chapter, by unmistakable parallels existing both on the concrete level of direct experience, and on the abstract level of psychological explanation. We have noted in particular that privileged moments tend to follow a characteristic pattern of development. They begin with the heightened awareness of a particular object which detaches itself from the flux of everyday impressions. Consciousness then passes through progressive stages of intensification and unification, culminating in the ecstatic identification of the self and the world. In other words, there is in the privileged moment an underlying continuum, a progression from a lower to a higher state of development. A main purpose of the psychological discussion in this chapter has been to demonstrate the existence of this continuum, the progressive heightening of awareness having been seen to correspond to the progressive expulsion of conceptual thought from consciousness.

It is, above all, this continuum of related states of consciousness, in which it is possible to 'situate' any particular manifestation of heightened awareness, that makes it justifiable to speak of 'the' privileged moment. It is hoped that this chapter has shown the continuum to be latent in any privileged moment. This does not mean, of course, that each one will necessarily pass through all the stages of the continuum, from the lowest to the highest level of intensity. But it implies that every privileged moment *could* do so, that the possibility of the full development exists in advance, as it were, of each particular experience, and also that the stages of this possible development are subject to a predetermined order.

There are of course many reasons why in practice this possibility might not be realised to its full extent. The most obvious reason is the natural tendency of the logical mind to re-assert its authority, to try to understand what is happening, and in so doing, to dispel the quality of experience it is attempting to grasp. Individual privileged moments may therefore be only fragmentary and partial realisations of the 'ideal' continuum underlying the experience. But if allowed its full development, a privileged moment will necessarily follow the pattern established in this chapter and summarised above.

The descriptions of privileged moments quoted so far have been broken up so that individual aspects could be compared; this has unavoidably blurred the outline of particular experiences. To restore this outline, and to show how an experience may conform in practice to the ideal continuum referred to above, a passage will now be quoted in which a privileged moment is described in full. It is taken from Flaubert's first *Temptation of St Anthony*. The beginning has already been referred to: at certain moments the saint's attention had been suddenly transfixed by a previously insignificant object. The passage goes on:

> The object you were contemplating seemed to encroach on you as you bent closer to it, and links formed; you clasped one another, touching each other by innumerable delicate adherences; then, through looking so intently, you no longer saw anything; listening, you heard nothing, and your mind itself finally lost the notion of particularity which kept it on the alert. It was like an immense harmony engulfing your soul with marvellous palpitations, and you felt in its plenitude an inexpressible comprehension of the unrevealed wholeness of things; the interval between you and the object, like an abyss closing, grew narrower and narrower, until the difference vanished, because you both were bathed in infinity; you penetrated each other equally, and a subtle current passed from you into matter while the life of the elements slowly pervaded you, rising like a sap; one degree more, and you would have become nature, or nature become you.[61]

This 'one degree more', too, is experienced by St Anthony at the climax of his 'temptation', when he proclaims: 'immortality, boundlessness, infinity, I have all that, I am that! I feel myself to be Substance, I am Thought! ... I understand, I see, I breathe, in the midst of plenitude ... how calm I am!'[62]

To conclude this introduction to the privileged moment it should be noted that the experience ends as abruptly as it began, and that the return to everyday reality is as disagreeable as the leaving of it was intoxicating. Moreover, the glimpse of another world in the privileged moment serves, by contrast, further to devalue the experience of ordinary life. There is no need to quote from all five writers to illustrate this inevitable and natural phenomenon. Here is the relevant passage from *Nausea*:

> When I found myself once more on the boulevard de la Redoute I no longer felt anything but bitter regret. I said to myself: 'There is perhaps nothing in the world I value so much as this feeling of adventure. But it comes when it likes; it goes away so quickly and how arid I feel when it has gone!'[63]

Roquentin goes on to ask a last question – the ultimate question towards which the privileged moment points: 'Does it pay me these ironic little visits to show me that I have wasted my life?'

# CHAPTER TWO

## Proust and Rilke: the Beginnings

HAVING established what a privileged moment is, we can
begin the study of its role in the development of Proust and
Rilke. For reasons given in the Introduction, this study must
be a chronological one. Our first task, therefore, is to discover how
important the experience was for the two writers at the beginning of
their development. Did they have privileged moments, and if so, how
far did these influence what they wrote?

The earliest text which throws light on these questions in the case
of Proust is a school essay entitled 'Clouds', written when he was about
sixteen. It deals with the impressions and reflections aroused by the
contemplation of clouds at evening. Proust chose the subject himself,
and is no doubt describing an experience of his own, although he does
so in generalised terms. The man contemplating clouds, he writes, is
'religiously moved by the solemn and majestic calm of this poetic
hour'; his 'exalted imagination' discovers giants, towers and other
'brilliant fantasies' in the clouds:

> Then, giving himself up almost involuntarily to an absorbing reverie, he
> gradually forgets the things around him; no longer seeing or hearing any-
> thing near him, he takes his illusion for reality.

This undoubtedly has something in common with the experience
which Valéry called 'absence': the mind, totally absorbed by a visual
impression, becomes oblivious of all else. The end of the experience,
too, follows the pattern we noted in the last chapter: 'the illusion is
destroyed, the vision gone, and you return to earth with the disagreeable sensation you have in the morning after a beautiful dream'.[1]

Undeniably, there are traces of the privileged moment in this
passage. But at the same time it is clear that Proust's experience cannot be equated with those discussed in the last chapter. His response
to the sunset, unlike the privileged moment, is in no way surprising or
exceptional. He experiences an abnormal intensity of sensation – 'a
play of dazzling colours' is referred to elsewhere in the passage – but
this is inherent in the spectacle; it is not, as in the privileged moment,
put there by the mind. The same applies to the heightened imaginative
activity he describes: the fluctuating shapes of the clouds lend themselves naturally to imaginative interpretations, whereas the objects
involved in the privileged moments discussed earlier – Chandos' watering-can or Roquentin's white post, for example – clearly do not. In

their case the mind imposes a heightened meaning on an object whose significance is normally limited by an unambiguous practical function. In other words, Proust's experience, though it has some qualities of the privileged moment, owes them to the nature of the spectacle contemplated rather than to an intensified activity of the mind itself. And even with this help from outward reality his awareness remains at a far lower level of intensity and unity than was the case with the writers in Chapter One. This experience, then, though distinct from everyday awareness, is far closer to it than the privileged moments discussed so far.

There is another aspect of this essay that must be noted. Although Proust's experience of the privileged moment is limited, it is sufficiently developed to show ordinary existence in a contrasting and unfavourable light. This is evident from the reference to the disagreeable return to earth after the experience has ended, and towards the end of the essay the contrast is presented in more general terms. The clouds are seen as the comforters of all those who are unhappy; the poetic state they induce lifts men above their misery. A sense of the deficiency of normal life, contrasting with higher states of consciousness, is therefore present in Proust's mind at a very early stage. Even before this, in an essay written at about thirteen, he spoke of an atmosphere of poetry which lifts men above 'life and its miseries'.[2]

Let us look now at another text which is relevant to our inquiry:

> There sometimes comes an hour that he would not like to forget. At about five or six in the evening, when the clouds high up in the sky take on such fantastic shapes and colours, towering suddenly like mountains behind the flat lawns of the 'English Garden' and making you think: Tomorrow I will climb those peaks. And then tomorrow is a rainy day and the mist lies thick and heavy along the endless streets. Mornings like that are always coming and leaving you empty-handed, and the young man waits for things to change.[3]

This is taken from Rilke's early autobiographical story *Ewald Tragy*, written when he was twenty-two. The extract makes plain an important parallel between Rilke's experience and Proust's. This does not lie, of course, primarily in the repetition of the cloud-motif, which is little more than a coincidence. More important is the underlying dissatisfaction with normal life which the passage reveals, and coupled to it the sense of a possible escape glimpsed in moments of heightened awareness. Tragy's experience here is not, any more than Proust's, a privileged moment; it is at most a first step towards one and even this step is only made possible by the 'fantastic shapes and colours' of the clouds which, as for Proust, have the effect of liberating the imagination. Everyday existence is for Tragy an oppressive burden, and his

B

occasional glimpses of higher states of consciousness only serve to make it heavier. Later in the story he sums up his situation as follows: 'We are really made for dreaming, we lack the organs needed for living; but we are fishes that insist on trying to fly.'[4]

The same duality between two contrasting levels of consciousness is the central theme of one of the few other surviving examples of Proust's very early writings, a sketch written at seventeen for a schoolboy review. It has two parts, the first dealing with his impressions on going to bed at the age of fifteen, the second with the same scene two years later. The two sections embody the duality we are concerned with: the first expresses a sense of being crushed by 'the horror of usual things';[5] in the second the oppression is lifted, and a scene is described which is clearly being experienced in a state of heightened awareness. The writer hears 'the fresh, cold breath of all the sleeping things'; the street outside his window, transfigured by the bluish light, is like 'a polar landscape electrically illuminated'. The language, becoming increasingly exalted, moves towards a climax:

> The divine hour! As with nature, so with the usual things, being unable to conquer them I have consecrated them. I have clothed them with my soul and with intimate or splendid images. I live in a sanctuary, in the midst of a spectacle. I am the centre of things and each one allows me to enjoy sensations and sentiments which are magnificent or melancholy. Splendid visions are before my eyes.[6]

Reading this, we may be reminded of Baudelaire's characterisation of the privileged moment in the last chapter: 'the mind casts a magic, supernatural light on the natural obscurity of things'. But it is doubtful whether the comparison with the experiences in Chapter One can be taken very far. The more elevated Proust's language becomes at the height of the passage, the more it becomes general and empty. He does not seem to be describing a particular experience any longer, but elaborating on his impressions, inflating them verbally, in order to bring out more strongly the contrast with 'the horror of usual things'. And he shows the overcoming of this horror not as a momentary experience, as in the privileged moment, but as a permanent achievement. In other words, if there is a privileged moment at the origin of this sketch, it can only be an incipient, undeveloped one.

The discussion of this passage exemplifies the difficulty of interpreting texts produced by writers before they have reached maturity. The language lacks the precision on which a reliable analysis can be based. With Rilke in the very early period the problem is still more acute. Whereas Proust wrote relatively little, and early acquired a sure

literary taste from his family background and his education, Rilke had
none of these advantages: his early writing was as prolific as it was
without self-criticism.

This early work will not be studied in detail here. Rilke himself later
dismissed it as valueless, and the motives which produced it were less
an inner creative necessity than the desire of the adolescent Rilke to
assert himself against his philistine background.[7] Those parts of his
output which did have a genuine creative impulse at their origin sur-
vived this early period to be synthesised in his first significant work,
*The Book of Hours*, which will be studied in a later chapter. Here,
only a few indications of the role of privileged moments in the early
period need be given.

Traces of moments of heightened awareness can be found in Rilke's
early poetry and prose, though these experiences do not reach a high
degree of intensity or occur very often. A noteworthy example is the
prose passage 'Sunday' of 1896, describing an early-morning walk. The
language reveals a heightened awareness of sensation, an intensified
feeling of existence: the tree-trunks 'glow', the houses appear much
whiter than usual and their windows much brighter; the morning
seems to have passed close in front of him – its 'golden tracks' are on
the ground. He finishes standing on the shore gazing out into the
'glittering splendour' of the sea: 'Like a child who has been given a
beautiful toy, I would have liked to call to all those who are dear to
me: "Come and look, isn't that — magnificent?!"'[8]

Clearly, this experience, as well as its sentimental expression, is far
removed from those in Chapter One. It remains, like that of Proust just
discussed, close to the level of normal existence, though it does show
sufficient characteristics for it to be recognised as an undeveloped
form of the privileged moment.

Rilke's early poetry also contains indications of impressions related
to the privileged moment. A poem of 1895 describing an aristocratic
residence ends with the line: 'that I call atmosphere, yes, that I call —
magic'.[9] But apart from this statement there is nothing in the poem to
explain what gives the impression its magical quality. In a poem of
1896, contemplating the night sky, he feels a vague affinity with the
stars. Something within him, which he calls 'a piece of eternity', is
struggling to free itself and rise up to join the stars.[10] Here, the poet
does not so much experience 'eternity' as the possibility of it and the
longing for it. Longing – *Sehnsucht* – is a word characteristic of this
early poetry in which the privileged moment is not so much experienced as sensed as an absent possibility.

This preoccupation becomes steadily more prominent in succeeding
collections of poems, and in *Celebration for Myself* (which Rilke later
thought worth re-touching and publishing with other poems from the

same period as *Early Poems*), *Sehrsucht* in this sense is the theme of the introductory poem which sets the tone for the whole collection. Longing, says the poet, means having no home in time, and wishes are 'quiet dialogues that daily hours hold with eternity'. He goes on to introduce a development which is of considerable importance for this study. The second stanza reveals that there is a way in which the object of longing can be approached: memory. A past hour can rise up, detaching itself from those around it, and 'look silently towards eternity'.[11]

In this early poetry, although the privileged moment nowhere emerges as a clearly defined experience comparable to those in Chapter One, its various concomitants, particularly longing as defined above, move steadily towards the centre of Rilke's literary preoccupations.

But more important for his creative life than anything Rilke wrote in this period was his love-affair with Lou Andreas-Salomé. The mention of love brings a new and central theme into our discussion. The relationship between Rilke and Lou began in the early summer of 1897 when they made an excursion together from Munich to Wolfrat-shausen. During the stay there, walking in the meadows, Rilke experienced a blissful awareness of existence which resembles the privileged moments in Chapter One more closely than any of his experiences described so far. In a letter to Lou a week later he writes in these terms of the 'fairy-tale morning' in the meadow:

> That was one of the rarest hours. In such hours it is like being on an island with flowers clustering all around: from beyond the spring's sea-walls comes the soft breathing of the waves, and there is no boat coming in from the past nor any that wants to put out into the future.

Rilke's image makes very clear the suspension of normal time – of the orientation towards past and future inseparable from everyday consciousness. Other important resemblances to the privileged moment can also be recognised: 'That there is then a return to everyday reality can do no harm to these island-hours. They remain cut off from all others, as if they were lived in a second, higher existence.' And he now goes on to make a statement which points far ahead in the direction this study must take: 'This kind of higher island-existence is, it seems to me, the future of the very few.'[12] What we shall be concerned to find out is how far Rilke, or Proust, was to be numbered among the 'very few'.

It is evident that this experience which, as other letters show,[13] took place in Lou's company, is closely bound up with the heightened feeling of existence that accompanies falling in love. A poem in *Celebration for You*, a collection written for Lou and commemorating their love, throws light on the connection between the two experiences. Like the privileged moment, falling in love produces a radical change in self-awareness. The idea of the self can no longer be separated from that of another person; and because the other is as unknown and un-limited as the 'I' is known and limited, this prolongation of the indi-viduality seems to have no end: it seems (until the other, too, becomes familiar) to embrace the whole of existence.

> Ich hab das 'Ich' verlernt und weiß nur: *wir.*
> Mit der Geliebten wurde ich zu zwein;
> und aus uns beiden in die Welt hinein
> und über alles Wesen wuchs das *Wir.*
> Und *weil wir Alles sind, sind wir allein.*[14]

I have forgotten the meaning of 'I' and only know: *we.* With the beloved I became two; and out of us both, into the world and beyond all being, grew the *we.* And *because we are everything, we are alone.*

The lovers are at the same time identified with the whole cosmos and cut off from the everyday world; Rilke's use of 'alone' has much the same meaning as Valéry's 'absent'.

Coupled to this feeling of universal participation is an intensification of sense-impressions, as the letter just quoted makes clear. Flowers, for example, which before he met Lou had 'shivered in listless solitude', are now 'bright, full of light movements, their heads almost touching the heavens that shine back from deep within you'.[15] Falling in love has therefore given Rilke the ability to experience reality with the intensity of the privileged moment, but this has a necessary corollary: he can only do so through love. Even a privileged moment he experiences alone is only made possible by the inner presence of Lou; in a letter of later in the same year, after describing such a moment, he goes on: 'Only your soul was with me in that quiet hour, for to it I owe the deep joy that all this can give me.'[16] Rilke is therefore dependent on love for his ability to enjoy privileged moments, and the connection between the two is so direct that the question arises whether his love for Lou was not rather a love for the privileged moments she made it possible for him to enjoy. His dependence on her subsequently became such that she felt obliged to break off the relationship.

Before this, however, in the spring of 1898, Rilke had made a journey alone to Italy, and as a means of remaining in inner contact with Lou during their separation, he kept a notebook addressed to her. In it we find a further important passage relating to the privileged moment. He writes of 'creative moments' in which things seem to shed their outer shells and to reveal themselves as totally unlike what they normally appear to be. He does not go on, however, to give further details of particular impressions, but describes in general terms the vision of reality that is given to him in such moments. The whole cosmos appears in the form of great trees, with their roots formed of earthly causality, their leaves of the stars, and their trunks of human generations rising between the two.[17] These notions are expressed in vague, grandiose language which, unlike that used to describe privileged moments discussed so far, is bereft of all reference to direct sense impressions. Such conceptions are likely to have been derived from stock 'mystical' vocabulary rather than from a specific experience. Like Proust earlier, Rilke seems to be using words to inflate an undeveloped experience of the privileged moment. However that may be, what is of importance here is that these 'creative moments', too, owe their existence to Lou, whose inner presence, as the notebook shows, permeated the whole of Rilke's Italian experience.

The relationship with Lou points to two general conclusions. First, the privileged moment is already a central preoccupation of Rilke's, to the extent that love is valued primarily as a means of experiencing it. Secondly, connected to this, he cannot experience the privileged moment intensely without some form of external stimulus – here, that of love. These are at the same time the two main conclusions to be drawn from the chapter as a whole; they apply to Proust as much as to Rilke. We have seen that the privileged moment early on became the highest value for both of them, and that both, to experience it, needed some form of 'help', either from the material contemplated, which was predisposed to incite heightened awareness, or from the psychological stimulus of love. In this, of course, they differed from the writers in Chapter One, for whom an essential feature of the privileged moment was its lack of any apparent cause.

In the case of Proust these conclusions have been less fully documented than in that of Rilke. This is because the creative writing done by Proust during and immediately after his last years at school was collected and published as a coherent entity in *Pleasures and Days*, which is best discussed in a separate context. The role of the privileged moment in this book is the subject of the next chapter.

## CHAPTER THREE

# *Pleasures and Days*

AS a critic has noted,[1] *Pleasures and Days* is written in two entirely different styles. In some parts Proust uses a concise, analytical prose which has been compared to that of Voltaire, in others the language is evocative, poetical, in the manner of late nineteenth-century aestheticism. Clearly, it is to the latter parts that we should look for material relevant to the privileged moment. But before doing so, to see the role of the privileged moment in the perspective of the book as a whole, the relation between these two apparently separate, analytical and poetic, halves of the book will be briefly examined.

In the analytical section Proust deals with two main themes, love and society, both of which are viewed with total pessimism. The pessimism concerning love has a number of main aspects. The first is a sense of guilt attaching to erotic pleasure, a guilt often directed towards the mother, and seen most clearly in 'A Girl's Confession'. It is not necessary to probe deeply into Proust's personal life to see the relation between this guilt and his own experience. During the years in which he wrote *Pleasures and Days* he was making the progressive and painful discovery of his sexual abnormality. This discovery culminated in his first passionate homosexual relationship, with Reynaldo Hahn, beginning in 1894, in connection with which 'A Girl's Confession' was probably written.[2]

But it is not only guilt that makes love a source of pain for Proust. Another main theme of the book is jealousy, which is seen as inseparable from love and as a cause of suffering inherently more intense than the happiness which love can provide. This is because the jealous lover, unlike his successful rival, sees the loved woman through his imagination 'which magnifies everything'.[3]

But the deepest source of the pessimism attaching to love is the conviction that the fulfilment of the experience can never satisfy the aspirations first awakened by desire, that reality inevitably falls short of imagination, that love returned is therefore love destroyed, and that the only tenable attitude in the face of this experience is resignation. So Proust, describing the beginning of an affair, writes characteristically of 'an immense desire, disenchanted in advance', coupled with a 'wise mistrust'.[4]

The pessimism concerning society is closely related to that aroused by love. Society is presented as a distraction from 'bad desires' and the

guilt attending their satisfaction,[5] or as a compensation for humilia-
tions suffered in love.[6] The most elevated reason for entering society
is, for Proust, a sense for the poetry of aristocratic names.[7] But the
only desires which society is able to fulfil are those of egoism; the
most successful social situation is incapable of satisfying the aspirations formed in solitude and in childhood. The heroine of one of the
stories, having exchanged solitude and obscurity for a brilliant social
situation, 'offered the sumptuous, desolate spectacle of an existence
made for the infinite and gradually reduced almost to nothingness,
touched only by the melancholy shadows of the noble destiny she
might have fulfilled and which every day drew farther away from
her'.[8]

It is not difficult to recognise here and elsewhere in the treatment of
society a reflection of Proust's own situation. He too was preoccupied
with social success during these years and in his stories and sketches
there are traces not only of the numerous wounds to which this exposed
his vulnerable sensibility, but also of his feeling that he was dissipating
his talents in pursuing the facile successes which society offered. In
'The Stranger' society and conversation are shown as a betrayal of the
true self which can only be realised in solitude, and in the introductory
'dedication' this pessimistic view is given wider application: life itself,
in so far as it implies activity in the world, is a flight from the true
self: 'I had to start living again, turning my back on myself.'[9]

The pessimism of *Pleasures and Days* is therefore ultimately directed
at life itself. The inadequacy of the satisfactions provided by love and
society is only a symptom of 'an incurable imperfection in the very
essence of the present',[10] and the sufferings caused by love and society
are only two forms of the suffering inherent in human existence. So
Proust arrives at a definition of life as that which causes pain: 'Life is
a hard thing which fits too tightly, perpetually hurting the soul.'[11]

When life is experienced in this way as a constant menace and a
source of pain, it is natural that faculties capable of mitigating the
pain will be highly developed. The intelligence is the weapon with
which the over-exposed sensibility can defend itself; by discovering
the laws according to which pain and disappointment occur, it can
help both to forestall them, and to make possible a certain detached
superiority over the things producing them. When Proust wrote
sentences like the following:

> Violante was in love, that is to say, a young Englishman called Laurence
> was for several months the object of her most insignificant thoughts, the
> goal of her most important actions[12]

he was no doubt providing himself with a necessary innoculation
against the anguish and remorse produced by his own infatuations,

just as he was arming himself against society when, for example, describing a dinner-party, he pointed out beneath the diners' elegance 'their one common trait, or rather the same collective madness, the same rampant epidemic infecting them all, snobbery'.[13]

Proust's powers of psychological analysis and lapidary formulation developed early, together with his precocious sensibility and his capacity to suffer through his contacts with other human beings. An early manifestation of this parallel and interrelated development of intelligence and sensibility is seen in a letter of several pages written while he was still at school to a classmate, in which Proust analysed minutely and systematically another boy's possible reasons for refusing to greet him.[14] In one place in *Pleasures and Days* Proust uses an image, describing the rigging of ships in a harbour, which suggests that he was himself aware of this role of the highly-developed intelligence as a defence against life:

> The marvellous scientific complexity of the ropes was mirrored in the water like a precise, prudent intelligence immersed in the destiny which sooner or later will break it to pieces.[15]

At this point the relation between the analytic and poetic sections of the book begins to emerge: both are products of the same basic experience of life. For although life, for Proust, is normally 'a hard thing which fits too tightly' and provokes the anxious response of the intelligence, it also allows brief moments of respite: 'Feeling its bonds loosen for a moment, we can be filled with lucid delight.'[16] It is these moments that are described in the 'poetic' part of the book:

> The moonlight, in evoking the keeper's house, the foliage, a sail, from the night which blotted them out, had not awakened them. In this sleepy silence, it illuminated only their vague, ghostly forms, without showing the distinct outlines which made them so real during the day and oppressed me with the certitude of their presence, the perpetuity of their banal closeness.

In this experience described in 'Moonlight Sonata' the oppressive familiarity of the outside world – its 'cruelly undeniable, monotonously habitual reality' – is dispelled by moonlight. The world's power to inflict pain is likewise suspended: 'My sadness had vanished. I heard my father scolding me, Pia making fun of me, my enemies plotting against me, and none of this seemed real to me.' The writer of this passage (in which Proust transcribes an experience of his own near Honfleur in 1892)[17] has left behind the world of everyday cares and entered a new reality in which sensation is heightened and becomes a source of self-evident delight: 'The only reality was in this unreal light which I invoked with a smile.'

B*

This experience is closer to the privileged moments in Chapter One than any other of Proust's discussed so far. Apart from the heightening of sensation, there is the same use of dynamic rather than static terms to describe it; a patch of light between two rows of trees is called 'a river of brightness flowing between these two dark banks'. There is also the same feeling that outer reality possesses a dreamy consciousness of its own: the things around the writer seem like 'the strange, insubstantial, luminous dream of the slumbering trees enveloped in darkness'. And as the experience reaches its climax there is the same sense of unity between the self and the outer world, together with the suspension of abstract thought processes:

> I did not understand what was the mysterious likeness joining my sorrows to the solemn mysteries being celebrated in the woods, in the sky and on the sea, but I felt that an explanation, a consolation, a pardon for them was being held out, and that it was of no account that my intelligence was not in the secret, since my heart understood it so well.[18]

But in spite of all these characteristics this experience must still be distinguished from the privileged moments in Chapter One. In them the transfiguration of reality was brought about by the heightened receptivity of the onlooker alone, whereas here it is largely the result of the disorientating effect of moonlight. In other words, as in the 'Clouds' essay, Proust still needs 'help' from outwardly predisposed reality before he can experience the privileged moment with any intensity. In addition, as we shall see, love, too, plays a part in this experience.

Another, though less intense, privileged moment induced by moonlight is described in the sketch 'As by Moonlight'. The things outside his window at night seem, says Proust, to be recalled, rather than revealed, by the pale moonlight; darkness still covers them 'like forgetfulness'. And this scene no longer suffers from what Proust elsewhere called 'the incurable imperfection of the present'; it has a quality of 'absence', of something imagined or remembered:

> And I spent hours looking out into the courtyard at the mute, vague, pale and enchanted memory of things which, during the day, had given me pleasure or pain with their shouts, their voices, their din.

This 'remembered' quality of the spectacle now leads Proust to draw a parallel which has crucial importance for this study: he compares the quality of external reality in this privileged moment to the quality of his own past life seen in memory. Like the moonlit scene, life re-experienced in memory has lost the power to inflict pain, it no longer 'fits too tightly' but takes on an atmosphere which is moving and poetic. The joys and sorrows of past loves seem now to look at him mutely like the things outside his window: 'Their silence moves me

‘PLEASURES AND DAYS’ 43

while their remoteness and their uncertain paleness intoxicate me with sadness and poetry. And I cannot stop looking at this interior moonlight.'[19]

The theme of memory appears frequently in *Pleasures and Days*, both in the involuntary form produced by a coincidence of past and present sensations, as at the end of 'The Death of Baldassare Silvande', and in the more usual voluntary form as in 'Memory's Genre-Paintings'; in both forms it is a source of happiness denied by the present. And, as we have seen, Proust's concern with memory has the same origin in his preoccupation with the privileged moment.

The section headed 'Regrets and Reveries' contains numerous other descriptions of privileged moments. None of them reaches the intensity of those in Chapter One, but each shows recognisable qualities of the experience. In 'Tuileries' an intensification of sensation is rendered by the use of 'dynamic' language: 'Ardent with sun, the heliotrope burns its scents. Hollyhocks spring forth in front of the Louvre';[20] and the characteristic 'return to earth' at the end of the privileged moment is emphasised by the sun suddenly disappearing behind clouds. 'Inner Sunset' evokes an intoxicated feeling of participation in the evening landscape reminiscent of Flaubert's seashore privileged moment discussed in Chapter One, though Proust's experience does not reach the final ecstasy described by Flaubert. But in Proust's description the writer does feel an extraordinary intensification of his inner life, and sees his tumultuous thoughts mysteriously reflected in the sky. In 'Underwood' he enjoys the same 'joyful agility of the mind',[21] and has an intuition, communicated by the 'strange' yet 'natural' attitudes of the trees, that their lives are the 'dark, inexhaustible reservoir' of our own.

It was probably this dim perception he had during privileged moments of a deep life in nature related to his own – a perception which we also found in 'Moonlight Sonata' – that Proust referred to in a letter when he said that he had expressed in *Pleasures and Days* 'a certain feeling of metempsychoses'.[22] There is nothing in the book apart from the privileged moments which would answer this description. And it is worth noting that Proust here called these feelings of metempsychosis 'the things I value most'.

In another sketch, contemplation of the sea produces a unification of the inner and outer worlds. The writer's feelings, rising and falling in harmony with the waves, 'confuse their destiny with that of things'.[23] The mind is able to achieve this identification because the sea, being in constant movement, lacks the fixed, confining significance of objects in the everyday world: 'It refreshes our imagination because it does not make us think of human life ... it enchants us in the same way as music which, unlike language, does not bear the traces of things and tells us nothing of men.' The sea is one of those indefinite, fluctuating realities like moonlight and clouds which, as we have already seen, are conducive to heightened awareness. Again, Proust needs an external stimulus in order to experience a privileged moment.

The fullest account of a privileged moment in *Pleasures and Days*, apart from 'Moonlight Sonata', is in 'Real Presence', a sketch based on an experience of Proust's in the Engadine about 1893.[24] In this passage the flight of butterflies across a lake at evening takes on the quality of an inner experience:

> As they crossed the lake these little butterflies passed back and forth across our souls – across our souls taut with emotion in the face of so much beauty, ready to vibrate – passed back and forth like the voluptuous bow of a violin. As they flew their light movements never brushed the water, but they caressed our eyes, our hearts, and at each beat of their little pink wings we almost passed out.

Like the writers in Chapter One, Proust uses numerous musical analogies in his attempt to convey the harmonious and unified quality of his awareness during this experience, and the description concludes as follows:

> Our souls had become sonorous and in the butterflies' silent flight they listened to a music full of charm and freedom, and all the soft, intense harmonies of the lake, the woods, the sky and our own lives, accompanied it with a magical sweetness that made us melt into tears.[25]

It is noticeable that Proust says 'we' and not 'I' throughout this passage; his partner in the experience is the absent person he loves. Just as Rilke, as we saw in the last chapter, was only able to experience the later privileged moment at Wolfratshausen because of the inner presence of Lou, Proust here is able to enjoy his privileged moment through the inner 'real presence' of his beloved. Love therefore acts as a stimulus in this experience, as it does also in the other outstanding privileged moment in *Pleasures and Days* – that described in 'Moonlight Sonata' where the experience quoted earlier is immediately followed by the appearance of 'Assunta' and a tearful embrace.

In view of the rôle of the absent beloved in 'Real Presence' and the sentimental tone of the description of nature, it might be thought that Proust's experience can be accounted for as the re-direction on to nature of frustrated erotic desire. We might also be tempted to explain the privileged moment in general along vaguely Freudian lines as a phenomenon of sublimation.

Proust's accounts of the experience and the psychology underlying them do not, however, lend themselves to such an interpretation. In 'Real Presence' the memory of the experience of nature outlives, and is seen as intrinsically far more significant than, the love which accompanied it; and in general in *Pleasures and Days* Proust regards erotic pleasure as a substitute for the privileged moment, not vice versa. This is explicit in a passage of 'The Girl's Confession'; the girl's ability to enjoy privileged moments has been destroyed by her preoccupation with social success:

> It was then that, searching for an inverse remedy, and because I lacked the courage to will the true cure which was so near and, alas, so far from me, within myself, I gave myself up once more to guilty pleasures, believing I might thereby rekindle the flame that society had extinguished.[26]

Love, for Proust, is a manifestation not of sexual desire alone, but of sexual desire indissolubly mingled with imagination. It is not until it has become absorbed by an aspiration of the inner life that erotic desire takes on the obsessive quality characteristic of love in Proust. This process is described in detail in the story of Madame de Breyves. The heroine's helpless attachment to a man she knows to be insignificant draws its invincible strength from the power of her imagination, which is ultimately to blame for her plight:

> Finally she cursed her thought in its most divine forms, the supreme gift she had been given, which has been called by every name – poetic intuition, religious ecstasy, deep feeling for nature and music – though its true name has never been found. This gift had placed summits and infinite horizons before her love, bathing them in the preternatural light of love's charm, and lending her love in return a little of its own; it had involved in this love, combined and confused with it her highest and most intimate inner life.

Proust goes on to show still more clearly that the 'poetic intuition', 'deep feeling for nature', etc., which he sees as a fundamental ingredient of love, is the experience we have called the privileged moment:

> she cursed that inexpressible feeling of the mystery of things when our mind is engulfed in a radiance of beauty, like the sun going down into the sea; she cursed it for having made her love deeper, more immaterial, more vast – for making it infinite but not less tormenting, 'for (as Baudelaire has said, speaking of the late afternoons in autumn), there are sensations whose vagueness does not exclude intensity, and there is no point sharper than that of the infinite'.[27]

The allusion to Baudelaire's prose-poem 'The Artist's Confiteor', already discussed in Chapter One, underlines the rôle of the privileged moment in Proust's conception of love.

Madame de Breyves has invested the mediocre M. de Laléande with all the prestige of the world experienced in a privileged moment. It is this, rather than any personal or even sexual fulfilment, that she is pursuing in the arbitrarily chosen figure of a particular human being. In the light of this it is not difficult to see why, for Proust, love could never lead to a satisfying personal relationship. The story of Mme de Breyves shows also how the privileged moment, by its dominating if hidden influence, tends to devalue other experiences and to make them appear in advance as 'bitter and vulgar'.[28]

It can be seen from this analysis that Proust had already evolved a fixed hierarchy of experiences by the time he wrote *Pleasures and Days*. The highest value is given to the experiences of nature and imagination possible only in solitude and in childhood – the privileged moments. Below them is love, which incorporates some of the aspirations towards the privileged moment, though it is by its nature incapable of satisfying them. Below love, and redeemed from total sterility only by a minimal degree of imaginative content, is society. The relationships between these different experiences are explored in the narrative sections of the book – the stories of Mme de Breyves, Violante, etc., which combine the elements of poetry and analysis referred to earlier.

As a corollary of his pessimistic view of life as a whole, Proust sees in death possibilities of access to a more rewarding existence. This theme appears in 'The Death of Baldassare Silvande' and 'The End of Jealousy', as well as in the epigraph from Renan at the beginning of the book, which speaks of 'those truths which have power over death, which prevent us from fearing it and almost make us love it'.[29] But although Proust once mentions the possibility of 'conscious immortality' emerging from 'our marriage with death',[30] his intuition of another life outside our present existence owes little to Christian notions of an after-life. It seems rather to be rooted in the sense of 'metempsychosis' referred to earlier, the feeling that there is an invisible realm of consciousness beyond the compass of the senses, which is dimly perceived in moments of heightened awareness, as in 'Moonlight Sonata' and 'Underwood'.

This invisible realm was partly experienced by Violante in her communings with nature before she entered society: 'Violante felt the whole of the visible and had a presentiment of a small part of the invisible.'[31] But the influence of society destroys her contact with this realm. A similar pattern is present in other stories – 'The Girl's Confession', 'Mme de Breyves', 'Baldassare Silvande': all experiences are seen as greater or lesser aberrations from this first ideal.

There is, therefore, a coherent view of life underlying the disparate elements and styles of *Pleasures and Days*. This view of life may appear somewhat restricted and schematic; it nevertheless remained unchanged, in its main outlines, in all Proust's subsequent works.

# CHAPTER FOUR

## *The Book of Hours*

THE subject of *The Book of Hours* is a reality beyond the world of the senses, a reality which Rilke calls God. The book is an attempt to discover God through experience, at his 'origin and source',[1] rather than through faith or dogma. It was ostensibly written by a Russian monk and icon-painter, with whom Rilke appears to have identified while writing the poems. But throughout the book he ignores the fact that Russian monks worship the Christian God, and in one place he openly rejects Christianity: 'for the Christians/ mean nothing to you'.[2]

If it is asked why the poet, independently of Christianity, should be interested in the existence of God and metaphysical reality, a large part of the answer is no doubt to be found in his dissatisfaction with the 'here and now'. The book is full of a sense of the insufficiency of ordinary life. 'Nobody lives his life', he writes in one poem, and he goes on to sum up human existence as haphazard, fragmentary, banal and afraid:

> Zufälle sind die Menschen, Stimmen, Stücke,
> Alltage, Ängste.[3]

Related to this feeling of insufficiency is the poet's intuition that his own real life is somehow absent from the moment in which he is living: 'My life is not this uphill hour/ in which you see me hurrying so'.[4] The conviction that his existence contains the unrealised possibility of another life comes to him in moments of insight in which his senses 'grow deep'. These moments bring him the knowledge that he has a second life which is 'timeless and wide'.[5]

He calls these experiences *Dunkelstunden* – hours of darkness; and darkness is a foremost attribute of the God of *The Book of Hours*: 'My God is dark and like a hundred/ matted roots that drink in silence.'[6] Coupled to this attribute of darkness, as the root image suggests, is one of depth: *Gott aber dunkelt tief*: 'but my deep God is dark'.[7]

Rilke's God is the antithesis of light, which restricts the sphere of possibility to the area it illuminates: 'You darkness from which I came,/ I love you more than the flame/ which limits the world.'[8] Darkness has no such limitations – it 'holds all things to itself'. The night may contain the powerful reality which the poet feels to be absent from normal life:

> Und es kann sein: eine große Kraft
> rührt sich in meiner Nachbarschaft.
> Ich glaube an Nächte.[9]

It may be that a mighty force is stirring near me. I believe in nights.

The poet senses that the sphere in which God exists is very close, separated from him only by 'a slender wall'.[10] This wall is built up, he adds, of the images, or names, which men have created for God. Name is another antithesis of Rilke's God. A third antithesis is time; the life towards which the poet aspires is, as we saw earlier 'timeless and wide'. Time, in these poems, has an implication of superficiality opposed to the deep reality of God; it is 'the shining garment/ discarded by God'.[11]

The God of *The Book of Hours* is therefore a being, or a plane of being, characterised by a number of attributes, in particular by darkness, depth, timelessness and namelessness.

Coupled to this notion of God, as a kind of extension on a mythical and historical plane of the attributes we have discussed, is a religious conception of world history in which Rilke takes over but re-interprets numerous elements from the Old Testament. Just as God is the antithesis of light and time, he is seen in this historical scheme as having existed before light and time, which he created: 'The first of all your words was: Light:/ then Time began.'[12] God created the world in order to overcome the nothingness which preceded it: 'The void was like a wound to you,/ so you cooled it with the world.'[13]

But creation too was a source of pain to God, because it involved time, his 'deepest woe'.[14] As a result he threw off the 'garment' of time, and, while persisting as a deep presence in his creation, withdrew from the realm of light and time:

> als Er, der immer Tiefe war,
> ermüdete des Flugs
> und sich verbarg vor jedem Jahr,
> bis ihm sein wurzelhaftes Haar
> durch alle Dinge wuchs.[15]

when He, who always had been depth, grew tired of soaring and hid himself before all years, until like roots his hair grew through all things.

In this way God has become *der Dinge tiefer Inbegriff*[16] – the deep essence of things – a kind of subliminal presence marginally perceived in the physical world. He is felt most strongly in organic nature, and this is emphasised by the root-image which we have already met twice.

Numerous other passages show the connection between God and the landscape; he 'breaks out of the earth with trees', and 'rises softly from the earth as scent'.[17] In conventional religious terms Rilke's God is closest to the deity of pantheism, an immanent, not a transcendent God, to whom the Christian idea of eternal life is alien: 'No waiting for the life beyond, no peering at the other world.'[18]

Now that God has withdrawn into nature, human history and civilisation, which in Rilke's scheme belong to the realm of light and time, have become estranged from him:

> So blieb das Dunkel dir allein,
> und, wachsend in die leere Lichte,
> erhob sich eine Weltgeschichte
> aus immer blinderem Gestein.[19]

So darkness was left to you alone, and, growing into empty brightness, world-history rose up out of ever blinder stone.

Rilke's picture of creation and history also contains an account of the relation of man to God. But if an attempt is made to systematise this, a number of contradictions appear. On one hand, God is seen as evolving in the course of history: 'God ripens',[20] and this evolving God is the creation of man, or at least of the artists among men: 'Workmen are we: apprentices and masters,/ building you up, you high cathedral-nave.'[21] In this way God becomes a kind of total work of art conceived by humanity, and there is a sense of confidence in the builders: 'Dimly your coming contours loom./ God, you are great.'[22] God is therefore projected into the future, and his realisation is bound up with the creative activity of man. It is to be noticed that at one point the poet of *The Book of Hours* assigns to himself the culminating rôle in this process of creation: 'And I see: my senses/form and fashion/ the last decorations.'[23]

There is already a contradiction between this idea that God is dependent on man for his existence, or realisation, and the idea mentioned earlier that God created the world, and therefore man. But a similar contradiction is latent in Christian dogma and is perhaps inherent in any theological system in which man is not to become irrelevant. But there is another, more serious, contradiction which is peculiar to Rilke's system. At one moment the poet asserts that God is in the process of becoming, that he has never yet existed fully: 'your beauty never yet took place'.[24] But at another moment he writes: 'You are no more in the midst of your glory.'[25] God is said now to be on the decline, on the point of exhaustion; his great epoch has already passed. In this situation too, however, the poet assigns to himself the supreme rôle: without him, God will cease to be heard at all: 'you live in the last of all your houses./ Your whole heaven is hanging on my words'.[26]

In this latter situation the artists who preceded Rilke, far from building up God, are accused of having dispersed and destroyed him; the rôle of the poet of *The Book of Hours* is to restore God to his former state: 'You have been scattered by the bards/ ... But I will gather you in again.'[27]

What these two conflicting situations have in common is, therefore, the important rôle which in each case the poet allocates to himself. This might suggest that the need for self-justification which, as we saw in Chapter Two, played a large part in Rilke's early literary efforts, is still present in *The Book of Hours*. Rilke has in effect re-written the scriptures, replacing Christ as redeemer by the poet, by himself. No doubt there is an element of self-justification here, but this fact cannot be used to explain *The Book of Hours* away. It explains in part Rilke's interpretation of poetic inspiration, but not that inspiration itself. While he wrote the first part of the work he was experiencing for the first time the full scope of his poetic powers and it was this overwhelming experience which impelled him to attribute an absolute and redeeming power to creativity.

The element of self-justification in the work is of interest here for a different reason: it reveals an important parallel with Proust, and at the same time a basic difference between the two writers. Rilke, like Proust, felt exposed and insecure in the face of experience and, more than Proust, he suffered in childhood and adolescence through an uncomprehending and brutal environment. Both writers, like all sensitive and vulnerable beings who cannot dominate life directly, began early to attempt to disarm the hostile forces around them by the power of intellect. They both belong to the type of artist exemplified by Tonio Kröger, who tries to take his revenge on 'Life' by the cultivation of 'mind and word'.

But whereas Proust, whose mind tended naturally towards logical analysis, developed primarily this faculty as his defence against life, with the results we saw in *Pleasures and Days*, Rilke shunned purely logical argument; his mind tended towards synthesis rather than analysis. As his defence he built up the systematic, all-embracing but illogical structure which we have studied, in which his own place and importance were guaranteed, as it were, in advance of the contingencies of actual experience.

But just as this need for self-justification cannot explain the inspiration which produced *The Book of Hours*, it cannot account, either, for the logical inconsistencies in the work. The source of these is to be found rather in the nature of Rilke's inspiration. He wrote later that the poems came to him as an 'inner dictation';[28] they seemed to embody a deep, self-evident truth beside which logical inconsistencies were insignificant.

This does not necessarily mean, of course, that we should follow Rilke in his belief. The metaphysical system of *The Book of Hours*, in so far as it can be reduced to abstract terms and shown to be self-contradictory, is clearly of little value, and is open in addition to Rilke's own condemnation of all such abstract interpretations of God: 'Every concept is contrived,/ you can feel fine stitching in it/ and that someone spun the thread.'[29]

But *The Book of Hours* does not consist only of abstract speculation. Fundamental to Rilke's position is the belief that God can only be known concretely, through experience: 'You are only grasped by deeds';[30] and it is with the sections where the concrete experience of God is conveyed that this study must be primarily concerned. The metaphysical system is no more than a superstructure erected on this experience, and the interest of this system, including its contradictions, lies only in the meaning it takes on when seen in relation to the underlying experience.

The experience on which the notion of God, and the whole of *The Book of Hours*, are based appears first in the opening poem of the book. The poet records a moment in which his awareness seems to tremble on the verge of revelation:

> Da neigt sich die Stunde und rührt mich an
> mit klarem, metallenem Schlag:
> mir zittern die Sinne. Ich fühle: ich kann –
> und ich fasse den plastischen Tag.[31]

Now the hour sinks, touching me with a clear, metallic stroke: my senses quiver. I feel: I can – and I grasp the plastic day.

The experience of God takes place in a moment when the senses grasp reality in an intense, plastic way. Rilke emphasises throughout the book that it is through the senses that God is apprehended, though by an extremely tenuous and marginal perception: 'I *feel* you. At my senses' fringe/ you fitfully begin, as if with many islands.'[32]

God appears as a kind of knowledge or reality beginning at the extreme limits of human awareness. This reality normally lies beyond the senses' reach: 'And my senses, which soon weaken,/ are cut off from you, without a home.'[33] Because of their limitations they can be seen as an obstacle to the ultimate awareness of God: 'If the noise my senses make/ did not so mar my being awake/ then I could, in a thousandfold thought,/ think you to the very end.'[34] The 'thousandfold thought' referred to here must not be understood as a purely mental concept: it is a multiplied awareness in which all the senses are involved and which lies ultimately beyond them all, in a deep knowledge of the blood, a participation in some pre-conscious organic sympathy:

> Lösch mir die Augen aus: ich kann dich sehn,
> wirf mir die Ohren zu: ich kann dich hören,
> und ohne Füße kann ich zu dir gehn,
> und ohne Mund noch kann ich dich beschwören.
> Brich mir die Arme ab, ich fasse dich
> mit meinem Herzen wie mit einer Hand,
> halt mir das Herz zu, und mein Hirn wird schlagen,
> und wirfst du in mein Hirn den Brand,
> so werd ich dich auf meinem Blute tragen.[35]

Put out my eyes: I can see you, shut up my ears: I can hear you, and without feet I can walk to you, and without a mouth I can call you. Break off my arms, I grasp you with my heart as with a hand, strangle my heart, and my brain will beat, and if you throw firebrands into my brain, then I will bear you on my blood.

Having explored the rôle of the senses in the experience of God, we can proceed with the interpretation of the opening poem. In the second stanza the next stage of the experience is described. In the poet's intensified sensory awareness things seem to achieve a definitive state, a perfection, as if their existing in time is culminated: 'Nothing was finished before I beheld it,/ all coming-to-be stood still.'[36] There is an alteration in the awareness of time, which seems to hesitate, to be arrested. The man experiencing God exists outside time: 'and every circle drawn around you/ opens his compasses outside time'.[37]

We find here the origin of the idea we met earlier that God exists outside time. The way in which Rilke's metaphysical system is related to his poetic experience is beginning to become apparent. In constructing this system he takes 'time' to mean both the everyday sense of passing moments and historical, biblical time. The changed awareness of everyday time expressed in such lines as: 'You are the enigmatic one/ about whom time stood wavering',[38] is translated from the plane of individual experience in which it originates to the universal plane of history, and takes on cosmic implications. The poet's growing sense of the closeness of God in a moment of inspiration gives rise to the notion of a God drawing nearer in historical time: when he writes of 'hushed, somehow hesitating times when something nears',[39] he refers simultaneously to his own experience of God in nature and to an event which takes place on the level of mankind.

We can go further: having noted the connection between the poet's experience and the metaphysical system, we can now explain also the contradiction in the metaphysical system, where God was projected sometimes into the past, sometimes into the future. The moments of inspiration from which the historical conception of God is derived, when they were not being actually enjoyed, were for the poet both in the future as intuitions and in the past as memories. When he felt the approach of such a moment, he projected the historical realisation of God into the future; when the splendour of this moment was past, God too was no longer 'in the midst of his glory', and so on.

This extrapolation from personal experience to a universal plane was not, of course, a deliberate or conscious process. Nor was it in any way harmful to the poetic qualities of the work. On the contrary, it is the main source of these qualities; it gives rise to the sonorous language and to the memorable, prophetic utterances which, if their value as literal truth is questionable, have an immediate appeal as poetry:

> Die Wurzel Gott hat Frucht getragen,
> geht hin, die Glocken zu zerschlagen;
> wir kommen zu den stillern Tagen,
> in denen reif die Stunde steht.
> Die Wurzel Gott hat Frucht getragen.
> Seid ernst und seht.[40]

God, the root, has brought forth fruit; go and dash the bells to pieces; we are come to the quieter days in which the hour stands ripe. God, the root, has brought forth fruit. Be grave and see.

Further aspects of Rilke's poetic experience must now be examined. We have already seen that while God is being apprehended the everyday sense of time is suppressed. When this happens, human knowledge, which for Rilke belongs to the sphere of time, also vanishes: 'Knowledge only is in time./ You are the dark unconscious one/ from eternity to eternity.'[41] There is complete discontinuity between human thought processes and the timeless reality of God: the poet 'knows', he says, whenever '[his] thinking measures out/ how deep, how long, how wide –:/ whereas you are and are and are,/ and round you trembles time'.[42]

In the state of awareness in which God is apprehended, logical connections and distinctions vanish and contradictory elements are reconciled. God is called 'the forest of contradictions'[43] and is described in terms which deliberately overthrow the normal logical implications of language: 'You are the deepest soaring thing,/ the envy of divers and towers.'[44] And given the relation we noted between the metaphysical system and the experience underlying it, it is hardly surprising that the absence of rational thought during the experience should be reflected by the illogicality of the superstructure.

The reconciliation of logical contradictions takes place not only in God but in the poet experiencing him. This is seen when the poet says, for example: 'for all my twigs/ lie deep below and only wave in the wind'.[45] Here he not only confuses the functions of roots and branches and the ideas 'up' and 'down': he ceases to distinguish between his own identity and that of a tree. The breakdown of normal logical thought processes leads to a loss of the sense of the self as a single, limited entity. The poet's relation to the external world is blurred, objects outside him take on an exceptional interest and value for him, and in them he feels a release, a liberation of his soul. This is the experience described by Rilke (who, it should be remembered, speaks through the mouth of an icon-painter) in the third stanza of the opening poem:

> Nichts ist mir zu klein und ich lieb es trotzdem
> und mal es auf Goldgrund und groß,
> und halte es hoch, und ich weiß nicht wem
> löst es die Seele los ...[46]

Nothing is too small to me, I love it all the same and paint it large on a background of gold and hold it high, and I do not know whose soul it is setting free ...

He writes: 'I do not know whose soul' because, at the moment when his soul is liberated, he has lost the sense of his own identity.

At this stage of the experience the limits of the poet's awareness are broken down; he is able to identify himself with surrounding reality in an expanding circle, and perhaps finally with the totality of God. Understood in this way, the second poem of *The Book of Hours*, can be seen to grow out of the first:

> Ich lebe mein Leben in wachsenden Ringen,
> die sich über die Dinge ziehn.
> Ich werde den letzten vielleicht nicht vollbringen,
> aber versuchen will ich ihn.[47]

I live my life in growing rings which spread out over things. I shall not complete the last, perhaps, but I shall make the attempt.

In the next stanza the final ring, the total experience of God, becomes the centre of the circle, and the poet confuses his identity with the things circling round God and with his own song, while experiencing a sense of endless time:

> Ich kreise um Gott, um den uralten Turm,
> und ich kreise jahrtausendelang;
> und ich weiß noch nicht: bin ich ein Falke, ein Sturm
> oder ein großer Gesang.

I circle round God, the ancient tower, and I circle for thousands of years;
and I do not yet know: am I a falcon, a storm or a mighty song.

The image used in this poem of a circle which expands to become its
own centre is a very apt one for an experience in which subject and
object are identified. Like the centre and the circumference of a circle,
the poet and God are totally interrelated and interdependent, so that
Rilke writes in another poem: 'If you are the dreamer, I am your
dream.'[48] The poet in his turn is 'One who dreams of completing you/
and: that he will complete himself.'[49] In this way, by the merging and
reversing of the rôles of subject and object, the poet becomes the
creator of God: 'O how beautiful did I create you/ in an hour which
held me taut.'[50]

Here we see the origin of further aspects of Rilke's metaphysical
system: the idea of the interdependence of God and man, and the connected idea that artists are creating God. A point-to-point correspondence is emerging between the characteristics of the theological
structure and those of the state of awareness expressed in the opening
poems. The connection between the two goes still further. The process
whereby Rilke expanded his personal experience on a cosmic scale can
itself be seen to result from the special nature of this experience. For
during his states of poetic inspiration Rilke was able, as we saw, to
identify himself with external objects. This expansion of his existence
could extend to include absent, imagined realities such as, in one
instance, the city of Jerusalem; the poet hears the inhabitants' foot-
steps within himself; his life becomes generalised, all-embracing: 'For
am I not the Universal,/ am I not, weeping, *everything*,/ and you
the one who hears?'[51] In view of the nature of this experience it is not
surprising that he should describe it in terms giving it the maximum
extension and universality; in other words, that he should present it as
a metaphysical experience involving all history and the whole cosmos.

In constructing his universal system Rilke synthesises a number of
disparate elements. He draws not only on his reading of the Old Testament but also from his study of art history and from his impressions
on his Italian journey of 1898. The combining of these elements
begins as early as the third poem of the book, where Rilke introduces
the theme of Renaissance art. Other constituents of the synthesis are
the influence of Lou, to be discussed in more detail later, and his impressions on the Russian journey of 1899. This provided him with the
characteristic landscape of *The Book of Hours*, and with his mouth-
piece the monk, together with the idea he incarnates of a life dominated by the quest for God. In other words, the religious system unites
all Rilke's predominant concerns in the years leading up to the work.

But underlying all this, and providing the unifying principle, is the poetic experience we have now studied. Not only does the religious speculation grow spontaneously out of the experience described in the opening poems: the system reproduces within itself the essential characteristics of the poetic experience. And the 'God' who is approached during the moment of inspiration constitutes the focal point, the goal giving the whole work coherence and direction.

But even this supreme moment of inspiration, as the poet experiences it, is not completely satisfying. It provides only an image, which falls short of the full reality of God: 'the most quivering picture my senses invent me,/ you by your simple being would blindly surpass it'.[52] His most intense experience is no more than a 'poor substitute'[53] for God, not only because its intensity is limited but because it is transient and cannot be prolonged; God is 'the guest who passes on again'.[54] And because loss is implicit in the moment of possession, the poet is, even while the experience lasts, 'a man who smiles and yet is half in tears'.[55]

Once this moment is past, its absence dominates the poet's life, casting over it a shadow of nostalgia and melancholy, a mood of longing so deep-seated that he comes to see it as his innermost nature: 'I am made up of longing'.[56] God in his turn becomes a 'great homesickness'.[57] The monk is 'homesick' not only for the intensity and splendour of the moment when God is apprehended, but also for the feeling of unity and completeness the experience gave him. As he says in one poem, he longs for 'a bond, a single understanding' looking on him 'as on *one* thing'.[58]

The absence of God gives his life a kind of inner direction; every step he takes, he says, is a step towards God.[59] In this way the whole of life becomes a kind of pilgrimage; and the second part of *The Book of Hours*, which is dominated by the sense of the absent God, bears the title: 'The Book of Pilgrimage'. For the pilgrim-poet nothing is real in life except God's absence and the sense of being drawn towards him:

> Es *ist* nichts andres dennein Schweigen
> von schönen Engeln und von Geigen,
> und der Verschwiegene ist der,
> zu dem sich alle Dinge neigen,
> von seiner Stärke Strahlen schwer.[60]

There *is* nothing apart from a silence of beautiful angels and of violins, and concealed by this silence is he towards whom all things bend, heavy with the rays of his power.

The longing for God is, for Rilke, inseparable from life; it is the human condition. And to feel God's absence, it is not necessary to have already felt his presence: the knowledge of him is intuitive. In Rilke's mythical scheme, longing – *Sehnsucht* – is implanted in man before his birth, by the only words God speaks to him directly. 'Go out to the limits of your longing',[61] man is told; he is seen as a kind of pioneer sent out by his senses; he must keep advancing through experience, for 'No feeling is the farthest'; he must let nothing come between him and God. And he is given final words of encouragement: 'Near is the land/ they give the name of Life.'

We return here to the point from which this chapter started – Rilke's conviction that men are not fulfilled by the lives they lead, and his intuition that their true lives are lived elsewhere. This theme is re-stated early in 'The Book of Pilgrimage'; everyone is imprisoned in himself as in a cell 'that hates and holds him',[62] and is struggling to escape. And yet, says the poet, there is a great miracle: 'I feel: *all lives are being lived.*'

But this intuition in itself does not satisfy the poet; he goes on at once to ask: 'Who lives it, then?' – where is the fulfilment that seems vaguely near him, yet withdrawn from his experience? Is it in the landscape around him, in the things standing 'like an unplayed melody/ in the evening as in a harp'? These things – trees, breezes, flowers, birds – seem pregnant with a possible significance, but it is not revealed. The poet is filled with doubts, and finally questions even his God: 'Who lives it then? Do you, God, live it – Life?'

So his attitude to the world becomes an anxious searching: 'You see, I am a seeker',[63] he says to God. But at the same time he knows that a search of this kind must be fruitless, that the very act of asking prevents God from revealing himself: 'You are the soft-tongued one who said his name,/ yet when a coward's question came/ you revelled in your reticence.'[64] The attitude of conscious questioning, with its need for proof, is dismissed as a 'temptation' of God, an appeal to his vanity.[65] Man's true duty towards God is different; it is to grasp him 'as the earth does'.[66] The poet must abandon all intellectual questioning for an attitude of simplicity and patient openness; he must become like a thing.[67] The notion of the 'Thing' takes on a strongly positive meaning for Rilke, contrasting with the inadequacy of normal human attitudes.

In approaching God through things the poet is returning to the attitude of children who, says Rilke, have not yet 'gone away' from God.[68] The theme of the child's instinctive closeness to God recurs throughout *The Book of Hours* and need not be illustrated in detail here. But childhood is fated to pass away, and its ending is marked for Rilke by a moment of choice. As he crosses the threshold of the adult world of sensuality and self-consciousness, the child is suddenly divided against himself, torn by conflicting impulses: 'All at once I have so many senses,/ and each one has a different thirst.'[69] This is the voice of a 'young brother' expressing the shock of the child's first conscious exposure to his own sensuality, when 'suddenly all arms are naked'.

At this moment the child, for Rilke, can choose between the way of ordinary humanity, into the blindness of an endless pursuit of sensual satisfaction, and the way of the monk of *The Book of Hours*. When sexual desire is at its height there are, for the monk, deeper voices to which he must listen: 'But then, as through dark alleyways/ rumours of God pass darkly through your blood.'[70] The monk's longing for God is more essential and of another kind than sexual desire: 'there are so many noises in my blood,/ and yet I know, I am made up of longing'.[71] So he is able to look beyond the woman his senses desire, drawn by his distant, absent goal:

> Es war ein Weib in meiner Nachbarschaft
> und winkte mir aus welkenden Gewändern.
> Du aber sprichst mir von so fernen Ländern.
> Und meine Kraft
> schaut nach den Hügelrändern.

There was a woman close by me, beckoning me from wilting garments. But you tell me of such distant lands. And my strength looks out towards the hills.

There is a clear parallel between this view of the way in which erotic desire is related to the impulse towards God, and Proust's conception, discussed in the last chapter, of its relation to the impulse towards the privileged moment. In fact, the two writers' interpretations of childhood and love resemble each other to the point of identification. Both see the onset of sensuality as marking the end of the child's instinctive harmony with the world. On the other hand love can, for both, provide an escape, though only a brief and partial one, from the arid world of adult life to a more imaginative sphere. Rilke sees lovers as temporarily closer to God: 'They are the poets of a fleeting hour',[72] and Proust writes in *Pleasures and Days*: 'lovers, when they begin to love, like poets at the times when they sing, ... feel closer to their souls.'[73]

Both writers see the two impulses – towards sensual satisfaction and towards God or the privileged moment – as initially separate but so closely related that they frequently become confused and inextricably intertwined. In *Pleasures and Days* this appears most clearly in the story of Mme de Breyves. How far the same situation is present in Rilke's work is suggested by Lou Andreas-Salomé's claim that the poem quoted earlier, 'Put out my eyes, I can see you', which in *The Book of Hours* is addressed to God, was originally written as a love-poem to her. Although there are strong factual and stylistic reasons for questioning this claim,[74] there is no doubt that in his letters to Lou Rilke did adopt a tone strongly reminiscent of the Russian monk speaking to God: 'I have never seen you except in such a way that I would pray to you. I have never heard you except in such a way that I would believe in you.'[75]

Rilke's fullest treatment of love in relation to the experience of God is given in the third part of *The Book of Hours*, 'The Book of Poverty and Death'. Here he introduces a vision of St Francis as a man in whom human possibilities were fully realised. He has an attitude of intense openness to all existence, in which erotic desire is fused with the love of nature; he was 'The warmest and most loving of them all/ ... in whom were wonder and contentment/ and a capture with the earth.'[76] He is also gifted with the power of poetic utterance, a creativity in which, again, erotic and artistic elements are indistinguishable:

> Dann aber lösten seines Liedes Pollen
> sich leise los aus seinem roten Mund
> und trieben träumend zu den Liebevollen
> und fielen in die offenen Corollen
> und sanken langsam auf den Blütengrund.[77]

But then the pollen of his song softly parted from his mouth's red lips and drifted, dreaming, to the love-filled ones, and fell into the open corollas, and slowly sank into the flowers' folds.

Rilke's vision of St Francis – which is clearly a projection of his own aspirations – shows that for him at this point the erotic and creative impulses had become so close that he saw them as the same thing. And in a letter written three days after the poem just quoted he expressed the same view explicitly:

artistic experience does indeed lie so unbelievably close to the realm of sexuality, to its pain and its joy, that the two phenomena are really only different forms of one and the same longing and bliss.[78]

It is significant, however, that these two statements were made within a very short space of time; they need not represent a view held permanently. Elsewhere in *The Book of Hours*, as we have seen, the two impulses were clearly distinguished and even opposed.

The vision of St Francis culminates in the idea that a man whose life has been so intimately and fruitfully fused with nature cannot be annihilated by death. When he died his being was 'divided out': 'his sperm ran/ in the streams, and in the trees it sang/ and out of flowers it calmly looked at him'.[79] Death is a central theme of 'The Book of Poverty and Death'. Shocked, on his arrival in Paris, by the meaningless, impersonal way of death in the city, Rilke is preoccupied in this book with conceiving an idea of death as a necessary part of life. He comes to see what he calls 'one's own death' as a positive experience; it is the crowning achievement of a life intensely lived like that of St Francis, or of another idealised figure introduced in this part, a future man who is called 'the one who gives birth to death'.[80]

Like his interpretations of childhood and love, Rilke's view of death comes close to that of Proust; in *Pleasures and Days* we met with a notion of 'conscious immortality' which owed nothing to the Christian conception of an after-life. Connected to the idea of death and oblivion, there is a further important parallel between the two writers: the positive value both attribute to memory. For Proust, as we saw, memory transfigures experience in a manner analogous to that of the privileged moment. In *The Book of Hours* it is a way of approaching God who, in one poem, is said to inherit the autumns that lie 'like sumptuous clothes in poets' memories'.[81] St Francis's creative existence likewise involves the remembrance of the past: 'And when he sang, even the yesterdays/ came back, and what had been forgotten.'[82]

The two writers are therefore in marked agreement in their interpretations of particular experiences as they are in their general view of the inadequacy of normal life. They are also alike in their evaluation of experiences. Proust, as we saw, built up a hierachy in which the places of particular experiences were determined by their degree of divergence from an ideal provided by the privileged moment. Rilke likewise valued them more or less according to their greater or lesser proximity to the experience of God.

Rilke's God therefore plays exactly the same rôle for him as the privileged moment does for Proust. And, as we have seen, the experience of God has all the main features of the privileged moment: heightened sensory awareness, the suspension of normal time, the expansion of the self. Should we not, therefore, see 'God' as another name for the privileged moment? There is an important reason why we cannot do so. Although Rilke emphasises direct experience and even sensory perception as the only means of contact with God, *The Book of Hours* does not contain descriptions of direct experiences like those in Chapter One. The book begins, it is true, with two poems describing a moment of heightened awareness in which the characteristics of an incipient privileged moment are clearly recognisable. But after this the distinct outline of a particular experience is lost and the poems become concerned with God in a far more general way, as prayers addressed to him.

These prayers are the poet's means of approaching God, who can never be directly experienced or possessed. He can only be invoked by prayer: 'when someone grasps you in the night,/ so that you have to come into his prayer'.[83] God is apprehended in or through prayer, in so far as he is apprehended at all. And because prayer is the only means of contact with God, it becomes for the poet the only real experience: 'There are at bottom only prayers.'[84] The poems of *The Book of Hours* (which Rilke originally planned to call 'The Prayers') are all prayers in this sense.

This is the fundamental difference between Rilke and the writers in Chapter One. For him the privileged moment, though it remains the ultimate goal, can only be experienced indirectly, through the creative process. The nature of this process will be studied in the next chapter.

## CHAPTER FIVE

# *Incantation: the Creative Process in the Early Period*

THE 'prayers' of *The Book of Hours* are Rilke's means of experiencing God. The words of the poems do not merely record or accompany the experience of God; they are an inherent part of it, and in some way they even cause it to take place.

There is one poem in which this appears particularly clearly. The poet begins by expressing a sense of expectancy, of a possibility latent in the evening scene; the landscape is 'ready for everything'. There is something, he does not yet know what, towards which he is drawn: 'Tell me, my soul, what you long for.' The soul's answer makes up the main body of the poem; it is a plea for identification with the landscape and, through this, for liberation and expansion: 'Be heathland and, heathland, be vast.' The possibility in the landscape is revealed as the experience of God, and identification with the landscape as the way of realising it: 'Be heathland, be heathland, be heathland,/ then maybe the old man will come/ whom I hardly can tell from the night.'[1]

This poem does not describe an event which has already taken place; the poet approaches the experience of God in the course of the poem. In another place we find a similar plea for identification with the evening landscape: 'Now be the earth and evening song/ and land that fits the sky.'[2] A further point is noticeable here: the poet wants to be identified not only with the landscape but also with a song. There was a similar situation in the opening sequence of poems: 'am I a falcon, a storm/ or a mighty song'.

It is as a song, or a poem, that Rilke seeks to reach God. In a number of places this is made explicit, for example when he says to God: 'I also am a song, hear mine/ which is so lonely and unheard.'[3] The same identification of poem and poet is apparent in the closing lines of the first part of the book: 'Then to his knees I come:/ and into him his songs/ flow thunderously back.'[4] The poem acts as a kind of bridge joining God and the poet; it joins them because God too, like the poet, is identified with the poem. In one place he is called 'God, the rhyme',[5] and in another he is 'the syllable in the song/ which, more and more vibrantly, the strong/ voices force to reappear'.[6] Quite literally then, Rilke experiences God in the poem, particularly in recurring parts of it such as rhyme. And he adds: 'You never showed yourself in any other way.'[7]

The way to God lies through language. More exactly it lies through creative language; God is in words used as they have not been used before: 'I believe in everything as yet unsaid.'[8] This line comes immediately after those expressing the poet's belief in God as ' a great power' near him in the darkness. At the beginning of 'The Book of Pilgrimage' he writes that he is resuming his prayers 'because my depths have in their power/ resounding words not heard before'.[9]

To experience God the poet depends on verbal inspiration, and this in turn has its negative side. When inspiration fails he feels deprived, alienated from himself: 'I am no longer master of my mouth/ which only wants to close up like a wound; .../ You force me, Lord, to an unfriendly hour.'[10] These lines appear early in the third part, which contains numerous pleas for inspiration such as: 'let me be the new Messiah's mouth,/ one crying out, the Baptist'.[11]

The writer confronted by the empty page is therefore facing, in a real sense, the emptiness of his own existence. But it is an emptiness which contains the possibility of infinite fulfilment: 'You feel the gleaming of a fresh-turned page/ on which all things may yet be done.'[12] The same image, the unwritten page pregnant with possibility, appears in another poem: 'Seven days I want, no more/ on which no writer yet has put himself,/ seven sheets of solitude.'[13] As he waits for inspiration the poet can compare himself to God on the point of creating the world; God too felt the oppression of nothingness and filled it with his voice:

> Gott, wie begreif ich deine Stunde,
> als du, daß sie im Raum sich runde,
> die Stimme vor dich hingestellt;
> dir war das Nichts wie eine Wunde,
> da kühltest du sie mit der Welt.[14]

God, how I understand your hour, when you put your voice before you that it might be round in space; nothingness was like a wound to you, so you cooled it with the world.

Here we can see how another aspect of Rilke's metaphysical system – the conception of Creation – has its origin in his own experience of writing poetry.

In the light of the foregoing the connection between Rilke's God and the act of poetic creation can now be clearly stated. Without poetry God is at best experienced as a remote possibility on the frontiers of awareness, yet separated from the poet only by 'a slender wall'. Poetic utterance is the means of removing this wall: 'a cry from your mouth or from mine – / and it breaks down';[15] the cry can be equally God's or the poet's since both are identified with the poem. God is a deep meaning in reality, but a meaning which is only partly revealed: 'You are the deep essence of all things/ which keeps its last word silent.'[16] Poetry is this 'last word' which fully reveals God. It is the means of completing, or realising, an experience which would otherwise remain marginal; it brings God from the fringes to the centre of consciousness. And since, as we saw in the last chapter, the experience of God itself embodies all the main attributes of the privileged moment, poetic creation can be defined as Rilke's means of realising the privileged moment.

This definition has been derived from the poems themselves, but it is also supported by evidence of a more external kind. Among the poems of the first version of *The Book of Hours* Rilke interspersed notes giving a kind of commentary on the writing of the book. In one of them he speaks of the 'harmony and serenity' which the verses brought to the monk;[17] in another he describes a state of intense awareness and of total identification with reality: 'the monk's depths grow bright and he feels himself lavished on all things, omnipresent in every joy'. This state is brought about and progressively heightened by the act of writing: 'he climbs up his verses as if they were steps and never grows tired.'[18] We see here that the creative process, once it has begun, generates, as it were, its own energy. The words the poet writes attract others spontaneously, effortlessly, and as they do so there is a sense of moving through rising levels of intensity. Looking back later on the writing of *The Book of Hours* Rilke recalled how the act of noting down fragments that came to him had 'strengthened and lured the inspiration'.[19]

Writing a poem, then, induces and progressively intensifies a state of consciousness having the essential characteristics of the privileged moment. This is stated most explicitly of all in a poem which Rilke wrote early in 1900, between the first and second parts of *The Book of Hours*. The language of the original is somewhat precious and need not concern us here, but the content is all-important. The first part of the poem, in prose translation, is as follows:

A single poem that I achieve and my boundaries fall like fences in the wind; there is nothing in which I do not find myself: not only my voice sings: all is sound. Things grow brighter and metallic, and as they, breathing, touch in space they are like bells, with silken cords, which fall into the hands of children playing:

The first sentence describes how the words of a poem, as he utters them, bring a sense of liberation from the normal limits of the self and a feeling of universal participation. Next we find a reference to the heightened awareness of objects followed by the sense of their total interrelatedness in space, conveyed by the image of bell-cords. The remaining lines show this feeling of unity leading to the state of ultimate bliss, which in *The Book of Hours* is called God:

> The children pull on all the strands at once that they find, astonished, in their hands, so that at heaven's gates, which open much too slowly, – the sounds are already clamouring.[20]

For Rilke, therefore, creative writing in this period was a means of realising the privileged moment, that is, of completing an experience which would otherwise remain latent or marginal. How far can this definition also be applied to Proust? It is more difficult to analyse the creative process in the case of Proust than of Rilke, because *Pleasures and Days* is less directly concerned with it than is *The Book of Hours*, and also because other sources of information are fewer. In his correspondence Proust is far less communicative about his writing than is Rilke.

*Pleasures and Days* does contain some indications of a connection between the creative process and the privileged moment, such as the remark in the dedication that poets while they write are 'closer to their souls'. But such indications are slight in themselves, and to obtain a more definite picture we shall have to look at passages in later works where Proust recalls the inspiration he experienced during this period. His miscellaneous writings contain a fragment entitled 'The Decline of Inspiration'; it is undated but its style and subject matter place it clearly in the period of *Jean Santeuil*, some years later than *Pleasures and Days*. Proust here looks back regretfully on the inspiration he had enjoyed earlier; he must therefore be thinking of the composition of parts at least of *Pleasures and Days*. He writes of inspiration as a 'sudden enthusiasm' which, when it appears, 'sends us galloping after it and at once makes words malleable, transparent, reflecting one another'. As with Rilke, words seem to attract each other and link up spontaneously. There is also in Proust's experience a feeling of liberation from the normal limits of the self reminiscent of Rilke's 'my boundaries fall like fences in the wind'; he calls inspiration:

> that enthusiasm, that cerebral renewal when all the partitions seem to fall and no barrier, no rigidity is left in us, when our whole substance seems a sort of lava ready to be cast, to be given the form we wish, without anything of us being left over and holding back.[21]

In this passage we also see how, during inspiration, the writer identifies himself entirely with the words he writes.

A very similar account of the inspiration which produced Proust's first works is given in *Jean Santeuil*, where he describes the literary

c

beginnings of a writer in whom it is easy to see a self-portrait. The young writer first becomes aware of his talent when he is asked by a school-friend for contributions to a boys' review; we should bear in mind that a number of the essays in *Pleasures and Days* as well as the sketch discussed on page 34 were originally written for schoolboy magazines. Proust even said in one place that the whole of *Pleasures and Days* had been written at the age of seventeen, though this is certainly an exaggeration.[22] The young writer's first inspiration is described in *Jean Santeuil* as follows:

> He began to write and suddenly, feeling the ideas crowding into his mind, the words moulding each other, embellishing and reflecting each other willingly under his hands, he felt a pleasure which is in truth the only reward of the man of letters.[23]

From the first, then, inspiration was for Proust a means of realising a particular pleasure; and this pleasure, as we see here, is the goal towards which the activity of writing is ultimately directed.

All these scattered references point to a conclusion similar to that reached in the case of Rilke. But the connection between the creative process and the privileged moment was only made fully and decisively explicit by Proust much later, in *In Search of Time Lost*. In this novel Proust no longer describes his experiences directly, but symbolises them in a way which will be discussed more fully in Chapter Sixteen. In doing so he reveals what he believes to be their essence. Early in the novel the hero, as a boy, is suddenly filled with delight by an effect of sunlight on a roof. He feels an impulse to express this delight but the only words that come to him are the uncontrolled expletive: *Zut, zut, zut, zut.*[24] Some time later he has a similar but more pronounced impression while looking at a group of steeples. He feels that the pleasure the steeples give him is not the whole of his impression, that there is something behind them, 'something they seemed at once to contain and to conceal'. This is markedly similar to Rilke's impression of God as a deep meaning partly revealed by the physical world, as 'the deep essence of things/ that keeps its last word silent'. And just as for Rilke this 'last word' is revealed when he writes a poem, the reality behind the impression of Proust's hero proves to be 'something analogous to a beautiful phrase'. He begins to find words for his experience and at once the hidden reality is revealed, the initial joy multiplied:

> Soon their outlines and their sunlit surfaces, as if they had been a sort of outer skin, split open, a little of what had been hidden from me in them was revealed. I had a thought that did not exist for me the moment before, which took the form of words in my head, and the pleasure which the sight of them had given me just before was so much increased that, seized by a kind of intoxication, I could no longer think of anything else.[25]

He writes a page of poetic prose describing the steeples, and when it is finished he has an intense feeling of liberation and fulfilment. A partial experience of heightened awareness has been realised by the creative use of language.

But in this passage Proust is symbolising his earliest creative experiences, not directly describing the writing of *Pleasures and Days*; we cannot draw specific conclusions from it concerning the latter work. Nevertheless, it does provide a valuable cross-reference to the study of Proust's early writing.

It is possible now to make a number of general statements about the creative process in the early period. These are based chiefly on the study of Rilke, but they are supported also by the available evidence relating to Proust. Both writers, as we saw in earlier chapters, have a general sense of the insufficiency of normal life, together with the intuition that somewhere a more real existence is possible. From time to time these feelings manifest themselves concretely through a particular object which seems to conceal a deep meaning beneath its superficial everyday appearance. Rilke calls this deep meaning 'God', and Proust, though far less systematically, 'the invisible'. This sense of a half-revealed meaning can be explained, in accordance with the arguments developed in Chapter One, as the intuition that the object concerned could be experienced in an entirely different and incomparably more intense and satisfying way: in a privileged moment. Each impression of God or 'the invisible' contains a latent privileged moment. Neither of the writers is capable of realising the latent experience directly, but both find instinctively that it can be realised indirectly, through the mediation of language. As they write about their impressions they experience the progressive intensification and unification of awareness which are characteristic of the privileged moment.

Creative language, then, induces heightened awareness; we must now consider how it does so. The first point which is of significance here is that privileged moments realised by language in this period do not occur in broad daylight. Evening is the time at which Rilke's God is invariably experienced: 'The more the day with ever fainter/ gestures bends towards evening,/ the more you are, my God.'[26] The point could be illustrated with almost unlimited quotations. In *Pleasures and Days* all the more intense privileged moments – 'Real Presence', 'Moonlight Sonata', 'Inner Sunset', 'As by Moonlight' – are experienced either in the evening or by moonlight. The incident of the steeples in *In Search of Time Lost* also takes place in the evening. The reason why half-light is propitious to the realisation of privileged moments can be readily given. As the light grows dim reality, while remaining visible, loses its everyday familiarity. The outlines of things become blurred and equivocal, so that they can no longer be instantly identified. The concepts through which we normally recognise the world around us adhere less tightly to our perceptions. We saw in Chapter One that it is these concepts which limit the intensity of consciousness; the connection between half-light and heightened awareness is therefore apparent.

The link between daylight and conceptualisation is reflected in the imagery of *The Book of Hours*. 'Light' and 'name', as we saw, are antitheses of God, and they are virtually equated in their tendency to dazzle and blind us to God: 'Name for us is like a light/ placed hard by our brow.'[27] The imagery here further indicates the connection between 'name' and cerebral activity. 'Name' is more or less a synonym for knowledge (*Wissen*), and can be taken in general to mean abstract throught-processes and the conventional language in which they are embodied. A similar view of conventional language as a limitation of consciousness is found in Proust. For him language is marked by the imperfection of everyday experience, it bears 'the trace of things'.[28] It is this trace which is effaced in the half-light when the world ceases to be a 'cruelly undeniable, monotonously habitual reality'.[29] The need to escape the sphere of conventional language also explains Proust's love of contemplating the sea and music, which he expressed in sketches in *Pleasures and Days*. And it was no doubt for similar reasons that the Russian steppes, like the sea a vast and featureless expanse, played an important part in the forming of Rilke's conception of God.

But the suspension of conventional language is only a part of the process of realising the privileged moment: it is the precondition for a new, creative use of language. Rilke calls the state in which conventional language is suspended 'silence'; but this silence of everyday speech is only the necessary background for poetic utterance, so that God is called 'you song we sang with every silence'.[30] Once conventional language is silenced it is possible to apply new names to reality, which means, above all, to create metaphors. Metaphor is for Rilke the essence of poetic activity; poets, he says, 'ripen through comparisons',[31] and contemplating the poor in Paris his reaction is characteristic: 'Consider them and see what might resemble them.'[32]

In a similar way the process of experiencing or creating God is one of giving new names to reality. God never receives a fixed, permanent designation, he is evoked by a constantly changing stream of images, frequently introduced simply by the words 'you are'. This is seen most clearly in one poem where, within sixteen lines, God is 'named' in the following ways:

Du bist der raunende Verrußte
Du bist der dunkle Unbewußte
Du bist der Bittende und Bange
Du bist die Silbe im Gesange
Du bist der Schlichte, welcher sparte
Du bist der Bauer mit dem Barte[33]

You are the sooty whisperer; You are the dark unconscious one; You are the anxious suppliant; You are the syllable in the song; You are the parsimonious, simple man; You are the peasant with the beard.

The same process takes place, in a less concentrated form, throughout *The Book of Hours*. The essence of God is therefore metaphor and transformation. Indeed, the notion of God is itself essentially a metaphor for the deep meaning that Rilke senses in reality. He sees a half-revealed meaning in the evening landscape and evokes it by calling it God. The idea of God has little or no specific content as he uses it. It is given content by the metaphors he constantly applies to God and, through God, to the landscape before him. God therefore acts as a *tertium comparationis*, a link between the external scene and the poet's images. In this way, by interposing 'God', Rilke gives his language greater freedom and flexibility; his images are only indirectly linked to the visible reality confronting him.

Proust's prose in *Pleasures and Days* is not, of course, directly comparable to Rilke's poetry; nevertheless, in the passages evoking privileged moments there is an extensive use of metaphor. In 'Real Presence' the lake is compared to 'a great fading flower',[34] and the onlooker's soul to the strings of a violin. In 'Moonlight Sonata' the moonlight flows like a river, and in 'Tuileries' metaphors are particularly numerous. The same is true of the passage on the steeples in *In Search of Time Lost*.

The use of metaphor makes heightened awareness possible by replacing the names which normally limit the awareness of reality by other, less familiar names. But this does not in itself explain why these unfamiliar names should be experienced more intensely by the poet than those which they replace. To understand this we must look more closely at the kind of metaphors the writers use. In the list of Rilke's metaphors for God quoted above it is noticeable that what they all have in common is not any visible or logical connection between the things they evoke, but a quality of sound. All the metaphors involve either alliteration or assonance or both, and this tendency is present throughout *The Book of Hours*. The most immediate and obvious links between words and ideas in the poems are those of repeated sounds, alliteration, assonance and rhyme. The work is above all a rich and complex tissue of repeated and interrelated sounds. It is unnecessary to quote to illustrate this – every poem and almost every line would serve as an example.

Why should this repetition of sounds affect the intensity of awareness? We saw in Chapter One that the everyday sense of time is bound up with the practical and rational attitude to reality which limits the intensity of normal consciousness. We also saw that this everyday sense of time, founded on abstract thought, can be supplanted by a more concrete sense of time provided by a rhythmically repeated sound or event. When this happens, awareness is given a temporal unity sufficient to allow the mind to disregard other factors, the sensations and preoccupations which normally unify experience. In particular, rational thought tends to be eliminated from consciousness.

The poetry of *The Book of Hours* acts in a similar way: the network of sound-patterns gives to the mind experiencing the poetry (as creator, and, to a lesser extent, as reader) a temporal unity serving to eliminate normal thought-processes. By this means the poems induce the heightened awareness and the identification with the outer world characteristic of the privileged moment. It is significant that when the desire for identification is most evident, as in the poem quoted at the beginning of this chapter, the impulse to repeat sounds is most insistent, to the extent that the same words are uttered again and again: 'be heathland, be heathland, be heathland'. In the German the assonance is still more powerful: *Sei Heide, sei Heide, sei Heide*.

Because of this tendency to use the repetition of sounds and formulae as a means of summoning up an invisible reality – God – and at the same time of achieving a trance-like state of identification with the outer world, Rilke's use of language in *The Book of Hours* may be called incantation. 'Incantation' in this sense is necessarily an involuntary and, to a large extent, unconscious process: the poet is led on by the inner dynamic of his inspiration, not by a rational or conscious control of his material. In a letter, Rilke wrote that the first part of *The Book of Hours* 'formed itself in a constant progression out of the following-up of an inner acoustic'.[35] That normal consciousness is excluded from the creative process is made clear in one of the poems where the poet describes himself as producing his work 'with eyes averted'.[36]

This form of inspiration, which depends on the ability to produce involuntarily a flood of resonant and harmonious language, Rilke spoke of as *Klang*, which might be translated as 'resonance'. In a notebook entry written on 12th September, 1900, between the first two parts of *The Book of Hours*, he describes an experience of this kind of inspiration:

I uttered a lot of verses which I do not remember today. I had resonance for everything and a thankfulness which I hurled out into the unknown, scarcely daring to address it to a God.[37]

The inner presence of *Klang*, of a possibility of creation through incantation, appears here to exist in advance of the particular content of the poem it produces. *Klang* might be defined, in the terms established in Chapter One, as an incipient state of heightened awareness, in which sound predominates over vision, time over space, and containing the possibility of realisation through an incantatory use of language.

This use of language, in which the predominant elements are rhythm and the repetition of sounds, has much in common with the most obvious and perhaps also the most superficial aspects of music. Rilke's attitude to music in this period, though not without ambiguities, is generally favourable. In a poem in his notebook of 1900 he calls music 'she who orders sounds';[38] like his poems, music creates a pattern and a unity out of the previously disconnected contents of awareness. Like the poems too, it releases the deep reality concealed in objects; in the same poem he describes music as setting free forms long imprisoned in things.

We find a similar emphasis on the musical quality of awareness in Proust's descriptions of privileged moments. The musical element is implied in the title of 'Moonlight Sonata', and 'Real Presence' contains an extended analogy between the soul of the onlooker and a musical instrument. There are also, in Proust's use of language in these descriptions, elements of what we have called incantation. In 'Moonlight Sonata', when the privileged moment is at its highest point, the incantatory element is made explicit: 'I called by her name my holy mother the night.'[39] It is also present concretely in Proust's style. Since he is writing in prose, he cannot use incantatory devices – alliteration, repetition and so on – as extensively as Rilke; but traces of these devices are to be found, for example, in the alliteration of the metaphor comparing the lake to 'a great fading flower' (*une grande fleur qui se fane*), or in the repetition of words in the sentence which comes soon after this:

> As they crossed the lake these little butterflies passed back and forth (*passaient et repassaient*) across our souls – across our souls stretched taut with emotion before such beauty, ready to vibrate – passed back and forth like the voluptuous bow of a violin.[40]

Here Proust is using language not only to describe an experience, but to bring about in awareness the state of disorientation and trance which he refers to explicitly in the next sentence: 'we almost passed out'.

It is clear that in this 'incantatory' manner of writing, sound and hearing are the chief factors involved; vision is of secondary importance. In Proust's evocations of privileged moments, above all in 'Real Presence', the visual element is extremely vague. In *The Book of Hours*, despite the brilliance and 'colour' of Rilke's language, there is virtually no description of the visible world. Visual impressions may serve as the starting-points of poems, but they are at once converted into 'God', and into sound patterns only tenuously related to visible reality. Even in the third part of *The Book of Hours* where Rilke is somewhat more concerned with describing visual impressions, he does so characteristically by relating them to, or transposing them into, sound. He writes, for example, of 'young women who, to the strange/ sound of their laughter, added a flower',[41] and of silk dresses which 'ring out' on a gravel path.[42] A similar transposition of visual impressions into sound is fundamental to Proust's method in 'Real Presence':

> Our souls had become sonorous and in the butterflies' silent flight they listened to a music full of charm and freedom, and all the soft, intense harmonies of the lake, the woods, the sky and our own lives accompanied it with a magical sweetness.[43]

Some conclusions may now be drawn. It was argued earlier that at the beginning of this early creative period Proust and Rilke were unable to experience the full continuum of the privileged moment as defined in Chapter One. Various 'helps' were discovered, primarily love. But now the most direct and effective 'help' of all has been found: artistic creation.

The creative process in the early period involves an incantatory use of language making it possible for the writers to realise the privileged moment to a degree of which they would otherwise be incapable. But this realisation of the privileged moment takes a particular form: it involves a unification of awareness in which the inner and outer worlds are identified through language, but in this identification the inner and outer worlds are not equally balanced. The predominant element is the words and images contributed by the mind; visual impressions from the outside world are reduced to a minimum. The normal separation between subject and object has been overcome, but by the suppression of the object rather than by a fusion of the two. The possibility of realising the privileged moment has been bought at the cost of a loss of contact with the visible world.

# CHAPTER SIX

## The First Crisis

ABOUT their mid-twenties, both Proust and Rilke showed a marked change in their way of experiencing reality. Whereas they had previously neglected visual sensation, they now became preoccupied with the act of seeing. 'I am beginning to see something new', Rilke wrote from Paris in 1903, 'already flowers often have such an infinite meaning for me, and I have had strange kinds of inspiration from animals ... I look at everything more calmly and with greater justice.'[1]

The origins of Rilke's new vision are to be found in his stay with an artists' colony at Worpswede in 1900. The notebook he kept there is full of references to his new-found vision: 'You really learn to see something new here'; 'How big the eyes grow here! They always want the whole sky'. The landscape, 'near and powerful and so real that you cannot overlook or forget it', is a dominating presence which totally absorbs the attention. Under its impact conversations with his companions invariably meet with the same end: 'for a while you walk on in conversations which the wind quickly destroys. Then one of you stops and after a while the other. So much is happening. Under the huge skies flat colourful fields are growing darker ...'[2]

Proust's new vision, in the corresponding period, was having a similar effect:

> We were passing in front of a border of Bengal roses when suddenly he fell silent and stood still. I stopped too, but then he started walking again and I did the same. Soon he stopped again and asked me with the soft, childish and slightly melancholy tone he always had in his voice: 'Would you be angry if I stayed behind a bit? I'd like to have another look at those little roses.' I left him. At the next turning in the path I looked behind me. Marcel had gone back to the rose-trees. When I had walked round the *château* I found him in the same place, looking fixedly at the roses. With bent head and a grave expression on his face he was screwing up his eyes and frowning slightly as if he were making a passionate effort of attention.[3]

In this anecdote Reynaldo Hahn recalls an incident which occurred in 1894 when he and Proust were staying as guests at a country house. He adds that he witnessed the same thing on many other occasions.

Proust himself describes numerous similar experiences of contemplation in the writings of this period, in *Jean Santeuil* and in a passage in his miscellaneous writings entitled 'Artistic Contemplation' which, though undated, contains abundant stylistic and thematic evidence that it was written at this time. In this passage a poet, who is clearly Proust, stops before a cherry-tree in blossom as if it were an apparition: 'He stays in front of this tree trying to close his ears to the noises from outside and to recapture the feeling he had just now when, in the middle of this public garden, alone on the lawn, this tree appeared in front of him.' The poet remains for an hour in this position, lost in contemplation.

These intense visual experiences may remind us of the privileged moments described in Chapter One, particularly that of Valéry on London Bridge; but they are far closer to everyday life. There is no mention of the ecstasy of the privileged moment, or of the identification with the thing contemplated. Although these experiences begin like the privileged moment with a sudden delight given by a visual impression, this is followed by a conscious and deliberate concentration of awareness on that impression, whereas the true privileged moment develops involuntarily and spontaneously. How much an effort of concentration is involved is made clear in 'Artistic Contemplation', where Proust says the poet is 'in front of things like a student endlessly re-reading the text of a problem he has been set and which he cannot solve'.[4]

This strenuous clinging to visual impressions clearly marks a radical departure from the attitude of the early period; what has brought the change about? To find the answer we must first examine some of the implications of the creative process discussed in the last chapter. We saw that the poet achieved an intensified feeling of existence by releasing a flow of incantatory language. He only exists intensely while writing, and from this it might be expected to follow that he will wish to write continuously. Such a wish is indeed expressed by Rilke in a poem of 1899: 'Oh, night after night after night/ I want to write/ and always, always be bending over pages.'[5] But the creative process we are concerned with is essentially involuntary, as the poet goes on to acknowledge. The words he writes are not of his own hand; they show 'that I myself am the hand of one/ who does strange things with me'. And yet his existence is wholly bound up and equated with these uncontrolled words – 'words whose closing syllable my life/ mysteriously covers'. Rilke, then, is not in control of his own destiny. His existence is in the hands of another on whose favour he depends. When this alien power abandons him he is exposed to non-being, he is an instrument without a player: 'You have made me like a lute:/ be, then, like a hand.'[6]

The note of abandonment and reproach discernible in these lines is expressive of Rilke's predicament. Similar sentiments are voiced by Proust, who was equally dependent on the favour of inspiration and no less disconsolate when it abandoned him. 'So the time when these transports are no longer renewed is a very sad one', he writes in a fragment already quoted, 'The Decline of Inspiration'. Only what he has writen during inspiration has any value for him. Anything that was produced by a mere conscious effort, however highly praised it may be, is totally indifferent: 'We should give all that for a minute of the strange power we had then, which nothing can restore to us.'[7]

The situation of both writers at the end of the early period is summed up in the following passage from a letter of Rilke's to Rodin of 1902:

> my work, because I so loved it, has become in these years a solemn thing, a feast-day, attached to rare inspirations; and there have been weeks when I did nothing except wait with infinite sadness for the creative hour.[8]

It is clear that this situation, in which the writers were dependent on a power beyond their control for the highest and perhaps the only happiness of which they were capable, must lead to a state of acute insecurity. In the crisis which marked the end of the early creative period these stresses undoubtedly played a major part.

But there is another way in which the early creative manner was bound to lead to an impasse. The two writers used language in an incantatory way to produce a kind of trance, a state on the verge of dreaming. Near-darkness was the condition most favourable to this form of inspiration, which was essentially verbal rather than visual. The severance from the visual world which this brought about was bound sooner or later to produce dissatisfaction and a sense of impoverishment.

Such feelings began to appear in Rilke's notebook even before his stay at Worpswede. They are expressed most clearly in a fictitious letter writen in April 1900 with the title 'From a Girl's Letter'. Despite the tone of whimsical sentimentality into which Rilke was prone to fall in such contexts, this letter is worth studying in some detail. It is ostensibly written by a girl who has just finished a journey, to another girl, her friend, who has stayed at home. But in the letter Rilke is clearly externalising a dialogue in himself between a part of him which is changing, and another part which he is leaving behind. It is in fact a dialogue between the future writer of *New Poems* and the writer of *The Book of Hours*.

The essential message of the letter is a condemnation of the state of 'dream' in which the two girls had lived together before the journey. In the light of her visit to a bright southern climate', even the most splendid of their dreams appears to the writer of the letter as pale and lustreless, 'like a Christmas-tree in the daytime'. What is more, the dreams had impoverished the girls' lives, they had swallowed up the energies which should have been turned outward: 'all your thoughts go there, there is no room in your eyes for the day'.

As the letter continues it becomes plain that these all-consuming dreams stand for the trance-like inspiration of the early period. During their dreams the girls had the power of utterance, and this is now presented as an impoverishment of their lives, a draining away of their vital energies into an unreal garden. Just as Rilke had been constantly trying to perceive God behind the outward appearances of things, the girls had spent their time looking for a reality beneath the surface of the visible world. They had 'thought all walls transparent' and thus had failed to notice the most immediate realities – their parents, the colour of the walls of the rooms they lived in, and so on. But the girl writing the letter has now discovered the reality of the visible world, and that all things, if contemplated with attention, will return and enrich her gaze: 'the more we look, the more splendid are the looks we receive in exchange'. She has thus discovered a new and unsuspected source of happiness, and hastens to warn her friend of the dangers of further cultivation of dreams. They are 'enemies who drink our eyes empty': in contemplating them we fix our eyes on something which lacks reality and will not return our gaze. She finishes the letter with the hope that her friend will soon be 'as far as I am'.[9]

We must remember, however, that this is, in effect, a dialogue and that when he wrote the letter one part of Rilke was not yet 'as far as' the other: the change in his vision was not yet matched by a modification of his poetic style. And soon after writing this letter Rilke left on his second journey to Russia with Lou, the tendency of which was necessarily to reinforce the old manner of writing of *The Book of Hours*.

But as soon as he arrived back from Russia Rilke went to Worpswede, and the first entry in his notebook there shows that the crisis had now arrived and had only been postponed by the journey. He is full of dissatisfaction with the fruits of the journey; instead of being enriched by what he has seen he feels impoverished and empty, though he does express a faint hope that something might still be salvaged: 'After all I did live through it all, I can't only have dreamt.'[10] But later in the same month this hope has disappeared; the journey has been wasted because his perception of reality is obstructed by inner visions:

> The Russian journey with its daily losses is such a distressing proof to me of the unreadiness of my eyes; they are unable to receive, to hold on to or even to let go of anything; weighed down with tormenting images they pass beauty by on their way to disappointments.[11]

Rilke, then, has repudiated the early manner of experiencing reality; it involves an impoverishment of existence which he can no longer accept.

In the case of Proust, in the absence of documents comparable to Rilke's Worpswede notebook, it is, again, more difficult to trace a similar pattern of development. His letters, as mentioned already, throw little light on his inner life. On the other hand the novel *Jean Santeuil* is very much concerned with his inner development and there is a passage early in it which, because of its relevance here, may be mentioned in advance of the study of the novel as a whole. It is a passage which symbolises the essential difference between *Jean Santeuil* and *Pleasures and Days*; in it Proust seems, perhaps even consciously, to 'unwrite' certain typical parts of the earlier work, such as 'Real Presence'.

The passage in *Jean Santeuil* begins, like 'Real Presence', with a description of the effects of half-light on water. But this is not an evening scene leading to darkness and trance – it is early morning, and gives way to daylight and wakefulness. Proust goes on to draw attention explicitly to the questionable aspects of his earlier preoccupation with half-light:

> Instead of fading into an ever vaster silence, the light grew brighter and brighter as the noise of the waking birds grew louder, so that those magical tints, the dreams of evening and morning which, if they were not so quickly effaced, would warp our perception of things, were gradually blended into the brightness of daylight and life.[12]

The half-light now does not transfigure, it merely distorts. And whereas daylight previously served only to reveal the cruel banality of reality, it now heralds a world of colour and joyful vitality. But Proust, like Rilke in the 'girl's' letter, has not himself fully completed the development symbolised in this passage. He admits to a regret at abandoning the enchantment of evening, and the persistence of the mood of 'Real Presence' is further indicated when he adds that a part of these enchantments lies in their promise to fulfil impossible desires. We saw that these – clearly erotic – desires played an important part in the sketch in *Pleasures and Days*.

For Proust, therefore, the early non-visual, dream-orientated creative process involves a distortion, for Rilke an impoverishment, of reality; this is the second major cause of the crisis. Like the first – the sense of insecurity resulting from the uncontrollable nature of their inspiration – this cause is of an existential kind, bound up with the effects of the creative process on the lives of the writers. But there was in addition a third main cause, which was less existential than artistic in nature.

The early creative process had been verbal rather than visual, had involved sound rather than sight. Rilke himself used the term *Klang* for the inner state from which the poems spontaneously emerged. *Klang* is a potentiality for utterance which is used up by the poem. On his return from his second trip to Russia, however, he had new doubts about this kind of creation. He noted that on one occasion the same experience of *Klang* had given rise to two quite different poems. Clearly there is no very necessary relationship between the inspiration and the specific content of the poem, and Rilke is faced with the conclusion: 'my seeing is by no means as closely linked to my creating as I then thought'. Indeed, *Klang* may not in the first place be bound up with words at all: 'I do not know one word from this web of sounds, I do not even remember whether they went with words.'[13]

The description of external reality therefore plays only a minor part in his poems. Some years later Rilke remarked in a letter that nature, in the early period, had been no more than a 'general occasion' for his poems: 'As I walked I did not see nature but the visions it aroused in me.'[14] In this situation where the words of the poem are only tenuously connected to the objective world, reality offers no limit or check to the utterances of the poet. As Rilke himself later observed: 'I could have gone on writing similar verses indefinitely, and what then?'[15] As a result, his early work, including *The Book of Hours*, is marred by a looseness and facility which the poet himself dismissed long afterwards as 'a lyrical superficiality and a cheap ... *à peu près*.'[16] On the artistic level too, therefore, the early creative process led to failure and crisis.

A similar sense of artistic failure contributing to the crisis can be detected in the case of Proust. He was painfully conscious that *Pleasures and Days* had not been a success with the reading public. His hypersensitive reaction when his friends playfully ridiculed the work probably indicates that he inwardly shared their misgivings, as does the following otherwise inexplicable remark to a friend in a letter of about this time: 'You alone of us have created a work.'[17]

Apart from these external indications, the artistic failure of *Pleasures and Days* is evident in the work itself. It is true that the psychological and analytical parts of the book have certain qualities of subtlety and elegance, but the poetic parts with which we are concerned here, and which Proust himself valued most, have obvious shortcomings of which Proust, an astute literary critic, can hardly have been unaware. The lacrimose vagueness and artistic nullity of 'Real Presence', for example, need no detailed demonstration here and are sufficient to condemn the creative process which produced them.

The crisis which for both writers marked the end of the early creative period was not a sudden break with the past – its effects were spread over a number of years. Rilke continued to write poems in the old manner after the revelation of the Worpswede landscape. For a long time he did not express his new vision in poetry at all; it was confined to prose descriptions in his notebook. But in these passages we find what his poetry lacks: a precise notation of physical detail, even when he is describing an evening scene:

> The evening is always large when I come out of this house. The slender new moon hangs like bright glass in the amber sky. The woods are black, and coolness comes from them without wind across the path and the meadows that lie beside the water. There the trees have already lost more leaves and the whole of space has grown. Things stand out against the plain with soft contours, like many islands in the dim air.[18]

To see how far Rilke's prose style is from his poetic manner in this period, the passage can be compared with a characteristic poem which deals with the same subject-matter – heightened awareness at evening. That the prose passage is concerned with heightened awareness is clear from the reference to the expansion of space. In the poem, the attempt to 'realise' a privileged moment through language is quite apparent; but in this attempt, in forcing his words to yield a maximum of rhyme, assonance and alliteration, he neglects their descriptive value and deprives the scene of all sense of physical reality:

> Die Abende sind warm und zart,
> und ihre sanfte Gegenwart
> macht alle Dinge gut;
> ein jedes neigt sein Haupt und lauscht,
> und in den stillen Dingen rauscht
> die Schweigsamkeit wie Blut.
> In diesen leisen Stunden wird
> machtlos und müd die Zeit:
> Die Dinge rühren sich, befreit,
> und jedes wandert unbeirrt
> zu seiner Ewigkeit.[19]

The evenings are warm and delicate, and their mild presence mollifies all things; each one, listening, bows its head, and in the peaceful things the silence makes a rushing noise like blood. In these gentle hours time grows powerless and tired: things, set free, begin to stir and each one moves, unwavering, towards eternity.

In addition to its failure to convey any definite visual impression, this poem also exemplifies another aspect of the artistic bankruptcy to which the early creative process was bound to lead. It begins, like all poems attempting to realise a privileged moment through language, with an impression of nature. But whereas most of Rilke's poems, particularly in *The Book of Hours*, are carried far from the initial impressions by the internal resonance and associations of the poet's language, here the poem is confined strictly to the immediate scene. As a result, the particular privileged moment is realised more clearly and completely than in most other poems, but this serves only to show up more sharply the limits of such art. For if the subject-matter is restricted to the privileged moment only, there is very little for the poet to say. He can only describe more or less clearly the successive stages of heightened awareness, as in this poem. Poetry produced in this way is bound to be repetitive and monotonous, unless it takes the other course, discussed earlier, of escaping into facile verbosity, into a 'lyrical superficiality' divorced from reality.

In the poetry of this period reality – particularly landscape – is seen as a formless, undifferentiated totality permeated, in *The Book of Hours*, by the unifying presence of God. But in the prose, for example the passage just quoted, a change in the vision is apparent: there is a new sense of form, of the contours of separate things which Rilke calls 'islands'. That he was himself fully conscious of this change is made clear by another passage written at Worpswede:

> Things always seemed to me like arms and extremities joined to the great body of the earth; but here there are many things which are like islands – isolated, bright, with the air, never still, flowing round them on all sides. That makes their forms so powerful.[20]

Although Rilke did not at this stage possess the means to realise his new sense of form in poetry, a number of the later poems written at Worpswede express at least the desire to do so, as well as dissatisfaction with the present lyrical manner. The 'soaring song' is not enough, he writes in one poem; he must dare to express his intuitions in a form which will be 'visible far and wide'.[21] Another poem contains what seems to be a repudiation of the whole idea of *Klang*, in favour of form: 'I am an image./ Ask not that I speak ... My life is this: the stillness of a form.'[22]

But these poems are only statements of Rilke's intent, not realisations of it. Lacking a new technique to replace the old, which was now highly developed, he was obliged to go on writing in the manner of *The Book of Hours*, two more books of which were produced before the style was finally abandoned. But in the later books there are significant changes, in subject-matter if not in style. The predominant darkness of the first book gives way in the last to a world of light and colour: 'he came from light to light forever deeper,/ his cell was set in bright serenity'.[23] Similarly, in the later passages of *Pleasures and Days* such as 'Underwood' and 'Chestnut Trees', both dated 1895, there is an increased tendency to describe daylight scenes.

In their search for a new style more adequate to a highly visual awareness of reality, both writers were instinctively drawn to visual art. In September 1900 Rilke wrote: 'It seems I am only now beginning to learn how to look at pictures',[24] and his notebook contains numerous exact descriptions of paintings. Proust in the period of roughly 1895–1900 frequently visited the Louvre with his friends, and wrote numerous essays on paintings.

In addition both writers, uncertain of their own resources, looked anxiously for guidance from other artists. Rilke, again in September 1900, expressed the need for a teacher even before he was fully aware who the teacher was to be: 'For everyone there is no doubt a mentor somewhere.'[25] The teachers they turned to were both artists primarily concerned, though in different ways, with visual art: Rodin and Ruskin. Proust began reading Ruskin about 1895, and Rilke's Worpswede notebook already contains lengthy discussions of Rodin's work. But their interest in their respective masters was not to crystallise into absolute allegiance until some years later – about 1900 for Proust and 1902 for Rilke.

During the years in which the future revelation was, as it were, gestating, Proust was writing *Jean Santeuil* and Rilke *The Book of Images*. We shall have to examine these books, both of which are essentially works of transition, before the importance of Ruskin and Rodin for the two writers can be fully appreciated.

# CHAPTER SEVEN

## *Jean Santeuil*

'CAN I call this book a novel?' Proust asks at the beginning of *Jean Santeuil*. To answer his question we should have to begin by defining the novel – a task which cannot be attempted here. What can be said, however, is that at least up to Proust's time an essential requirement of the novel was plot, that is, a unified narrative, a chain of significant incident. This in turn implies character, for, in the words of Henry James: 'what is character but the determination of incident? What is incident but the illustration of character?'[1] For our purposes, then, plot, incident and character will be taken as necessary criteria for a novel.

*Jean Santeuil* has incidents, but it has neither plot nor a convincing central character. It might be argued that a plot is provided by the theme of Jean's intellectual development, which appears to be the main subject of the book. But this development, which is in any case inconclusive, is not the book's organising principle. Jean is frequently only marginally involved in the events narrated, and their influence on his development is clearly not Proust's reason for including them. Nor is Jean as a character able to provide a centre of interest which might give the book unity. He never takes on sufficient substance and identity to arouse the reader's interest or concern. He is too passive to provide the impulse required for the unfolding of plot.

The book therefore clearly fails to satisfy the requirements for a novel set out above. It fails so completely that we are bound to look for an explanation. Was it that Proust was ignorant of these requirements or that, knowing what they are, he felt he had good reason to ignore them? With this question in mind it is instructive to examine in some detail the opening pages of the 'novel' proper – the chapter entitled 'Evenings at Saint-Germain' where the narration of Jean's life begins. A critic has remarked on the competence with which these pages are written;[2] they are clearly the work of an accomplished novelist fully in control of his material. The characters are drawn with insight and detachment; Proust is able to present a number of people together, showing their interaction with an impressive economy of means and sureness of timing. From the scene in the garden interest switches at the appropriate moment to the mind of Jean himself, and Proust gives a convincing portrayal of the child's reactions.

So far so good – the reader becomes absorbed in a convincing illusion of reality, as in so many other novels. But then there is an unexpected development: when the incident comes to an end the narrator, previously concealed behind the action in the manner of a 'realistic' novelist, suddenly emerges and comments directly on the scene that has just been described, in particular on its relation to Jean's later life. In so doing he begins himself to take on a definite personal identity; remarking that we shall not have occasion to return to this childhood scene, that Jean's life will carry us far from it as it carries Jean himself, he adds this wistful afterthought: 'and no one, alas, can live his childhood twice over'.[3]

The effect of this intrusion of the author's emotions is to detach the reader abruptly from the scene in which he was previously immersed. He becomes still further estranged from Jean and the action as the narrator goes on to analyse the scene's general significance and to relate it to later incidents which are only vaguely sketched in. This is followed by more abstract discourse and further references to Jean's later life.

The next chapter, 'Evenings at Dieppe', follows a similar pattern. It begins with the description of a physical scene, but the narrative soon gives way to general discourse and then to another reference to Jean's later life:

> Ten years later, when his life had become very different, one day in the rue du faubourg Saint-Germain he felt a vague regret for the lost years of his irreplaceable childhood and his life in the open air ...[4]

But the reader has not been shown the substance of the lost years referred to, so that the word 'irreplaceable' seems gratuitous. He is unable to enter sympathetically into the experience of this older Jean who appears from nowhere. As a result he is left unmoved by a scene which is so poignant for Jean that he sees it 'through his tears'.[5]

It is clear by now that Proust's method of proceeding from one point of time to another in this seemingly arbitrary way does not produce an effective novel. Situations, characters and plot are not allowed to develop in their own right, but are abruptly manipulated with insufficient use of concrete detail to support the illusion of reality on which the reader's attention depends. But it is also clear that Proust is not attempting to write a novel on the conventional pattern. He has shown that he is able, if he wishes, to construct a connected chronological narrative, but that he is really interested in something quite different: the moment when the focus changes, when the scene that is being described recedes abruptly, giving a sudden perspective of the depth of past time. This effect, as we saw, is closely bound up with the direct intrusion of the novelist into the narrative and, as he states explicitly in two separate places in *Jean Santeuil*,[6] it was this device which Proust valued above all else in a novel. He also wrote in a letter that the opening pages of *The Mill on the Floss*, where such a change of temporal perspective is used with great poetic effect, moved him to tears.[7] He tries repeatedly to achieve something similar at the beginning of *Jean Santeuil*, to the detriment of his narrative.

Why, then, did Proust so value this device that he was willing to sacrifice to it what might have become a successful novel on the conventional pattern? This is not only a question of technique: it leads to very fundamental issues. For to answer the question why Proust wrote as he did, we must first answer the question why he wrote at all. And we cannot do this without an understanding of his basic experience of life. We must look first, therefore, at what the novel tells us about this underlying experience.

Throughout *Jean Santeuil* there is a feeling, either attributed to Jean as he grows older, or expressed more directly by the narrator, of dissatisfaction with life, of a duty left undone, of bad conscience:

> The thought of the four years which he had completely wasted since leaving school never left him, filling him with irritation and despair. Each of his empty, sterile days was, in diminished form, their desolate and sterile image.[8]

The same pervasive mood also appears frequently when the narrator addresses the reader directly with a general reflection. In one place he remarks, for example, that whenever we revisit a place after a long absence we are reminded how little we have done in the interval to approach the happiness it had seemed to hold out to us when we were last there.[9] In the passages of this kind there appears both a remorse for a neglected duty – that of discovering happiness – and at the same time a partly-contradictory belief, reminiscent of *Pleasures and Days*, that life is in any case incapable of satisfying the desire for happiness: 'Life is only beautiful from a distance. In reality it holds nothing more in store for us than is to be found in the most tedious schoolday.'[10]

This underlying sense of the nullity of life, and of the futility of action as a way of achieving happiness, explains why the novel lost its direction after the first few pages. For to take an interest in creating a plot, that is, a chain of significant actions, it is necessary to have some belief in the significance of action itself, of its rewards or failure. But Proust had no such belief, and was unable as a result to generate in his narrative the momentum of unfolding action which gave the traditional novel its inner necessity and unity. Instead, his novel meanders without apparent cause between past and present, taking root in neither, and the attention of novelist and reader wavers between the hero Jean and the narrator who is clearly also Jean looking back in later life, and who so easily eclipses the insignificant puppet he is supposed to animate.

Proust's fundamental experience of life therefore explains why he rejected the traditional form of the novel, even if it does not yet account for the new form which he tried to put in its place. It also points to the answer to the other question raised just now: the question why Proust wrote at all. For his belief that life could not be fulfilled through action was coupled to an intuition that it could be fulfilled in a different way: through artistic creation. It is very likely that he wished to illustrate this in *Jean Santeuil* by making the hero become a successful writer; but he could not do so convincingly until he had become one himself, which no doubt he hoped to do in the process of writing the novel. Unfortunately, for reasons which we shall see, this plan came to nothing: the novel was a failure. Jean, accordingly, is unable to advance beyond the state of a would-be artist full of impotent remorse, and Proust is obliged to introduce his conception of the successful artist through a number of much more peripheral figures. In them we can see the kind of writer he was himself trying to become; and by examining what he says about them we can discover why he saw art as the only possible fulfilment of life.

For these writers art is the supreme and only duty. When C., the ostensible writer of the novel, is found to have a predilection for social excursions – a taste he shared with Proust – this is treated as a moral weakness. Balzac is taken to task for saying that if he could live his novels he would not need to write them.[11] This is for Proust a fundamental error: it ignores the fact that art is intrinsically superior to life, that what is important in a book is not the material the writer uses but 'the nature of the work carried out on it by his mind'.[12] Literature should not imitate life but transcend it: Naturalist and Impressionist novels are therefore dismissed as 'a useless competition with inexhaustible and unsatisfying reality'.[13] For the same reason character-drawing is not the novelist's main task: 'we have more profound things to do than to fix character traits, however general or particular they may be'.[14] What are these 'more profound things'? Proust goes on to give the answer: they are moments when 'nature dictates revelations which we feel it is essential to write down'.

To see what this means in practice we must look at Proust's successful writers at work. They all have a similar manner of creating, based on inspiration. The act of writing grows out of an intense inner state which gives rise to words and images – 'a certain enthusiasm which preceded the arrival of his thoughts and which they exalted as if they were something real that he must hold fast and record without changing anything'.[15] Here Proust is describing the inspiration of the novelist Traves; C.'s manner of writing is essentially the same. In the case of the poetess Mme se Réveillon, Proust goes further and indicates the source of the creative enthusiasm; it springs, he says, from 'the marvellous gift of feeling one's own essence in things, or feeling the essence of things';[16] it arises, therefore, from an experience which we have seen to be an essential aspect of the privileged moment. This form of inspiration, originating in an exalted fusion of the self and the world and producing an intensification of that state, bears an unmistakable resemblance to the creative process discussed in Chapter Five.

But in *Jean Santeuil* a number of important additions are made to the conception of the creative process that has emerged in previous chapters. Firstly, involuntary memory – the resurrection of the past through a coincidence of past and present sensations – is given much greater importance than it had either for the writers in Chapter One or in the works of Proust and Rilke discussed so far. The narrator even asserts in one place that involuntary memory was the only source of his inspiration,[17] which would mean that it gave rise to the whole novel. It is unlikely, however, that this statement should be taken literally. Elsewhere Proust writes that inspired moments often – not always – involve remembrance of the past.[18] In fact he has two separate conceptions of the creative process at this stage. Both involve inspiration, but in one case this gives rise to memories and in the other to new ideas which spring from 'the feeling of a great power to go beyond, to bring to light a thousand thoughts'.[19]

The writer to whom this last statement is applied is Silvain Bastelle, another member of the gallery of successful artists in the novel. The account of Bastelle's creative experiences contains many echoes of 'Artistic Contemplation', the sketch discussed in an earlier chapter; the similarities are so pronounced that the two passages must have been written close together in time. Fundamental to them both is the idea that visual contemplation is at the origin of artistic creation, and this emphasis on visual contemplation is Proust's second major addition to the notion of the creative process in the period of *Jean Santeuil*. It plays a part in both the conceptions of inspiration just discussed, that involving memory and that producing new ideas. In addition, it is treated as a valuable experience in its own right, even when it does not lead to creation. In other words, experiences of this kind have a central importance in the novel, and Proust's descriptions of them must now be examined more closely.

The first appears in the section entitled 'Étreuilles'. The narrator experiences an 'infinite pleasure' at the sight of an apple tree in blossom. There seems to be a deeper reality beneath the surface of his impression, 'a life quite different from that which we sometimes call life'. The parellels to the privileged moments in Chapter One are evident, but there is also a characteristic difference: the deeper reality is revealed here as 'a past time when we saw similar apple trees',[20] evoked by the coincidence of sensations. An experience of the same kind, this time involving the contemplation of a rose-border, appears later in the novel.[21] Here Proust is in fact transcribing the incident which Reynaldo Hahn refers to in the anecdote quoted at the beginning of the last chapter. The intense delight the roses give Jean is again attributed to the recollection of the past.

But shortly after this incident a number of strongly visual privileged moments are described in which memory plays no part. Jean feels an intense unity existing in all the things around him:

> The woods, the vineyards, the stones themselves were harmonised with the sunlight and the clear sky; and when the sky clouded over, as if by a change of tone, the multitude of leaves, the earth of the paths and the roofs of the town all remained united in a new world.[22]

As in the privileged moments in Chapter One, particularly those described by Valéry, a system of harmonious relationships unites all parts of the scene. And these relationships extend to include the inner world of Jean: 'each of Jean's feelings too seemed to remain effortlessly in unison with everything, and he felt the perfect enjoyment that results from harmony'. There is no doubt that this is one of the most intense privileged moments described by Proust so far, though even this does not seem to be as highly developed as some of those in Chapter One. Here, the relationship between the self and the outside world is one of harmonious participation rather than of total identification.

No attempt is made to relate this experience to the remembrance of the past, and the same is true of another privileged moment described at length later in the novel. Here Jean is filled with a sense of intoxicated delight by the spectacle of a winter day; again, all parts of the scene are interrelated, every detail is significant; 'there was so little empty space, everything was so tightly-knit in this living matter trembling in unison' that, for example, a moving horseman and his shadow seemed to Jean to answer each other like two instruments in an orchestra.[23]

From the numerous descriptions of privileged moments in *Jean Santeuil*, of which only a small cross-section has been given here, two facts emerge clearly. Firstly, Proust is nowhere able to experience privileged moments with the same intensity as the writers in Chapter One. Secondly, his privileged moments fall into two distinct classes: those involving involuntary memory and those involving the direct perception of the present. He does, however, frequently speak of involuntary memory as the explanation of all such phenomena. There is therefore the same inconsistency here as in his explanation of inspiration discussed earlier.

It is worth investigating why Proust should have been so manifestly inconsistent on this point. One reason is no doubt that he wrote the novel over a long period; while he was working on one episode he probably had only a vague idea of what he had written elsewhere. But there may also be a more fundamental reason. Proust was anxious not only to describe his experience but to understand it, and the attraction of involuntary memory for him was that it seemed to offer a total explanation for the experiences that seemed most important to him.

In one section, 'Impressions Regained', this need for a comprehensive explanation becomes particularly clear: Proust attempts here to derive a whole philosophy of life from a moment of involuntary memory. A period of his past life that had been quite indifferent to him while he lived it is suddenly filled with beauty and meaning when he re-experiences it through involuntary memory. What has caused this transfiguration? The answer which Proust gives can be summarised as follows. The only way in which we can truly enjoy reality is through the imagination, and the imagination is incapable of experiencing the present. It is prevented from doing so by the personal element – what Proust calls *ce quelque chose de personnel*[24] – which is inseparable from experience in the present. By this personal element we are to understand the egoistic, active preoccupations which attach themselves to the impressions we receive in each moment: 'it was my will which experienced them, directing them towards some goal of pleasure or fear, vanity or malice'.[25] An effort of will, says Proust, can never reveal to us the essence of our experience, because it remains tied to our egotistical preoccupations. For this reason voluntary memory too is denied access to essential reality. Only involuntary memory can sever experiences from the personal element and reveal their true essence, which for Proust does not belong only to the past but is the 'common essence' of past and present.

The implications of these ideas with regard to the creative process will be discussed in a later chapter. What is more important here is the light they throw on Proust's conception of the novel. They have shown us why action was for Proust intrinsically incapable of satisfying man's desire for happiness: it prevents us from experiencing life through the imagination. But action, and *ce quelque chose de personnel*, are precisely what had provided the subject-matter and indeed the *raison d'être* of the traditional novel, and a view of life which seeks to eliminate the personal element from experience is difficult to reconcile with the idea of writing a novel.

Proust however is not deterred by this. The experience of involuntary memory has given him the conviction that there is something deeper and more real in life than the personal and temporal level of existence; it seemed to him as if 'our true nature were outside time, made to enjoy the eternal and dissatisfied with the present, saddened by the past'.[26] Our true self, for Proust, is not the part of us which is involved in action and is confined to a single moment of time. It is something much vaster: the essence of all the moments of our past life, preserved in a timeless dimension which normally lies outside our experience, but which can occasionally be glimpsed through involuntary memory. This dimension constitutes reality for Proust; it is not surprising, therefore, that he did not share the Naturalists' conception of literature as the imitation of empirical reality. The task of literature as he saw it was to make visible the true but normally hidden reality of our experience – 'a reality which we spread around us as we write pages which synthesise the diverse moments of life'.[27]

We have now arrived at the answer to the fundamental question raised earlier: the question why Proust wrote at all. We have also seen more clearly why he rejected the traditional form of the novel. What still remains to be discussed is how far he was successful in *Jean Santeuil* in creating a new form more appropriate to his conceptions of the self and reality.

It is not possible within the scope of this chapter to engage in a detailed technical analysis of *Jean Santeuil*. And we must remember that the arrangement of the material as it is published is the work of an editor and does not necessarily correspond exactly to Proust's plan, in so far as he had one. However, a number of clear points do emerge and can be established briefly. As noted earlier, Proust abandons the attempt to write a chronological narrative of Jean's childhood after the first few pages and becomes increasingly preoccupied with relating Jean's, and other characters', experiences directly to later periods in their lives. The notion of a common sensation linking two moments is introduced early on and throughout the first section there is a repeated attempt to weave the narrative thread into a wider temporal fabric. The effect produced, however, is not that of a synthesis, but of a series of disconnected episodes.

In the next section, 'Étreuilles', this approach is taken further. There are numerous, sometimes lengthy, descriptions of moments of involuntary memory, in the course of which an important technical difficulty arises. In order to relate different moments together Proust is obliged to introduce numerous sketches of the hero at different times of his life without having time to develop any of them. This leads to constant confusion as to which of the many 'Jeans' who appear is experiencing any given moment. Sometimes experiences are attributed to the child which clearly belong to the older man, and the account of Jean's childhood often seems to be no more than a pretext for describing things – notably privileged moments – which preoccupy the author.

Another major technical problem which becomes apparent is that Proust's concern with coupling together widely-separated moments fails to provide a dynamic driving the narrative forward. It leads to the description of moments, or pairs of moments, for their own sake, but provides no way of linking these fragments in a wider unity. The narrative is only a starting point for analogies with other times, and Proust returns to it only because there is nothing else for him to do when a particular analogy has been exhausted. This constant switching from one point in time to another, bewildering as it is, soon becomes monotonous. Proust does what he can to vary it, sometimes making the transition without warning or explanation, a procedure which, if it breaks the monotony, only adds to the bewilderment. In one place he even attributes an impression he is introducing to the reader: 'And have you not, reader, ... sometimes yourself had the feeling ...';[28] he now gives a detailed account of what is clearly a recent experience of his own. This is no doubt an attempt to avoid the repetition yet again of the formula: 'Later, Jean had a similar impression ...' It also has a further significance which will be discussed in a later chapter.

Proust's preoccupation with involuntary memory and with his special conceptions of reality and the self did not, of course, lead him to exclude all traces of the traditional novel. Despite his assertion that the novelist has more important things to do than to 'fix character traits', his evocations of the past are interspersed with character sketches combining humour with psychological penetration. The novel also contains a necessary element of action. This, however, characteristically takes the form of repeated or typical events narrated in the imperfect tense, and is thus absorbed into the dominant, descriptive mode of writing.

The next section of the book in which Proust's attempt to realise his special conception of literature appears most clearly is that entitled 'Réveillon'. This is largely a transcription of Proust's stay at a country house referred to in Reynaldo Hahn's anecdote quoted in Chapter Six. Here, description is again the dominant mode, but it now has a brilliance and an immediacy which we have not met before in Proust's writing:

> The whole lawn was sunlit, not only made blond, golden by the sun, but saturated, soaked with sunlight, nourished with it as a woman who has slept too long seems nourished with sleep, sunlight that now and then appeared visibly at the tip of a blade of grass, sparkling.[29]

In this and the many similar passages in this section we can see how far Proust has advanced beyond *Pleasures and Days* in the rendering of intense visual sensation, and how his emphasis on the importance of visual contemplation in inspiration during this period is reflected in his style.

Involuntary memory appears in this section, notably in the transcription of the rose-border incident referred to in Reynaldo Hahn's anecdote, but it does not account for the pervasive joy in the visual world which is present throughout the section. Proust is less concerned here with explaining heightened awareness than with describing it for its own sake, and he shows that he now has a prose style which is fully equal to the task.

In section VI of the novel, however, involuntary memory is again his central preoccupation; numerous descriptions and analyses of the experience are accumulated, giving a repetitive effect which may be due in part to the editing, but which does show strikingly Proust's almost obsessive concern with the privileged moment. After this the experience appears less frequently, though in significant contexts. At one point Jean is brooding over the impermanence of human attachments when the sight of a group of trees suddenly reminds him that beyond the world of normal experience – 'mediocre, soon finished for us, utterly human and familiar' – there is another world which is 'eternal, eternally young, mysterious, full of wonderful promises'.[30]

Proust's fervent and somewhat breathless language in this passage gives the impression that he is making a last attempt to gain access to the mysterious world he has glimpsed. So, after the sentence just quoted, forgetting his narrative, he evokes a series of similar impressions, letting his inspiration take him where it will. But this carries him barely half a page before the description, which inevitably turns into narrative as it becomes more particularised, begins leading him in a direction he cannot follow, and the passage breaks off inconclusively.

In a similar way the novel itself was abandoned unfinished. Proust as we saw, was convinced that to write his novel, and in so doing to discover the meaning of his life, he had to concern himself with the privileged moment; but he had little idea of what this involved in practice. He wrote without any clear plan, including experiences for their own sake rather than for their relevance to a wider structure. He wrote about the moments of his life that had been most intense, most significant, or simply most pleasurable. In places this pleasure-criterion becomes quite overt: 'Many other moments besides these were agreeable at Étreuilles ... '[31] But as he accumulated more and more of these moments in his book he became aware that, far from constructing something significant, he was, in his own words, 'amassing ruins'.[32] Sooner or later he would have to break off.

The discussion of the novel so far has inevitably given the impression that privileged moments constitute the bulk of its subject-matter. This is by no means the case; whole sections of the book are devoted to other themes, in particular to those of society, love and public affairs. All these themes, however, are related to, and ultimately subordinated to, the privileged moment. As was the case in *Pleasures and Days*, Proust opposes social existence to the life of the imagination; his descriptions of society serve to emphasise by contrast the value of the privileged moment. Love is shown as having the power to transfigure reality in the manner of a privileged moment, but it is by its nature self-limiting: in a formulation which is particularly worth noting in a comparison with Rilke, Jean's mistress is called 'that mysterious face interposed between him and the happiness whose rays could come only from her'.[33] Being inseparable from a human relationship, the happiness of love is imperfect and transient, and Proust contrasts it explicitly to that of the privileged moment which, so involuntary memory seemed to him to prove, is eternal.[34]

The treatment of love and society, then, can be seen as an extension of Proust's preoccupation with the privileged moment. It might seem more difficult to make the same assertion with regard to the other main area of subject matter – that devoted to public affairs and in particular to the Dreyfus trial and the 'Marie affair'. Certainly, in these parts of the book Proust seems closest to the rôle frequently assigned to him of the Balzacian chronicler of his time, describing political events for their own sake. Even here, however, the privileged moment exerts a decisive influence. Proust's chief interest in the Dreyfus trial lies in the chance it gives him of playing off one of the protagonists, Picquart, whom he sees as exemplifying the philosophical and poetical intelligence and to whom he attributes privileged moments manifestly drawn from his own experience,[35] against the sterile would-be writers like Rustinlor who, incapable of the effort demanded by creation, feverishly dispense their unused energies in external activities such as politics. The defence of Dreyfus turns into a defence of Proust's conception of literature, with its emphasis on inwardness and solitude, against the 'engaged' literature of 'all those crows who just by beating the air with their cries thought they were portending the future'.[36]

Proust's concern with the 'Marie affair', admittedly, has no such motivation. In Marie, who was 'neither a dreamer nor melancholic', he seems to be going out of his way to create a character as unlike himself, or Jean, as possible. Nevertheless, Proust here is far from being merely a detached observer; the episode is profoundly related to his own personal existence. Its theme is guilt and the horror of discovery, coupled with an attempt to justify what the world condemns. Proust's life, dominated secretly by his homosexuality and the impossibility of revealing it to his mother, offers a parallel situation. The actual form taken by Marie's guilt in the novel seems contrived and unconvincing in relation to the anguish and catastrophe it causes. But Proust's description of the consciousness of a man at the moment of realising that he has been discovered and disgraced has the ring of intense personal experience: 'A certain heaviness in the head and the sight of that blue vase on the cupboard, that was the form in which horror suddenly came upon him.'[37] Marie is the first embodiment in Proust's work of the guilty man leading a double life, who carries his secret with arrogance but is finally humiliated and crushed. Perhaps it is not far-fetched to see in the last picture of Marie – 'His hair was now quite white, he was broken, prematurely decrepit, with a sadness at being removed from power that his despair no longer dared avow to his pride'[38] – a first glimpse of the Charlus of 'Time Regained'.

Another episode which has its roots in the same conflict in Proust's life is 'Daltozzi and Women'. Daltozzi, in his obsessive pursuit of his all-too-physical dreams, is clearly a reflection of Proust's vision of himself, or of his fears of what he might become. There is even a clumsy confession of the link between himself and his creation in an 'Author's Note' where Jean, having seen a photograph of Daltozzi's mother in his room, the scene of his orgies, swears never to expose his own mother to a similar spectacle.

What is striking about both this episode and the Marie affair is that they are alive in a way which makes them stand out from the rest of the novel. They come closest to satisfying the criteria for the novel outlined at the beginning of this chapter; their theme – guilt – gives unity to plot and character and a sense of drama to the action. Marie and Daltozzi, though peripheral figures in the novel, are far more impressive as fictional creations than Jean himself. This is because they are animated by an important emotional conflict, or 'drama', in Proust's life: Jean, on the other hand, is allocated only the least compromising, and least interesting, of the author's experiences. The theme of vice and homosexuality is relegated to minor characters, not only to Marie and Daltozzi, but to numerous others. Proust fails to bring his main character to life because he is not yet willing to make the truth about himself the central theme of his novel.

But apart from his homosexuality there was a second and equally tormenting 'drama' in Proust's life. It was his feeling, already mentioned, that he was wasting his life, procrastinating from day to day instead of devoting himself to the work which he knew he must write. But this theme too he fails to express through his protagonist. The reason may be bound up with his use of third-person narration, which separates the hero from the intimate concerns of the narrator. These find expression only in passages where the narrator brushes Jean aside and addresses the reader – or himself – directly, in a tone of anxious communing close to despair. The immediacy of the emotion conveyed in these passages makes Jean and his problems seem, by contrast, doubly unreal and remote.

For these reasons Proust failed to write a satisfactory novel of plot and character, which, in parts of the book at least, he was no doubt trying to do. But we have seen that his main concern was to write an entirely different kind of novel giving expression to his special conceptions of reality and personality. In this too he failed, because he was unable, as we saw, to solve the technical problem of turning the privileged moment into literature.

We can now return, therefore, to Proust's opening question: 'Can I call this book a novel?' He goes on himself to give a kind of answer: 'This book was never made, it was gathered.' It is true that, in *Jean Santeuil* he has gathered together, though sometimes only at its periphery, all the themes and ingredients needed for his novel. But in so doing he has not yet written the novel. Having gathered his book, as J. M. Cocking remarks,[39] he still has to make it.

# CHAPTER EIGHT

## The Book of Images

THE *book of images* consists of poems written before, during and
after the crisis discussed in Chapter Six. It is a work of transition, in which Rilke can be seen looking for subjects and for a
style. As might be expected with a collection produced under these circumstances, the poems vary widely both in subject-matter and in
quality. The range of themes is so wide as to give an impression of confusion; and the question we must be concerned with in this chapter is
whether, underlying this disparate material, there is a fundamental
unity.

In many of the poems Rilke restates and develops themes which
were prominent in *The Book of Hours*, notably those of childhood and
love. As in that work, the poems are permeated by a sense of the
inadequacy and incompleteness of life: 'Life is only a part..... Of
what?/ Life is only a note..... What in?' And, again as in *The Book of
Hours*, this dissatisfaction is coupled to an intuition that somewhere a
more intense consciousness is possible: 'Life is only the dream of a
dream,/ but wakefulness is elsewhere.'[1] But though the poet normally
feels only the absence of this intensity, there are moments when it is
present. His life, he says in one poem, is 'now confined, now comprehending',[2] it alternates between intensity and the lack of it.

The mood of the poems moves between the same two poles. Many
express anxiety and deprivation: 'How remote all is/ and how long
past./ I think the star/ that sends me light/ has been dead for thousands of years.'[3] But in another poem, 'Prayer', the poet is moving
closer to the life he desires; he asks the night more hopefully to bring
him into contact with the things it harbours. In the next poem, 'Progress', the desired state is reached: 'And once again my life runs deeper,
louder/ as if it flowed within a broader bed.'[4] He feels an expansion of
his inner life, and an increased participation in the scene around him:
'Things become more and more akin to me/ and images more closely
looked upon.' This feeling leads to a merging with nature, a penetration of the normally impenetrable:

> Dem Namenlosen fühl ich mich vertrauter:
> Mit meinen Sinnen, wie mit Vögeln, reiche
> ich in die windigen Himmel aus der Eiche,
> und in den abgebrochnen Tag der Teiche
> sinkt, wie auf Fischen stehend, mein Gefühl.

I feel more acquainted with the nameless: with my senses, as if with birds, I reach from the oak-tree into the windy sky, and into the broken-off daylight of ponds my feeling sinks as if it were resting on fishes.

This expansion of awareness into nature closely resembles the experience of the monk of *The Book of Hours*, as expressed, for example, in the lines: 'I live my life in growing circles/ spreading outwards over things.' A poem in *The Book of Images* contains a markedly similar formulation: 'Life has meaning only when joined/ to many circles of far-widening space.'[5]

This experience of expanded and heightened awareness – in other words, the privileged moment – is therefore the positive pole contrasting to the negative experience of life discussed earlier. Round these two poles the other themes of the book are clustered.

One of the foremost of these, as already mentioned, is childhood. The child's experience of external reality as an undifferentiated totality, as in the poem 'Childhood', is clearly related to the kind of awareness enjoyed during the privileged moment. Love is valued for similar reasons; it characteristically takes the form of unrequited longing – a state which confers heightened awareness, a sensitivity to normally imperceptible sensations: 'Do you hear, beloved, how I raise my hands –/ do you hear the sound it makes.' In this state, the things around the poet seem to 'listen' to him, to participate attentively in his existence. This sense of participation is such that his smallest actions seem to involve the whole cosmos: 'On my breathing's rise and fall/ the stars are carried.' This cosmic implication of the experience is taken still further: in his state of heightened receptivity, the unsatisfied lover gains an awareness of 'distant angels'.[6]

The angel is one of the principal motifs of *The Book of Images* and, as we have just seen, it is directly related to the privileged moment. Rilke's angel, like the other biblical elements in the book, has little in common with Christian conceptions. It is a being which, in a similar way to the God of *The Book of Hours*, answers the poet's call for inspiration. In 'The Guardian Angel' it comes to him when he calls in the night; and he calls it, the poem says, not by its name, which is a chasm too deep for him to sound, but only with wild gestures. The summoning of the angel, then, is bound up with the problem of verbal expression, with the naming of the unnamable: 'what shall I call you? See, my lips are crippled.' Here again there is little apart from nomenclature to distinguish the angel from the God of *The Book of Hours*.

In summoning the angel, the poet is trying to call back the moments when he escaped the apathy and mediocrity of normal existence; often, he says, the angel lifted him out of darkness, hoisting him 'like scarlet flags and draperies'.[7] Rilke's use of the flag to symbolise the colour and splendour of his existence in these moments must be noted, as must the definition he now gives of the angel as the being in whom this intensity of awareness is constantly achieved:

> Du: der von Wundern redet wie vom Wissen
> und von den Menschen wie von Melodien
> und von den Rosen: von Ereignissen,
> die flammend sich in deinem Blick vollziehn, –[8]

You: who speak of miracles as if they were common knowledge, and of men as melodies, and of roses: as things that happen, blazing, in your gaze.

Here we can see not only that the angel is a symbol of the privileged moment, but also, in the same way as in *The Book of Hours*, that the experience which it symbolises is closely bound up with the use of language: in the lines just quoted 'speaking' is an integral part of the angel's experience.

We noted that the flag is another motif connected to the privileged moment. If this image is pursued in the poems, further links between the disparate elements making up *The Book of Images* are discovered. The image appears, for example, in one of the historical poems, in a description of a battle seen through the eyes of a young king: 'the wind, lean as a panther,/ leapt into the flags'. The context in which the motif appears here is highly significant for this study. The king, in the midst of danger, is overcome by a sense of dream and wonder. He falls into a state of intense contemplation in which every detail of the scene before him is perceived with exceptional lucidity: 'he had woken up to seeing'. He has achieved the state of 'wakefulness' normally absent from life which was referred to earlier in this chapter. In this state, the poem continues, all things seem to speak to each other, they all have voices, and their souls are suspended 'as if in many bells'. It is clear that the king is experiencing a privileged moment, in which all parts of awareness are united by a sense of *Klang*, in which familiar things take on a new significance – 'even the wind raged differently' – and in which time is suspended: 'Sluggish vapours filled the darkness,/ and the darkness was not time'. The description becomes increasingly grandiose, and finally, the stars seem to be involved in the experience, as in the love-poem quoted earlier, and the flag-motif appears once more.[9]

Extreme danger is therefore another of the experiences, like love and creative writing, that can stimulate the awareness of the privileged moment. For Rilke the idea of danger was inseparably bound up with the boyhood dreams of military glory, fostered by his father, which led to a rather romantic interest in history and even to the writing, in adolescence, of a study of the Thirty Years' War. The boyhood enthusiasm for military adventure is expressed in *The Book of Images*

D

in 'The Boy': 'I would I were like one of those/ who ride by night on fiery horses.'[10] A few lines later the boy sees himself raised up like a flag at the head of the troop. The reappearance of the flag-motif here indicates the connection between the theme of the boyhood interest in military history and that of the privileged moment; through this connection Rilke is able to bring his interest in history and battles into the sphere of his creative preoccupations. This helps to explain the large number of poems with historical subjects that are included in *The Book of Images*.

The link between the flag image and the privileged moment enables us to interpret the poem 'Anticipation' as forming a sequence with two poems already discussed, 'Prayer' and 'Progress', which directly precede it. In this poem the flag, which senses the approaching storm long before the things on the ground are stirred by the wind, symbolises the approach of a privileged moment: 'I know the storm already and am tossed like the sea.'[11] The image of the flag beating in the storm-wind is particularly appropriate to the poet during inspiration: both are shaken and totally possessed by an elemental force. Storms, too, are frequently the subject of poems in *The Book of Images*. In 'Storm', the poem following 'Anticipation', the poet's consciousness reflects the stormy skies to the point that he identifies himself with the landscape. Here the connection between the storm of the privileged moment is still implicit; in other poems it is more directly stated. At the beginning of the cycle 'From a Stormy Night' the landscape during a storm is described as transcending its normal limits in space and time; it is spread open like a fan, 'as if, before, it had been tucked away/ within the petty pleats of time'. As in those experienced by the lover and the hero-king in the poems discussed earlier, this privileged moment induced by the storm takes on a cosmic dimension in which the star-motif appears, while the normal limits of individuality are also transcended: 'where the stars withstand it the night does not end/ … nor at my face,/ nor with your form'.[12]

By tracing various motifs in *The Book of Images* we have seen how the different areas of subject-matter are linked together through their common connection with the privileged moment. The situation is therefore similar to that in *Jean Santeuil* where the apparently unconnected elements of the book were united below the surface by the pervasive preoccupation with the privileged moment. This does not mean, of course, that either work has artistic unity, only that each is animated by a single predominant concern. The parallels between the two works extend to the treatment of particular themes and experiences. We have just noted Rilke's treatment of storms; Proust in *Jean Santeuil* reacts to them in a similar way: the sound of the wind, obliterating all human thoughts, induces heightened awareness.[13]

There are other, more central, parallels between the two books. For Rilke as for Proust, reading is a means of inducing heightened awareness. In one poem, the act of reading interrupts the flow of time, which builds up round the reader like dammed water. This is coupled to an intensified awareness of reality, not of the reality described in the book, but of that actually surrounding the reader, which is filled with harmony and interrelatedness:

> Und jetzt wird Sommernacht, soweit man sieht:
> zu wenig Gruppen stellt sich das Verstreute,
> dunkel, auf langen Wegen, gehn die Leute,
> und seltsam weit, als ob es mehr bedeute,
> hört man das Wenige, das noch geschieht.

And now, as far as the eye can see, is the summer night: the scattered things converge into few groups; darkly, on long paths, people move, and strangely distant, as if more important, one hears what little is still happening.

The inner and outer worlds are unified, and the limits of normal life disappear: 'Out there is what I live within,/ and here as yonder all is limitless.' This privileged moment finally reaches the same cosmic proportions as those discussed earlier in the chapter; the earth seems to expand to embrace the whole sky, 'the nearest star is like the farthest house'.[14] The introduction of the star-motif in such contexts occurs so regularly that it must be taken as fundamental to Rilke's conception of the privileged moment.

A still more important parallel between *The Book of Images* and *Jean Santeuil* is the value attached in both to memory. In the poem 'Memory' we see that for Rilke the longing for the privileged moment is at the same time a desire for remembrance: 'You wait, await the single thing/ by which your life is endlessly increased'; this increase is felt when the depths of the past are opened. The poem does not say exactly how this happens, but the experience is shown to involve a visual impression – the sight of old bookcases – which sets off a train of recollection until suddenly a past year's 'fear and form and prayer'[15] appears before the poet as an intensely present reality.

There is undoubtedly something here of the experience of involuntary memory as described by Proust. But Rilke's conception of memory differs from Proust's in that for him the recoverable past extends beyond the memories of his personal life; experiences are inherited from generation to generation. In 'The Singer Sings before a Young Prince' the boy is told that the past is the substance of his true life; his immediate temporal existence is no more than a dream. According to the singer, the function of the past is to provide images corresponding to actions and feelings in the present; experienced in this way the past becomes an inward possession without which the present is impover-ished. It is because Rilke saw the past as incorporated in heirs such as this young prince, frequently the last of their line, that he makes them the subjects of a number of poems in this collection. Seen in the light of this poetic intuition, Rilke's much-derided attempt to establish an ancient lineage for himself may have had something more than snobbery at its origin.

Rilke's sense of the nullity of ordinary life therefore leaves room for another, more inward, sphere in which past and present co-exist. Memory is one way of reaching this sphere; another way, in this col-lection, is blindness. In 'The Blind Woman' the loss of sight leads to a heightening of awareness through the other senses; the blind woman hears inaudible things: time flowing over her hair, silence ringing in fragile glasses, the breath of a rose passing close by her hand. She possesses the world inwardly, freed from its normal imperfections: 'Now all things go about in me,/ secure and nonchalant'; and because, as the poem says, she has already 'died to the world', she is no longer subject to death.[16]

Connected to the notion of an inward sphere independent of time, a special conception of death is beginning to emerge in Rilke's poetry. Those who achieve a state of inwardness in their lives, and detach themselves from the world of the senses normally experienced by adults, gain access to a kind of immortality. This idea is taken farthest in 'Requiem', a poem about a girl who dies in childhood. As a child she existed outside and above the world of adults, aware of its poverty: 'for you knew: that is not *the whole*'. In death she has passed into a realm of intensity, and enjoys a deep contact with the beauty of nature. In this sphere the heaviness of human existence is removed, the earth is 'full of balance', and like the God of *The Book of Hours* she no longer distinguishes as men do between the ideas 'up' and 'down': 'You will no longer be able to tell/ what rises or falls.' The dead girl has reached a state in which what was only a longing on earth is a possession; in other words, Rilke sees death in this poem as the per-manent enjoyment of the total awareness of the privileged moment:

> Jetzt weißt du *das Andre*, das uns verstößt,
> so oft wir's im Dunkel erfaßt;
> von dem, was du *sehntest*, bist du erlöst
> zu etwas, was du *hast*.[17]

Now you know *the Other* that rejects us whenever we grasp it in the dark;
from what you *longed for* you are delivered to something that you *have*.

In this notion of a realm of inwardness independent of time, in which the distinction between life and death has no place, we can recognise, with the advantage of hindsight, an early configuration of the world of Rilke's late poetry. In addition, we have already found in this collection a number of motifs which were to be central to the *Elegies*: the angel, the unrequited lover, those who die young, the child, the hero. And most important of all for this study, all these fundamental conceptions of the late poetry have been seen to grow directly out of Rilke's preoccupation with the privileged moment.

But Rilke still has, of course, a long distance to cover before he can write the late work. Elements of it can be traced in *The Book of Images*, and synthetically unified as in this chapter, but as they actually appear in the poems they are far too fragmentary, and overlaid with too much extraneous material, to give unity either of style or subject-matter to the book. In this respect too, Rilke is in roughly the same position as Proust in *Jean Santeuil*. Both are aware of the importance of the privileged moment, and derive from it a notion of reality departing radically from empirical experience. But they have little idea of how they are to turn this into a work of literature; frequently they can do no more than list the impressions received during privileged moments. An example of this in Rilke's case is the poem 'On Fountains'; he begins by describing a vague sense of revelation given by a fountain, and this leads him to recall other moments of heightened awareness; the poem becomes a series of disconnected fragments and finally tails off inconclusively in much the same way as similar passages in Proust's novel.[18]

Although *The Book of Images* reveals an unmistakable lack of purpose in its author, it begins with what appears to be a statement of a definite artistic programme. The opening poem contains the following directions to the artist: 'With your eyes ... you slowly raise up a black tree/ and set it before the sky: slender, alone./ And you have made the world.' Contemplated in this way, the tree takes on the significance of the whole world; and this awareness of its significance leads to expression: the tree is 'like a word still ripening in silence'. But at the moment of expression, visual contemplation comes to an end: 'And as your will encompasses its meaning,/ tenderly your eyes let go their hold ...'[19] This poem, written in February 1900, prefigures Rilke's attempt to achieve the more visual approach to reality which, as we saw in Chapter Six, was to begin in earnest at Worpswede later that year. But his practice does not generally correspond to the programme expressed here.

Numerous poems, such as 'At the Night's Edge', written a month before that just quoted, show Rilke still entirely under the influence of the early ideal of *Klang*: 'I am a string/ stretched over wide/ rushing resonances.'[20] In 'The Blind Woman', written after the stay at Worpswede, he still expresses the belief that visual impressions benefit from being transposed into sound.[21] In a similar way the angel, which, as we saw, symbolises the privileged moment realised through language, is associated with music rather than with visual art. In a poem already quoted the angel 'speaks of men as if of melodies',[22] and in another the angels are called 'many, many intervals/ in the might and melody of God'.[23]

Elsewhere, however, an ambivalent attitude towards music appears. In 'Madness', written in November 1899, the perception of reality in terms of music is virtually equated with insanity,[24] and in a poem written some months earlier, music is seen as a force undermining life.[25] The later poems in the book reflect a definite progression away from *Klang*. In 'The Blind Man's Song' (1906), Rilke goes far towards reversing the positive evaluation of blindness he expressed earlier in 'The Blind Woman'. Now the blind man is aware only of pain and deprivation; with his grey hand on the 'grey greyness' of his wife's arm he is led through 'utter emptiness'.[26] In the privileged moment described in 'The Reader' (1901) the visual scene is no longer experienced as an undifferentiated totality, but, in the terms of the Worpswede notebook, as 'islands': in the passage quoted the scattered things surrounding the poet 'converge into groups'. The brilliant rendering of light and colour in 'The Confirmands' (1903) shows the value Rilke now attaches to visual sensation.[27]

'Evening in Skåne', written in 1904 and revised in 1905, expresses a moment of heightened visual awareness. The self becomes totally absorbed in contemplation of the clouds; the colours are meticulously described, and the whole spectacle is grasped as a self-contained structure, moving and resting within itself:

> Wunderlicher Bau,
> in sich bewegt und von sich selbst gehalten[28]

In the revised version, Rilke removed the last remaining subjective elements. He had reached the opposite position to that of the early period, where the visible world was submerged and lost in the self. This poem points clearly towards *New Poems* and the middle period. But to see how Rilke reached this position we must now examine in more detail the part played in his development by his admiration for Rodin.

# CHAPTER NINE

## Ruskin and Rodin

I N 1903 Rilke was in despair over his art. He had achieved nothing, he wrote to Lou; everything he had written so far was worth-
less, he must start again at the beginning.[1] The first edition of *The
Book of Images* had been published the previous year: we must infer
that it had not been a success in Rilke's eyes. It is not difficult to see why
this was so. The title implies that the poems should be pictures, separate
visual unities; but the poems in this collection are not capable of existing as pictures in their own right. The main reason for this is that Rilke
is still using the style, and particularly the rhythm, of *The Book of
Hours*: a strongly unified, musical language with a fast, unbroken
*tempo* carried by the rhythm. This language is not well suited to the
creation of images; it does not allow the mind's eye to rest long enough
on a single point to produce a visual impression. 'Evening in Skåne',
where the rhythm is slower and the visual effect correspondingly more
satisfactory, was of course written later than the poems of the first
edition.

When Rilke went to Paris to study Rodin in 1902, he temporarily
abandoned the writing of poetry as his main occupation. Before he
could return to creative work, he was determined to learn the 'handicraft' of his art, starting from the 'lowest, humblest point'.[2] His problem was to find this point. In another letter of this time he has begun
to glimpse it: 'Is the handicraft perhaps in the language itself?'[3] It
seems as if, whether consciously or instinctively, his purpose in writing
his monograph on Rodin was to school his language. In the monograph he describes a large number of works of art which are, for him,
totally successful; he forces himself to re-create them in his own
language, and in so doing he gives his language new powers of expression. This was the way in which he sought to escape from the
impasse he had reached.

In about 1900, when he abandoned *Jean Santeuil*, Proust was in a
similar deadlock; he had come to see his creative activity as one of
'amassing ruins'. He too began to look for a way out of the impasse,
and like Rilke he turned to a non-creative activity – that of translating
Ruskin. The parallel between Proust and Rilke is therefore very close
here. Both have chosen models who oblige them to render into words
the most visual and concrete of all arts: sculpture. In particular, both
have become concerned in this way with the sculpture of Gothic
cathedrals.

The value of sculpture for them was that it gave clear expression to that which in them was 'unsayable, confused and enigmatic'; it came to the help of a time 'whose torment it was that all its conflicts lay in the realm of the invisible'.[4] The words are Rilke's, but they apply to Proust's situation as much as to his own. Both writers, as we have seen, had been trying unsuccessfully in their works to express 'the invisible': a reality transcending the empirical world, a realm of eternity and inwardness intimated through privileged moments. In turning to sculpture, the most tangible of the arts, they are not re-pudiating their intangible higher reality, but trying to approach it in a different way. What attracted them to Rodin and Ruskin was that, in them too, they found a belief in a higher reality; but these artists, unlike Proust and Rilke, were able to express this reality.

Ruskin, as seen by Proust, was a writer whose life was dominated by a sense of the presence close to him of 'an eternal reality intuitively perceived through inspiration'.[5] Similarly, Rodin's art for Rilke was concerned with revealing in his model 'that piece of eternity through which it had a part in the great course of eternal things'.[6] It was because Rodin and Ruskin seemed to have gained sure access to an eternal reality that Rilke and Proust saw in them, and in the imitation of their lives and work, a way to their own salvation. Each spoke of his respective master in tones of an almost religious reverence; each called him a prophet.[7]

The importance of the two masters lies, however, not only in the fact that they believed in a higher reality, but in the manner in which this reality manifested itself to them. The reality which Ruskin 'intuitively perceived through inspiration' was revealed to him, Proust wrote, by 'the feeling of beauty, in nature as in art'.[8] An example of such an experience of beauty in nature is to be found in *Praeterita*, a work which Proust claimed to know by heart in 1900.[9] Ruskin writes of a day of depression in France, when he lay down under some trees to try to sleep. His attention was attracted by a visual impression: 'the branches against the blue sky began to interest me, motionless as the branches of a tree of Jesse on a painted window'. This heightened awareness of the tree led to a creative act which further intensified the impression:

> Languidly, but not idly, I began to draw it; and as I drew, the languor passed away: the beautiful lines insisted on being traced, – without weariness. More and more beautiful they became, as each rose out of the rest, and took its place in the air. With wonder increasing every instant I saw that they 'composed' themselves, by finer laws than any known of men. At last, the tree was there, and everything that I had thought before about trees, nowhere.[10]

This privileged moment, realised by artistic creation, is described by

Ruskin as a major formative experience in his life. Rilke saw similar experiences as the source of Rodin's art. In his lecture on Rodin he asks the audience to recall such moments in their own experience, moments when a previously indifferent object is suddenly transfigured:

> one day you were struck by its intense, imploring look, the peculiar, almost despairing seriousness which they all have; and did you not then notice how there came over this spectacle, almost against its will, a beauty that you had not thought possible.[11]

The artist's task, says Rilke, is to facilitate such apparitions, to create circumstances favourable to 'that which sometimes is disposed to come among us'.[12] In the first version of the lecture he states this idea still more directly: objects are 'vessels', and the artist's task is to attract into them 'something which under certain conditions came'.[13]

We can see here how close Rilke still is fundamentally to his position in *The Book of Hours*. The function of art is still to lure an elusive 'something', which we have seen to be the quality of awareness during a privileged moment, into consciousness. What Rilke has changed is the method by which this is to be achieved, and his terminology. He no longer calls the true reality of the world – and here the change is most apparent – God, but a surface. The desired quality of awareness is not now to be summoned by the incantatory use of language, but by manipulating this surface. But the underlying purpose is unchanged; the disciple of Rodin is pursuing the same thing as the monk of *The Book of Hours*, and Rilke himself is fully aware of this. He writes in one place that the man whose meditations led him to the conclusion that 'everything is God' was as much saved and redeemed as he was who concluded that 'there is only a single surface, filled with a thousandfold movement'; this man, too, has had his life's task placed 'simply and entirely in his hands'.[14]

In view of this it is not surprising that Rilke continues to speak of the artist's task in terms of religious humility and awe; in creating favourable circumstances for the appearance of beauty, he writes, one is only providing 'an altar and fruits and a flame – the rest is not in our hands'.[15] This may be compared with the terms used by Proust in an essay on a painter written during this period; he calls the artist 'a sort of priest whose life is devoted to serving this divinity, nourishing the sacred animals which please him and burning the incense which facilitates his appearances'.[16]

But this conception of the artist does not imply that he is entirely at the mercy of the divinity of inspiration. He has a measure of control over it, conferred by work. Work can prolong inspiration; it is, Proust writes in the same essay, 'the effort to remain in it entirely'.[17] He saw Ruskin as exemplifying this conception of work, and quoted

D*

approvingly one of his master's favourite dicta 'Work while you still have light.'[18] Rilke, when he went to Rodin to ask how he should live, received the same commandment: 'One must always work – always.'[19] He saw Rodin as an artist who, by a lifetime of work, had achieved complete mastery over inspiration; he could even deny the existence of inspiration since, experiencing it permanently, he no longer felt it coming and going. From this Rilke went on to derive the simple dogma underlying his long infatuation with Rodin's work: 'one can rest assured: he who works is happy'.[20]

Through the example of Ruskin and Rodin, Proust and Rilke were able to believe in the possibility of identifying work with spiritual and artistic progress, and this provided them with the remedy to the crisis discussed in Chapter Six. It gave them not only a doctrine of salvation, but also a practical programme. For Proust, this took the form of translating and annotating Ruskin, and visiting Gothic cathedrals. For Rilke the programme was still more specific; his aim was to adapt to his own medium the creative powers he saw in Rodin: 'Somehow I too must learn how to make Things; not plastic Things: written ones.'[21]

Rilke here uses the term 'Thing' in a special sense; and by analysing the meaning he gave the term, we can go far towards an understanding of what he hoped to achieve by his emulation of Rodin. The concept is developed from the 'Thing' of *The Book of Hours*, but through the study of Rodin it has acquired a far more specific meaning. In its new form it is introduced in the 1907 lecture on Rodin as follows:

*Things*
As I pronounce this word (do you hear?) a stillness forms; the stillness surrounding Things. All movement comes to rest, turns into contour, and out of past and future time something lasting is composed: space, the great tranquillity of Things which nothing drives onwards.[22]

It is at once evident that the qualities attributed here to the 'Thing' closely resemble those of an object seen during a privileged moment. And in fact, the notion of the 'Thing' is derived directly from the privileged moment: in the passage referred to earlier in this chapter where he describes moments in which familiar objects suddenly take on an unaccountable beauty, he says that such moments are those 'in which Things enter your lives again',[23]

But the notion of the 'Thing' is important not only because it was originally derived from the privileged moment, but because it provided Rilke with a number of principles for turning the privileged moment into art. These were based on the essential qualities of the 'Thing'; these qualities, therefore, must now be examined. In the passage introducing the 'Thing' just quoted, the most striking phenomenon is the change in the awareness of time : past and future merge. In the earlier version of the lecture this idea is expressed more fully: 'time, taken up in the great simultaneity of space, shows its full circle and goes back into itself'.[24] In the 'Thing' time is not confined to the present moment; it shows its whole span at once, so that the sense of its passing disappears. Two distinct conceptions of time are therefore involved here: everyday time, in which moments are successive, and what might be called 'total time', in which moments are simultaneous.

How is this latter concept to be understood? Its meaning can be made clearer by considering it in relation to Rilke's conception of space. 'Total time' is for him identical with space; in the quotations just given he speaks of 'something lasting: space' and 'the simultaneity of space'. The 'Thing' exists in space, but not in everyday time. It might be objected, of course, that the first part at least of this statement is meaningless, since all objects exist in space. Here again, however, Rilke is giving his terms a special meaning: he does not only mean that the object exists in space, but that is existence in space is far more intensely felt than that of other objects. To turn an object into a 'Thing', he says, the artist must 'fit it more intensely, more tightly, a thousand times better into the breadth of space, so that it would not move, so to speak, if you shook it'.[25]

How does the artist achieve this? Rilke takes Rodin as his example; the sculptor had learned how to make 'Things' by observing nature and great works of art. They had revealed to him 'a secret geometry of space'; he had learned that 'the contours of a Thing must be ordered in accordance with a number of planes inclined towards one another, if this Thing is to be really taken up by space, acknowledged by it, so to speak'.[26] Through this experience Rodin, in Rilke's view, had come to see surface as the only fundamental reality; his work consisted in seeing an object in terms of its surfaces and organising these into a rigorously unified structure. This is the activity which Rilke referred to in the earlier quotation when he said the artist's task was to create conditions favourable to the appearance of beauty. The beauty of Rodin's sculptures 'arises from the feeling of balance, of agreement between all these surfaces in motion'.[27]

This brings us to a further essential characteristic of the 'Thing': its surfaces are 'in motion'; their relatedness to one another, the interchange between them, gives an impression of movement. This movement, which Rilke also calls 'life', was, he said, a property of all great sculpture, and it was present to the highest degree in each of Rodin's works: 'What was to be found in the face ... was written on the smallest part of this body; each spot was a mouth saying it in its own way. The most critical eye could not find a place on this figure that was less alive.'[28] Interrelatedness, movement and 'life' are therefore essential and inseparable qualities of the 'Thing'.

In developing his theory of the 'Thing', Rilke was not only learning how to describe works of art: he was also clarifying his own experience of reality. His letters of this period show how the concepts derived from the study of Rodin helped him to take account of his visual impressions of Paris. This was particularly the case when they involved heightened awareness. An important example of such an impression is to be found in a letter of 1907; he begins by noting an intensified awareness of colour – 'a red that cannot hold itself back' – and goes on to describe the scene in terms of its surfaces: 'everything is simplified, reduced to a number of correct, bright planes, like a face in a portrait by Manet'. The impression also involves a sense of the interrelatedness, the mutual significance, of all its details:

> Nothing is trivial or superfluous. The *bouquinistes* on the embankment open their boxes and the fresh or faded yellow of the books, the violet brown of the bindings, the green of a portfolio: everything is right, everything has its say, adding its note to the unison of bright connections.[29]

In another letter concerned with heightened awareness he writes of 'houses in a background of bluish dove-grey, closed together in planes, with rectilinear surfaces like quarried terraces'.[30] We see, then, that the relationship between the 'Thing' and the privileged moment is 'two-way': the notion of the former was in the first place derived from the latter, but the terminology of the 'Thing' is now being applied back to the experience of the privileged moment, and helping in this way to bring it within the compass of Rilke's language.

There is another way in which the passages just quoted are of interest: as Rilke's careful rendering of colour indicates, he is now looking at external reality not only through the eyes of a sculptor but of a painter. When he wrote these letters his cult of Rodin was waning, to be replaced by an equally fervent admiration for Cézanne. This change of allegiance did not, however, mark a break in his development; Cézanne was a continuation and extension of what Rodin had begun. He had the same way of looking at reality in terms of surfaces, a fact which did not escape Rilke's notice: 'There he sat for hours, busy finding and taking in the "planes" (of which, very curiously, he constantly speaks, using the same words as Rodin).'[31] More important, the essence of Cézanne's paintings, as of Rodin's sculptures, was for Rilke the total interrelatedness of all their parts: 'It seems as if each place knows of all the rest.'[32] This quality gave the paintings the movement characteristic of the 'Thing': 'In this to-and-fro of multiple reciprocal influences the picture vibrates internally, rising and falling back into itself without a single stationary point.'[33]

Rilke's ideas on painting show striking parallels to those of Proust in this period. Chardin, one of Proust's favourite painters, appealed to him because of his use of colour, which produced an interrelatedness, or 'friendship' as Proust called it, between the different parts of his paintings.[34] It is worth noting in this connection that Rilke saw Chardin as Cézanne's forerunner in the use of colour,[35] and that Proust shared Rilke's admiration for Cézanne. Proust saw the same unity and interrelatedness as the essence of Rembrandt's paintings, this time produced by the use of light.[36]

The quality of internal interrelatedness which both writers considered the essential quality of visual art was also, as we have seen, a primary feature of the 'Thing'. But this feature introduces what might seem an inherent contradiction into Rilke's concept. For it was this internal interrelatedness which gave the 'Thing' movement, whereas Rilke had earlier stressed its intense stillness. In fact, however, there is no inconsistency here, since the stillness of the 'Thing' was itself composed of 'hundreds and hundreds of movements holding each other in equilibrium'.[37] But there is one kind of movement which is hostile to the nature of the 'Thing': 'the movement which does not come to an end, which is not balanced by others, which points outside the frontiers of the Thing'. In contrast to this the movement proper to the 'Thing' is a complete or 'closed' movement giving the work a self-contained unity:

> However large the movement in a piece of sculpture may be, it must, though it be from infinite distances, though it be from the depths of the sky, it must return to it, the great circle must be closed, the circle of solitude in which an Art-Thing spends its days.[38]

Rilke here introduces a number of further concepts which must be noted. He uses the term 'Art-Thing' to refer to a work of art as distinct from a 'Thing', which might be any object perceived with heightened awareness; it has the same essential qualities as the 'Thing'. 'Solitude' – the total isolation from its surroundings produced by its closed movement – was a further essential characteristic of the 'Thing'. An expression frequently used by Rilke to denote this quality was 'absorbed in itself' (*mit sich beschäftigt*) and, as might be expected, he also found it in Cézanne's paintings.[39] In being cut off from its surroundings, the 'Thing' is isolated from the arbitrariness and uncertainty of normal reality. It is totally governed by law (*gesetzmäßig*), exempt from chance. It is for this reason that Rilke sees the 'Thing' as existing outside everyday time, the passing of which is marked by random changes in its environment: in this sense time for Rilke is equated with chance.[40]

As a further consequence of its isolation from the everyday world, the 'Thing' is also unrelated to everyday language. Abstract thought, Rilke writes, passes over Rodin's sculptures 'like shadows', unable to impinge on their meaning.[41] It is the fact that nothing in them has been 'thought out' that gives them their pristine intensity.[42] In creating them, Rodin has progressively converted the conceptually recognisable element in his subject-matter into something 'objective and nameless', giving his material 'a new meaning related only to the plastic fulfilment.'[43] Apropos of Ruskin, Proust expressed ideas which reveal a similar underlying conception of art; painting, he said, can only attain reality if it gives up emulating literature, and 'the beauty of a picture does not depend on the things represented in it'.[44]

It might appear from this that Proust and Rilke were moving towards an Impressionist view of art as the exact representation of appearances undistorted by intellectual intentions. In fact, the conception of art which they saw exemplified in their masters includes Impressionism but goes beyond it. It would be wrong to call Rodin an Impressionist, Rilke writes, and yet his art is drawn from a rich stock of impressions. From these the artist selects the important elements and synthesises them in his work.[45] Proust's ideas were in complete agreement with this. 'No one', he writes, 'was more scornful than Ruskin of those who see the purpose of art as the imitation of simple appearance ... If he attaches such importance to the appearance of things, it is because this alone reveals their essential nature.'[46] On the other hand, neither Rodin nor Ruskin allowed the artist to us his imagination to alter or supplement what was provided by observation.[47] The work of art was therefore derived solely from observed reality, but was more 'real' than so-called reality: it was, in Rilke's words, the 'fulfilment of the wish to be which is manifested by everything in nature'.[48] In making it the artist had concentrated the meaning which was present only much more diffusely in his model. Not all art-forms, however, are capable, in Rilke's view, of achieving this. Music even tends to produce the opposite effect: it turns 'the apparent realities of the everyday world into something still more unreal – light, drifting appearances'.[49] Rilke's attitude to music in this period was unambiguously negative; in Proust, a similar, though less vehemently expressed, preference of painting to music may be inferred not only from his interest in Ruskin, but also from the fact that he wrote numerous essays on painters in this period but none on musicians.

The 'Thing' or 'Art-Thing' is therefore a piece of more intense reality isolated from the everyday world. It is impervious to conceptual thought, and this has an important consequence: from the standpoint of this art there is ultimately no distinction between people and things. If we look long enough at the men and women created by Rodin, says Rilke, we finally see only: 'Things'.[50] Proust drew a similar lesson from his study of painting: 'We had learned from Chardin that a pear is as much alive as a woman'.[51] Art of this kind therefore eliminates the personal element from experience. By a related process, the artist producing such art escapes – or so Proust and Rilke thought – from the conditions and limitations of individual existence. Proust writes of one painter that his art enabled him to break through 'the barrier of the individual self'; as he worked, 'gradually the moments when ... he was the man that he also was became fewer and fewer'.[52] Rilke spoke of his master as having himself become a 'Thing'; he had completely thrown off the trammels of personal existence: 'his daily life and the people who are a part of it lie there like an empty river-bed that he no longer flows through'.[53]

In addition to this depersonalising effect, the isolation of the 'Thing' has a further consequence of decisive importance for the conception of art towards which Rilke is developing. Because it is unrelated to its immediate surroundings, the 'Thing' takes on unlimited, exclusive significance: it becomes a world in itself. Everything Rodin contemplates, says Rilke, becomes such a world; when he forms a hand 'it is alone in space, and there is nothing but a hand'.[54] As we contemplate a 'Thing', surrounding reality is expelled from consciousness. This can happen with almost unnerving violence; as we look, for example, at one of Rodin's wash-drawings, 'space hurls itself from all sides into the page and surrounds the figure with so much nothingness that one's head swims'.[55]

The 'Thing', then, has no environment. This can also be expressed differently: lacking an immediate environment the 'Thing' is able to relate itself to surrounding space in a wider, more absolute way. It carries, as Rilke put it, its environment within itself;[56] the system composed by its surfaces seems to propagate itself throughout all space.[57] Similarly, a landscape contemplated during a privileged moment 'throws out space',[58] in one of Rilke's formulations. In Rodin's sculptures this effect is so marked that they seem to involve the whole cosmos: 'When there is a rising up in them, it seems as if they were lifting up the heavens, and the flight of their fall draws the stars in its train.'[59] Taking this idea further, he sees the sculptures themselves as circling among the stars: they are 'as if placed over us, in the universe, beneath the stars, in a wide, infallible circling'.[60]

This notion of the 'Things' circling in the cosmos is clearly related to the idea of the closed, circular movements contained within them. So too is the idea mentioned earlier that the 'Thing' embodies eternity, the 'full circle' of 'total' time. It is clear, then, that the circle-image is taking up a central position in Rilke's artistic preoccupations.

In attributing cosmic implications to the 'Thing', Rilke has taken further an idea which appeared persistently in *The Book of Images*. There we found that descriptions of privileged moments generally culminated in a sense of being related to the stars. Here again, the connection between the 'Thing' and the privileged moment is apparent.

As a further implication of the vision of Rodin's works as heavenly bodies circling in the universe, Rilke sees them as forming 'a new solar system' among themselves.[61] They exist together, he writes in a letter of 1908, 'in an instant of eternity, held in a celestial equilibrium between music and geometry'.[62] He goes on to imagine Rodin himself as possessing within him such a timeless dimension 'in which all is simultaneous and awake and nothing passes away' – without this, he says, Rodin could not have created his works.[63]

In this way the timelessness of the 'Thing' becomes connected to the rôle of memory in art. Rilke frequently stresses the importance of memory in Rodin's work, and Proust calls Ruskin 'a man for whom there is no death ... no forgetting'. In Ruskin he finds support for the intuition that we found underlying *Jean Santeuil*: 'nothing dies of all that has lived' – in Ruskin's words we can still breathe the scent of biblical roses that have not faded.[64] In turning to Ruskin and Rodin and through them to sculpture, the most tangible of the arts, the two writers have therefore found confirmation for their most intangible belief: that there exists beyond the empirical world a realm of eternity which is also a realm of memory and inwardness.

This is perhaps the farthest point to which the study of their two masters carried them. It remains only to be added that we have been concerned here not with Ruskin and Rodin as they actually were but as they appeared to their two disciples; and above all we have been concerned with what Proust and Rilke hoped they might themselves become. Through their masters they recognised their own needs and potentialities. Proust has given a precise summing-up of the part played in their development by these 'influences': 'There is no better way of finding out what one feels oneself than by attempting to recreate in oneself what has been felt by a master.'[65]

# CHAPTER TEN

## *New Poems*

ILKE'S *New Poems* are often referred to as 'static'.[1] If this
were an accurate description, it would be in surprising contradiction to the theories of the 'Thing' outlined in the last
chapter, on which these 'Thing-poems' (*Dinggedichte*) are supposedly
based. We saw there not only that Rilke saw movement as an inherent
property of a work of art, but that it played a fundamental part in the
formation of his special conceptions of time and reality. The question
of the movement, or lack of it, in *New Poems* is not, therefore, only of
technical interest: it leads to a discussion of the central meaning of the
work.

How static, then, are the *New Poems*? An examination of a number
of examples will give us the answer; let us look first at one of the most
well-known and successful of the 'Thing-poems', 'Roman Fountain':

> Zwei Becken, eins das andre übersteigend
> aus einem alten runden Marmorrand,
> und aus dem oberen Wasser leis sich neigend
> zum Wasser, welches unten wartend stand,
>
> dem leise redenden entgegenschweigend
> und heimlich, gleichsam in der hohlen Hand,
> ihm Himmel hinter Grün und Dunkel zeigend
> wie einen unbekannten Gegenstand;
>
> sich selber ruhig in der schönen Schale
> verbreitend ohne Heimweh, Kreis aus Kreis,
> nur manchmal träumerisch und tropfenweis
>
> sich niederlassend an den Moosbehängen
> zum letzten Spiegel, der sein Becken leis
> von unten lächeln macht mit Ubergängen.[2]

Two bowls, one above the other, rising from an old, round marble basin,
and from the top one water gently bending towards the water waiting
underneath

which meets the murmur with its silence and shows the top bowl secretly,
as in a hollow hand, sky behind green and darkness like a thing unknown;

in its own bowl calmly spreading, ring upon ring departing without
regret, only sometimes, dreamily, in drops,

letting itself down by the mossy hangings to the lowest surface which, from underneath, makes its bowl smile softly with reflected rippling.

Compared to the rhythm of Rilke's earlier work, this poem may give a first impression of stillness. But once the change in *tempo* is allowed for, it is apparent that the poem, far from being static, is pervaded and indeed constituted by movement: the downward movement of water in the first quartet, the upward movement of reflection in the second, the outward movement of ripples in the first tercet, then a further downward movement of water going over to the last tercet where there is again an upward movement of reflections.

This is not all; if these movements are examined it is found that they are carefully organised to form a balanced and symmetrical pattern. The downward *neigend* ('bending') of the first stanza is balanced by *entgegenschweigend* (a verbal invention which imparts to the lower bowl's silence a movement towards the upper one) and *zeigend* ('showing') of the 'upturned' second stanza. These movements complement and in a sense cancel each other out: they are followed by a moment of stillness which comes in the 'middle' of the poem, that is, in the first line of the first tercet, traditionally the point where the critical break or transition in the sonnet occurs. The next lines show that this stillness is also movement, but outward movement, as if held in a weightless equilibrium between the 'pull' of the upper and lower parts of the poem. Then the downward movement resumes – the water 'letting itself down' – and is again balanced by the reflections 'from underneath'.

The pattern formed by these movements is repeated and reinforced by the rhyme scheme. The two quartets have a self-contained scheme, the 'still' line with its last word *Schale* is related by rhyme to no other line, and the remaining lines of the tercets have another scheme. Content and form are therefore finely organised to express a movement, or system of movements, fundamental to the poem. But this movement is of a particular kind; it is the complete, self-contained, 'closed' movement which Rilke specified for the 'Thing' and the work of art. In 'Roman Fountain', then, his practice corresponds exactly to the principles discussed in the last chapter.

An objection might be made, however, to the use of this poem as an example: the movement it embodies is inherent in the object described, so that a static representation would in any case be inappropriate. To answer this we must turn to other poems in which the object described presents no such inherent movement, for instance, the group of poems on the porch of Chartres cathedral: 'The Portal', I–III.[3] Here Rilke is describing something which is obviously static, but to do so he introduces a movement, different in each poem, and the poem is made up only of those elements in its object which are embraced by this movement. In I the movement is that of an imaginary tide which washed the stones until they were formed and has now receded, leaving behind the figures which are themselves 'removed' (*fortgerückt*) into the empty porch. In II the movement is that of the darkness, personified as an actor, which 'steps, engaged in action', on to its own stage. In III the apparent stillness of the figures is shown to be maintained by the multiplied movements of the carvings below them, which 'only make such jerky, wild gesticulations/ to keep the baton balanced on their brow'.

The same device is used in the poems that follow 'The Portal', which are also concerned with describing Gothic architecture. In 'The Rose Window' the movement is introduced by a comparison of the window to the eye of a beast of prey: 'So, in other days, out of the cathedrals'/ darkness huge rose windows/ seized a heart and tore it into God.'[4] It is noticeable that the movement used here is 'two-way' or 'closed'. The same is true on a larger scale in the next poem, 'The Capital'; here the pillars and vaults are united by a composite movement in which rising and falling elements form a cycle. This has its source in the ferment of movements in the carvings of the capital, which generates, as it were, the motive force,

> alles aufwärtsjagend,
> was immer wieder mit dem Dunkel kalt
> herunterfällt, wie Regen Sorge tragend
> für dieses alten Wachstums Unterhalt.[5]

driving up all that which constantly descends again, cold with the dark like rain assuring this old growth's support.

Movement therefore, and particularly circular movement, is a fundamental law of the descriptive poems which form the bulk of the two parts of *New Poems*. This law is too pervasive to be demonstrated in full; only a few further examples can be given. In 'The Ball' the double movement of rising and falling is represented perfectly in the poem, to the exclusion of all other elements. Here, more than in any other poem perhaps, the movement and the poem are one, and it may have been for this reason that as late as 1918 Rilke regarded 'The Ball' as his best poem.[6] The movement in 'Lady at the Looking-Glass' consists in her first 'pouring' her reflection into the mirror, then 'drinking' it back from it. 'Black Cat' has a similar movement: the gaze of the onlooker is first absorbed by the unreflecting coat of the cat, then reappears sinisterly in the fixity of its eyes turned towards him. It is significant that in both these latter poems the circular movement is provided by the act of looking, which is the fundamental act of a descriptive poem.

The closed movements embodied in Rilke's poems give them their unity, their clearly defined shape. In the poems, as in the 'Thing', 'all movement comes to rest, turns into contour'. We should recall that Rilke does not mean by this that movement is abolished, but that it is enclosed in a circular configuration of the kind he saw in Rodin's sculptures. It would be misleading, however, to take the parallel with sculpture too far. The poems clearly cannot have the same kind of contour or outline as a piece of sculpture: even the subjects taken by Rilke do not necessarily have outline in this sense. The flowers in 'The Bowl of Roses', for example, are for Rilke the epitome of 'Thingness' (*Dinghaftigkeit*) yet he speaks of them as something almost without outline: *fast nicht Umrissen-sein wie Ausgespartes*. The space in which the flowers exist is not cut out from the surrounding space by their outline but 'reserved' or 'hollowed out' (*ausgespart*) from within, by the reciprocal movements and relationships contained in them. The roses are *lauter Inneres* – an inside without an outside – which 'shines on itself – to the very edge'. They create their own space, independent of that of the everyday world in which objects, but not works of art or 'Things', exist: the process by which this space is created Rilke calls 'using space and yet not taking from the space/ that things all round make smaller'[7] – 'things' it should be mentioned, has its everyday meaning when used in the poems.

Because of the movement in them these roses are symbolic of the poem itself. As in them, the movement represented in a poem creates the space in which the poem exists: in this sense it is the poem's 'contour'. And it is only through this movement that we can apprehend the poem and the space it creates. In the medium of language, we cannot be presented simultaneously with all the data needed to build up a picture. Unlike sculpture and like music, poetry is an art-form which exists in time, not in space. Or, to be more exact, it exists in time before it exists in space: its elements must be apprehended in succession before they can be related together in a spatial system. This is why movement is essential even in descriptive poetry. Even when a poet wishes to reproduce spatial relations, he must first convert them into succession, into temporal relations, into movement. For this reason Rilke, when he is describing the eternal stillness of the statues in the cathedral porch, uses a temporal term: 'only rarely, out of the fall of folds,/ steps a gesture, upright, steep as they'.[8]

But the order of time introduced into the poem in this way is entirely different from that of everyday time: the statue's gesture, 'after half a step, stands still/ where centuries pass it by'. While moments in everyday time continue to pass and vanish, the time and movement embodied in the sculpture are eternalised. In an analogous way, the poem itself creates an order of time in which a movement can be eternalised, because all the points making up the movement are related together in a pattern in which each implies, and in a sense contains, all the others. The movement in the poem, once it has been apprehended, therefore remains visible in its entirety, a situation impossible in normal time where one moment excludes all others. In this way, by the movement in a poem, time as succession is converted into time as simultaneity, or 'total' time.

It can be seen that a poetic theory, and underlying it a special conception of reality, is emerging from the study of the poems. To complete the exposition of this theory, a further point has to be made: the 'total' time of the poem is the same thing as its *ausgesparter Raum* – the space it creates from within. This is again symbolised in 'The Bowl of Roses', where the movement in the roses is 'eternal': the flowers 'open without end'. What we have in a poem, therefore, is not really, as is often thought, a conversion of time into space in the simple sense that moments of time are represented as points in space. Rather it is a more dynamic phenomenon in which time continues to flow and yet remains fully visible as if it were space. In the poem we have a new dimension in which, in Rilke's words, 'time, taken up by the great simultaneity of space, shows its full circle and goes back into itself'.[9]

Such a conception, as formulated here in theoretical terms, must remain problematical. But it becomes clearer as embodied in the poems. In some it is represented symbolically, even allegorically, above all in 'L'Ange du Méridien' where the angel is asked whether he does not see how the hours we live slip from the sun-dial he holds, 'on which the day's whole sum at once,/ each real as each, stands deeply balancing,/ as if all hours were ripe and full'.[10] The two orders of time-as-succession and 'total' time are clearly opposed here, and the latter is symbolised by the full circle of the sun-dial. The image of the full circle is used elsewere in contexts where 'total' time is explicitly contrasted to normal time. The 'round face' of a child is 'clear and whole like an abundant hour/ starting and striking to an end'; but the child's time is alien to the everyday world: 'the others do not count the strokes'.[11] More generally, the circle-image is associated with the space and the movement of the poem: 'a whirlpool's circle' and 'the smallest of all circles' are central motifs in 'The Rose Window' and the well-known 'Panther' respectively. The connection between this image and the closed movement of the poem is too obvious to need lengthy demonstration.

The circle embodied in a poem does not necessarily correspond to the actual visual form of the object described. In 'Early Apollo', for example, Rilke completes the movement in the sculpture by imagining a cycle made up by rose-petals floating outwards on the breath from the mouth, and the future songs of Apollo being drawn in by the mouth. In 'The Unicorn' a similar device is used to 'close' the poem at the end: 'Yet his gaze, which nothing limited,/ threw out in space around him images/ and closed a blue and legendary cycle.'[12] Here the poem, like a landscape described by Rilke in the last chapter, 'throws out space'; and like Rodin's sculptures it contains its own surroundings. In the case of the 'Thing' we saw that this projection of its movement outside itself culminated in the identification of the 'Thing' with the stars and the universe; this too is realised in some of the poems. Three are devoted to Buddha,[13] and were probably inspired by a Buddha figure in Rodin's garden. In the first, Buddha is seen as a star surrounded by other stars invisible to us, and then he is described simply as 'everything'; in the others the same idea is followed through: he 'touches space as if it were himself'; he is the 'centre of centres', the kernel of a fruit which contains the stars. The Buddha poems are also connected to the circle image and through it to the dimension of eternity or 'total' time. What draws us to the Buddha has 'circled in him many million years'; another of the poems states that he will outlast time altogether.

In these poems Rilke seems to be deliberately and somewhat programmatically putting into practice ideas which he had expressed elsewhere in prose, to the extent that their value as poetry has become a secondary consideration. The same is true of 'The Scarab' which directly precedes the last of the Buddha poems and has a similar subject and meaning. The scarabs too are seen as existing in the vicinity of the stars and as all-embracing in space and time, and they too embody the circle-image: at the end of the poem they 'close drowsily'.[14]

The poems which 'close' in this way also embody another of the characteristics which Rilke attributed to Rodin's sculptures. They are indifferent to their surroundings; they do not 'look out' at the onlooker, who is situated in a world which for them does not exist. For example, Buddha: 'Really, do we wait/ for him to see us? Should he need to?/ ... who forgets what we encounter/ and encounters what refuses us.' Similarly the poet asks 'L'Ange du Méridien': 'What do you know, stony figure, of our life?' Such figures are, like Rodin's sculptures, totally self-absorbed; so too is the piece of sculpture in 'Tanagra' which is described as 'touching only on itself'.[15] The figures who achieve this total self-absorption are raised out of the human world and are immune to its pain; they are symbolised by Saint Sebastian who is 'entwined in himself like a wreath' and is thereby 'far removed', inaccessible to suffering; as the arrows pierce him he smiles, 'unharmed'.[16]

In 'The Coat of Arms' Rilke seems likewise to be putting into practice another, related idea which he had expressed abstractly in the Rodin monograph; he had said there that the sculptor 'could, with a living surface as with a mirror, capture the distances'.[17] The coat of arms acts in a similar way: it 'takes in, like a mirror' things coming 'from far off' – in this case from the distant past.[18] The same image of the mirror reflecting distant realities is used in other poems, particularly those describing flowers. In 'Blue Hydrangea' the colour of the flowers is seen not as a part of them but as a reflection from far off, and in 'Within the Rose' the sky is reflected inside the flowers. An idea of reflection similar to that in 'The Coat of Arms' is expressed at length in 'The Bowl of Roses': the minute movements in the flowers would remain invisible, says the poet, if they were not projected outwards into the universe; through these prolongations the roses contain the whole of space within them.

We saw earlier that the circle, or self-contained movement, is the basic vehicle through which the *New Poems* take possession of their object and draw it into their inner space as the cat's eye in 'The Rose Window' draws the gaze of the onlooker into 'a whirlpool's circle'. We have now seen also that the image of the mirror frequently appears in poems where this movement is present, for example in 'Lady at the Looking-Glass', 'Roman Fountain' and 'The Coat of Arms'. In these three poems it is noticeable that the mirror, by its action of reflecting, provides the movement of the poem; still more important, in the first two poems the mirror is instrumental in providing the balanced or 'two-way' movement with which Rilke was concerned. It is clear from this that the mirror and circle images are not associated by accident: the mirror is by its nature a source of the circular movement. As such it is one of the fundamental images of *New Poems*; its presence is too pervasive to need detailed demonstration and will become apparent as the argument continues.

One feature of the mirror must, however, be noted here. The world it reflects, while being recognisably like that outside it, is at the same time strange and unfamiliar. In 'Roman Fountain' the sky and foliage reflected in the water are 'like a thing unknown'. In 'The Island' the bizarre world of the islanders is seen reflected in mirrors which 'stand crookedly on chests of drawers'.[19] In 'Quai du Rosaire' the nature of the mirror-world is made clear; the town landscape, reflected in the still water of a canal, becomes 'as real as these things never are'. The reflected world, for Rilke, is more 'real' than the real world. In such contexts Rilke uses the word 'real', as he does in the essays and letters on Rodin, to mean the heightened reality of the 'Thing' as opposed to the 'apparent realities of the everyday world'. Life, as it passes into the mirror, is strippped of the unreality of everyday experience: the reflected town is 'distinct and wide awake', 'as if there life were not so rare'.[20] For related reasons, the object reflected in the mirror is frequently one which is too beautiful to be merely a part of the décor of normal life. So the colour of the blue hydrangea, for example, seemed to be, not a part of the flower, but a reflection from far off.

It is becoming apparent that there are in *New Poems* certain key images, such as the circle and the mirror, which recur from poem to poem. We notice also that these streams of imagery are bound up with the central themes of the poems, Rilke's special conceptions of time and reality. If these strands of imagery are pursued they are found to be interwoven with others. The mirror image, for example, is frequently associated with that of the smile, as in the last line of 'Roman Fountain' and in 'Lady at the Looking-Glass', where she 'puts in her smile, entire'. The colour of flowers, which we have just seen related to the mirror image, is seen as 'smiling from the air' in 'Pink Hydrangea'.[21] The smile is the quality of the work of art in 'Archaic Torso of Apollo'; and it characterises too the onlooker's reaction to art, as in 'Lace-Work' and 'Tanagra'. In the latter poem the smile image is connected to a further important motif of *New Poems*, 'clear' (*klar*), which elsewhere, as in 'Quai du Rosaire', is in its turn related to the mirror. The smile also appears in connection with the circle and the related idea of 'total' time, above all through the smiling figure of 'L'Ange du Méridien'. In this poem another central motif, 'blissful' (*selig*), is also used to describe the angel's face. A further word with similar connections to the smile imagery is 'heedless' (*sorglos*), which is applied to flowers on numerous occasions and also to the perfectly balanced movement described in 'The Ball'. The ball at the apex of its flight is in equilibrium between rising and falling and is, in this sense, weightless. The state of weightlessness – a further key motif of the poems, frequently denoted by the word *schweben* – is the antithesis of the characteristic heaviness and difficulty of human life which in a well-known poem is compared to the laborious and impeded gait of a swan on dry land.[22] Contrasting with this heaviness is the sense of liberation given by a work of art, which allows us 'to smile and be weightless'.[23]

The idea of weightlessness is in turn connected to another basic concept of *New Poems*, expressed by the formula: 'driven on to (or by) no goal' (*zu* [or *von*] *nichts gedrängt*). *Schweben* implies not only weightlessness in the physical sense, but freedom from the feeling of being constantly impelled from moment to moment by desire or practical need, a feeling which, for Rilke, gives normal life the heaviness and wretchedness characterised in 'The Swan'. This is absent from the world of the mirror; in 'Quai du Rosaire', for example, the town, balanced now by its reflection, becomes 'weightless', freed from imperfection.

> und kostet langsam und von nichts gedrängt
> Beere um Beere aus der süßen Traube
> des Glockenspiels, das in den Himmeln hängt.

and slowly savours, driven by no haste, berry upon berry from the sweet grape-bunch of bells hanging in the sky.

The same formulation, with similar connotations, appears in 'Portrait of my Father as a Young Man', and it may be recalled also that Rilke used this phrase in the passage introducing the 'Thing' in the Rodin monograph: 'the great calm of the Things which nothing drives onwards'.

The motif *zu nichts gedrängt* is also associated with a further quality of the 'Thing', its self-absorbed detachment from the outside world. In 'The Roundabout' this is linked to the circle image: 'it only circles, turning round without a goal'.[24] The piece of sculpture in 'Tanagra' has a gesture which 'reaches out to nothing' and the flight of steps in 'The Orangerie Staircase' climbs 'towards the sky and nowhere'.[25] The same serene freedom from external compulsions, again connected with the circle image, is expressed in 'Roman Fountain' by the ripples spreading outwards 'ring upon ring, without regret'.

The sense of weightlessness fundamental to these motifs is the product of equilibrium, and this in turn is connected to the smile. In 'L'Ange du Méridien' the whole circle of time carried by the smiling angel on his sun-dial 'stands deeply balancing'. A further connection between these strands of imagery is seen in 'The Unicorn'; the poem evokes an animal whose whole being is expressive of unearthly joy and whose movements embody a perfect equilibrium:

> Der Beine elfenbeinernes Gestell
> bewegte sich in leichten Gleichgewichten,
> ein weißer Glanz glitt selig durch das Fell[26]

The ivory structure of the limbs was full of lightly balanced movements, a white sheen shimmered blissfully across the coat.

In the last line we find 'balance' and 'blissful' linked with a further important motif: *Glanz* ('gleam' or 'sheen'). This latter appears in another poem evoking near-mythical creatures representing an ideal of more-than-human happiness – 'blissful, heedless and invulnerable' – the dolphins, who are 'happy, as if they felt the water gleaming'.[27] In the cycle of poems entitled 'Parks' 'gleam' appears again in conjunction with the key motifs already discussed; to give one example among many, nature, personified as an artist, is described in one poem as painting the evening scene with a brush 'that gleaming seemed to hold/ a melted smile as clear as varnish'.[28] 'Gleam' again expresses the quality of a work of art in 'Early Apollo'; in the piece of sculpture there is 'nothing to shield you from the almost lethal gleam/ of every poem'.[29] Here 'gleam' expresses an intensity of experience heightened to the point where it becomes alarming and dangerous.

These examples have served to show how densely certain strands of imagery are woven round the special conception of reality which is fundamental to *New Poems* as it was to the discussion of Rodin. It is apparent that the most central of these images is the mirror. It is from the mirror that the other images derive an essential part of their meaning: by 'balancing' each object with its reflection, the mirror produces the states of equilibrium and weightlessness and the attendant emotional states: 'smiling', 'heedless', 'blissful'; its surface is 'gleaming' and 'clear', and the circle too, as we saw, is an expression of the mirror's fundamental act of reflecting.

The mirror, then, is the central image of the poems, but it is also significant for another, equally fundamental, reason: it is bound up with the poet's use of metaphor. In a metaphor, as in a mirror, an object is 'balanced' by its equivalent; between the two terms of a metaphor there is the same relationship as between an object and its mirror image. This is made explicit by Rilke in one of the poems. 'The Flamingoes' begins with the statement that the reflections of the birds in water reveal as much of their colours as someone would reveal who said of his lady-friend: 'she was still soft with sleep'.[30] The reflections of the flamingoes are equated with the comparison between the birds and the girl. Rilke's image here, as E. C. Mason has noted,[31] seems somewhat far-fetched and unconvincing as poetry; the reason may be that Rilke is trying too consciously to express his idea about the link between the mirror and metaphor. In other poems the connection is less explicit, and more convincingly a part of the natural process of the poem. In 'Blue Hydrangea' the flowers seem to reflect their own colour, but they 'reflect it in a blurred and tearful way/ as if they would be rid of it again'. These lines are followed by a series of metaphors which, by assimilating it into a new context, do in a sense 'rid' the flowers of their colour: 'and as in old blue writing-paper/ there is yellow in them, violet and grey;/ the washed-out tints of children's pinafores'.[32]

In other poems the act of describing is equated with that of discovering metaphors; in 'The Lute', for example, we are told that to describe the shape of the instrument we should have to speak of that of a ripe fig; to convey the true reality of a thing metaphor is necessary, just as the world only becomes real when it passes into the mirror. 'The Gazelle' begins in a similar way; the poet asks how the usual devices of poetry can ever equal the 'rhyme' which appears in the animal. The poem immediately passes over into metaphor: 'From your brow rise foliage and lyre', and the use of metaphor becomes self-conscious and explicit as in 'The Flamingoes': 'all that is yours comparison can pass/ through love-songs that have words as soft/ as roses' petals'; we must close our eyes and contemplate these images if we are to see the animal truly:

> um dich zu sehen: hingetragen, als
> wäre mit Sprüngen jeder Lauf geladen
> und schösse nur nicht ab, solang der Hals
> das Haupt ins Horchen hält.[33]

to see you: borne along as if each leg were a gun-barrel loaded with leaps, only holding its fire while the neck keeps the head cocked listening.

Again a metaphor is used to show the essence of the animal; and this is followed immediately by a further metaphor concluding the poem, in which the physical appearance of the animal disappears almost entirely.

Metaphor is the second basic vehicle through which the *New Poems* take possession of reality, the first, as we saw earlier, being circular movement. In a sense metaphor too involves a circular movement; an object and its metaphorical equivalent together form a self-contained structure in which the meaning of the poem circulates, so to speak, in isolation from the rest of reality. This kind of circular movement is used by Rilke as an alternative to the other, more literal, kind which is absent, for example, from 'The Gazelle'. The 'mirror' image, as we have seen, expresses both kinds of movement; its relevance to metaphor is indicated again in the last line of 'The Gazelle' where the animal's head is compared to the face of a bather reflecting a forest lake: *den Waldsee im gewendeten Gesicht.* Metaphor can therefore be seen as a kind of verbal mirror by means of which an object is projected out of the world or normal existence into that of true reality – into the world of 'Things'.

But the symbolic meaning of the mirror is not exhausted by its relevance to the closed movement and to metaphor. It also symbolises memory; it can reflect the past. In 'Quai du Rosaire' the water seems to reflect not only the town's present, but its past preserved in the present: 'Did this town not pass away?' The church window in 'Béguinage II' reflects 'beneath the summer day's unsteady scenery/ the grey of ancient winters'.[34] There is a similar phenomenon in 'Before the Summer Rain' where the wallpaper reflects 'the faltering light of childhood afternoons'.[35] In 'The Pavilion' the gaiety of past years is reflected in the glass doors of a deserted summer-house:

> Aber selbst noch durch die Flügeltüren
> mit dem grünen regentrüben Glas
> ist ein Spiegeln lächelnder Allüren
> und ein Glanz von jenem Glück zu spüren[36]

But even through the folding doors, their green glass dimmed by rain, reflections of those smiling ways, a gleam of that past joy can still be felt

When Rilke describes such scenes in the present, he does so in very different terms. Then, social life is presented as a painful and difficult play we are forced to act, mechanically repeating our lines.[37] But as soon as it is seen reflected in the past, life takes on the qualities of 'gleam' and 'smile', as in the quotation above. Because the past is exempt from the imperfections of the present, memory is a further way of approaching the world of 'Things'. But remembrance of the kind we are concerned with here does not eliminate the present from awareness but rather fuses the two, producing a temporal disorientation which appears also in a number of other poems: 'In a Strange Park', 'The Apple-Orchard', 'The Sun-Dial'. In the last poem the connection between this form of memory and 'total' time is indicated: the sun-dial, which can only register time as a succession of points, 'pauses' – it has no measure for the intense moment the poem describes.

There are, then, in *New Poems*, three major preoccupations: with the closed movement, with metaphor and, to a lesser extent, with memory. The mirror image has been seen to symbolise all three, and may be called the master-image of the poems. The function of the mirror, and of what it symbolises, might be summed up by saying that it serves to translate objects or experiences from the context of the present into a world, characterised by the motifs of the smile, weightlessness, etc., from which all the faults and limitations of human existence in time are removed. The world of the mirror is clearly a development of the notion of a higher reality which we have met before in Rilke's work. His main advance from his earlier position is that, through the study of Rodin, he has now developed the poetic means by which to transplant reality successfully into the dimension he perceives intuitively beyond the world of appearances. It is above all the poems themselves which are symbolised by the mirror. Through them, things are lifted out of their everyday contingency and, like the flamingoes in Rilke's poem, 'step, separate, into the imaginary'.

The world of the mirror is the dimension in which works of art exist. And as we saw in 'Tanagra' and in 'Lace-Work', art is able to transmit the quality of this dimension – the 'smile' – to the onlooker. But this has an important consequence which must now be noted: in showing him the existence of another world, the work of art makes the onlooker aware of the defects of his actual existence, which is suddenly called into question. In 'The Reliquary' the finished work seems to become aware of the artist who has made it and, 'suddenly questioning his life,/ looks at him as from dynasties'. In 'Archaic Torso of Apollo' the message conveyed by the sculpture is still more peremptory: 'there is no place/ that does not look at you. You must change your life.'

In this way the study of Rilke's imagery leads to a discussion of his interpretation of life. The basic movement underlying the imagery – the movement away from the everyday world to a higher dimension – becomes, when translated into practical terms, the directive to 'change one's life'. To follow the implications of this command we must turn now from the descriptive to the narrative poems in the collections. Here, in such poems as 'The Departure of the Prodigal Son', 'The Elopement', 'The Recluse', and 'The Stranger', the attempt to escape from the familiar world to a more satisfying existence appears as a recurrent theme.

What the characters in these poems are trying to leave behind is the power of normal life to impose on them an existence which is not really theirs. The people and things surrounding a human existence are incapable of reflecting its true reality; as the Prodigal Son discovers, they 'mirror us tremblingly, and the image breaks'.[38] In the human world, unlike that of art, the pure mirror does not exist. Instead, a fictitious identity is made up by other people and projected on to us. In 'Eranna to Sappho' the young girl, to whom Sappho's poems have given an awareness of her true nature, realises that her sisters are 'thinking her' as they sit weaving in the familiar house from which she is now estranged.[39] Similarly in 'Corpse-Washing', the fact that a man is dead does not prevent other people from giving him an identity: 'since they knew nothing of his fate,/ they made him up another out of lies'.[04] The illusory nature of the self conferred by the home environment is the theme of 'The Scene of the Fire', in which the son of a burnt-down house finds himself stripped of his identity: 'And he was changed. Like someone from a distant land.'[41] An analogous experience is described in 'Snake-Charming'; the music entrances not only the snake but the onlooker, who is suddenly transported from his familiar world to a distant tropical unknown; over his head burning skies seem to rush. In these alien surroundings a split appears in the awareness of identity: 'A crack/ runs through your face.'[42] Likewise the man transported into the world of his book in 'The Reader' would be unidentifiable even to his mother.

The fictitious reality in which we normally live is, for Rilke, maintained largely by the visual sense, as is stated in 'The Dog': 'Up there
the image of a world/ is constantly renewed from glances and holds
good.'[43] But in the context of *New Poems* this idea must not be taken
as a denigration of the visual sense itself, but only of the narrowly
practical use to which it is put in normal life. Blind people in the poems
are exempt from the normal limitations; the 'Woman Going Blind',
for example, detaching herself from the sterile clatter of social intercourse, seems about to take flight to a higher world: 'as if, after a
passing-over,/ she would no longer walk, but fly'.[44] By severing herself
from the everyday world she can reach the realm of weightlessness.

It was the premonition of such a transition to a higher sphere which
caused the solitary figures in the other poems mentioned to tear themselves away from their familiar worlds. The Prodigal Son has an
intuition of a realm devoid of personal implications – 'a warm and
unrelated land' – in which he would be able to look again, 'as if at a
beginning, from close to', at things which had become so familiar that
he no longer saw them. The girl in 'The Elopement' has a similar
though misdirected desire to experience nature in a way which was
impossible in her home surroundings. 'The Recluse' breaks human
bonds in order to experience the full intensity of reality, knowing that
this painful exposure will make him, paradoxically, 'ever more blissful'.[45] In a similar way 'The Stranger', having abandoned all his possessions and material aspirations, is able to possess reality itself in a
different and more universal way; sometimes in a strange town the
worn stone of a well was 'like a thing he owned'.[46] This pattern of
'losing one's life in order to gain it' is repeated in the numerous poems
about saints and hermits who isolate themselves from humanity, and
after struggling to rid themselves of the 'daily demons'[47] of their personality, are rewarded by the feeling that they hold within themselves
'all living things'.[48]

The implication of these attempts to 'change one's life' is therefore
that by turning one's back on communal human life one can approach
the higher world. But solitude is not for Rilke the only way of escaping
the nullity of normal existence. Within the human world there are
certain 'privileged' experiences which give us at least a glimpse of true
reality. These experiences, as we might by now expect with Rilke, are
primarily: childhood, love, heroism and death. It would be repetitive
to discuss these themes in detail; here we need be concerned only with
the development their treatment has undergone in *New Poems*. This
is largely bound up with the way in which the themes are related,
through the special imagery studied earlier, to the world of 'Things'.

That the child exists in this higher world is symbolised, as we saw
earlier, by its face which is 'clear and whole like an abundant hour'.

Other symbols of the child's world which we have already met with are the flight of the ball and the roundabout which 'circles, turning round without a goal'. Like the roundabout the child is free of external compulsions, *zu nichts gedrängt*, but the end of this state of grace is foreshadowed in this poem by the older girls, who look out from the circling roundabout, 'somewhere, over here'. They are beginning to have a 'goal' which, as E. C. Mason points out,[49] is erotic, and which marks the end of childhood. But the girls' outward look is also 'a smile ... a blissful one',[50] for they can see, not the sterile world of normal adult experience, but the world of love.

The lover too exists in the realm of weightlessness: 'I thought that I was floating. How far does my life extend'; these are the words of the 'Woman in Love' who experiences the same kind of cosmic awareness as Buddha in the poems quoted earlier. The relation between love and the mirror complex of imagery appears in numerous other poems.[51] But love is unlike childhood in that it has a goal, or more exactly two goals, as is seen in 'Girl's Lament', which expresses the irruption of erotic desire into childhood at puberty:

> wenn, auf meiner Brüste Hügeln
> stehend, mein Gefühl nach Flügeln
> oder einem Ende schreit.[52]

when, standing on my breasts' hills, my feeling cries out for wings or for an end.

One goal, the 'end' in this quotation, is the meeting with the lover, physical satisfaction and personal involvement. The other goal, implied by the 'wings', is the higher world to which love can give access. But if the first goal is reached the second cannot be, so that the girl longing for a lover is 'both calling and afraid/ the call might be heard'.[53] Sappho, who possesses the wings referred to above, rudely rejects her would-be lover: 'what has my soul to do with you'.[54]

For Rilke, therefore, it is the duty of lovers to separate, to lift their souls 'over you to other things'.[55] As a consequence of his view of unrequited love as a positive experience, Rilke sees Don Juan as performing a valuable task: he is entrusted by an angel with the almost sacred duty of leading many women into loneliness. Because of this rôle Don Juan, too, has contact with the higher world; even as a child, under the gaze of women: 'he smiled'.[56]

The conception of Don Juan, the man who will be held by no human bond, is extended in the figure of 'The Adventurer', who refuses to take on any fixed identity, accepting only the appearance of one: 'among all those who *were/* stepped suddenly the one who *seemed*'. In this way he can assume any number of different identities --

'there was always an existence to be had' – but he is constantly
threatened by the possibility of contracting a human bond and thereby
becoming 'somebody': 'Often not a spot in him was safe,/ and he
shook with fear: I am.' Through constantly confronting and overcoming this danger he takes on heroic qualities and in this way links
the figure of the lover with that of the hero. Danger gives his existence
a quality of heightened reality; he exists, in fact, in the world of
'Things', as the imagery reveals: there was 'a gleam as if of dangers/ in
the space that opened round him/ which he smiling crossed'. The word
which Rilke uses to describe this space – *ausgespart* – is the same as
that used in the poem quoted earlier to define the inner space of the
roses. As we might expect, this being who resembles but never is, whose
existence is a constantly-renewed metaphor, is at home in the world of
the mirror: he holds all the feminine glances falling on him, 'and even
those that fell in mirrors counted'.[57]

The same imagery is frequently related to the theme of heroism in
*New Poems*. As a young count in one of the historical poems decides to
die a heroic death 'a smile of noble women' falls on him.[58] In 'Corrida'
the circle of the arena seems to be formed by the 'gleam' and 'darkness'
of the matador's eyes, and in 'Falconry' heroism, with its concomitant
cruelty, is represented by the falcon 'thrown gleaming from the hand'
in pursuit of its prey. It is noticeable that the motif predominantly used
in relation to heroism and danger is 'gleam', a connection which was
noted previously in 'Early Apollo'.

Closely connected to the theme of heroism is that of facing and
accepting death. In 'Death Encountered' Rilke shows that the awareness of death, normally expelled from the 'play-acting' of normal existence, permits a more intense awareness of life. In 'The Swan' the act
of dying is seen as an entry to a new world of serenity, and the same
idea appears in 'Roman Tombs'; the poet suggests that death may fill
us with a new kind of existence as the tombs were filled with water
which 'mirrors now and runs and gleams in them': death too is linked
through imagery to the world of 'Things'.

But all these experiences give no more than a partial or doubtful
contact with the higher world. The only being who lives completely
and permanently in it is the angel, who has the awareness of total time
and reality which for men is only a distant longing: 'through his heart,
gigantic and erect,/ passes the circling that ever is to come'. In
numerous other contexts the angel is associated with Rilke's special
imagery; in 'Pink Hydrangea' it is the angel who receives the flower's
colour which 'smiles from the air'; in 'Falconry' the bird dives on its
prey 'like an angel', and so on.

The angel, with an inclination of the head, 'banishes far what limits
and constrains'.[59] The other being which in *New Poems* is exempt from

the conditions of the human world is the animal. 'The Dog', as we saw, exists outside the fictitious reality created by human intercourse, 'low down, unlike us, as he is'.[60] The animal's world is for Rilke both different and more real than ours, and for this reason he made a systematic attempt to enter it through empathy, or *Einfühlung*, an attempt which led to numerous poems on animals.

The animal is a particularly suitable subject for *Einfühlung* because its existence has important parallels to the artist's own. The artist tries to do voluntarily what the animal does involuntarily – to escape the human world and exist in the world of 'Things'. Poems explicitly about the artist are relatively few in *New Poems*, which might seem surprising were the artist not implicitly the subject of many, perhaps even of most of them. Rilke's choice of subjects for his poems was far from random, and in a large number of them he projects into various figures different aspects of his own situation as an artist. In other words, many of the poems have a symbolic meaning.

The symbolic implications of the animal poems have been indicated; the poems on solitaries already discussed have a similar function: in them Rilke projects the solitude inseparable from the artistic vocation as he conceived it. This isolation, with its liability to become eccentric and grotesque, is caricatured in 'The Island' and 'The Bachelor', which also parodies the predilection for the past. In the poems devoted to saints, hermits, etc., we find the problem of sexual deprivation inherent in Rilke's doctrine of non-possessive love. The same theme is present in 'David sings before Saul'. In two poems on lunatics,[61] there is a suggestion of the proximity of intensified artistic awareness to mental derangement.

The numerous poems on prophets, such as 'Saul among the Prophets', 'Jeremiah', 'A Sibyl', are concerned with the gift of inspired utterance and its problems. In two of these poems strikingly similar passages occur: 'he had prophesied/ almost still a boy, as if each vein/ has issued in a mouth of bronze' and 'What a mouth you burdened me with then/ when I was almost still a boy:/ it is become a wound.'[26] These passages, from 'Saul among the Prophets' and 'Jeremiah' respectively, contain what seems an unmistakable allusion to Rilke's own artistic development, his premature gift of compulsive inspiration, characterised as *Klang*, which produced *The Book of Hours* and led to the crisis which has been discussed.

Equally relevant in this connection are the poems on alchemy with its underlying quest for the absolute. In 'The Alchemist' the futility of this quest, and the impossible demands it places on human faculties – 'constellations in the brain/ and in the consciousness at least the sea' – are recognised. Abandoning the quest, the alchemist contents himself with 'the scrap of gold that he possessed',[63] which, however, suddenly

E

becomes more valuable to him than all he has renounced. Here it is not difficult to see another reflection of Rilke's artistic situation: his abandonment of the quest for God after *The Book of Hours* and his new-found creativity, based less on inspiration than on work and consciously applied technique, which was enabling him to write *New Poems*. In 'The Reliquary', the poem placed after 'The Alchemist', the artist is shown as a craftsman working with cold determination until his work is perfected.

The theme of the mistake of trying to proclaim God is present in other poems, in 'Elijah's Consolation': 'God, use me/ no more. For I am broken',[64] and in 'The Olive Garden', where the crisis produced by *The Book of Hours* is clearly visible: 'I find you no longer. Not in me, no./ Not in the others. Not in this stone.' The lesson of this poem is that such abandonment is the deserved fate of those who rely on forces outside their control: 'Those who lose themselves, everything lets go'.[65]

One of the most significant of the poems in which the theme of the artist is implicit is 'The Donor'. Here Rilke presents a man who prays but whose attitude is far removed from that of the monk of *The Book of Hours*. It is one of silent concentration and self-absorption which, if it is achieved, may be rewarded by an overwhelming vision:

> Daß wenn ein Ungeheueres geschähe,
> das nicht versprochen ist und nieverbrieft,
> wir hoffen könnten, daß es uns nicht sähe
> und näher käme, ganz in unsre Nähe,
> mit sich beschäftigt und in sich vertieft[66]

so that if the immense event should come to pass which is neither promised nor pledged, we might hope it would not see us and would come closer, come right up to us, busied with itself and self-absorbed.

The terms used in the last line show clearly that this hoped-for experience is a vision of the 'Thing'; and the experience of the 'Thing', as we saw in the last chapter, can be equated with the privileged moment. Rilke therefore has not abandoned the privileged moment as his goal, nor the idea of reaching it through 'prayer'. But he has changed his method: 'prayer' no longer involves involuntary incantation, which he now calls 'a howling',[67] but an attitude of patient and silent receptivity such as he saw practiced by Rodin.

The privileged moment can be called the invisible centre of *New Poems*; Rilke has now found a new way of embodying the experience in his poems. He no longer evokes it by involuntary language as in *The Book of Hours* or describes it for its own sake as in *The Book of Images*. On the one occasion in *New Poems* when the privileged moment appears explicitly, in 'The Poet', the poems begins, significantly, where the privileged moment ends: 'You are deserting me, my hour.'[68] But in another way the privileged moment is present in all the poems. Through his study of Rodin and the 'Thing' Rilke has been able to isolate the essential attributes of the privileged moment and to derive from them principles of poetic composition. It is as the laborious application of these principles that he now conceives his task as a poet.

This conception of art is illustrated in 'The Mountain', describing Hokusai at work. By a process of unremitting labour the painter, in the manner which Rilke noted in Rodin and Cézanne, produces a progressive heightening – 'intensified from form to form' – until he achieves the desired result: 'suddenly, the secret learned, to rise/ like apparition filling every rift'. Here the artist appears to be finally identified with the vision realised in his painting. In the process of creation, having thrown off all personal attributes – 'unparticipating, vast, without opinion'[69] – he has objectified himself and become what he has created. He has himself entered the world of 'Things'.

The study of Rilke's interpretation of life in *New Poems* has therefore led to the conclusion that for him artistic creation is the true way of 'changing one's life'. In arriving at this conclusion we have seen that his work contains a self-consistent view of life; all the important experiences, represented by themes – love, childhood, heroism, etc. – are related together in a coherent way. The presentation of this view of life in *New Poems* is further enhanced by the arrangement of the poems in a kind of pattern. Those dealing with related themes are grouped together in clusters which in turn are ordered in such a way as to produce an interweaving of themes. A further pattern is created by the time-scale of the poems. Generally speaking, the earliest historical subjects appear first, but again there is a blending of different groups to avoid an excessively chronological order.

This arrangement of the poems to form a balanced whole gives each of the two parts of *New Poems* a certain degree of unity of its own, over and above that of individual poems. We may at this point recall Rilke's admiration of the collective unity which he saw in Rodin's works: 'He started by making Things, many Things, and when they were made he formed the new unity out of them, or let it form itself.'[70] It seems clear that Rilke has tried to achieve a similar effect in his own collections. His emulation of Rodin in this respect becomes even rather obvious if we note that both parts of *New Poems* begin with a poem on a piece of sculpture, and that the final poem, 'Buddha in Glory' sounds the theme of heavenly constellations, with which Rilke had compared the totality of Rodin's work. The two other poems on Buddha placed elsewhere reinforce the impression that Rilke is trying to create his own 'universe' in which his 'Things' exist together, like Rodin's, 'in an instant of eternity'.

It must be admitted, however, that in this attempt Rilke has been only partly successful. His poems are, by their nature, 'closed', cut off from their surroundings. Like the flamingoes, as mentioned earlier, they 'step, separate, into the imaginary' – but it is the word 'separate' that must now be stressed. These intensely self-contained poems cannot be integrated together simply by being juxtaposed. If they are to form a wider unity among themselves, they must, in the terms used by Rilke of Rodin's sculptures, contain their environment within themselves. By this he meant that their internal structure should imply, and in a sense contain, the wider structure of which they are a part. In other words, they should be related formally in their surroundings. Rilke's poems, however, are related together only by their themes, their content; the unity of *New Poems* is that of the coherent view of life mentioned above. This as an abstract, intellectual unity, not the concrete, formal unity of a work of art.

Nevertheless, the embryo of such a concrete unity is present in the poems, in the special use of imagery discussed in this chapter. In this imagery Rilke has begun to create a 'field' or 'space' formed by inter-related words and motifs, which, by recurring in different poems, link them together in an autonomous structure. But this system of imagery, which is only visible after patient inspection, does not provide the main unifying principle of *New Poems*. It is at the most an adjunct to the far more obvious intellectual system we have discussed.

*New Poems*, therefore, despite Rilke's immeasurable advance in the use of language in comparison to his early poetry and even to *The Book of Hours*, fails to satisfy one of the deepest aspirations which led him to Rodin. Many of the individual poems are totally successful, but together they do not form the wider structure, glimpsed through Rodin's work, which Rilke called 'a celestial equilibrium between music and geometry.'

# CHAPTER ELEVEN

## Contemplation: the Creative Process in the Middle Period

M ANY of the *New Poems*, we noted in the last chapter, were the outcome of a process of empathy or *Einfühlung*. This was particularly the case with those about animals. In this connection we may recall Rilke's reference, in a letter of 1904 describing his new vision of reality, to the 'strange kinds of inspiration' he had received from animals.[1] There is clearly a connection between his new vision and the creative process in this period; it is confirmed in another letter where he writes of 'changes affecting in equal measure my vision and my creation'.[2] We must now examine the nature of this connection.

The 'strange inspiration' which Rilke received from animals is described at greater length in another letter, written in 1914, but which clearly refers back to this period: 'how splendid it is, for example, to see into a dog as you pass, *to see into it* ... to get inside it, to its exact centre, the point where it starts being a dog'. He goes on to say that his 'supreme feeling', his 'earthly bliss' had been experienced in 'the indescribably quick, deep, timeless moments of this divine seeing into things'.[3]

From these words it is clear that *Einfühling* or, to use Rilke's more precise term, *Einsehen* (seeing-into), is a form of the privileged moment. For Rilke it is only during such moments that we are able to know the world as it really is. Our everyday awareness of things, and the terminology we use to express it, serve only to obscure their true nature. 'What has been discovered?' he asks in another letter. 'Is not everything around us almost as if it had never been spoken, and most of it even never seen? Are we not the first to be face to face with every thing that we really (by "really" I mean without haste and without prejudice) look at.' He goes on to draw this revealing conclusion: 'and is not everything worthy of being expressed somehow, if we first discover it in this way?'[4]

For Rilke the act of seeing things truly, and that of naming them, are inseparable. The nature of the connection between them is described most fully in another important letter which must be quoted at some length:

> Contemplation is such a wonderful thing about which we know so little.
> It turns us completely outwards, but just when we are most turned outwards things seem to take place within us that have been longing for us to

stop observing them, and while these things, intact and strangely anonymous, are being accomplished in us, without involving us, in the object outside its meaning is growing up, convincing, powerful – its only possible name. And in this name we blissfully and reverently recognise the event that has been taking place within us, comprehending it only very faintly, from far off, under the sign of a thing which just now was strange to us and which the next moment is estranged from us again. [5]

There are a number of points here to which particular attention must be drawn. Firstly, the moment of recognition, though it may be prepared by a period of contemplation, is itself brief and precarious, and it is accompanied by a feeling of intense joy – Rilke uses the word 'blissful' (*selig*). It is clear, therefore, that this form of the creative process still involves an element of inspiration. Secondly, this process demands the total suppression of self-consciousness; it takes place anonymously, 'without involving us'. Only when self-consciousness is absent is it possible for the object which is recognised, and the part of the poet's mind which recognises it, to come together. Thirdly, and most important of all, the act of recognition takes place through the mediation of language, through the 'only possible name' of the object.

In this process, then, seeing a thing truly means naming it, and naming it means making a connection, finding an analogy between the object and something within the mind. The analogy can consist of a symbolic equivalence between the object and a feature of the poet's life, as Rilke states elsewhere in the letter just quoted and as we found to be his practice in many of the *New Poems*. But more generally the finding of analogies means the use of metaphor, often without specific symbolic implications. As we saw in the last chapter, metaphor is fundamental to *New Poems*. It is for Rilke a means of producing the sense of anonymity, the suspension of self-consciousness, referred to in the passage quoted. That he was himself conscious of this property of metaphor is indicated by a passage from another letter, of 1906: 'a situation, taken up by a comparison in a literary work, loses the distressing, rootless, drifting quality that belongs to the moment, and is filled with significance and inner validity the moment it passes entirely into an image'. [6]

How does metaphor produce this effect? We must return for a moment to the argument developed in Chapter One. We saw there that recognition involves abstract thought: when an object is recognised it is related to the group of similar objects to which it belongs. We saw also that the recognition of objects involves self-awareness: we see them in relation to our immediate personal preoccupations. Both these circumstances limit the intensity of awareness – abstract thought by reducing the quantity of sensation involved in perception, and self-consciousness by restricting our interest in objects to the part they play in our immediate desires or fears. If the object were isolated from these abstract and personal associations, it would therefore be perceived with far greater intensity than in normal life. But an object cannot be perceived in isolation: it must be related to something if it is to be 're-cognised' at all. An artist who wishes to produce an intensification of perception must therefore find a way of presenting objects which are recognisable yet are isolated from their normal abstract and personal associations.

Metaphor is a way of achieving this effect. In a metaphor the abstract relationship of the object to similar objects is replaced by one which is concrete and unique. Similarly the practical relationships of the object to its surroundings are superseded by a context from which practical and personal associations are absent. An example of this function of metaphor is seen in 'The Rose Window'. If we look at such a window we are likely to see it in the context of what we know about Gothic architecture and about similar windows. But by comparing it to the eye of a beast of prey Rilke shows what is for him the intense reality of the window: the hypnotic spiritual impact it had on souls in a different time. This example shows how metaphor enables us to by-pass the conventional abstract notions through which we normally perceive reality. In other poems we see how it is able to remove an experience from the context of our personal interests. In 'Parting', for example, an experience ceases to cause pain once it is embodied in a metaphor; the parting from the woman he loves has, by the end of the poem, no more relation to the poet's personal existence than 'a plum-tree, say,/ from which a cuckoo hastily took flight'.[7]

The use of metaphor is, of course, not new in *New Poems*. In Chapter Five we saw that it was one of the means through which the poet procured the experience of God. But although in the early period metaphor did play a part in producing an intensified consciousness, it was a consciousness in which the objective world had only a minimal part. In *New Poems* the reverse is the case: metaphor is used to concentrate awareness exclusively on things and experiences in the outside world.

For Rilke now the ideal metaphor is one which reveals wholly the intense reality of an object while excluding all the contingent elements normally attached to it. In 'The Gazelle', for example, the whole being of the animal is contained, for the poet, in the metaphors of the poem: 'all that is yours comparison can pass/ through love-songs', etc. It is noticeable that abstract concepts such as 'gazelle' or 'animal', which would reintroduce a sense of familiar reality into the poem, are entirely excluded. In general in *New Poems* it is Rilke's practice to use the conventional names of things only in the titles: in the poem itself the thing portrayed is introduced either by a more specific and expressive attribute such as 'Enchanted one', which stresses the gazelle's unique quality of being as it is, rather than its being like other gazelles, or by a non-committal term such as 'This', 'It', 'Something', etc., which gives us a powerful sense of the immediate presence of the object while withholding all familiar associations pending its assimilation into a metaphor. Or again, Rilke may begin, not with the object, but with its metaphorical equivalent, as in 'The Rose-Window', 'The Orangerie Staircase' and in the many poems beginning with 'Like' or 'As'.

But if a metaphor is to be successful it must strike a delicate balance. It must not only equate two objects which in conventional terms are entirely dissimilar; it must also show that there is a real and convincing equivalence between the two objects, a link strong enough to hold them together in the mind and to keep conventional notions in abeyance. If the link is not sufficiently strong, the metaphor will merely be refused by the mind as absurd or meaningless; the 'convincing, powerful, only possible name' will not have been found.

In *New Poems* such instances are rare; generally the elements of surprise and convincingness are perfectly balanced. But occasionally we find a metaphor where the two terms do not give a perfect equation; for example the opening metaphor in 'The Flamingoes', as noted earlier, seems far-fetched, seems to give not one but two separate events; and the metaphor defining the glance of 'The Adventurer': 'as if he had from roses/ children being brought up somewhere else' is so bizarre that it fails to give an impression at all. It is worth noting, however, that in both these cases the metaphor is not purely descriptive but appears to have been introduced for an extraneous reason. In 'The Flamingoes' it is intended to make explicit an abstract idea: the connection between metaphor and the mirror image. In 'The Adventurer', in which Rilke is clearly projecting an important aspect of his own life, the image, though not comprehensible in the context of the poem, is clear enough if we remember Rilke's personal situation: his daughter was being brought up by his wife's family while he contemplated roses in Paris.

The balance between the two terms of a metaphor is obviously a matter of crucial artistic importance to a poet like Rilke. He wrote relatively little on the technical aspects of his own art, but his criticism of painting reveals that he was acutely aware of this problem, translated into the terms of another medium. We have seen that it is the function of metaphor to transplant an object from the context of its familiar associations to a realm of intense being; Cézanne's work, as Rilke saw it, had a similar function: it 'concentrated reality so infallibly into its colour-content that it began a new existence, without earlier memories, in a Beyond of colour'.[8] The painter's task, weighing each element of his painting 'in the scales of an infinitely mobile conscience',[9] was to achieve a perfect balance betweenn an object and the colours representing it. That is to say, the object remains recognisably itself while being entirely severed from everyday reality. It was this achievement that Rilke admired in Cézanne:

> and yet the colour has no preponderance over the object, which appears so perfectly translated into its pictorial equivalents that, however successfully it is reproduced, its everyday reality nevertheless loses all heaviness to a definitive image-existence.[10]

If we substitute 'metaphorical equivalent' for 'colour' in this quotation we have a perfect description of Rilke's own practice in *New Poems*. He did in fact speak modestly, in another letter on Cézanne, of having achieved 'the beginnings of a similar objectivity' in his poems, mentioning 'The Gazelle' in particular: 'it is good'.[11]

But metaphor is not Rilke's only means of removing objects from their everyday contexts. As we saw in the last chapter, he achieves a similar effect by 'transplanting' things and experiences into the past. This is done in *New Poems* in two distinct ways. The first is by taking a historical subject and re-creating it as vividly as possible, so that it seems as 'real' as present experience, but without the oppressive associations of the actual present. This escape from the present by evoking the past is, however, a rather simple way of trying to solve the poet's problem, and the poems it produces – 'The King', 'Resurrection', 'Esther', etc. – are perhaps the least impressive and most conventional of the *New Poems*.

The second way in which the past is used to intensify the awareness of the present is more significant for this study. Sensations from the past are fused with those of the present to such an extent that the distinction between the two times is blurred. This experience is described most fully in 'The Apple Orchard':

> sieh das Abendgrün des Rasengrunds;
> ist es nicht, als hätten wir es lange
> angesammelt und erspart in uns,
> um es jetzt aus Fühlen und Erinnern,
> neuer Hoffnung, halbvergeßnem Freun,
> noch vermischt mit Dunkel aus dem Innern,
> in Gedanken vor uns hinzustreun.

see the evening green of this grass-plot; is it not as if we had long collected and saved it in ourselves in order now, from feeling and remembering, new hope, half-forgotten joy, still mingled with darkness from within, to scatter it in thought before us.[12]

E*

This poem evokes a 'spiritualised' awareness in the sense used in Chapter One: the mind seems no longer merely to 'take in' external reality, but to shed on it a radiance from within itself. A similar effect can be produced by reading, which temporarily transports us outside the context of our personal lives. In 'The Reader' the intense world of the book is projected on to outward reality 'with eyes that, far from taking, giving/ struck against the world's awaiting fullness'.[13]

It is because memory can play a part in producing this intense, 'spiritualised' awareness of the present that it is of extreme importance to Rilke in the middle period. In the entry in the Worpswede notebook which may be taken as marking the beginning of this period, he wrote the following:

> I have a great longing for the past. I do not wish to think back over it. But I want to experience its values, half unconsciously, in the things now surrounding me.[14]

This may be compared with a further quotation:

> He needed memory, not exactly memory itself, but memory transmuted into a reality directly experienced.[15]

The second quotation is from *Jean Santeuil*: the ideas of the two writers tally exactly on this point. In moments when present sensations are accompanied and enriched by past sensations 'like those ageing singers whose weakening voices are backed up by an invisible choir', Jean too experiences a 'spiritualised' awareness of reality: 'The past opened its heart to the present and the passing hour had become like spirit through which Jean was rapturously making his way.'[16] And, for Proust as for Rilke, this state of awareness, in which the content of the mind is merged with sensations from the outward scene, can be stimulated by reading; when Jean puts down his book 'the sun struck and lit up in him all the thoughts which his reading had sent flooding through him'.[17]

With regard to involuntary memory, then, and to the related activity of reading, the two writers are in marked agreement. But there is a difference which must also be noted. Whereas involuntary memory played a relatively minor part in *New Poems*, Proust claimed in *Jean Santeuil* that it was his only source of inspiration. This divergence between the writers is, however, more apparent than real. In practice, we found that involuntary memory did not account for all the privileged moments in *Jean Santeuil*, and the case was similar with the descriptions of inspiration attributed to fictitious writers in the novel. Memory played a part in inspiration for the novelist C. and for the comtesse de Réveillon, but not for Traves, Silvain Bastelle, or the poet in 'Artistic Contemplation'.

The creative process, in Proust's accounts, takes much the same form whether or not memory is involved. It begins with an impression of beauty and meaning encountered generally in a visual object. But this impression is not complete in itself; it demands a concentrated contemplation of the object, as when Jean gazes at the rose-border, or when the poet stands for an hour in front of the cherry tree. The impression cannot be fully enjoyed by contemplation alone, however, and this activity finally gives way to writing. This does not normally take place with the object directly present, but is derived from an image of it assimilated during contemplation; 'Wrapped up in this image, as it were, he took his thoughts away with him',[18] Proust writes of Silvain Bastelle. Through writing, the joy contained in the original impression is at last fully realised, and 'the word "writing" is quite incapable of suggesting the charm of the precious substance in which he cast his thoughts.'[19]

Inspiration here does not involve remembrance of the past but the writing down of 'thoughts' which are not further defined. Similarly in 'Artistic Contemplation' the poet extracts from his impression something which Proust calls rather vaguely 'the thought of the mysterious laws, or poetry'. In this essay, however, we are given a very exact account of the part played by language in realising fully the joy and meaning that had first appeared in the experience of visual contemplation:

> No doubt, if it [the thought of the mysterious laws] was close enough to escaping to have already found a few vague words, by repeating the words one day when he feels it to be charged with energy, having preserved it up to then under his words like a fish under grass, he will perhaps be able to recreate it. And when, shut up in his room, he has begun to take hold of it again, his mind throwing to him at each moment a new form to animate, a new vessel to fill, – what frenzied, sacred work![20]

When Proust adds that 'At this moment has has exchanged his soul for the universal soul', it is clear that we are concerned, here again, with a form of the privileged moment. Proust's creative process in the middle period therefore has much in common with that of the early period: in involves the use of language to realise a privileged moment which would otherwise remain incomplete. In addition, the process is not wholly voluntary; it contains an element of spontaneous inspiration. The voluntary part of the process is the effort of contemplation which precedes inspiration, when the writer applies himself to his impression in a way which Proust compares to a student reading and re-reading the text of a difficult problem.[21]

Proust's description of the creative process is therefore essentially the same as that given by Rilke earlier in this chapter, where a period of contemplation culminated in a moment of joy and recognition of the object's 'true' name. As we noted, an element of inspiration was involved there too; early in his acquaintance with Rodin, Rilke had realised that he could not follow the sculptor in completely replacing inspiration by work. This was made impossible by the essential differences between the two media – 'the incompatibility of two artistic worlds'.[22] What Rilke was able to learn from Rodin was the attitude of concentrated contemplation which facilitated the appearance of inspiration: 'I must learn from him, not how to make things, but how to compose myself deeply in order to make them.'[23] This effort of contemplation was an important part of the 'work' which produced *New Poems*; he himself summed up the collection as follows: 'It is a book: work, the transition from inspiration that comes, to that which is called up and held fast.'[24]

Inspiration, therefore, for Rilke as for Proust, is still a necessary part of the creative process. The advance they have made since the early period lies in the degree of conscious control they have gained over inspiration through the technique of contemplation.

But how can a conscious effort of contemplation facilitate inspiration? First, we must consider the nature of inspiration. In the study of *Jean Santeuil* and *New Poems* we found that, for the two writers in this period, inspiration means the escape from the narrow confines of personal existence in time to a higher world of timelessness. To see how contemplation can assist this process we must now look more closely at what is meant by the 'confines of personal existence in time'. We noted earlier that normal awareness means the awareness of the practical and personal preoccupations constituting our intentions for the immediate future and our memories of the immediate past. It is in relation to these preoccupations that we situate ourselves, and the things around us, in time and space. In this way we spread around us in each moment a kind of plan or 'map' of the outside world as it affects us. This is a map not so much of our surroundings themselves, as of our attitudes to them, our ways of approaching the problems in them, of avoiding what we wish to avoid, etc. It is through this net of aims and attitudes spread around us that we interact with people and things. It therefore constitutes our personality, our 'self', as it exists from moment to moment. Self-consciousness can be equated with the awareness of this 'map' of relationships and preoccupations; we cannot say or think 'I' without implying this vague network stretching around us.

It is through this system of practical relationships that we see the outside world. We do not consciously see the whole of reality, but only those parts of it which at a given moment are involved in our personal 'map'. This is why self-consciousness has a limiting and impoverishing effect on awareness. Anything which does not fit into the context of our immediate preoccupations is virtually non-existent. 'Our own lives' far too great proximity / forever overwhelms our gaze, as if / no other thing were happening'[25] – so Rilke expresses this phenomenon in 'The Cathedral'.

Contemplation is the attempt to remove these limitations of awareness by eliminating self-consciousness. It involves an effort to concentrate awareness, to prevent it from spreading outwards along the familiar channels of the 'map' or system of relationships which it normally occupies. This is the effort that is expressed in 'The Donor':

> zu knien: daß man die eigenen Konturen,
> die auswärtswollenden, ganz angespannt
> im Herzen hält, wie Pferde in der Hand.[26]

To kneel in such a way that one's own outward-pulling contours are held in tightly in the heart like horses in the hand.

Once this inner concentration is achieved the outside world is not lost to view but, on the contrary, is seen far more fully and intensely than before. Precisely at the moment when all our normal relationships to outward reality are suspended we are, to use Rilke's words in the account quoted earlier, 'turned completely outwards'. There is nothing paradoxical in this: when self-consciousness is removed, for the reasons just given the network which normally obstructs our vision of reality is drawn aside like a veil. In Rilke's case, the beginnings of this experience of self-less contemplation, of 'being nothing but eye', as he called it, are described at length in his Worpswede notebook:

> There is something like selflessness in this kind of participation in nature ... This daily attentiveness, wakefulness and readiness of the outward-turned senses, this thousandfold looking and always looking away from oneself.[27]

Similarly in Proust's 'Artistic Contemplation', the momentary return of self-consciousness masks the vision which the poet is contemplating: 'at moments something inside him hides from him what he sees, and he is obliged to wait for a moment'.[28]

Contemplation therefore involves deliberately 'forgetting' that one has a personal identity and objectives and needs in the outside world. It is the state of perfect absorption in the present which Rilke called Zu-Nichts-Gedrängt-Sein. In the midst of this state when all personal preoccupations are absent creative utterance can take place, as when in the passage quoted earlier Rilke 'anonymously' discovered the true name of the thing he had been contemplating. In the same way the

poet in 'Artistic Contemplation' can only write when he has detached
himself from all personal goals:

> every time he is aridly pursuing something, with a goal that transports
> his person from within to outside himself, he ceases to be in that part of
> himself where he can be in communication, as in a telephone or telegraph
> booth, with the beauty of the whole world.[29]

The technique of contemplation enables the writer to see things in
isolation from their normal practical contexts, and so makes it easier
to give them names relating them to other contexts of metaphor or
memory. Creative writing is therefore a natural extension of contemplation; but it is also, as we see from Proust's and Rilke's descriptions,
a way of further intensifying and completing the process begun by
contemplation. It is as if contemplation acts as a kind of 'starter' which
sets the creative process in motion; but once this has begun it carries on
with its own momentum and its own sources of energy.

How does the writer's use of language extend the transformation of
consciousness begun by contemplation? In writing creatively the poet
uses language in a special way; he modifies and in a sense violates a
number of its essential functions. One of the most basic functions of
language is to classify reality according to universally accepted,
abstract categories. As we saw earlier, the poet, in discovering metaphors, replaces these categories by particular, concrete links and in so
doing intensifies his consciousness of reality.

A second basic feature of language is its function as a means of communication between people. Communication, of course, involves the
awareness of 'I' and 'you', a human relationship. But human relationships, because they imply self-consciousness, are hostile to contemplation and creation. For example, in the letter describing the experience
of *Einsehen* involving the dog quoted earlier in this chapter, Rilke
remarked that such an experience would be impossible if he were in
love, because of the constant presence of his beloved and his personal
situation at the back of his mind. Conversation, he says elsewhere, has
a similar effect.[30] Proust repeatedly makes the same criticism of love,
conversation and all similar human relationships.[31] How, then, is the
poet to use language in a way which does not involve communication
and its concomitant self-consciousness?

This question may conveniently be studied on the level of the
writer's use of personal pronouns. In *New Poems* 'I' is never used
except in contexts where the poet is participating in a personal or
social situation, as in 'Woman Going Blind'. When he is describing his
poetic awareness of objects he uses the impersonal 'one' or 'we'. In
*Jean Santeuil* the situation appears to be similar. Proust uses third-

person narration, no doubt because he is aware that the 'I' would be hostile to the atmosphere of the privileged moment with which he is so persistently concerned in the novel. In practice, however, he might equally have written 'I': Jean is transparently a projection of the author's personal self and is frequently used as a means of vicarious wish-fulfilment. Proust has not yet learned that he cannot change his attitude to life by a change of personal pronouns. Instinctively, however, he seems to realise that Jean suffers from the same limitations as an 'I', and in his evocation of privileged moments ostensibly experienced by Jean he frequently slips into the illogical but more convincing use of 'one' or 'we'.

There is therefore an attempt by both writers to eliminate the 'I' from language. This attempt must, however, ultimately come into conflict with the nature of language itself. In so far as language is essentially a means of communication between people, it is inseparable from self-consciousness; the realm of language is co-extensive with the 'I'. The poet during inspiration must therefore preserve a residue of self-consciousness if he is to find words in his mind at all. Otherwise he might experience still more intensity and meaning, but would lack the means to express it, as is the case with mystical experience. On the other hand, of course, too much self-consciousness would put an end to inspiration.

During inspiration the poet is therefore constantly on a 'knife-edge' between having too little self-consciousness and too much. His consciousness must in fact be split into two, a 'personal' and an 'impersonal' part, an 'I' and an 'other', so that he can express the experience of the latter in the language of the former. We can imagine that there is a constant 'to-and-fro', as the 'I' plays with words in his mind until he finds the formula which brings the potential meaning of the object within the compass of his mind and at the same time tends to transport him outside the frontiers of language altogether. But a poet whose hold on language is secure will never quite cross this frontier; or, more exactly, he will never quite be able to: language is too deeply embedded in his personality and in his capacity for experience. So he compensates for a kind of impotence to experience full mystical awareness by developing his special use of language by which he manœuvres his consciousness to the borderline where it can, by the activity described above, draw parts of the previously unexpressed into the realm of the expressible.

Such theoretical discussion is necessarily somewhat speculative, but it is supported by concrete evidence in the writers' works. This can again be seen clearly on the level of personal pronouns. We saw that this creative act involves a kind of split personality: one part of the poet's mind is still in the familiar world of accepted signs and meanings, the other is exploring a nameless unknown. Expressing a similar experience of disorientation and 'split personality' in 'Snake Charming', Rilke writes: 'a crack runs through your face'. The use of the second person (*du*) is significant here: it is the syntactical form which most adequately expresses this kind of experience. In saying 'you' he presupposes the 'I' who is speaking, but the 'I' is describing not his own experience but that of the 'other' who is involved in the poetic experience. The use of 'you', unlike the impersonal 'we' and 'one', preserves the essential function of language as communication. But this communication is not between individuals forming a human relationship, but between two parts of the poet's mind. The degree of self-consciousness and the restriction of awareness normally insepar-able from communication is therefore avoided.

Rilke's use of *du* in *New Poems* is systematic, and it is particularly noticeable in contexts where the poetic atmosphere is most strongly conveyed, for example 'In a Strange Park'. Proust has of course no opportunity to use a similar device within the terms of the third-person narrative of *Jean Santeuil*. But on one occasion, in trying to find a more satisfactory variant of the 'one' or 'we' he uses so fre-quently to present the experience of privileged moments, he openly addresses the reader: 'Have you not, reader, sometimes yourself had the feeling ...'[32] and goes on to describe a poetic experience at Versailles which he attributes to the reader. But this is really Proust's own experience, and in addressing the reader he is addressing himself. This lapse into the second person, which is more significant for being entirely without justification in the context of the narrative, suggests a tendency in Proust running parallel to that of Rilke in *New Poems*. But, of course, the form of Proust's novel forbids him to follow this tendency except as an aberration.

We have seen, therefore, that by modifying certain fundamental characteristics of language, the writers are able to alter their con-sciousness of reality. Moreover, these modifications of language are of a kind which can to a large extent be applied consciously, as is above all the case in *New Poems*. This use of language, with the technique of contemplation to which it is coupled, therefore gives the writers a con-siderable measure of voluntary control over the quality of their con-sciousness.

Contemplation and creative expression enable the writers to isolate an object from its everyday context, and to eliminate self-conscious-ness from their perception of it. In consequence, their awareness of the object is intensified, and the normal subject-object relationship is sus-pended. In these respects too, therefore, the creative process of the middle period, like that of the early period, is essentially a process of realising the privileged moment. But this process has now been brought under voluntary control to a degree which was impossible with the incantatory inspiration of the early period. One of the major factors which produced the first crisis has therefore been removed. There is a second important difference between the two creative processes. In the early period the division between the self and the world was overcome largely by the suppression of the latter from awareness; this led to the loss of contact with the visible world which was another source of the first crisis. But in the middle period the division between self and world is overcome by the opposite means: by the suppression of self-consciousness and total absorption in objective reality. As a result, the visible world, the world of light and colour, appears in the work of this period with an unprecedented brilliance. This may be regarded as the major artistic gain of the two writers in the middle period.

To see what this development involves in terms of descriptive style, and to see also whether the theoretical parallels between the two writers which have been established in this chapter are borne out in practice, a comparative 'practical' examination of texts from this period must now be undertaken. A convenient way of beginning such a study is by comparing passages in which both writers deal with the same subject-matter, for example Proust's description of the rose-border at Réveillon and Rilke's description of roses in 'The Bowl of Roses'. The two passages are as follows:

> Quel bonheur alors de voir, comme c'était dans cette plate-bande de Réveillon, tous les chefs-d'œuvre de rosiers, s'élevant à la suite, offrant au cœur embrasé d'amour par le premier rosier blanc plus qu'il ne pouvait concevoir, un rosier aux profondes roses de pourpre, un autre aux petites roses roses comme des coupes peu creusées, un rosier aux pétales violets et simples comme une fleur d'églantine; c'était une longue galerie de rosiers dont chacun paraissait le plus beau, toujours un rosier comme on le reconnaissait à sa personnalité voluptueuse et grande, mais chaque fois s'étant enchanté d'une imagination différente, tantôt de la richesse de la pourpre et tantôt de la candeur des pétales blancs, comme un artiste dont chaque toile enferme un nouvel amour pour un autre rêve dans de particulières couleurs.[33]

> What joy it is then to see, as in this flower-bed at Réveillon, all the rose-bush masterpieces rising behind [the first], offering to the heart that the first white rose-bush had inflamed with love beyond imagining, a rose-bush with deep crimson roses, another with little pink roses like shallow cups, a rose-bush with violet petals, simple like those of a dog-rose; it was a long gallery of rose-bushes, each one seeming the most beautiful, always recognized as a rose-bush by its tall, voluptuous personality, but each time enchanted by a different conception, now by the richness of its purple, now by the innocence of its white petals, like an artist's paintings that each enclose a new love for a different dream in particular colours.

Sieh jene weiße, die sich selig aufschlug
und dasteht in den großen offnen Blättern
wie eine Venus aufrecht in der Muschel;
und die errötende, die wie verwirrt
nach einer kühlen sich hinüberwendet,
und wie die kühle fühllos sich zurückzieht,
und wie die kalte steht, in sich gehüllt,
unter den offenen, die alles abtun.[34]

See that white one which unfolded blissfully and stands in the big, wide-opened petals straight as a Venus in the sea-shell; and the blushing one, bending over as if in confusion to one that is cool, and how the cool one draws back unfeelingly, and how the cold one stands, wrapped in itself, among the others who take off everything.

It is noticeable that both passages consist of a single long sentence in which a number of roses are evoked in quick succession. By embracing the whole scene in a single sentence the writers preserve its unity, and at the same time compress a maximum of sensation within a minimum of space, with a minimum use of abstract particles of speech. The attention moves from one part of the scene to another with a kind of urgency, which is conveyed in Rilke's passage by the repeated 'and' and in Proust's by the rapid succession of phrases linked by 'behind [the first]', 'another', 'always a rose-bush', 'now … now', etc. This use of words serves further to bind all parts of the sentence into a unity. In Proust's case this need for unity and denseness of sensation is allowed precedence over clarity and elegance; there is much heavy repetition of 'rose-bush', *roses roses*, etc.

There is some use of metaphor in both passages, the roses being compared to paintings and to other flowers by Proust, and to human figures by Rilke. Proust too uses personification, referring to the 'voluptuous personality' of the flowers. But his use of metaphor is limited: he is concerned in this passage less with metaphor than with relating the impressions to the past. Rilke, however, uses metaphor more extensively to describe the roses: 'What can they not be?', the poet goes on to ask, and the question introduces a section of fifteen lines consisting almost entirely of metaphors.

There are further ways in which these passages exemplify the use of language discussed theoretically earlier in this chapter. Proust's description is presented through anonymous eyes and at an unspecified time: 'one of those moments in life when … we feel that there is nothing more delightful to love' than what is before us. The sentence describing the roses is without a personal pronoun of any kind: 'What a joy it is then to see', etc. In the rest of the passage Proust uses impersonal terms such as 'the delighted admirer', 'one', and 'we'. Rilke, in his passage, uses the second person in the way discussed earlier: 'See that white one', etc.

Both passages contain evidence that they originated in a state of contemplation involving the suspension of the normal sense of time and place. In Proust's description the present is indissolubly fused with the past, and for Rilke the roses seem to embody an almost infinite sphere of time and space contained 'in a hand full of inside' (*in einer Hand voll Innres*). In both cases the state of contemplation began with a sense of delight caused by sensation. In Proust, the sense-impressions produced by the flowers are linked immediately to an inner, emotional response: 'The pleasure which Jean felt then was as much in him as in the rose-bush'; in Rilke's poem there is a similar direct coupling of perception with emotion: 'a feeling caused/ by petals touching petals'.

In addition to this internal evidence there is also external, bio-graphical proof – Reynaldo Hahn's anecdote quoted earlier – that Proust's descriptive passage resulted directly from an experience of contemplation such as he describes in 'Artistic Contemplation'. For this reason the passage is valuable in giving a reliable basis to this textual study. But in itself it is not among the most satisfying descriptions in *Jean Santeuil*. When he wrote the novel Proust was already a master of nature description, a fact that has been noted by André Maurois;[35] as an example of his descriptive style at its most successful, the following extract from a passage, too long to be quoted in full, evoking a garden on a summer morning, probably could not be surpassed:

Ainsi entrelacées entre les feuilles, les fleurs des capucines suspendues aussi entre ciel et terre, les volubilis blancs avec au coeur une nuance plus ardente, comme dans le ciel certains reflets de soleil, se penchant sur la rivière et y égouttant le soleil qui s'y brisait en poussière lumineuse, les iris se suivant les uns les autres le long de la petite bordure, les myosotis levant l'un à côté de l'autre leur petite fleur d'un bleu profond comme un petit morceau bleu du ciel tendu vers lui, toutes ces fleurs, en rang comme les myosotis ou enlacées comme les pois de senteur, semblant de-scendre du ciel à la suite des reflets du soleil en se laissant glisser le long du treillage par le mur du jardin, semblaient comme les innombrables anges d'une sorte de Jour, comme ceux qu'ont représenté les grands peintres de la Renaissance, des anges peints d'un rose, d'un bleu, d'un orangé aussi vifs, les uns capucines, pois de senteur, volubilis semblant dans les airs se laisser glisser à terre en s'entrelaçant, les autres comme les violettes et les pensées à l'ombre dans la terre chaude semblant dormi ou paresser à terre, les uns entrelacés comme ici deux pensées gardant à l'ombre les plus merveilleuses couleurs de la lumière, les autres seules, dans toutes les poses mais toujours bienheureuses, donnant à qui les regarde un bonheur inouï, l'idée que le jardinier est un bienheureux, que ce jardin est le paradis, mais ayant moins que ces anges des peintres l'air de célébrer cette joie que de la remédier, d'y participer. Joie à laquelle n'échappait pas davange l'arbre indulgent qui ne cesse de verser aux fleurs extasiées a ses pieds, coucous, herbe et violettes, ici l'ombre, là la lumière, ou le cygne qui passe lentement sur la rivière portant aussi la lumière et la joie sur son corps éclatant, puis entrant dans une région d'ombre, ressortant dans la lumière, ne dérangeant en rien la joie autour de lui et laissant paraître par son air heureux qu'il la ressent, mais sans que sa démarche lente et calme an soit en rien changée, comme une femme noble voit avec plaisir ses serviteurs dans la joie et passe en souriant prés d'eux, sans mépriser leur gaieté, sans la troubler, mais sans s'y mêler autrement que par une calme sympathie et le charme majestueux que son passage répand autour d'elle.[36]

So entwined with the leaves, the nasturtium flowers hanging too between heaven and earth, the white convulvulus, with a fierier tint at their heart like certain gleams of sunlight in the sky, bending over the river and splashed by the sunlight that broke there in a luminous dust, the irises following each other the length of the little border, the forget-me-nots, side by side, lifting up their little deep-blue flowers like small blue pieces of the sky held out towards it, all these flowers, in rows like the forget-me-nots or entwined like the sweet peas, seeming to come down from the sky in the train of the glinting sunlight and slipping along the trellis by the garden wall, seemed like the numberless angels of a sort of Judgement-Day, as they are depicted by the great Renaissance painters, angels painted in just as bright a pink, blue or orange; some of them, nasturtiums, sweet peas, convulvulus, seeming in the air to glide down to earth entwined together, others, like the violets and pansies shaded in the warm earth, seeming to sleep or drowse on the ground, some entwined like two pansies here, preserving in the shade the most splendid colours of the light, others standing alone in all postures but always in bliss, giving the beholder an inconceivable joy and the idea that the gardener is one of the blessed, that this garden is paradise, but appearing less to celebrate this joy like the angels in the paintings, than to perfect it, to participate in it. It was a joy that the indulgent tree, too, could not escape as it shed ceaselessly on the flowers basking in rapture at its feet – cowslips, grass and violets – here shade, there light, nor could the swan passing by slowly on the river, he too carrying light and joy on his dazzling body, then penetrating a region of shadow, emerging again into the light, not in the least disturbing the joy around him and showing by a visible happiness that he shares it, but without this affecting in any way his slow, calm progress, as a noblewoman is glad to see her servants joyful, and passes smiling close by them without despising or disturbing their gaiety, but without being involved in it except through a calm sympathy and the majestic charm she spreads about her as she passes.

Such a style does not make for easy reading or immediate comprehension. The reader is constantly aware of an obscurity which positively resists the formation of distinct impressions. But it is an obscurity from which, once the passage as a whole has been absorbed, there emerges in the imagination a glowing reverberation of colour, freshness and sunlight. The sensations and images in the passage interpenetrate retrospectively to form a total impression which is complex yet full of specific detail.

To see how this effect is produced it is revealing to study Proust's use of syntax. The most striking syntactical feature of the passage is that it consists of only two sentences. Proust is clearly unwilling to break his sentences until he is absolutely forced to by the demands of comprehensibility. The division between the sentences is itself minimised by the repetition of the word 'joy' from one sentence to the next. In addition the sentences are unified internally by words and phrases which link together the various parts of the scene: 'entwined', 'following each other', 'here ... there', etc. The repetition of nouns contributes to this effect.

These unbroken sentences, consisting almost entirely of subordinate clauses, force the reader to hold together in his mind an abnormal quantity of impressions. He is unable to 'put down' the data at comfortable intervals as is possible with sentences of more normal length and with more frequent main verbs. In this way, if he makes the effort demanded by the prose, his consciousness is dilated to embrace an impression which is abnormally extensive and unified. The syntax therefore reproduces the sense given by the scene that all its parts are interrelated, a sense which Proust makes explicit later in the description when he calls the garden 'the happy realm in which nothing had secrets for anything else'.

A second striking feature of the passage is the extensive use of metaphor. It is significant too that here, as in the passage describing the roses, Proust's metaphors relate the scene to visual art, a reminder of the important influence of painting on his vision during this period. In addition, metaphor has the function of animating the scene: the personification of the flowers gives movement and a kind of alertness to what would otherwise be static and inert. Even where metaphor is not directly involved, Proust uses verbs denoting movement rather than those denoting fixed postures; for example, the flowers are described as: 'bending', 'following', 'lifting', 'coming down', etc. This use of present participles is also important in giving the scene a kind of indefinite duration, a sense of 'eternity'.

It is also noticeable that, as in the passage on the roses, Jean is entirely absent from the description. The only mention of a subjective consciousness experiencing the scene is contained in the phrase: 'giving the beholder an inconceivable joy'. In fact it is clear that this scene could not have been seen through the eyes of Jean as a boy, to whom it is attributed in the novel. The references to paintings, which are an integral part of the impressions, are sufficient to show that this is the experience of the mature Proust, who indeed uses the first person later in the passage. It may be assumed, therefore, that this description is not pure recollection of childhood, but is based on scenes more recently contemplated by Proust when his eyes had been opened by painting and his visual awareness was acute. Memory may, of course, have played a part in combining diverse impressions into a single picture. What is certain, however, both from the style of the passage and from its context in the novel, is that it describes heightened awareness. But the use of the word 'describe' here must be qualified. For we saw in the earlier part of this chapter that creative writing of the kind we are concerned with here does not merely record a finished experience: it is itself instrumental in completing, or 'realising', the experience. Proust did not fully experience the scene described until the moment he expressed it in language. In this context the meanings of the words 'describe' and 'experience' therefore become identical.

There is a further conclusion to be drawn from the passage: for Proust as for Rilke, metaphor is a primary means of expressing heightened awareness. The device is equally in evidence when he describes the impressions made on him by paintings; in a passage describing a Chardin interior he uses thirteen metaphors (excluding partly-metaphorical uses of language) in twenty-six lines. We may assume, then, that metaphors figured prominently among the vaguely-defined 'thoughts' mentioned earlier, which Proust's fictitious writers wrote down as a result of contemplation.

Rilke's work during this period allowed little scope for passages directly comparable to that of Proust just discussed. But in *Malte Laurids Brigge* there is a passage which shows that Rilke was attentive to the same kind of impressions as we find in Proust's description. This too is a description of a sunlit garden in early morning:

Es muß dies eine von jenen Tagesfrühen gewesen sein, wie es solche im Juli gibt, neue, ausgeruhte Stunden, in denen überall etwas frohes Unüberlegtes geschieht. Aus Millionen kleinen ununterdrückbaren Bewegungen setzt sich ein Mosaik überzeugtesten Daseins zusammen; die Dinge schwingen ineinander hinüber und hinaus in die Luft, und ihre Kühle macht den Schatten klar und die Sonne zu einem leichten, geistigen Schein. Da gibt es im Garten keine Hauptsache; alles ist überall, und man müßte in allem sein, um nichts zu versäumen.[37]

It must have been one of those early morning hours, of the kind that occur in July, new, rested hours when everywhere something joyfully unpremeditated is happening. A million tiny, irrepressible movements compose a mosaic of the most unwavering existence; in a mutual vibrancy things merge with each other and with the air, and their coolness gives limpidity to the shadow and makes the sunlight appear like a light, luminous spirit. Then there is nothing that predominates in the garden; everything is everywhere, and you would have to be in everything if you were to miss nothing.

Here we find the same intensity, the same cool play of light and shade and above all the same sense of interrelatedness and joyful participation, as in Proust's passage. But Rilke's theme in this novel did not permit him the lengthy nature descriptions which would be necessary for a close stylistic comparison with *Jean Santeuil*.

To find another German prose-writer of this time whose rendering of visual sensation, of colour and light, equals that of Proust in *Jean Santeuil*, would be difficult, perhaps impossible. But there is a writer in another language whose descriptive style, when translated into German, resembles Proust's to a striking degree. This writer is J. P. Jacobsen, the Danish novelist whom Georg Brandes called 'the greatest colourist of present-day prose'.[38] In his novel *Niels Lyhne*, for example, we find this passage:

> Durch die herabhängenden Zweige einer uralten Esche sickerte das gelbe Sonnenlicht in Strahlenbündeln auf die Treppe herab und bildete in dem kühlen, halbklaren Schatten eine Schicht leuchtender Linien, die die Luft um sie herum mit goldenem Staub erfüllten und klare Flecke auf die Stufen der Treppe, auf Tür und Wand zeichneten, Sonnenfleck neben Sonnenfleck, so daß es aussah, als leuchte das alles durch einen durchlöcherten Schatten dem Licht mit eigenen Farben entgegen, weiß von Edeles weißem Kleide, purpurblutig von den Purpurlippen und gelb wie Bernstein von dem Bernsteingelben Haar. Und ringsumher in hundert anderen Farben in Blau und Gold, in Eichenbraun, in glasblankem Spiegelglanz und in Rot und Grün.[39]

> Through the downward-hanging branches of an ancient ash sunlight trickled on to the steps in sheaves of yellow rays, and formed in the cool, half-bright shadow a screen of glowing lines which filled the air around her with golden dust and cast bright patches on the stairs, the door and the wall, patch of sun beside patch of sun, so that it looked as if all this were shining back towards the light through a perforated shadow with its own colours, white from Edele's white dress, blood-crimson from her crimson lips and yellow as amber from her amber-yellow hair. And all around in a hundred other colours, in blue and gold, in oak-brown, in a glassy mirror-sheen and in red and green.

Here, as in Proust, we find the use of a long sentence to embrace simultaneously a multiplicity of visual impressions, and the use of words such as 'around her' and 'all around' to bind together the various parts of the scene. The repetition of 'patch of sun', 'amber', 'white', 'purple', 'yellow', serves the same purpose. The effect of light is dazzling, and the shadow is luminous as in an impressionist painting. Metaphor, though present, is sparingly used. The reason may be that Jacobsen did not wish to isolate the scene from its context in the narrative, an effect which, as was shown earlier, metaphor would tend to produce. He therefore concentrates on expressing the brilliance of the scene directly, without forgetting the presence of the heroine who is made a part of the total colour-pattern. At this stage of his development Proust lacked Jacobsen's ability to integrate description into an unbroken narrative.

Rilke's admiration for Jacobsen is too well-known to need documenting here. Beside Rodin, the Danish writer was undoubtedly the most important influence on Rilke's style during this period, and in so far as his medium was words, his influence was more direct than Rodin's. Rilke liked to point out the agreement he found between his two masters: 'his words and Rodin's often coincide exactly'.[40] He saw Jacobsen and Rodin as possessing two essential features in common: 'contemplation of nature', and the ability, in their art, to recreate what they contemplate as 'reality intensified a thousandfold'.[41]

It was this intensified rendering of reality which first attracted Rilke to Jacobsen's works. In a letter of 1916 he recalls his first reaction to them as 'astonished joy at finding such things felt and given form'; they showed him the world as 'richer and closer to us than has previously been imagined'.[42] He also realised that Jacobsen's special use of language was an inseparable part of his vision. Like all great artists, said Rilke, Jacobsen had created his own language, word by word: 'Everything that is one's own ... demands a language of its own. Without it there is nothing.'[43] He was spurred by Jacobsen's example to create in his turn his own language, through which he would be able to experience reality with similar brilliance; he later spoke of the Danish writer's work as 'an obligation to achieve a more intense and living kind of writing than was then known and practised'.[44]

Jacobsen therefore played an important part in furthering Rilke's development from his early style, with its characteristic darkness and lack of visual impressions, to the clear daylight world of the middle period. The stages of this development have been noted in earlier chapters: in the third part of *The Book of Hours*, written in 1903 at Viareggio where Rilke had only Jacobsen's works and the Bible with him, colour and daylight become prominent, and the process is taken further in poems such as 'The Confirmands' (1903) in *The Book of Images*. By the time of *New Poems*, Rilke's mastery in the rendering of light and shade, and of the freshness and brilliance of the moment, was complete:

### Begegnung in der Kastanien-Allee

Ihm ward des Eingangs grüne Dunkelheit
kühl wie ein Seidenmantel umgegeben
den er noch nahm und ordnete: als eben
am andern transparenten Ende, weit,

aus grüner Sonne, wie aus grünen Scheiben,
weiß eine einzelne Gestalt
aufleuchtete, um lange fern zu bleiben
und schließlich, von dem Lichterniedertreiben
bei jedem Schritte überwallt,

ein helles Wechseln auf sich herzutragen,
das scheu im Blond nach hinten lief.
Aber auf einmal war der Schatten tief,
und nahe Augen lagen aufgeschlagen

in einem neuen deutlichen Gesicht,
das wie in einem Bildnis verweilte
in dem Moment, da man sich wieder teilte:
erst was es immer, und dann war es nicht.[45]

## Meeting in the Chestnut Avenue

The green seclusion of the entrance was laid around him like a silken
cloak that he was still taking and arranging: when at the other transparent end, far off,

emerging from green sunlight as from green panes of glass, a single white
glowing form appeared, staying long in the distance and at last, with cascades of light undulating over her at every step

bringing to him a bright, changing play that shyly ran back in the blond-
ness. But of a sudden the shadow was deep and, close to, eyes lay open

in a new face, quite distinct, which lingered as in a picture the moment
they parted: first it was always, and then it was not.

The use of metaphor in this poem is relatively limited. The reason
may be that the poem embodies a movement so perfectly contrived
that metaphor is scarcely needed in order to give the scene the necessary quality of isolation from contingent reality. The movement begins
at the moment when the poet and the woman enter the avenue at
opposite ends, and finishes when they meet; it is therefore balanced,
symmetrical and exactly coterminous with the poem.

But metaphor is, as we have seen in this chapter, the most important single feature in the descriptive styles of Rilke and Proust. As a
means of intensifying reality it serves equally well the purposes of the
poet and of the novelist. There is, however, an essential difference in
the way in which they use metaphor, dictated by their different genres.
For Proust, the axis around which his metaphors are clustered is the
thread of his narrative, however faltering this may be. The starting-
point for the metaphors is a scene in his novel, for instance the garden
scene quoted earlier, to which the images of women, angels, etc., are
attached. Rilke has no such continuous thread in his collections of

poems, and takes as an axis for groups of metaphors an object or an imaginary scene. As a result of his continuous axis Proust generally begins with a natural scene through which he evokes other things, whereas Rilke, with his discontinuous axis, often begins with other things in order to evoke nature. For example, in the garden scene quoted earlier Proust compares the freshness of the flowers to that of women emerging from water.[46] In 'Birth of Venus', with an interesting symmetry, Rilke uses a woman emerging from water as a starting-point for an extended evocation of nature. The parts of her body are linked to numerous impressions of nature: 'Like a young green leaf ... Her knees rose luminous like moons ... like a young fruit ... like a birch-grove in April ... like a fountain ... like a flower-stem ... like swans' necks ... the trees of her veins', etc.[47]

The technique used in this poem indicates that there is not always a simple 'one-to-one' relationship between the moments of contemplation and creation. Admittedly, the short descriptive poems most characteristic of *New Poems* appear to be the products of single acts of contemplation. In 'Birth of Venus', however, impressions assimilated during numerous moments of contemplation are synthesised in a single poem, which may itself have originated in a further act of contemplation, this time of a painting. But the poem is as much about Rilke's experience of nature as about Venus or the painting. Similarly, Proust's garden scene seems likely to have been a synthesis of various moments of contemplation.

The practical study of texts has therefore served two purposes: it has illustrated and corroborated the theory developed earlier in the chapter; and it has also now provided a useful corrective to the necessarily simplified account of the creative process that was given there. That account was of course only a schematic representation of what in reality must be a far more subtle and continuous interchange between the artist and his surroundings. The examples of the creative process given in the passages quoted were, for reasons of clarity, the simplest and the most highly developed. It need scarcely be said that this process, in the full complexity of its practical application, could never be completely analysed.

# CHAPTER TWELVE

## The Notebook of Malte Laurids Brigge

MALTE Laurids Brigge is a man who begins to live permanently in the state of contemplation discussed in the last chapter. Early in the novel he notes that his visual awareness of reality is undergoing a transformation: 'I am learning to see ... everything goes deeper into me and does not stop where it used to.'[1] The normal limits of awareness disappear and he experiences an unrestricted openness to impressions.

This total exposure to reality leads to distress and fear. About a page after the quotation above he writes: 'I am afraid. Against fear something must be done.'[2] What he does is to write; he sits up all night noting down an apparently unconnected series of episodes drawn from his family's past and his childhood, and from his recent impressions of Paris.

But his fear increases, despite the lack of external causes: 'I tell myself: nothing has happened.'[3] The cause of his fear, he realises, is internal – he is beginning to lose contact with reality: 'something is going on in me that is beginning to separate me and cut me off from everything'.[4]

After this realisation, which occurs fairly early in the novel, we hear less and less about Malte's actions. He visits a hospital, falls ill, appears sometimes in the streets of Paris. His fear seems to grow, but the bulk of the notebook towards the end deals with his recollections from the past and from reading.

When the notebrook breaks off at the end we are to understand that Brigge is dead, in some way overcome by his environment.

This is the plot of the novel, in so far as it has one at all. These are the more or less external events which enable us to discern a chronological axis along which the action advances. But even these events are concerned more with Brigge's state of mind than with his actions.

In fact, of course, the book is not about Brigge's actions, but about his inner development. Early in the novel, at the point where he mentions his new visual awareness, he also writes: 'I have an inner world that I knew nothing about. Everything now goes there. I don't know what happens there.' The 'action' of the novel is, precisely, 'what happens there'.

In trying to write a novel derived from his own experience in Paris, Rilke realised that the traditional form of the novel based on action, in the manner of a chronological biography, would not suit his purpose. He had already tried this approach once, in *Ewald Tragy*, and had produced a competent but rather insipid work. He now saw clearly that an external, chronological approach could not give access to his essential experience. For him, all human reality was now inner experience; the notebook states this explicitly: 'life, our life ... had withdrawn into the interior, so deeply that there were hardly even conjectures about it any more.'[5]

In order to approach this reality, Rilke abandoned the depiction of external action. In so doing, he forfeited the unifying narrative thread which made the traditional novel artistically possible. He was aware that his book lacked this kind of unity and compared the finished novel to a mass of papers found in disorder in a drawer, admitting that it was 'a bad unity' from the artistic point of view. But, he went on, 'from the human viewpoint it is possible, and what rises up behind it is, all the same, a projected existence, a shadow-pattern of connecting forces.'[6]

For Rilke, then, although his book may lack unity in the old sense, it has a coherence of its own, derived from the human personality it portrays. His standpoint here has much in common with that of Proust in writing *Jean Santeuil*, although Rilke goes further than Proust in abandoning chronological narrative. The parallel becomes still more pronounced if we look in more detail at Rilke's underlying conception of the unity of the personality. In a letter written much later, but in which he expresses a belief which, he maintains, he has held throughout his life, he describes the human personality as a kind of pyramid with normal consciousness at its apex, but with its base spreading further and further into a realm independent of space and time. If we could reach the lower levels of this pyramid, he says, we should be able to experience 'simple being ... that inviolable simultaneity and presence of everything which, at the upper "normal" tip of self-consciousness, we are only permitted to experience as a "sequence of events".'[7]

The 'normal tip of self-consciousness' referred to here is clearly that part of the personality which operates in social and personal intercourse and provides the material for the characters of the traditional novel. In his novel Rilke dispenses with this as with the 'sequence of events' of chronological narrative in order to capture 'simple being'; he tries to show, he says in the same letter, a character capable of experiencing 'what is past and what is yet to come simply as, in the highest degree, present'.

In the novel Rilke does present, through Malte's eyes, several characters who have this kind of experience. The first is Malte's grandfather, Count Brahe, in whose house a long-dead ancestor is seen walking, since the Count pays no attention to such notions as time and decease: 'death was a minor incident that he completely ignored'.[8] He also lacks a clear-cut personality and a fixed identity; it seemed to Malte as if 'no definite name could adhere to his personality which at certain moments was so sharp but which would always dissolve away again'.[9] Coupled to this lack of a consciousness of time or identity is an absence of normal personal relationships: on the few occasions when he spoke, 'his voice addressed nobody'.[10]

In the figure of Brahe, then, many of the essential features of the artistic consciousness discussed in the last chapter are to be found. Another such figure is the Marquis von Belmare, who is presented through the recollections of Count Brahe. Belmare carried the past within him, in his blood, and had access to any part of it: 'he could open it at any page he liked, there was always something written there'.[11] Like Brahe, he was characterised by a quality of anonymity; he was, for example, in the habit of receiving letters addressed to nobody. But although Belmare lacked the characteristics which would give him a definite identity, he had, Brahe maintains, one attribute which was all-important – that of 'being': 'at that time, of course, I could not judge whether he had wit, or this or that quality to which people attach importance –: but he *was*'.[12]

There are other characters in the novel who are able to perceive realities invisible to normal consciousness, for example Erik, or the dog who sees his dead mistress, and even Malte and his mother when they see a house which is no longer there. But no one has these powers to the same extent as Count Brahe, who can make others see his own reality, as when Abelone sees Belmare. In these figures who possess 'psychic' qualities Rilke has taken his conception of the 'pyramid of consciousness' to the extreme, and perhaps even deliberately to the absurd. But these are peripheral characters, and Malte himself, at the time of writing the notebook, is not concerned with extra-temporal and extra-sensory experience in such a literal sense. He illustrates the psychological, rather than the supernatural, implications of Rilke's special conception of the personality.

What Malte has in common with Brahe and Belmare is an uncertainty about his own personality, a lack of identity. 'What kind of life is this,' he writes early in the novel, 'without a house, without inherited things, without dogs? If one had at least one's memories. But who has them?'[13] He feels already that if there is a continuity in his personality it lies in the direction of his childhood; but this is closed to him, 'as if buried'.[14]

There is an early crisis in the novel when Malte realises the total nullity of his existence: 'Here I sit in my little room, I, Brigge, twenty-eight years old and unknown to anybody. Here I sit and am nothing.' Faced by his own non-existence, he poses to himself a number of

radical questions – questions which assert the superficiality and unreality of all human life: 'Is it possible that despite inventions and
progress, despite culture, religion and philosophy, we have remained
on the surface of life?' His questions all hinge on the contrast between
this 'surface of life' and the true, timeless depth of the personality,
which people normally forget: 'Is it possible that every single person
ought to be reminded that he has grown out of all who lived before
him, so that he knows it and should pay no attention to the others who
know otherwise?' The people who 'know otherwise' are those who
share the normal historical sense of the past as a succession of events,
which for Brigge is unreal, as is their chronological experience of life:
'Is it possible that all realities are nothing to them, that their lives are
ticking away, connected to nothing, like clocks in an empty room?'[15]
All this is possible, he concludes, and this being so it is necessary to do
something: Malte will have to write.

The next entry in the notebook is a recollection from his childhood – precisely the one describing his grandfather and his uncon-
ventional sense of time. From this point on, a large part of the
notebook consists of childhood recollections. Malte has realised that
he must renew contact with his childhood, or more exactly, that his
childhood is still in front of him, still has to be 'accomplished'. Rilke's
phrase for this – seine Kindheit leisten – has become well-known; it
occurs in a passage describing an earlier occasion when Malte had
realised that if he lost his childhood he would 'never have anything
else to appeal to'.[16]

The theme of childhood and its superiority over adult experience
is important in the novel as in New Poems, in connection with which
it has already been sufficiently discussed. What should be noted
regarding its specific treatment in the novel is that growing-up is
presented as a process of reducing and distorting experience to make
it fit into conventional categories; Malte writes of 'that thoroughly
communal life in which everyone expected to be backed up in his
feeling of being on familiar ground, and where people accommodated
themselves so cautiously to the comprehensible. Something was expected, and either it happened or it did not, anything else was out of
the question'.

In contrast, the child is constantly confronted with experiences
which do not fall within these 'agreed limits'.[17] Malte calls these
'one's own experiences' – eigene Erlebnisse[18] – and in the notebook
he describes several from his own childhood. One was the hallu-
cinatory encounter with 'the hand', when he seems to have crossed
into the realm of the supernatural; another was the irruption into his
life of 'the Huge' (das Große) during a feverish illness. 'The Huge' involves the exposure to normally hidden depths of the self. The inner

world, consisting largely of long-forgotten experiences, is thrown up into consciousness by the fever, and it is too large to be contained within the limits of normal consciousness: 'there I lay, heaped up with myself'. Malte is unable to put all this unmanageable material back tidily inside himself – there is too much of it. He is seized by desperation and panic: 'And then I screamed, half-open as I was, I screamed and screamed.'[19]

The formed personality is seen, therefore, as a kind of 'lid' or cover holding down the deeper levels of the self. In the child it is only precariously established and can be easily dislodged. Malte as a boy takes a pleasure in exchanging his real identity for that of a fictitious sister 'Sophie'. He also likes dressing up in costumes and looking at himself in a mirror. He notices that his personality – 'my movements, my facial expressions, even the ideas that came into my head' – is determined by the image he sees in the mirror. Still more disturbing, the being in the mirror seems to Malte to be far more 'himself' than does his normal personality: 'the more I rang the changes on myself, the more convinced of myself I became'.[20]

On the occasion when Malte discovers some masks and adds one to his costume, the experience becomes truly 'his own'. He accidentally knocks over a table bearing fragile objects, and in his panic-stricken attempts to free himself from his costume he becomes trapped in it. And now, he says, the mirror 'takes its revenge' – in it he sees: 'an image, no, a reality, an alien, incomprehensible, monstrous reality which steeped me through and through against my will'. The reality in the mirror is now so strong that the rôles are reversed. Malte is no longer the real being but the passive reflection: 'now it was the stronger of us and I was the mirror'. He loses his personality entirely, and the experience of losing it is terrifying:

> I stared transfixed at this terrible unknown figure looming before me and it seemed appalling to be alone with him. But at the same moment as I thought this the climax was reached: all sense deserted me, I simply ceased to be there. For the length of a second I had an indescribable, painful and fruitless longing for myself, then only he was there: there was nothing apart from him.[21]

He describes how he ran out of the room in terror and finally fainted, using the third person instead of 'I'.

The mirror presents a reality against which Malte becomes unreal. It therefore has the same rôle in the novel as in *New Poems*: it holds the world of true reality. And, because of this, those characters in the novel who really '*are*', such as the ghost who walks in Count Brahe's house, do not appear in mirrors. Little Erik 'explains' this to Malte: ' "Either one is in it", he dictated in his severe, precociously grown-up

way, "then one is not here; or, if one is here, one cannot be in it." [22]
This passage is placed, significantly, shortly after the incident of the
mask just described.

In the novel Malte's 'own experiences' of his childhood are repeated
by the grown man. He falls ill and encounters 'the Huge'; during the
experience he loses all sense of his own identity and of the meanings
of the normal world. The destination-boards of trams carry unknown
names; 'I did not know which town I was in and whether I had
lodgings somewhere here and what I should do in order not to have to
keep on walking'.[23] As he lies ill in bed he is overwhelmed by a re-
surgence of past experiences and anxieties: 'scattered on my bed-
spread are lost things from childhood, as if they were new. All the
fears I had lost are back again.'[24] In this state Malte no longer experiences time as a chronological succession, but as the 'total time'
discussed in the last chapters: 'my day, which nothing interrupts, is
like a clock-face without hands'.[25]

Malte is losing contact with his normal self and with the everyday
reality to which it belongs. In the light of the discussion in the last
chapter it is interesting to note that as he describes this sense of being
split from his former personality, he uses the second person:

> Your heart is driving you out of yourself, your heart is after you and
> already you have almost come out of yourself and you can't get back.
> Your insides are oozing out like a squashed beetle's, and your little bit of
> outer hardness and adaptation counts for nothing.[26]

As his adult personality gives way and the process of growing up is
reversed, Malte finds himself surrounded once again by the unmanageable world of his childhood; and he feels 'that it is still just as
difficult as it was then and that it has served no purpose to grow
older'.[27]

In his experiences in Paris, his encounters with his room-neighbours
and with the poor and outcast in the city, he re-enacts his childhood
experience with the mirror. Being without the 'outer hardness and
adaptation' of a formed personality, he is unable to separate his own
existence from those of the people around him. He is drawn to them
by curiosity and sympathy, shares their suffering and, in the case of
the hysteric and the student who is prevented from studying for his
examination by an uncontrollable eyelid, he gives away his will-
power to supplement theirs. Likewise he is exposed to all the impressions of horror and ugliness which the city offers. And he realises
that he is open to all these impressions because they correspond to
his own being; he is inwardly like them: 'For that is the terrible thing,

that I recognised them. I recognise everything of that kind here, and that is why it passes straight into me: it is at home in me'.[28]

Malte sees in external scenes a reflection of his own being which is far more 'himself' than in his normal adult personality. By a reversal of rôles like that in the childhood episode, he loses his identity and becomes both the mirror and the reflection in it. That is to say, he experiences himself no longer through self-consciousness in the normal way, but through his impressions of the outside world. External reality becomes a kind of metaphor for his own existence.

It is clear that this relationship between the self and the world is quite unlike that of conventional experience. To reach it from his relatively 'normal' standpoint early in the novel, Malte must pass through a crisis. This occurs early on, in the section where Malte writes that 'something is going on in me that is beginning to separate and cut me off from everything'. What he is leaving behind is his former personality and the familiar world to which it belonged; and just as in his childhood experience with the mirror he had felt a 'painful, fruitless longing for myself', so he is now filled with fear by the sense of losing contact with his familiar world: 'I fear this change with a nameless fear. I have not yet got used to this world, which seems good to me. What am I to do in another one?'[29] It is because of this fear in him that Malte's being coincides with, or 'reflects', that of other figures who are helplessly in the grip of a force beyond their control: the dying man in the *crémerie*, the hysteric and the student, so that he identifies himself with them.

Malte knows that the change he is undergoing will affect not only his identity, but the meaning of the things around him: 'I would so gladly stay among the meanings that have grown dear to me.' The change will therefore involve the meaning of words, and his ability to use language:

> For a while yet I shall be able to write down and say all that. But a day will come when my hand will be far from me, and if I command it to write it will write words which I do not mean.

Malte is approaching a position analogous to that of a writer during a creative moment, as discussed in the last chapter. The writer, too, is split between the 'I' who uses language and the 'other' who is involved in the poetic experience. Malte recognises that there is in his situation something similar to his own earlier experiences of creative writing: 'Despite my fear I am like someone who has a great event before him, and I remember that I used often to have a similar feeling before I began to write.' But now the experience is so extreme that the part of Malte which says 'I' will be entirely passive: 'But this time I shall be written.' As he earlier became the mirror and the

F

reflection in it, he now becomes the impression he will write down: 'I am the impression which will change.'

The impression will change; these words introduce a new and all-important possibility for Malte: the impression he reflects, which is at present one of fear and horror, might be different. If he can pass through his crisis, he may experience a world of ecstasy: 'Only one step, and my deep misery would be bliss.' As we saw in the last chapter, the moment of creation itself is one of intense joy: Rilke used precisely the word 'blissful' to describe it. It is only the process of leaving behind the normal personality and its preoccupations which is painful. But Malte is unable to go beyond this painful stage: 'I cannot take this step, I have fallen down and cannot get up, because I am broken.'[30]

We have seen that Malte's crisis involves the same transition from everyday reality to another, nameless reality as that achieved by the artist through contemplation and the creative use of language. But whereas, for the artists in the last chapter, this transition involved only brief moments of creation, after which they returned to everyday reality, for Malte it is an irreversible process involving the whole of his existence. The question posed by Malte as a projected existence is therefore the following: is it possible for the artist to experience constantly the reality he enjoys briefly during contemplation and creation, or, put another way: can he cross permanently into the world of the mirror?

Malte is unable to make this permanent transition, but he does recognise that it exists as a possibility: 'If my fear were not so great I should console myself with the knowledge that it is not impossible to see everything differently, and yet to live.'[31] But although he is unable to take the last step to reach the world of ecstasy, he is also unable to go back. He seems to remain permanently on the threshold, at the point of most acute suffering, strung between the two realities and existing fully in neither, until the experience destroys him.

He does not flinch from the pain of his exposure to reality, but realises that he must accept it if he is to take another step forward. Commenting on Baudelaire's poem '*Une Charogne*' ('Carrion'), he says it is the artist's duty to discover reality – *das Seiende*[32] – even in the most repugnant phenomena. So he too scrupulously records the reality experienced in a series of painful encounters, notably in his description of the inner wall of a house exposed by demolition. In places he goes to extreme lengths to confront and describe the horrible, for example the eyes of an old woman: 'running eyes that looked as if an invalid had spat green phlegm between the bloody lids'.[33] A similar preoccupation underlies the protracted descriptions of death-scenes in the novel.

Though Malte may not have reached the world of ecstasy, he does already live in a 'changed world', a 'new life full of new meanings'.[34] To some extent, then, he inhabits, like Count Brahe, the world of the mirror. And even before the crisis just discussed, Malte had a way of apprehending reality which was appropriate to the mirror-world: he experienced things, not directly in their presence, but through something else in their absence, in the manner of a metaphor. For example, he sees the face of his dead mother scattered in the features of his aunt: 'only now ... did I know once more what the deceased woman had looked like; indeed, I knew it perhaps for the first time'.[35] Similarly, he does not experience the beauty of Abelone, his first love, in her presence, but when he is away at an academy, looking out at nature: 'in such moments and at night the certainty grew in me that Abelone was beautiful'.[36] Later, in Paris, he again experiences Abelone while contemplating tapestries in which, in a multiplication of the mirror image, he sees her in the figure of a woman who is showing a unicorn its image in a mirror. On another occasion the figure of Abelone is experienced in a singer he meets in Venice, and he finds her too in Bettine von Arnim's letters:

> when I read them it is uncertain whether I think of Bettine or of Abelone. No, Bettine has become more real in me, Abelone, whom I knew, was like a preparation for her, and now, for me, she has passed into Bettine as into her own, involuntary being.[37]

In a similar way Malte, more and more as the notebook proceeds, ceases to have the reality of a separate individual: in the scenes and episodes he describes he too has 'passed as into his own, involuntary being'. Having lost his personal identity, he cannot experience himself directly through self-consciousness, but only indirectly in external realities analogous to his own inner existence. He must, as Rilke wrote later in a letter, grasp his life, which is 'constantly receding into the invisible' through 'phenomena and images', and he finds these 'now in his childhood memories, now in his Paris surroundings, and now in reminiscences from his reading'. In this way he experiences his life, not as chronological succession, but as simultaneity: 'and all this, wherever it may have been experienced, has the same validity for him, the same permanence and presence'.[38] Later in the same letter Rilke uses a formula which has become well-known: he calls the various figures recollected and evoked by Malte *Vokabeln seiner Not*[39] – the vocabulary of his distress.

The historical figures which occupy much of the second part of the notebook are metaphors for Malte's own being. In the gruesomeness

of many of the scenes Malte's inner distress is contained just as specifically as, in *New Poems*, the essence of the gazelle, for example, is
contained in the love-songs, etc., to which it is compared. This metaphorical 'vocabulary' reflects not only Malte's distress but other
related aspects of his existence, in particular his loss of identity. A
false Tsar who appears is presented as a man whose lack of a ready-
made identity gives him 'the will and the power ... to be everything'.[40]
Here, as in other historical episodes, the status of king or emperor confers ultimate identity. Charles the Bold tries to achieve such identity
in order to impose his stamp on his own rebellious blood. Charles the
Sixth, a mild, world-shy figure, part saint, part imbecile, is strengthened by the idea that he is king; but this extreme of identity also
gives him a feeling of confinement, and he eagerly attends the mystery
plays which impose their reality on his, so that the time in the verses
becomes 'the real time'.[41]

Here the loss of identity is related to the theme of time. In another
episode, that of Nikolaj Kusmitsch, Rilke's conception of time is reflected more fully. Kusmitsch becomes obsessed by the sense of passing
time, which he feels as a kind of perpetual wind. He can only overcome his malaise by continuously reciting poems which replace external time by an inner time of their own: 'If you recited a poem
slowly like that, with an even stressing of the end-rhymes, then to
some extent something stable was there that you could look to, inwardly of course.'[42] Kusmitsch therefore becomes a *Vokabel* of Malte's
tendency to live in the world of 'total' time, the time which he compared to a clock-face without hands.

In this way Malte's invisible inner life is presented concretely
through episodes which have the function of metaphors. But these
*Vokabeln* do not make up the whole of the notebook; Rilke also develops his themes in a more direct and abstract way. In connection
with Malte's Paris experiences, for example, he expresses ideas on art
and on the deficiencies of modern life. Characters such as Abelone
enable him to introduce his theory of love without possession. Finally,
in the legend of the Prodigal Son, suitably reinterpreted, Rilke is able
to present ideas on religion. At the same time, however, the Prodigal
Son is a kind of composite *Vokabel* for Malte; in this episode Rilke
draws together many of Malte's experiences into a form of conclusion.

*The Notebook of Malte Laurids Brigge* therefore presents a picture
of the hero built up from various episodes taken from different times
and sources. The figure of Malte is equated with the totality of these
episodes; as we saw, he is not limited, as in a chronological narrative,
to one moment at a time. For Malte, all moments are equally real and
present. 'Not for nothing', Rilke wrote in 1925, 'is Malte the grand-

son of the old Count Brahe who thought of everything, past or future, as simply "present": so too for Malte the stock of things that his mind has taken in in three different ways is present: his time of distress and the great time of distress of the Avignon popes ... are equated.'[43]

This, then, is the way in which Rilke attempted to realise in his novel his special conception of the deep unity of the personality which, he believed, would also provide the unity of the work. When he spoke of the book as artistically 'a bad unity', he did not mean to be taken quite literally, as Mason observes.[44] He meant that the unity was not that of the traditional novel but of a new kind. It remains to be seen, however, to what extent the human unity of Rilke's novel does in fact provide a principle of artistic unity capable of replacing the plot-principle of the traditional novel.

Rilke was aware of the problems involved by his conception of the novel even before he started working on *Malte Laurids Brigge*. His notebook of 1902 contains a comparison between two writers he admired, Jacobsen and Beer-Hofmann. The essential difference between them, as he saw it, was bound up with the use of plot as a principle of unity. Whereas everything in Jacobsen's novels is closely tied to the action, Rilke notes, Beer-Hofmann's has no such unifying time axis. Nevertheless, Rilke does not see the latter writer as altogether the inferior of the two: on the contrary, he considers his book 'more intensely experienced' than those of Jacobsen.

He goes on to enlarge on the way in which Jacobsen's use of coherent plot gives unity to his works. The writer is able to incorporate an essential part of himself in the narrative structure: Jacobsen's 'soul chose an expansive action, in the temporal and internal connections of which it might unfold itself'. The action is seen as a vessel for the unifying presence of the author; the whole 'world' of the novel is contained 'within the circle of his sun-filled soul'. Beer-Hofmann is unable to do this, because his soul is 'too much agitated by life. It knows nothing of calm paths through invented destinies.'[45] The more intense the writer's experience of reality, therefore, the more difficult it is for him, according to Rilke, to express it through the artifice of a constructed narrative. Beer-Hofmann can present only disconnected moments of beauty or intensity which are described for their own sake.

In this respect Rilke, when he began to try to use his Paris impressions for a novel, was in the position of Beer-Hofmann rather than of Jacobsen. His experience was too intense to be transferred to an imaginary world, and he was anxious to present it with the maximum of immediacy. And in the separate episodes of the novel he does achieve intensely luminous passages. The book is composed of such scenes, each one vivid in itself, but self-contained and self-sufficient, and frequently 'closed' by a final sentence full of resonance: 'and so we stayed, Mamma and I, until the house had quite passed away again.' 'Like an empty paper bag I drifted past the houses, back up the boulevard.'[46]

These intense, self-contained passages might well be called prose-poems, and indeed one work of which Rilke's novel is strongly reminiscent is Baudelaire's collection of prose-poems, *Paris Spleen*. In a letter of 1903 Rilke spoke of this as his favourite book;[47] he quoted from one of Baudelaire's prose-poems in the letter and later included the quotation in his novel. Like Rilke's episodes, Baudelaire's prose-poems end characteristically with a resonant last sentence: 'yonder... yonder... the marvellous clouds!' 'But implacable Venus is gazing at something far off, unknown to me, with her marble eyes.'[48]

But Rilke, unlike Baudelaire, wished to integrate his prose-poems into the wider structure of a novel. It might appear that by their 'closed' nature prose-poems would resist such an attempt, and the example of Beer-Hofmann supported this. But by 1904, the year in which he began writing *Malte Laurids Brigge*, Rilke seems to have thought he had found the solution to this problem. In that year he wrote a review, the relevance of which to his novel has been pointed out by E. C. Mason,[49] of a posthumous volume of the works of the Norwegian writer Obstfelder. Obstfelder had left behind a quantity of papers which had been subsequently edited and which Rilke refers to as follows:

> a mass of undated and unordered papers was discovered, containing various, constantly altered, jottings, not books but beginnings of books, not fixed but evolving, rising and falling life, a confusion which was really movement, and this world of moods and voices trembled and circled around the peculiar stillness which the dead leave behind them.[50]

Rilke's words 'movement', 'world', 'circled' and 'stillness' have a familiar ring: they are the terms he used to describe the formal qualities of the 'Thing' in the book on Rodin he produced during these years. The totality of Obstfelder's notebooks has for Rilke the unity of a 'Thing'; and he sees it as the task of the editor to capture and preserve this unity. He compares the editor to a man who goes into a ball-room and interrupts the dancers, so that the movement or 'figure' (*Figur*) of the dance is frozen before it has reached its natural end. 'But,' he goes on, 'we must believe that that was the end of the dance; that it was a dance, a new dance, which had to stop at precisely this point'.[51] The various fragments making up the notebooks are to be seen as forming a 'dance', a pattern of interrelated movements. Clearly, this pattern can only be seen if the fragments are perceived simultaneously, not in succession. The editor's task is therefore to preserve their simultaneity.

We know that when Rilke wrote about other artists he was concerned with possibilities he felt in himself rather than about the objective qualities of those artists. This was the case with his view of Rodin, and he himself admitted that what he said about art was always 'rather a provisional, personal insight than a fact derived objectively from the pages'.[52] With Obstfelder this seems to have been particularly the case; he even saw in the Norwegian's use of language a progression parallel to his own development from *Klang* to the visual style of the middle period: 'just as, at one stage of its growth his language became almost music, at another it realised itself to the point where it came within the sphere of painting'.[53]

The relevance of the review of Obstfelder to the conception of *Malte Laurids Brigge* is therefore indisputable. Rilke here is beginning to see his own rôle as the 'editor' of Malte's notebooks, and also to discover the new kind of unity – the 'new dance' – with which he would replace the old unity of plot. In practice, this unity would involve the simultaneous perception of the individual 'prose-poems' referred to earlier. That this was the kind of unity that Rilke aimed at is confirmed in a letter: 'This book must be accepted, not grasped through its details. Only in this way is everything given its right emphasis and intersection.'[54] All the parts of the book must be seen, not in succession, but together as a total impression: 'Fragmentary themselves, all these episodes have the function of complementing each other within the book in the manner of a mosaic.'[55]

This conception of the mosaic-like unity of Rilke's novel has been derived from what he wrote outside the book itself: how far is it corroborated by internal evidence? First, there are passages in the book in which the notion of simultaneous rather than successive perception is presented symbolically. In describing the tapestries in a letter to Abelone, before looking at each in turn Malte says: 'But first stand back and see them all at once.'[56] The tapestries themselves have qualities of the 'Thing'; in particular they contain the dimension of 'total' or simultaneous time; there is no sense of an absent future: 'Expectation plays no part in them. Everything is there. Everything for ever.'[57] In describing the tapestries, Malte is obliged to take them in turn, but in doing so he blurs the transitions between them, minimising the sense of succession and separation.

The same preoccupation with simultaneity appears elsewhere. The imbecile king who, it must be remembered, is a *Vokabel* for Malte, was frustrated by the fact that, in contemplating the pictures in his folios, he could only see them one at a time. But a solution is found: an old card game is revived which pleases the king because the cards were 'colourful, could be moved about independently and were full of con-figuration (*voller Figur*)'.[58] In these cards, contemplated simul-taneously, the king is able to experience what Rilke called elsewhere 'the figure (*Figur*) of the dance'.

In a famous passage of the novel Malte describes the inside wall of a house the rest of which has been demolished. On this wall all the rooms, which could normally only be seen in succession, appear simultan-eously. Malts responds to this impression with a passage of prose in which the past life in the house is compressed in time until it appears as simultaneous:

> The middays were there and the illnesses and the exhalations and the years-old smoke and the sweat from under the shoulders that makes the clothes heavy and the staleness from mouths and the smell of bad spirits that comes from fermenting feet. There hung the sourness of urine and the acridity of soot and grey steam from potatoes and the heavy, sleek stench of old dripping. The sweet, long odour of neglected babies was there and the smell of children's fear when they go to school and the sultriness from the beds of boys who have reached puberty. [59]

There are other passages in which an abnormal sense of unity is felt in an external scene. The first of them is a transcription, slightly modi-fied, from a letter which has already been quoted in an earlier chapter (cf. p. 108). It describes an impression of the Seine embankment with the *bouquinistes*, in which all sensations are harmonised: 'everything is right, everything has its say, takes part in a totality from which noth-ing is missing'.[60] The second of these passages has also been quoted already – it is the early-morning garden scene discussed in the last chapter (cf. p. 150). Here, as in the passage just mentioned, there is a sense of the inter-relatedness of all parts of the scene, which are per-ceived simultaneously: 'Nothing predominates in the garden, every-thing is everywhere, and you would have to be in everything if you were to miss nothing.'

These two passages, of course, describe privileged moments, and it is clear that the unity which Rilke was trying to achieve in his novel is significantly like that experienced during a privileged moment. The link between the two kinds of unity is further emphasised if we recall that elsewhere in the description just referred to Rilke called the garden scene 'a mosaic of the most unwavering existence' and that in a letter quoted earlier he spoke of the structure of the novel as 'mosaic-like'. Furthermore, we have already seen, in the discussion of Obst-felder, that the structure of *Malte Laurids Brigge* was first conceived in terms of that of the 'Thing', a concept which was directly derived from the privileged moment.

The privileged moment therefore played a fundamental part in the structure of the novel, as in that of the *New Poems*. It was noted in

*New Poems* that their structural principle, though realised perfectly in individual poems, was not extended to embrace the work as a whole. It seems possible that in writing the novel, which deals not only with the same themes as the poems but with the same particular subjects – the Prodigal Son, the burnt-down house, dogs, blind people, beggars, saints, Venice, etc. – Rilke was making another attempt at what he had failed to achieve in *New Poems*: to embody a wide expanse of experience in a single structure, to juxtapose different periods of time in 'an instant of eternity'.

What Rilke seems to be trying to achieve in *Malte Laurids Briggs* is a work in which the essential experience of his life – not only its content, as contained in the impressions and reminiscences, but also its meaning, as expressed in the 'themes' and the general reflections – is rigorously unified and presented as a 'Thing'. The success or failure of this enterprise depends of course on the extent to which the novel does in fact have the unity which was lacking in *New Poems*. So far, in discussing this unity, we have seen what Rilke intended, not what he actually achieved. It still remains to be seen whether the novel can indeed be validly compared to a mosaic or a dance.

The most obvious reasons why the novel might be expected to have a greater unity than the collections of poems are, firstly, that it has a single central character and, secondly, that prose is by its nature a more connected medium than poetry. But in themselves these reasons are not enough to ensure the kind of unity with which Rilke is concerned. Malte's presence is not necessarily a guarantee of a formal structure, and Rilke's prose, as we saw, has a tendency to split up into isolated prose-poems. We must therefore look further for the key to the work's unity.

J.-F. Angelloz finds in the novel 'a pictorial composition ... a composition by masses, planes and values, with incessant recapitulations'.[61] The first part of this description seems to refer, aptly enough, to Rilke's procedure of juxtaposing contrasting material to produce a rich and interesting texture. But concerning the 'incessant recapitulations', Angelloz gives no example, and in fact there does not seem to be any systematic use of repetition and organisation of motifs to produce a formal structure. There is some repetition of key-words such as 'stillness' and 'smile', which occur at significant points; but these verbal echoes, which are in any case far weaker than those in *New Poems*, are less easily perceptible in the fuller context of the prose work, and cannot provide an adequate basis for a structure. At the most, they might be a contributory element in a larger unity.

It may be, however, that Angelloz was referring to a repetition of themes. E. Buddeberg, too, speaks of a thematic structure with an exposition, ending with Malte's series of questions: 'Is it possible ...',

F*

which introduces all the themes of the novel.[62] But she demonstrates this method by reference not to this work but to the *Elegies*, and it would indeed be difficult to establish any rigorous structural development of themes in *Malte Laurids Brigge*. It is true, of course, that the same themes unavoidably reappear at different points in the course of the novel, but this does not in itself imply structure. It is true also that the themes can be related together on an intellectual plane to give a consistent view of life. But, as in *New Poems*, thematic unity in this sense is not the same as the formal unity of a work of art.

It seems unlikely, therefore, that the unity Rilke was trying to create was primarily one involving the organisation of themes and motifs. That he lacked any clearly preconceived structure is indicated by statements he made after the work was finished. He said for example that the work had reached only 'a kind of conclusion'[63] and that he could have gone on adding to the portrait of Malte's character indefinitely.[64]

In the absence of a deliberately contrived formal structure, we must look elsewhere for the unity of Rilke's novel. An indication of the direction in which it lies is given by Rilke in the review of Obstfelder. There he too asked the question with which we are concerned: 'Is this work a *whole* work?'[65] His answer was that a work whose writer has been able to contemplate all reality with the same intensity, and which includes even an affirmation of death, must be complete. In other words, for Rilke, the unity of the work is guaranteed by the totality of the experience expressed in it. In *Malte Laurids Brigge*, he presented a man who, precisely like Obstfelder, attempted to affirm all experience, including the most unpleasant. The unity of the work must therefore be sought in the unity and completeness of Malte himself.

Apropos of Jacobsen Rilke had noted how the unity of his novels was produced by the unifying presence of the author, who contained the whole action within the 'circle of his soul'. In general it might be said that the unity of a work of fiction depends ultimately on a total consciousness permeating all its parts, or expressed differently, on a 'commanding centre'[66] at which all the values and points of view in the book are focused and reconciled. For example, in *Emma* or in *Madame Bovary* the consciousness of the author, objectively built into the narrative, contains and transcends the consciousnesses of all the characters.

To what extent is such a unifying consciousness present in Rilke's novel? Since the author is ostensibly Malte, his consciousness must play this rôle. If the book is analysed from the point of view of Malte's consciousness, it is found that he does not occupy a single standpoint. His evocations of childhood and his experiences in Paris are both seen from the same point of view – that of Malte in Paris, which provides the centre of focus. In these sections, there is nothing 'beyond' Malte in

Paris, looking back on him from a later time or from outside his consciousness. But in other parts of the book we gain the impression of another, more generalised, presence, capable of standing back from Malte's experience in Paris. This is the 'voice' which describes the *Vokabeln*, gives the general reflections on art, modern life, etc., and relates the parable of the Prodigal Son.

But the Malte of the Paris scenes is totally absorbed by his immediate experiences and lacks this wider vision. As a result there is a split in the focus of the novel between these two centres, which are not made to coincide. It might have been possible, given these separate viewpoints of Malte's experience, to relate them together in a structure based on different levels of awareness, in which that of Malte in Paris is contained in the wider awareness of a more mature Malte beyond him. But such a structure would necessitate that the two are related together by some definite formal means. As it is they are merely juxtaposed. The only relation between them is a gradual but vague progression from one to the other, as the more 'personal' Malte of the early scenes gives way more and more to the impersonal narrator of the historical episodes. This progression, however, introduces a time axis into the book, an element of succession which prevents us from assimilating the beginning into the end in a full simultaneity.

There are, in short, two Maltes in the book, or perhaps there is Malte and his editor. And ultimately these two beings do not interpenetrate, they remain, so to speak, mutually ignorant. For this reason the different parts of the book cannot be contemplated simultaneously in the manner of a mosaic. Rilke has failed to give his book the pictorial unity he saw in Cézanne's work, in which 'it seems as if every place knows of all the others'.

Rilke's remarks on Cézanne also help us to understand why he failed to do so. For Rilke, Cézanne's uniqueness lay in his ability to convert subjective feeling into 'anonymous work'. Previous painters had lacked this ability: 'They painted: I love this thing here; instead of painting: here it is.' As a result, says Rilke, their feeling is not objectified in their work, but 'remains as an unconverted residue beside it'.[67] In his novel, Rilke too wanted to present objectively 'the simple being'[68] of Malte's existence. But in the Paris scenes, for instance that of the hysteric when Malte says: 'I felt a little fear beginning in me',[69] his feelings are not given objective or anonymous expression. It is true, he does not write: 'I love this thing here', but he does write in effect: 'I fear this thing here'. As a result, the 'personal' Malte with his subjective feelings and his individual existence 'remains as an unconverted residue' outside the descriptions, and it is this remnant of the 'personal' Malte which destroys the unity of the book. In his most successful descriptions, such as that of the wall of the house, Malte does succeed in objectifying his feeling entirely, but in other passages, particularly those referring to his everyday existence, his preoccupation with the state of his clothes and with the glances and smiles of the poor people who seem to number him among them, the personal element becomes obtrusive.

It might appear from this that the ideal form of the novel towards which Rilke was striving was one in which Malte was presented only through *Vokabeln* and from which day-to-day biographical material was entirely excluded. But at this point we may begin to wonder whether, presented in this extreme form, Rilke's ideal was not an impossibility. Is it possible to write about a character at all without showing him, at least as a starting-point, as a man who exists, not in the world of pure being and simultaneity, but in the world of everyday time? And does not Rilke's ideal of simultaneity and pictorial unity conflict with the nature of the novelist's medium: language. In Chapter Ten it was argued that literature is an art-form which exists primarily in time. The element of succession cannot be banished from the novel, and simultaneity cannot be achieved simply by juxtaposition, as David Daiches has argued convincingly in connection with Joyce's *Ulysses*.[70] Rilke, unlike the lunatic king in the novel, cannot make the pages of his book 'independently movable'.

In writing *Neue Gedichte* Rilke was faced, as we saw, by an analogous problem: that of isolating the 'Thing' of the poem from the world of everyday time. He solved this problem there, not by trying to suppress time altogether, but by introducing a movement in order to 'take up' the element of succession and contain it within the poem. For this, a special kind of movement was needed, a 'closed' movement in which time, as it were, circulated endlessly in isolation from that of the everyday world.

In *Malte Laurids Brigge*, in the poems of Nikolaj Kusmitsch and the verses of the mystery plays which create their own 'real' time, there are suggestions of this process; but Rilke does not apply the principle of the closed movement to the structure of the novel as a whole. Nevertheless it seems that he was aware of the need for an overriding movement to unify the book. In a letter of 1907, he said he now 'saw' the meaning of the novel: its subject was to be Malte's failure to stand the test of facing reality.[71] This provides the embryo of a plot, a direction in Malte's fate which, in a letter of 1912, Rilke called a downward direction.[72] It has been suggested that this downward movement was modelled on the 'falling curve' of the heroine's life which Rilke admired in one of Jacobsen's novels.[73] Rilke's conception of Malte therefore contains an element of movement which might have provided a means of unifying the work.

But the movement actually present in the novel, as we saw, is the vague progression from the personal to the more impersonal Malte.

Though Malte dies at the end it is not fully clear whether the 'curve' of his fate is really a downward or an upward one. Later Rilke said it was as much an 'ascension' as a 'downfall'.[74] What is certain about this movement is, however, that it is not a closed one. It is open in the sense that the end of the book is in no way related back to the beginning. The novel ends indeterminately and could have gone on longer in the same direction. Rilke therefore failed to achieve the 'dance' of balanced and circular movements which he originally saw in Obstfelder's notebook: 'rising and falling life, confusion which was really movement, and this world ... trembled and circled'.

It is therefore considered here that *Malte Laurids Brigge* failed artistically because Rilke was unable to give it the structural unity implicit in his conception of a work of art. But its failure as a novel has another aspect. Rilke's preoccupation with the notion of simultaneity and 'true being' interferes with his presentation of normal human existence, which he is obliged, by the fact of writing a novel at all, to introduce to some extent. His negative attitude towards normal experience prevents him from creating fictional characters who are convincing as human beings. Malte, despite his sufferings, is not given sufficient concrete reality to achieve stature or even pathos. Abelone, that 'pale Ophelia',[75] scarcely exists at all. This is largely because Rilke refuses to use the established methods of character portrayal: external description, narrated action and psychological analysis. Malte writes: 'I shall tell nothing of you, Abelone, ... because saying is always an injustice.'[76]

Nevertheless, Rilke believed that in his novel he was creating characters in his own way. He wrote to Rodin in 1908: 'Imagine that in this prose I am now able to make men and women, children and old men.' But the reason why these characters do not have the existence of powerful fictional creations becomes clear when Rilke goes on:

> Above all I have evoked women by taking great care over all the things around them, leaving a blank which would be only an empty space but which, tenderly and amply surrounded, becomes vibrant and luminous, almost like one of your marbles.[77]

We can see here how inappropriate Rilke's preoccupations are to the central demands of the novel. He seeks to create characters not from insight into human nature but by a juxtaposition of textures.

As might be expected from this, there is something unreal about the human relationships in the novel. Malte's relation to his mother is full of sterile preciosity which is aptly summed up by E. Buddeberg: 'What a way of spending time with a boy, this unfolding and unrolling of old lacework!'[78] His sparse conversations with Abelone have a cold, stilted quality which leaves the reader baffled when Malte writes of 'all our warmth'.[79] A similar incongruity is felt when Malte suddenly addresses Erik, an enigmatic and unlikeable character, as far as he exists at all, in the following terms: 'Dear, dear Erik; perhaps you were my only friend after all.'[80]

These relationships have their significance not on the human level but on that of Rilke's higher reality, to which they are symbolically related. They are typified by the understanding between Graf Brahe and Erik, which is based not on normal communication but on their perception of the invisible world of their dead ancestors: 'they went, hand in hand, along the rows of old dark portraits, without speaking, obviously communicating in a different way'.[81]

A further criticism of the characters in the novel must be made. They seem in many cases not to be characters in their own right but illustrations of ideas and themes which Rilke wishes to express. This is most obvious with minor figures like Graf Brahe and Nikolaj Kusmitsch, but it also applies to Abelone, through whom Rilke expresses his ideas on 'intransitive' love.

There is, therefore, in the novel an uneasy coexistence of elements from two incompatible spheres. The passages in which the interference between these elements is least disturbing are those in which the portrayal of character is least particularised, and which are farthest from the personal sphere of Malte. Thus the uniformity of tone is greater in the historical sections where Malte is absent than in the Paris scenes, and it is greatest of all where Rilke introduces a generalised mythological figure in the parable of the Prodigal Son. The parable brings with it a time-structure of its own in which all parts, unlike those of the main novel, are, so to speak, equidistant from the author, so that a unified focus is achieved. Moreover, the symbolic figure of the Prodigal Son is a more appropriate vehicle for demonstrating the general truths and themes with which Rilke is concerned than particular individuals involved in the narrative, such as Abelone.

Elsewhere in the novel there are passages in which Rilke seems briefly to find a point of view from which he can express directly and spontaneously the themes which preoccupy him. His prose takes on a heightened quality, a new rhythm and resonance which bring it close to the language of lyrical, elegiac poetry:

> Perhaps this is new, that we endure these things: the year and love. Blossoms and fruit are ripe when they fall; animals feel and find their way to each other and are content. But we, who have taken God upon ourselves, cannot have done. We postpone our nature, we need more time. What is a year to us? What are all years? Even before we have begun God we are already praying to him: let us endure the night. And then, illness. And then, love.[82]

In passages such as this we begin to hear a voice which leads beyond the middle period. This voice seems to have risen above the fate of Malte and to command a wider view. It is a generalised voice, which says 'we' but not 'I', but is full of a compelling urgency. It is quite unlike both the plaintive tone of the 'personal' Malte, and the hard objectivity of the descriptions constituting the *Vokabeln*. As such it is out of place in the novel, and appears only infrequently. But because of its combination of generality and urgent involvement, it is a more natural medium for expressing Rilke's general themes than the more limited voice of Malte. Therefore this voice points to a solution to the underlying problem confronting Rilke in the novel, that of expressing the general meaning of his life in a way which would produce a unified structure. But these infrequent intrusions of a different voice, detectable only with after-knowledge of Rilke's later work, give no more than a hint of a solution. The novel itself was a profound exploration of extreme possibilities of human experience; but as an attempt to embody a total vision of life in a unified 'Art Thing', it was ultimately not more successful than *New Poems*.

# CHAPTER THIRTEEN

## The Second Crisis

WHEN *Malte Laurids Brigge* was finished, early in 1910, Rilke entered a period of artistic sterility which he was himself unable to understand. In December 1911, writing to Lou after a long pause, as he did only in times of acute crisis, he said that the novel had left him 'helpless, unoccupied, no longer capable of being occupied'.[1] Despite all his progress in the use of language during the middle period he found himself in an impasse perhaps more hopeless than that which had followed *The Book of Hours*: 'How is it possible that now, prepared and schooled in expression, I remain without a calling, superfluous?'[2]

To find the answer to this question we must look back at his situation before he began the novel, and see what he had hoped to achieve by writing it. He started work on the book in 1904, and the period leading up to this was also one of inner distress and crisis. At that time too Rilke wrote a series of letters to Lou after a long silence. Early in the first of them he stated his fundamental problem: 'I have tried, with quiet self-discipline, to be constantly in my work, and my consternation is great when I realise that I have failed.'[3]

The problem he mentions here is still a part of the first crisis; Rilke has not yet succeeded in putting into practice the doctrine of work which he derived from Rodin. But his situation also has a new element which was not a part of the early crisis. In another letter, of November 1903, he wrote that he longed for a sense of reality, to be 'real, among real things'.[4] But he was able to achieve this only at rare intervals, through work. He explains that his normal lack of a feeling of reality is the result of his excessive openness to outside impressions: 'there are always things that repudiate me, events that go straight through me, more real than I, as if I did not exist'.[5] His over-exposure to experience prevents him from forming a solid personality: 'everything goes racing through me ... no core can form itself in me, no firm place'.[6] He is passive in the face of impressions: he cannot 'take hold' of them; instead, 'with their points and sharp edges they are pressed into my hand, deep into it almost against my will'.[7]

The attitude of visual openness with which Rilke attempted to overcome the limitations of his early manner has therefore created problems of its own. He is no longer at the mercy of capricious inspiration, but at that of his too-intense experience of reality. He knows that it is not his own will which controls his destiny but 'another great will which sometimes carries him away like a thing swept downstream by a river'.[8] This feeling of helplessness leads to a generalised dread in the face of reality – *Angst* (which will be translated here as 'fear'): 'a thousand hands have been at work building my fear ... Even in Wester-wede it was increasing ... And when Paris came it quickly grew very large'.[9] We can see here how closely Rilke's own situation is reflected by Malte's in his novel; and as in the case of Malte, Rilke's fear predisposes him to share in the distress of the poor people around him, with whom he is forced to identify against his will: 'I was torn out of myself into their lives, ... through all their burdened lives'.[10]

Faced with the presence of fear at the centre of his existence, Rilke sees only one possible response: he must use it as material for artistic creation:

> Had I been able to *make* the fears I experienced, had I been able to form Things out of them, real, still Things, to create which is serenity and freedom and which, when they are made, give out calmness, then nothing would have happened to me.

In this way he arrives at his well-known formulation of the artist's task: *Dinge machen aus Angst* – to make things from fear.[11]

Rilke's way of overcoming fear is therefore by re-doubling his efforts to achieve a new creativity. But this means further intensifying those tendencies – the attitude of contemplative openness and the doctrine of work connected to it – which, as we have seen, are the sources of fear. Rilke however is not deterred by this. In August 1903 he wrote: 'I always resolve to look at things better, to contemplate with more patience, with deeper absorption',[12] and in another letter he similarly re-affirms his determination to achieve his ideal of 'daily work' which he sees as his only task.[13]

Not long after writing this, early in 1904, Rilke began *Malte Laurids Brigge*, making use primarily of material from letters in which he had tried to describe objectively experiences which filled him with fear.

At this point an important aspect of Rilke's purpose in writing his novel must be noted. He was not motivated primarily by the desire to produce a work of art for its own sake, but by the need to overcome a problem which was existential rather than artistic: the problem of fear. In other words, considerations drawn from Rilke's life determine the course taken by his art. This may seem inconsistent with the fact that about the same time, through the experience of his marriage and the example of Rodin, Rilke was reaching the decision henceforth to subordinate all the claims of his personal life to those of his art: 'it must be so; this is *one* life and the other is another, and we are not made to have two lives'.[14] But this renouncing of his personal life must not be confused with an attitude of 'art for art's sake'. For Rilke, art is itself 'one life'; he chooses art because he sees in it the highest possible realisation of his life. It is only through creation that he can achieve a sense of reality in his existence: 'where I create I am true';[15] his attempt to build up his life on a basis of household and family had failed to give him this sense of reality: 'it was a reality *outside* myself, I was not a part of it, it did not contain me'.[16] It is therefore consistent with Rilke's conception of the relation of art to life that he should see his ideal of 'daily work, daily reality'[17] as a way of solving the problem of *Angst* and, in the full meaning of the words, as a way of life: 'so the inner void would be filled, and from the external distress the fear would be taken away; for he who *always works* can also live, must be able to'.[18]

Rilke was unable to complete *Malte Laurids Brigge* in 1904, and for a long period work on the novel was largely suspended while he concentrated on writing the two parts of *New Poems*. But when, in 1907, his attention began to return to the novel, his ideal of 'daily work' was not remotely realised: 'one is still so far from being able to work constantly'.[19] He was equally far from having overcome the sense of lacking a firm personality; his existence is undermined by the knowledge that whole stretches of his past life have been wasted in idleness: 'If only one had memories of work from early on: how firm the ground would be under one's feet; one would stand. But as it is one sinks in somewhere at every moment.'[20]

But in 1907, under the influence of Cézanne, Rilke believed that he now knew the reason for his inability to work continuously. It is bound up with the idea of 'making things from fear'. To achieve the necessary productive vision, all fear of reality, even in its most repugnant aspects, must be overcome: 'The artistic vision must first have so mastered itself that, even in the terrible and the apparently repulsive, it sees Being, which, with all other Being, is valid.' The slightest refusal of any aspect of reality would be enough to disrupt this vision and 'expel [the artist] from the state of grace'.[21] As we see here, Rilke speaks of this total acceptance of reality in religious terms; he also calls it 'lying down with the leper'. And, once accomplished, this acceptance will be rewarded by a kind of redemption, a 'new blessedness'. Beyond the 'pain threshold' Rilke visualises a terrestrial paradise, a state of openness and joyful affirmation of all existence:

> On the further side of this devotion, with small things at first, holiness begins; the simple living of a love which has passed the test, which, without ever glorying in it, goes to all things, unaccompanied, unobtrusive, wordless.

As a part of this 'state of grace' Rilke sees the power of creativity which he at present lacks: 'The real work, the abundance of tasks, everything begins only after this test has been passed.'[22] But it is noticeable that he praises this creativity above all for its existential qualities, as a blissful state of being, and only secondarily for the works of art it will produce.

These ideas are presented in a letter of October 1907; and at this point Rilke suddenly saw what had long eluded him: the nature of Malte's fate and the meaning of his novel. Malte is the man who, while being aware of the need of a total acceptance of reality, is unable to take the final step and to reach the state of 'blessedness'. But Rilke does not wish to demonstrate through Malte the impossibility of reaching this state. Malte is a negative example; where he failed, a stronger man might have succeeded: 'Brigge's death: that was Cézanne's life.'[23] Clearly, Rilke hoped it would be his own life too.

He now renewed his determination to complete the book. In 1908, while writing the novel, he described himself as one whose mission is 'to see everything ... to refuse nothing'. He believed that in concentrating all the horrors of life in his novel, he was preparing an essence of all possible poisons which, when consumed, would give a god-like immunity to fear.[24] Later he wrote that while writing the novel he had often felt like one who, in a battle, draws all the lances within reach into himself, in order to make them harmless to others.[25]

He was, according to his theories, able to withstand these potent and otherwise lethal realities because of the power of art, if totally objective – that is, totally affirmative – to convert even the horrible into a thing of beauty, into 'something which testifies to reality, which wants existence ... an angel'.[26] It was in this connection that Rilke wrote the 'Requiem' for Kalckreuth, in which he castigates the sentimental poets who, failing to achieve objectivity, 'describe the place that hurts them', instead of relentlessly converting their experience into words in the manner of a Cézanne. The ideal of art presented in this poem is one in which personal fate – Schicksal – is totally converted into an objective image and thus can no longer have any adverse influence on the existence of the artist. Rilke compares this image to a portrait of one of the artist's ancestors 'which seems to be his likeness and yet not his likeness'. The image is like the artist in that it represents his experience, but unlike him in that this experience is no longer seen from a subjective point of view.

Clearly, it was as a portrait of himself in this sense that Rilke conceived Malte, 'who is, after all, partly made of my own dangers'.[27] Malte was Rilke's means of rendering harmless the most dangerous elements in his life. It therefore became indispensable for him to create Malte if he was to progress towards the 'state of grace' which he saw as his goal: 'I can only go forward through him, he is in my way.'[28]

It can be seen, therefore, that Rilke's reasons for creating Malte during this second and final phase of activity on the novel, as during the first phase already discussed, were predominantly existential, concerned with his life rather than with art for its own sake. And there was a further way in which, for Rilke, the creation of a work of art could benefit the life of the creator:

> The immense help of an Art-Thing for the life of its maker is this: that it draws him together ... it is the ever-recurring proof to himself of his own unity and truth.[29]

Rilke therefore sees the creation of a work of art as a way of overcoming his sense of lacking a whole and firm personality referred to earlier. In other letters of about this time he enlarges on this question of the wholeness of the personality. Human relationships destroy the sense of wholeness; even in the most tenuous proximity to other people, Rilke feels himself 'a little as if under observation ... I am so excessively sensitive, and if an eye rests on me it cripples me in one place'. An individual person, capable of seeing only a part of the poet, limits his sense of existence. In contrast to this Rilke goes on to evoke another possibility, a state in which the whole of his being is perceived at once, so that he feels no limitations:

> Again and again I would like to have only the stars resting upon me, which from their distance see everything at once, in its wholeness, and so bind nothing, but rather leave everything free in everything ...[30]

Here Rilke touches, rather indistinctly, on an idea we have met before, the notion of an ultimate wholeness and relatedness in which the individual's existence is in some way bound up with the stars. The idea appeared in *The Book of Images* in connection with the privileged moment, and in Rodin's total work too Rilke had seen a stellar system of which the creator's existence was in some way a part.

This idea of a relatedness to the stars as an ultimate objective is still, at this stage, only a dimly-felt intuition. But in the letters Rilke wrote while he was completing his novel this theme occurs frequently, and it helps us to clarify what he means in the passage just quoted when he refers to the work of art as 'drawing together' the artist's life. Art for Rilke is a way of bringing his life into relation to the stars and thus of achieving wholeness; the artist feels a compulsion 'to cultivate and perfect his innermost world so that it may one day be able to hold the whole of the outer world, everything, as far as the stars, in balance, and be, as it were, equated with it'.[31]

In the important letter mentioned earlier in which Rilke suddenly 'saw' the meaning of Malte's existence, he also, by the same process, glimpsed this possibility in his own life of a wholeness, a sense of relatedness including the stars:

how much what we encounter is of one piece ... and our task really is just to *be there*, but to be there simply, urgently, as the earth is there, assenting to the seasons, bright and dark and wholly in space, asking for nothing more than to rest in the net of influences and forces in which the stars feel secure.[32]

We have seen, therefore, that in writing *Malte Laurids Brigge* Rilke was motivated by at least three major aspirations, all of which were of a predominantly existential nature: the desire to free himself from fear and reach the state of 'blessedness', the need for 'daily work', and the vaguely-felt but recurrent aspiration to feel his personality integrated into a wider totality, associated with the stars.

When the book was finished none of these hopes was even remotely fulfilled. Far from achieving his 'new blessedness', Rilke felt that he was 'going down into a barrenness which does not change'.[33] As for his hopes of working continuously: 'I deliberate much with myself why I am still not working, it is time, this long drought is really beginning to famish my soul.'[34] The sense of a wholeness in his personality likewise failed to appear; he describes himself characteristically leaving his room 'as a chaos',[35] and his uncertainty regarding himself is such that he is afraid of using the word 'I': 'there was no word which brought with it more inexactitude'.[36]

Moreover, as if to complete Rilke's disarray, Rodin, on whom the whole ethic of work had been built, was himself toppled from the throne on which Rilke had formerly placed him. In his old age he became the plaything of a banal erotic passion:

A moment of tiredness, a few days' slackening were enough, and life rose up around him as unmastered as it does around a schoolboy and drove him, just as he was, into the nearest, miserable trap. What shall *I* say, with my little bit of work that I am quite unable to stay inside, if he wasn't saved?

Rilke, witnessing the ruin of the ideals for which he had lived and worked for ten years, is clearly at the end of his tether:

what in all the world *is* this work if one cannot go through and learn everything in it, if one stands around outside it being pushed and jostled, grabbed and let go of, getting entangled in happiness and wrong and never understanding anything.[37]

It is significant that Rilke finally judges Rodin's ideal of work not by the works of art it produced but by its success or failure in bringing the artist 'salvation' in his life.

What Rilke witnessed in the aftermath of *Malte Laurids Brigge* was, therefore, the bankruptcy of his belief that a work of art will necessarily benefit its creator in an existential sense. This implies that his whole undertaking in writing the novel was based on a fallacy. But he did not immediately acknowledge this; he continued to look for the causes of his disappointment on an existential level. Writing to Lou, he asked whether he was like or unlike Malte, as if this decided whether or not he would have to share Malte's downfall.[38] In another letter, he expressed the fear that he had taken Malte's 'thoroughgoing despair' too far.[39] These 'diagnoses' refer to the author rather than to the book; it is possible, however, that the book itself, as a work of art, may provide a more valuable explanation of Rilke's dissatisfaction.

We saw earlier that Rilke believed that a work of art could provide a 'drawing together' of the author's life or personality. This might be understood to mean the following: if an artist succeeds in including in his work the important aspects of his experience which are disjointed in his life, and can interrelate them to form something complete and coherent, he may, in contemplating this work, gain a sense of his own 'unity and truth' which he would not otherwise have. As we saw in detail in the last chapter, Rilke tried in his novel to give such a unified representation of his life and personality. But the value of such a 'drawing together' is subject to two restrictions. Firstly, the unity produced in this way is not of an existential kind which would be automatically felt by the artist in his daily life. It is an ideal unity, and it can only satisfy the artist if he has given up all concern for the existential level of his life in a way which Rilke has not yet conceived of doing. Secondly, this ideal unity presupposes the creation of a perfectly unified work of art, which, as we saw in the last chapter, Rilke failed to achieve in his novel. It may be, then, that aesthetic factors, as well as the existential problems more usually considered, played an important part in the crisis which followed *Malte Laurids Brigge*.

Rilke himself seems during these years to have tacitly admitted that the book had been an artistic failure. He spoke, for example, of the impossibility of giving up artistic activities while nothing had yet been achieved, and of having realised only a fraction of his task.[40] Perhaps, when he spoke of his novel as 'artistically a bad unity' he meant, after all, to be taken literally.

But he continued to look for the causes of his crisis on the existential level, that is, by reference to the influence of the experiences treated in the novel. But even on this level, he could justify the book only on the rather doubtful grounds that it should be read 'against the current'.[41] He steadily distanced himself from the novel, calling it, in January 1912, 'already so old'[42] and, shortly afterwards, 'almost ... superfluous'.[43] He saw it finally not as a stepping-stone towards redemption, but as an obstacle which had created unnecessary problems by distorting and exaggerating reality.[44]

In a similar way he began to turn away from art itself, calling it 'the most passionate inversion of the world';[45] in another letter he spoke of art as the opposite to a joyful, natural response to life.[46] It had now become that which prevented him from achieving the state of 'blessedness'. And his readiness to dismiss art once it has proved incapable of bringing him salvation in his life is the logical conclusion of his fundamentally existential attitude to art.

This attitude, which places existential above artistic values, is inherent in Rilke's conception of art in the middle period. For at the basis of his conception is the technique of contemplation, which is a means of extracting the maximum of intensity from a given moment of existence. The ideal of working continuously is an attempt to extend these intense moments to fill the whole of life. To this end Rilke largely sacrificed the personal side of his existence and its pleasures, but he did so only in order to make possible the far greater pleasures of contemplation and creation. The whole of his effort in this period was directed towards achieving the greatest possible enjoyment on the existential level – the level of direct experience.

Here a significant parallel with Proust in the same period can be seen. Proust too valued contemplation and inspiration primarily for the pleasure they afforded. Apropos of Silvain Bastelle, he called this pleasure 'the only reward of the man of letters'.[47] In *Jean Santeuil* we noted Proust's tendency to describe experiences for no other reason than the pleasure they contained (cf. p. 91); he seems indeed in the novel to be almost greedily hoarding moments of recollected pleasure for his prolonged enjoyment. Proust, too, saw that the material and personal aspects of life are distractions from the kind of pleasure with which he was concerned. Silvain Bastelle's possessions, like Rilke's house and family, are an obstacle to inspiration.[48]

The pleasure with which both writers are concerned is ultimately that of the privileged moment. The artistic techniques they developed during the middle period are a means of maximising their experience of the privileged moment by bringing it under voluntary control. In this respect there is an underlying continuity between the early and middle periods, despite the outward changes. In the early period we saw that the goal of the creative process was to bring the whole external scene within the compass of the 'I' in a moment of supreme self-enjoyment. In the middle period, although the 'I" is abandoned, the tendency is no less towards the enjoyment of the moment. The only difference is in the means by which this is to be achieved.

This cultivation of the moment has repercussions in the form of the works which the two writers produced during this period. As we saw in Chapter Eleven, the creative process grows out of a particular moment of contemplation. What is created is therefore directly attached, and

confined, to this moment of experience. This leads to intensely
rendered but limited products – the short descriptive poems of *New
Poems* or the isolated moments of experience and descriptions in *Malte
Laurids Brigge* and in *Jean Santeuil*. The degree to which Rilke's
method of creation was tied to particular moments of experience is
indicated by the fact that he reproduced whole sections of his letters in
the descriptive passages of his novel. Similarly Proust, in the descriptions in *Jean Santeuil*, for example the passage on the rose-border, is
clearly writing down his own experiences with a minimum of alteration.

The result of this tendency is that both writers neglect the overall
unity of their works. In concentrating on particular moments of experience they lose control of the form of the work, so that Proust finds
himself 'amassing ruins', and Rilke remarks that he could have gone
on adding to Malte's notebooks indefinitely.[49]

In this sense the two writers' preoccupation with the privileged
moment as an experience to be enjoyed on the existential level can be
seen to have been detrimental to the unity of their works. On the other
hand, they both felt that the privileged moment provided them with a
principle of artistic unity to which they were prepared to sacrifice the
traditional unity of the novel. In Proust's case, as we saw, this was the
timeless unity of the personality, as glimpsed through involuntary
memory. In Rilke's, the mosaic-like unity of Malte's character which
he sought to present in his novel was clearly related to the mosaic-like
unity of awareness during a privileged moment. Both writers appear to
have believed that if they could embody their special conceptions of
the unity of the personality in their novels, then the artistic unity
would follow automatically.[50]

As we saw in both cases, this belief was unfounded. The disparate
material of their novels, composed of isolated scenes and fragments,
failed to coalesce. Both writers discarded the old unity of the novel but
were unable to put a new one in its place; for this reason they failed as
novelists.

Proust's reaction to his failure was to abandon creative writing and
devote himself to translating Ruskin. Rilke moved steadily away from
the ideals which had characterised his creative activity in the middle
period: work and contemplation. He dismissed the notion of writing
continuously as 'a completely theoretical and pedantic idea';[51] in
January 1912 he wrote what earlier would have been heresy: 'being
able to write constantly does not interest me'.[52] He no longer had the
ability to induce inspiration voluntarily, as had formerly been possible
by means of contemplation: 'It is as if I had completely lost the power
of summoning up the circumstances that can help me.'[53]

During a trip to North Africa in late 1910 and early 1911, which he
made in the hope of renewing his inspiration, Rilke's letters make it

clear that contemplation has lost its efficacy for him: 'brightness and looking have made me very tired, also there is practically nothing that I can say. I foresee that it will be a long time before I can speak out about all this.'[54] Contemplation now no longer gives rise directly, as in the middle period, to creation, to the 'only possible name' of the thing contemplated. In another letter, the technique appears to be more successful: Rilke describes his impressions at a bazaar:

> you went towards and simply into a piece of material, into its limpid green, through its violet, or simply onwards in a yellow that was still in front of you, bottomless, like a bright gleam in the sky. [55]

Rilke's consciousness here seems to be entirely absorbed in the colours he describes. But this example serves to show also the particular limitations of the technique of contemplation: it is appropriate to limited, highly-coloured, brightly-lit subject-matter contemplated at close quarters, as in the case of these materials and in many of the descriptive poems of *New Poems*. But Rilke is now becoming concerned with larger, more complex realities, which can no longer be encompassed by the process of visual contemplation. In other words, his creative crisis has a further aspect, not yet discussed. The cause of the crisis is not only that he has lost the ability to apply the technique of contemplation, but that this technique has outlived its time, it is no longer appropriate to the aspects of reality which are now beginning to interest Rilke. This is made clear in another of his letters from North Africa, in which he describes his attempt to apply the technique of contemplation to the temple at Karnak:

> I looked, looked, – heavens, one pulls oneself together, looks with all the willingness to believe that both trained eyes can muster – and still it begins above them, everywhere goes beyond them (only a god can command such a visual field) – there a column stands, alone, one that has survived, and one cannot encompass it, it so transcends one's life, one only grasps it somehow together with the night, takes it in the totality with the stars, related to them it becomes for a second human, human experience. [56]

This is clearly a form of the privileged moment, though not of the kind which can be induced by contemplation. The experience contains a dimension which includes the whole night – significantly it is not daylight – and the stars. Rilke is experiencing concretely the sense of a total relatedness of his being to the world which was mentioned earlier in this chapter, and which he hoped to achieve through writing *Malte Laurids Brigge*. The dimension in which this experience takes place contains a further element which distinguishes it sharply from the contemplation of the middle period: an element of human significance.

The meaning of the temple for Rilke is not one which can be given by a metaphor isolating it from the human world; it is a new kind of meaning, a symbolic meaning. It is because contemplation is unable to grasp symbolic meanings of this kind that it must be superseded as a creative technique.

The nature of the 'human' and symbolic meaning of experience with which Rilke is now becoming concerned is made more explicit in a letter of 1912:

> What speaks to me of the human, immensely, with a quiet authority which makes my hearing spacious, is the phenomenon of the young dead and, more absolutely still, more purely and inexhaustibly, *the woman who loves*. In both these figures something human is mixed into my heart whether I wish it or not. They make their appearance in me both with the distinctness of the marionette (which is an outward form empowered to carry conviction), and also as finished types incapable of further development, so that the natural history of their souls could be written. [57]

This passage introduces a whole range of new concepts which will play a central part in Rilke's later development. In the first place, however, its significance in relation to *Malte Laurids Brigge* must be noted.

In a letter written five days after this passage, Rilke said that his only admiration for his novel now was reserved for the way in which 'that which is great' had used this in itself totally inadequate book as a pretext for making its appearance. The term *das Große* is used here in an entirely different sense than in the book. From the letter just quoted we can see that Rilke must be thinking of those symbolic human figures who appear in the novel and fit rather ill into the narrative context: the 'young dead', Erik and Ingeborg, and above all 'the women who love', Abelone and the other women who dominate the later part of the book, and also the related figure of the Prodigal Son.

The value of the novel for Rilke now lies not in the portrait of Malte, but in the figures which symbolised more general aspects of human life. As we saw in the last chapter, the most successful realisation of this symbolising tendency was in the episode of the Prodigal Son. Through this figure Rilke not only expressed his ideal of 'intransitive' love, but also something of that wider dimension, which he later experienced at Karnak, in which the human figure is encompassed in the vastness of the night. But at the same time Rilke was aware of the inadequacy of the art then at his disposal to convey this vision: 'Which art is vast enough to evoke at the same time his slender, cloaked figure and the whole towering space of his gigantic nights.'[58]

The parable of the Prodigal Son was Rilke's first attempt to present one of the 'finished types' and the 'natural history of their souls' referred to in the letter quoted above. The symbolic narrative of the parable gave Rilke mobility and distance in relation to his subject-

matter, so that he could construct situations according to the requirements of the meaning he wished to convey, whereas in the other parts
of the book he was tied to the description of immediate sensation or
recollection, and the meaning had largely to look after itself.

The parable of the Prodigal Son was indeed less a conclusion to
*Malte Laurids Brigge* and the work of the middle period than the
beginning of a new creative development. It was no doubt because
Rilke found that the parable was leading him in a direction which
took him away from the rest of the novel that he found it necessary to
break it and the book off at a rather arbitrary point.[59]

The new conception of art towards which Rilke began to develop
after *Malte Laurids Brigge* is made clearer in a letter of May 1911 to
Max Dauthendey. He praises Dauthendey's work in terms which, as
so often with Rilke (cf. Rodin, Cézanne, Obstfelder, etc.), seem to be
concerned less with the work under discussion than with the possibilities he seeks to realise in his own art: he sees in the other writer's
work an 'intensity of being' resulting from his ability to 'take hold of
things and let go of them, ... barely to show them and then at once to
replace them by something else,' in such a way that 'none of them
pushes aside or overshadows the others, but rather they are all spread
out and preserved in the reader, making him, as it were, spacious,
although they seem merely to pass by'.[60] The 'letting go of things'
referred to here is in sharp contrast to the practice during contemplation of clinging to sensations until all else is excluded from consciousness. It is this 'letting go' of sensations which enables Dauthendey to
achieve what Rilke failed to achieve in *Malte Laurids Brigge*, a kind of
inner space in the work in which all its parts are present and interrelated.

The word which Rilke uses in connection with this inner dimension
– 'spacious' – recalls the passage in the letter quoted earlier, where he
spoke of symbolic human figures, the apprehension of whom 'makes
my hearing spacious'. It is significant that he does not refer to
vision, but to hearing, as the faculty appropriate to this kind of experience.

Rilke is nearing the end of the period in which the visual sense
dominates his perception of reality and his mode of creation. In a
letter of January 1912 he writes of a feeling of being cut off more and
more from the visible world; he compares himself to someone who has
allowed high walls to be built all round him and goes on: 'Perhaps
there is only one way out, to have the walls made higher and higher
until finally, from below, as from the bottom of a well, one can see the
stars even during the day.' Here again, the sense of a connectedness to
the stars appears as the ultimate goal; but to reach it Rilke will be
obliged, as he goes on to admit, to renounce 'the day's bright play'[61] –

the world of colour, light and sensation from which he had created *New Poems* and *Malte Laurids Brigge*.

But while he was abandoning his old method, Rilke was beginning to sense a world of new possibilities. In another letter of early 1912 he wrote: 'I long for work, and sometimes for a moment I have the feeling that it longs for me – but we do not come together.'[62] After his return from North Africa the previous year he had been aware that the impressions he had assimilated would not immediately give rise to renewed productivity: 'that will only be possible later, perhaps much later'.[63] He resigned himself to the only course open to him: as in the early period he must wait for the advent of inspiration: 'might it not be, after all, that for my nature only one thing is right: to endure?'[64] When Rilke wrote these more hopeful words, on January 24th, 1912, a development was taking place which may have led him to believe that his wait was already at an end; how long it was to be in fact, he can scarcely have imagined.

# CHAPTER FOURTEEN

## The Creative Process in the Late Period

### I. PROUST: 1904–1909

I N a letter of 1904 Proust expressed an idea on art which, he said explicitly, had just come to him for the first time. He now saw the 'primordial quality' of a work of literature as a 'coalescence', a 'transparent unity', in which all things, 'losing their first appearance of things, are arranged, one beside the other, in a kind of order'. The different parts of the work are totally interrelated, 'penetrated by the same light, seen one in the other, without a single word being left outside, remaining refractory to this assimilation'. The interrelatedness he describes is experienced as a unified atmosphere pervading the whole work. Commenting on the book by Mme de Noailles which was the immediate occasion for this letter Proust writes: 'Nothing has been "introduced" into the book, everything is bathed in an enchanted atmosphere'; and he adds that not a tone or a word could be changed 'without making all this life cry out in protest and dispelling at once the broken reflections'.[1]

It is clear at once that what Proust describes here as the essential quality of a work of art is also that of a privileged moment. His terms are strongly reminiscent of those used by the writers in Chapter One, and there are other echoes elsewhere in the letter. Moreover, the comparison with the privileged moment is made explicit. After referring to the unified atmosphere of the work he is discussing, Proust goes on: 'the colours command one another, they are complementary like those in a garden on a spring morning, seen from a dining-room with coloured-glass windows and a blind drawn half-down, where the breezes from the garden enter the parlour with its walls coated with whitewash and sunlight'.[2] The scene evoked here, with its obvious delight in sensation for its own sake and where 'everything communicates and mingles',[3] clearly has the heightened and unified quality of the privileged moment.

This conception of art, at which Proust first arrived in this letter, remained a central preoccupation from this time on. In a passage of *Against Sainte-Beuve* written in 1909 he described Flaubert's style in terms almost identical to those of the letter just quoted: 'All things are depicted there, but by reflection, without damaging its homogeneous substance. All that was different has been converted and absorbed.'[4]

Balzac's style, on the other hand, was for Proust totally lacking in this quality: 'Balzac uses all the ideas which come into his mind without trying to introduce them, dissolved, into a style which would harmonise them.'[5]

In the essay on Nerval in the same book Proust asserts that atmosphere, which he calls 'something vague and haunting like memory', is the fundamental quality of *Sylvie*. It is, he says, a 'dream atmosphere'; but what he is referring to is not a dream in the normal sense: it is a kind of waking dream produced in the author by a night of insomnia. He goes on to compare this with experiences of his own, mornings of intense lucidity similarly produced by a disruption of habits and a night without sleep. On such mornings he writes, 'you are intoxicated by the slightest beauty ... The rightness of every colour moves you like a harmony ... and if a faint light touches these colours ... you feel overwhelmed with beauty.' Here again, we can see clearly that the atmosphere with which Proust is concerned is that of the privileged moment. He goes on to speak of these mornings 'hollowed out by insomnia ... in the hard stone of our days' as magical grottoes in our memory, each one preserving its own dreamlike charm and its special atmosphere.

The privileged moment, then, is intimately bound up with Proust's new conception of unity of atmosphere as the primordial quality of a work of literature. He sees it as the writer's task above all to create the atmosphere of the privileged moment in his work. But this cannot be achieved by direct description, as Proust had attempted to do in *Jean Santeuil*. In the essay on Nerval he acknowledges that the atmosphere he is concerned with is inexpressible, that 'it is not in the words ... it is between the words like a morning mist at Chantilly'. This quality can only be suggested, evoked. The art form closest to this conception of literature is no longer painting, but music; the artist must try to express something 'which even words do not evoke, but which we sometimes see in dreams, or which music evokes'.[6]

Proust therefore has reached a standpoint departing radically from that of the middle period. The first piece of creative writing he produced after abandoning *Jean Santeuil* shows how far he has advanced in a new direction. It is the passage published as 'Days of Reading', written in a 'renewed burst of energy'[7] in April 1905, that is, not long after the letter to Mme de Noailles quoted at the beginning of this chapter. In this passage Proust achieved, for the first time, a unity of tone and atmosphere running through the entire piece. It is worth analysing the passage briefly to see how this effect is produced.

The atmosphere is created largely by the use of a rich and evocative prose. The sentences are crowded with references to the sensations experienced by Proust at the time evoked. More important, he does not confine himself in them, as in earlier works, to the impressions received at one particular moment, but clusters round the immediate scene fragments of memory giving a wider picture of the village where he lived and of this period of his life.[8] The atmosphere produced by this prose style is not, however, the only unifying factor in 'Days of Reading'. The passage has a definite structure which includes a chronological element. Its subject is a day spent reading; it is divided into roughly equal sections describing in turn the morning, the midday meal, Proust's bedroom in the early afternoon, the park in the late afternoon, and the bedroom at night. This extended evocation is preceded by an introductory paragraph giving a foreshortened view of the day's events, and establishing the general atmosphere of the passage.

The division into sections provides a framework; within this framework the individual episodes are further unified stylistically. The section evoking the bedroom in the early afternoon will serve as an example. The main part of this episode consists of description of the objects in the room. To unify the material Proust uses long sentences – one of them covers two pages – taking over a device already developed in *Jean Santeuil*. Within these sentences there is, however, a further unifying device not used in that novel. In a section of two and a half pages,[9] consisting of two sentences, there are ten major metaphors all of which relate the things in the room either to the spring flowers, or to the church. The flowers and the church are themselves related together by one metaphor which refers to the flowers on the altar. This systematic use of imagery serves, moreover, not only to unify the particular bedroom scene but to relate it to the scene outside, in which, precisely, the flowers and the church are the dominating elements. In this way the passage takes on a homogeneous quality: the atmosphere of the whole is present in the parts.

Unity is also given to the passage as a whole by the theme – reading – which runs through all the episodes. This theme is closely linked to the chronological structure – the series of events which might be called the 'plot' – so that the end of the day coincides with Proust finishing his book; the passage is rounded off with general reflections on reading.

The most fundamental way in which Proust has unified the passage is, however, his use of the first person. The narrator looks back on himself as a boy, but the narrator and the boy are always kept distinct. In this sense there are two 'I's in the passage. There is never a tendency for the narrator to merge with the protagonist, although the use of the first person might appear to encourage this. There is no question of Proust using his hero to achieve vicarious satisfactions in the way characteristic of *Jean Santeuil*. This does not mean, however, that the narrator is a detached, dispassionate observer. The whole narrative is pervaded by a strong sense of emotional participation – but this is not a participation in the particular emotions of the hero; it is a generalised, undifferentiated nostalgia for the whole world of his childhood, for the 'vanished days', 'the houses and ponds which no longer exist'.[10] Because he has accepted that this world is irrevocably lost, it is no longer related to his personal desires; he can begin to re-create it for its own sake.

This is the first appearance in Proust's work of *temps perdu* – 'time lost' – of a world so completely detached from his present existence that he can see his earlier life in that world as if it were the life of another person. He can now use the first person without danger of identifying himself with his protagonist.

In this way Proust achieves not only a consistent relation to his hero, but a consistent narrative tone or 'voice'. The narrative voice is separated from the world evoked by an immense and unbridgeable distance. It is a voice lacking in personal attributes, yet, as mentioned earlier, it is charged with an intense emotional quality, a tone which pervades the whole passage. When the narrator intervenes directly it is not to give a detail of Proust's present life, but to express, in language which in its rhythm and intensity rises to a kind of 'song', a single dominating emotion:

I am only happy when setting foot – in the avenue de la Gare, at the harbour, or on the place de l'Église – in one of those provincial hotels with long cold corridors where the wind from outside battles victoriously with the efforts of the stove ...

This dominating emotion is the longing for a certain quickening of the inner life, a sense of liberation from the habitual confines of the self, experienced when 'my imagination is exalted to feel itself plunged in the heart of what is not me [*non-moi*]'.[11] For Proust now, as we saw, the world of his childhood has become *non-moi*. His longing for imaginative exaltation therefore becomes focused on the world of the past. The nostalgia implicit in his evocation of the past gives his 'voice' throughout 'Days of Reading' its characteristic tone and thereby also, as a critic notes, 'what it had been waiting for for fifteen years: its unity'.[12]

The distance separating the two 'I's and the nostalgia pulling between them create in 'Days of Reading' a special tension which is a constitutive element in a new kind of structure. This is a structure in time, but it is not the same as the time-structure of chronological narrative, which the passage also has on a small scale. The new structure involves a sense of depth, of volume contained by the work. There are two 'levels' of time, or poles, which are intensely and exclusively interrelated, so that the work is structurally self-sufficient, closed on itself.

At this point an important parallel with the creative process in the

middle period can be seen. Proust's relation to the world of his childhood is analogous to that, for example, of the poet and the tree he
contemplates in 'Artistic Contemplation'. The past world, like the
object contemplated, is entirely severed from the interests of the 'personal' self, so that self-consciousness is eliminated from the process of
describing it. This means that Proust's interest in the world of his childhood is not restricted, as in actual life, to those aspects of it which play
a part in particular personal interests at a given time. He has now a
total interest, directed equally at all its details. For this reason the
world of the past has an intense radiance and significance; like the
object contemplated in the middle period, it takes on the quality of
reality perceived during a privileged moment. The past world therefore contrasts sharply with the present, which, of course, normally
lacks this quality. Proust's nostalgia for the past can be readily understood: it is a form of nostalgia for the privileged moment. To impart
the heightened and unified quality of the privileged moment to his
evocation of the past, Proust uses the techniques discussed in relation
to 'Days of Reading': a prose style expressing a rich profusion of
sensations, and a unified structure in which a systematic use of imagery
plays a part.

The new creative process can be seen, therefore, to be in important
respects a continuation of that of the middle period. There are also, of
course, fundamental differences: in the new process the quality of the
privileged moment is no longer confined to isolated objects or scenes,
but is extended to wide areas of experience. In addition, as we saw, the
polarity between the narrator and the world evoked provides an axis
for a new kind of structure; it makes possible an 'inner space' in the
work, which was notably lacking in the middle period.

It must be admitted, however, that the new creative process has been
exhibited so far only in a work of very limited length and containing a
minimum of action. In addition, the possibility of making use of the
inner space referred to has been scarcely explored. It remains to be
seen whether Proust can apply his new technique of narration to more
extended subject matter.

*Against Sainte-Beuve* was clearly an attempt to do so. In this work
Proust again uses the first person and the technique of different 'levels'
of time. But his procedure is considerably more complex than in 'Days
of Reading'. In the first chapter, entitled 'Sleep', Proust establishes
the time as that of a morning during the period when he was ill and
slept all day (this might be called 'level 1'). It is the events of this
morning, leading up to his conversation with his mother, which are to
supply the chronological axis of the work corresponding to that provided by the events of the day spent reading in the earlier passage. But
Proust does not at once evoke this morning; he goes further back to the

time, still near then, when he slept during the night (level 2). This time, which, says Proust, 'seems to me today to have been lived by another person',[13] clearly belongs to the realm of 'time lost'. Using this as a new starting-point he now goes still further back, calling up scenes and experiences from his childhood (level 3) as they cluster associatively round the experience of falling asleep in level 2. Including the present of the narrator, there are therefore four distinct levels of time in this chapter.

In the next chapter, 'Rooms', Proust uses a similar technique: different rooms he had slept in since his childhood are evoked, linked together by associations of sensation. The technique is continued in the third chapter, 'Days', where various days in different places are summoned up by the sights and sounds of early morning which filter into Proust's bedroom. The starting-point of these associations is level 1, the morning which appeared at the beginning of 'Sleep'.

Proust here has adopted a systematic technique for enlarging the scope of his evocations of the past. He takes as his starting-point a morning in the past, and attaches to different moments in this morning associations from different levels of time. In this way he creates a structure having two axes: the 'vertical' axis of the different levels of time, and the 'horizontal' axis of the chronological events of the morning. The vertical elements are attached to successive points on the horizontal axis: in 'Sleep' the associations are connected to the sensations of falling asleep, in 'Rooms' to those of waking up, and in 'Days' to those of the period following waking up. In this way Proust has attempted systematically to fill the 'inner space' discovered in 'Days of Reading'.

It should be noted, however, that he has not fully solved the problem encountered there. Instead of a single 'narrative line' Proust has now established a number of planes on which action can proceed. But a narrative line as such still exists only on one level – that of the morning first introduced; the different levels are not linked together by a continuous narrative. For this reason, Proust has failed to co-ordinate the two principles of structure existing in his work: the chronological structure of the narrative, and the structure in depth created by the distance between narrator and protagonist.

Proust's style, however, if not his use of structure, is fully equal to the tasks imposed by his new conception of literature. The atmosphere of this part of *Against Sainte-Beuve* has, to a still higher degree, the intensity and the abundance of sensation noted in 'Days of Reading'. Although Proust is now evoking a time more recent than his childhood, it is still one which appears to him as *non-moi*, as totally severed from his personal existence. Here, the sense of distance in time is no doubt supplemented by the fact that Proust is confined to bed by illness. He is prevented from participating in the world outside his room; his interest in this world is therefore not restricted to particular aspects connected with a personal project, it is undifferentiated and total. In the following passage, for example, he imagines the sensations of people living in the world which is closed to him, the ' "men with work to do" that I might have been', on their way home in the country:

> ils goûtaient déjà le plaisir de traverser tout un arc-en-ciel de parfums, dans le petit salon noir et fleuri dont un rayon de jour immobile semble avoir anesthésié l'atmosphère; et . . . après s'être dirigé dans l'office obscure où luisent soudain des irisations comme dans une grotte, et où rafraîchit dans des auges pleines d'eau le cidre, que tout à l'heure – si 'frais' en effet qu'il appuiera au passage sur toutes les parois de la gorge en une adhérence entière, glaciale et embaumée – on boira dans de jolis verres troubles et trop épais, qui comme certaines chairs de femme donnet envie de pousser jusqu'à la morsure l'insuffisance du baiser, ils goûtaient déjà la fraîcheur de la salle à manger où l'atmosphère – en sa congélation lumineuse que striaient comme l'intérieur d'une agate les parfums distincts de la nappe, du buffet, du cidre, celui aussi du gruyère auquel le voisinage des prismes de verre destinés à supporter les couteaux ajoutait quelque mysticité – se veinait délicatement quand on apportait les compotiers de l'odeur des cerises et des abricots.[14]

> already they were savouring the pleasure of passing through a whole rainbow of scents, in the small dark drawing-room full of flowers, with an atmosphere that seemed anaesthetised by a motionless beam of daylight; and ... after making their way into the dim pantry where an iridescent light suddenly shines as in a grotto, and where in buckets full of water cider is being freshened which presently – so 'fresh' indeed that it will press as it passes on all the walls of the throat in a total, icy and perfumed adherence – will be drunk from pretty glasses that are cloudy and too thick and which, as with the flesh of certain women, the inadequacy of the kiss gives one the desire to bite, already they were savouring the freshness of the dining-room where the atmosphere – its luminous congelation striated like the interior of an agate by the distinct scents of the tablecloth, the side-board, the cider and also that of the gruyère to which the proximity of the glass prisms destined to support the knives added a touch of the mystical – would be delicately veined, when the fruit dishes were brought in, by the scent of cherries and apricots.

It has been necessary to quote at length to show Proust's ability to weave together an abundance of sensations from different orders to form an atmosphere so rich and dense that, to use his word, it congeals. The passage illustrates an extreme point in the development of his style in the late period. By means of this style he is able to imbue whole stretches of his experience with the quality of the privileged moment. It is noticeable that Proust has now developed the well-known device of three contrasting but complementary adjectives – *une adhérence entière, glaciale et embaumée* – as a means of compressing a maximum of sensation into a minimum of words.

A further feature of 'Days of Reading' reappears in the opening section of *Against Sainte-Beuve*: the distinctive narrative voice and the sense of distance between the two 'I's, narrator and protagonist. When the narrator refers to his own present in relation to a memory from the past there is the same rising in the voice to a kind of 'song', the same expression of spiritual liberation coupled with nostalgia, and above all the same heightened rhythm, which is now becoming recognisable:

> Alors, dans ce grand silence de tout, que domine le bruit de mes râles, j'entends tout au fond de moi une petite voix gaie qui dit : il fait beau – il fait beau –, des larmes de souffrance me tombent des yeux, je ne peux pas parler, mais si je pouvais retrouver un instant le souffle, je chanterais, et le petit capucin d'opticien, qui est la seule chose que je suis resté, ôte son chapeau et annonce le soleil.[15]

> Then, in this universal silence where my dying groans are the only sound, deep in myself I hear a small voice gaily saying: the sun is out – the sun is out –, my eyes shed tears of suffering, I cannot speak, but if for a moment I could draw breath again I would sing, and the little capuchin friar in the optician's window, which is the only thing I have remained, takes off his hat and announces the sun.

But by creating a unified tone and atmosphere Proust has not solved all the problems involved in the use of his new techniques for a novel. His system is unable to include large narrative units or extended passages of general reflection, as is shown by the next chapter, 'The Countess'. The sense of distance between past and present, on which the atmosphere of the book depends, does not admit the sudden change of perspective and tone involved by the detailed presentation of a particular love affair, even though, in narrating this episode, Proust adheres to the imperfect tense. In this part of the narrative the tension between the two 'I's disappears, and there is a tendency, reminiscent of *Jean Santeuil*, for Proust to use the situations described as an occasion for boasting of his social successes in a way which destroys all sense of the narrator's detachment from the petty concerns of the moment. In addition, this episode does not fit into the structure of 'levels' established earlier.

In the following chapter, 'The Article in the *Figaro*', however, Proust returns to his temporal axis – the events of the morning introduced at the beginning of the book. He now describes reading his article in the newspaper, but in so doing he uses first the past historic, then the present tense. The episode is presented with such immediacy that the narrator and the protagonist are identified, and the atmosphere of *temps perdu* is entirely lost.

From this point on the original structure is abandoned; there is now only one centre of interest, only one 'level', and the characteristic 'voice' of the earlier part gives way to a more abstract, intellectual tone. In later parts, particularly in 'The Ray of Sunlight on the Balcony', there is some further evocation of the past, but now the associations of sensation are used to prove a theoretical point rather than to create an atmosphere.

In the chapter 'Conversation with Mother' it becomes clear why Proust was unable to maintain the detachment from his subject-matter noted in the early chapters. We see here that he had, as well as general nostalgia for the past, a strongly personal reason for writing about what he introduces at the beginning of the book as 'this morning whose memory, I do not know why, I want to fix'.[16] This reason, whether or not Proust was conscious of it, was his desire to re-live his past life with his mother, not as a detached, aesthetic experience, but as a sentimental experience, in which he could listen to the words of affection he puts endlessly into her mouth: *mon petit serin, mon Loup, ta Maman*, etc.

To point this out is not deny the value of such emotion, nor the skill with which it is embodied in this scene. But Proust here is producing a kind of literature entirely removed from that which he was seen developing towards in 'Days of Reading' and in the earlier parts of *Against Sainte-Beuve*. He has not yet been able to detach himself from his mother sufficiently to include her in the world of 'time lost'.

In the next chapter Proust moves still further from the form of the opening section by introducing a theoretical discussion of Sainte-Beuve's method, only perfunctorily presented as fiction. In so doing he finally forfeits all possibility of achieving unity of style. Why should he have tried to include such disparate elements in a single work? To find the explanation me must first see *Against Sainte-Beuve* against the wider background of Proust's development during this period.

From as early as 1905 onwards Proust appears to have made sporadic attempts to write a novel, without being able to advance far beyond what he had achieved in *Jean Santeuil*.[17] He was still unable to bind his isolated fragments into a larger unity. The last of these attempts before *Against Sainte-Beuve* seems to have been begun early in 1908.[18] Indications of the contents of this attempted novel are given in the editor's preface to *Against Sainte-Beuve*, and are based on a notebook or 'agenda' kept by Proust at that time. He gives a list of 'pages written' – a number of episodes in which the two 'ways' (*côtés* – at this stage called Villebon and Méséglise) appear, concluding with a section referred to as 'what the Villebon way and the Méséglise way taught me'.[19] He had therefore already seen the possibility of using the 'ways' and their lessons as a basis for a unified structure. But this structure seems rather peripheral to the main body of the incidents alluded to, and its discovery did not yet provide Proust with the key to his novel.

Towards the end of 1908 he abandoned this attempt and, moved by what Painter calls 'a deep intuition',[20] turned his attention to Sainte-Beuve. The critic attracted Proust because he represented an attitude towards reality and literature which was diametrically opposed to Proust's own. In refuting him Proust would clarify his own conception of literature. He would also be given the opportunity of expressing ideas which were important to him but which he had not been able to introduce naturally into his creative writing, for example, the opening sentence of his preface to *Against Sainte-Beuve*: 'Every day I attach less importance to the intelligence.'

For Proust, Sainte-Beuve typified the attitude which takes the scientific interpretation of reality as absolute truth, and therefore wishes to see literature and literary criticism as a branch of scientific study. This gives rise to Sainte-Beuve's method, which explains and evaluates works of art by explaining and evaluating the person of their author. Proust believed, however, and wrote in the chapter entitled 'Sainte-Beuve's Method', that 'a book is the product of a different self than that which we manifest in our habits, in society, in our vices'.[21] To the intelligence Proust opposed instinct and the irrational. The 'true self' who composes a book is that part of a man which is 'unconscious, deep, personal'.[22]

To present his argument Proust first chose the form of the classical essay in the manner of Taine, but, finding this unsatisfactory, he then adopted a dramatised form using the conversation with his mother. According to Painter, the 'classical essay' survives in *Against Sainte Beuve* as the chapter entitled 'Sainte-Beuve's Method'.[23] Proust's reasons for abandoning the essay form are easily understood. He was trying to use purely rational argument to prove the supremacy of the irrational – a doubtful undertaking. But in the dramatised form he was able to present his own conception of literature 'in action' by showing the artistic value of irrational impressions such as associations of sensation. The early sections of the book contain the concrete substance on which his argument is based.

Proust therefore had a definite reason for trying to combine the elements of 'atmosphere' and rational argument in the book. These two elements, however disparate, were interdependent. He could not present his argument without the early evocative passages; on the other hand the argument was necessary to provide the motive for writing these passages, and to supply a unifying theme without which the associations of sensation could proliferate at random.

Moreover, the theme – the attack on Sainte-Beuve and on the intelligence – enabled Proust to introduce other material which he urgently sought to express, and which hitherto had not found its way into a large-scale work. The chapter entitled 'The Accursed Race', dealing with homosexuality, was written about May 1908;[24] Proust was able to include it in *Against Sainte-Beuve* because he was able to see his defence of homosexuality as a part of his wider attack on the scientific intelligence: it was based on the belief that the subjective element, desire, rather than its external object, is the true reality involved in love as in the other relationships of man to the external world. The attack on the superficial view which equates literature with life – the error of Sainte-Beuve – also enabled Proust to include portraits of his social acquaintances of whom this mistake was characteristic. So he introduces the Guermantes, who fill the last sections of the book in its published form.

Despite its heterogeneous material, *Against Sainte-Beuve* therefore contains what Proust's previous attempted novels had lacked: a principle of unity. This is provided by a central idea with which all parts of the book are consistent, in meaning if not in style. Proust gives an indication of this new principle of unity permeating the work in an early note on *Against Sainte-Beuve* in his 'agenda': 'Everything is fictitious, laboriously so, for I have no imagination; but it is filled with a meaning which I have long carried within me.'[25]

The central idea of *Against Sainte-Beuve* is not a purely rational concept; as we saw, it did not lend itself to a strictly logical exposition. It is an intuition, rooted in the irrational levels of experience and expressing itself through an extended fictional representation of life. In other words, the unifying principle of the book is a myth, that is, a truth about life which cannot be contained in the forms of expression denoted since Aristotle by 'logos'. The relevance of myth, as opposed to logos, to this discussion, is made clear by Wellek and Warren in *Theory of Literature*:

> The 'myth' is narrative, story, as against dialectical discourse, exposition; it is also the irrational or intuitive as against the systematically philosophical.[26]

The idea of myth throws light on fundamental aspects of Proust's work in this period. The world of *Contre Sainte-Beuve* necessarily and naturally gives rise to elements of myth.

In 'The Ray of Sunlight on the Balcony' Proust reflects on the inadequacy of external, physical description as a means of conveying the meaning of impressions. The meaning of the sunlight does not lie in the sensations as such, but in the pleasure it causes him. The impression is related by association to his emotional life at the time of first seeing it as a boy: if the sun shines he will be able to go out to play

with a little girl he loves. Objects giving such impressions have not the
neutral existence which they have for the scientific or practical intelligence. Like the human face, they have a power of expressing
emotion; in this passage, for example, Proust writes of the sky's 'cloudy
smile'.[27]

It is this 'physiognomic' quality which Ernst Cassirer, in *An Essay on
Man*, describes as a primary feature the mythical world inhabited by
primitive man:

> what myth primarily perceives are not objective but *physiognomic* charac-
> ters ... Mythical perception is always impregnated with ... emotional
> qualities. Whatever is seen or felt is surrounded by a special atmosphere –
> an atmosphere of joy or grief, of anguish, of excitement, of exultation or
> depression.[28]

Proust's world, under the influence of emotion, is perceived in a
similar way. For example, a window in Venice, behind which he
knows his mother is waiting for him, takes on the quality of a face:
'From far off ... I saw it waiting for me, having already caught sight of
me, and the upward sweep of its arch added to its smile the distinction
of a slightly misunderstood look.'[29] Similarly the objects surrounding
the girl he loves are imbued with his emotion; her house, for example,
'cast a delightful spell so far around it that the mere name of the street
and of the adjacent streets and the number of the *arrondissement*
resounded in us with a painful and unhealthy charm'.[30] Emotion, we
see here, has the power of unifying things which would normally be
separated by the logical mind. The same tendency is present in another
scene where the protagonist, tormented by indecision after quarrelling
with his mother and threatening to leave Venice, listens to a singer:
'The serenade seemed incapable of finishing, and the sun of going
down, as if my anguish, the dusk and the metal of the singer's voice
were fused forever in a poignant, equivocal and imperturbable alloy.'[31]

The power of emotional atmosphere to override logical distinctions
is also an essential feature of the mythical world as described by
Cassirer:

> Myth is an offspring of emotion and its emotional background imbues all
> its productions with its own specific colour. Primitive man by no means
> lacks the ability to grasp the empirical differences of things. But in his
> conception of nature and life all these differences are obliterated by a
> stronger feeling: the deep conviction of a fundamental and indelible
> *solidarity of life* that bridges over the multiplicity and variety of its single
> forms.[32]

This sense of the unity of life, says Cassirer, influences primitive man's
view of death: 'The feeling of the indestructible unity of life is so
strong and unshakeable as to deny and to defy the fact of death.' He

goes on to say that this attitude to death is of fundamental importance in the mythical view of reality: 'In a certain sense the whole of mythical thought may be interpreted as a constant and obstinate negation of the phenomenon of death.'[33] A similar negation of death is essential to the experience underlying Proust's work; for example, the effect of light in 'The Ray of Sunlight on the Balcony' gives him 'a pleasure which nothing equals, and while it lasts we know that death has not the slightest importance'.[34]

The mythical view of reality has another aspect which is important for this study. Because primitive man experiences the world as an unbroken totality lacking the fixed categories and distinctions of objective thought, reality for him is essentially fluctuating and unstable: 'Nothing has a definite, invariable static shape. By a sudden metamorphosis everything may be turned into everything.' Cassirer goes on from this to point to the fundamental law of the world of myth: 'If there is any characteristic and outstanding feature of the mythical world, any law by which it is governed – it is this law of metamorphosis.'[35]

Proust's world is governed by the same law. As mentioned, objects for him are not inert stuff, they are imbued with emotion. To describe them, he does not reproduce their objective appearance, but exaggerates and concentrates sense-impressions to bring them into line with their emotional importance. Thus, when he is in love with 'the Countess', he sees her carriage in the following way:

> very slowly, drawn by enormous horses, with a footman whose hat reached the height of the first floors, the carriage, as long as the façades of the houses, passed from one house to the next, sanctifying the unfeeling streets with a perfume of aristocracy.[36]

When he first saw the Countess, the protagonist had only a fleeting glimpse of her profile: 'that sort of serpentine line which joined a trace of her glance with the inflexion of her nose and a corner of pouting mouth and left out all the rest'. But under the pressure of the anxiety she now causes him, this 'serpentine' aspect of his impression becomes the basis for a metamorphosis of the real into something concentrated which symbolises his emotion. Her profile now becomes 'the little sleeping serpent', and when he suddenly meets her unawares he feels 'stunned like a little bird that has caught sight of a snake'.[37]

To assist the symbolic metamorphosis of impressions, Proust frequently makes use of already existing myths and mythological figures. When he is timorously entering a social reception, unsure whether he has really been invited: 'I heard my name, hurled by a door-keeper gigantic as Jupiter, roll like an obscure and catastrophic peal of thunder.'[38] Similarly, the parents of a girl he loves are, according to their disposition to him, 'implacable divinities' or 'benevolent Eumenides'.[39]

Proust's mythical world is coloured and transformed by emotion – generally desire with its concomitant fear – which causes reality to appear as something unknown, open to the imagination. But this mythical world is subject to a law of impermanence. The unknown becomes the known, desire gives way to familiarity and habit. The world of imagination is inevitably 'demythologised' by experience. All the love-affairs in *Against Sainte-Beuve* take this course. The object of desire is finally possessed – 'but the suffering has gone and with it the dream'.[40] Proust's disappointment once he has gained the intimacy of the Countess is the occasion for the following generalisation: 'Our whole life is passed, with the aid of habit, in letting those great paintings of unknown people, which the first impression gave us, fade away.'[41]

This law applies in Proust's world not only to love, but to man's whole relationship to existence. Life is divided into successive phases in each of which the world is experienced in a different way. In the early phase reality is not yet split up into abstract categories; things are differentiated and coloured by the concrete properties of their names.[42] For Proust, names have a direct appeal to the imagination in advance of experience; he speaks of 'the mysterious current which the *Name*, that thing which precedes knowledge, causes to flow, unlike anything we know, as happens sometimes in our dreams'.[43]

The imaginative fascination of names, particularly those of places and of noble families, is for Proust at the root of the desire to travel, and of the more questionable desire to make the acquaintance of the aristocracy. A social invitation by people he has not yet met gives him contact with 'a pure name, still full of its beautiful images unsullied by any terrestrial memory'.[44] Before he has met them, the Guermantes are for Proust a part of the unknown world of myth: 'that mysterious race, a little as a race with animal or divine blood in its veins may have been for the ancients'.[45]

But the satisfaction of the snob's ambitions, like the arrival at the real place, is inevitably a disappointment. When he has become a familiar acquaintance of Madame de Guermantes, Proust realises that 'just as the town of Pont-Aven was not built of the wholly imaginary elements evoked by the sonority of its name, no more was Madame de Guermantes made of the legend-coloured substance that I saw when I pronounced her name'.[46]

So far, we have been presented with the familiar picture of a world 'where action is not the sister of dream'. But the pattern of imagination disappointed by reality has, for Proust, a further stage which is decisive for the development of his art. When the process of getting to know them has run its course and Proust has tasted his disappointment to the full, the Guermantes, who can no longer satisfy a snobbish desire, begin to exert a new fascination. He is now able to survey their prosaic reality with an eye unclouded by any emotion, and he begins to see that they have characteristics previously unnoticed: 'In truth the real Guermantes, if they differed in an essential way from my dream, were all the same, once granted that they were men and women, peculiar enough.'[47] He now notes their particularities as if he were observing natural phenomena, with no concern for their dignity. He describes in detail a characteristic asymmetrical quality in their physique and posture, their hooked nose, their complexion with its warts and its ruddy hue heightened by inbreeding. Then he concentrates all these impressions in an intense and generalised picture of the family, as typified by certain members:

> corkscrewing like all the Guermantes beneath the beak that projected between their garnet cheeks and their amethyst cheekbones, they looked like some swan majestically adorned with purple feathers vindictively attacking a clump of irises or heliotropes.[48]

By making the nose a beak, and so on, Proust has heightened his impression and gone beyond objective reality. In this way he has restored to the Guermantes a kind of mythical existence; now, thinking of their bird-like quality, he can say: 'I do not know which was the mythological race that was issued from a goddess and a bird, but I am sure they were Guermantes.'[49]

This, however, is a new kind of myth, entirely unlike that discussed earlier: 'this originality of the Guermantes which life gave me in compensation like a dividend, was not the originality I lost when I got to know them and which made them poetic and golden like their name'.[50] In achieving this new vision, the third stage of the pattern of experience mentioned earlier, Proust gained access to the source of the incomparable humour which he was henceforth able to extract from the human scene.

There are, therefore, two different kinds of myth in Proust's world. One is charged with imagination and desire, the other is characterised by a complete absence of feeling. Because the Guermantes can no longer satisfy Proust's personal desires, he becomes detached from their world and so gains a freedom he had previously lacked in his portrayal of society: he is no longer in danger of being drawn personally into the world he creates to seek an imaginary social satisfaction. The social world is now irrevocably separated from him; it too has become a part of 'time lost'.

But because the social world is now entirely lost, like the world of his childhood it becomes again, but in a new way, an object of desire and a source of poetry. Like one of the characters in *Against Sainte-Beuve*, Proust has achieved 'that intellectual detachment from the aristocracy which was sufficiently complete ... to find in them, as in something strange, useless and dead, an aesthetic charm'.[51] He now feels for the world of society the same total, undifferentiated nostalgia as for the world of the past. And just as the nostalgia for the world of the past gave rise to its poetic re-creation in 'Days of Reading' and in the early part of *Against Sainte-Beuve*, the nostalgia for society too is coupled with the impulse to create. In the last sections of *Against Sainte-Beuve*, many of them unpublished, Proust's fictional characters drawn from society proliferated until they outgrew the conception of the book and began to people a new world – that of *In Search of Time Lost*.

In this way Proust has found a means of extending the scope of 'Days of Reading' and of the early parts of *Against Sainte-Beuve*. He can now assimilate material from society into the world of his childhood; two major areas of his experience are now made of a homogeneous substance. He has taken an important step towards achieving in his work what he saw in Flaubert: 'every part of reality has been converted into the same substance. All that was different has been converted and absorbed.' He has begun to create the pervasive atmosphere which he saw as the unifying quality of a work of art: the atmosphere of 'time lost' which, as we saw at the beginning of this chapter, is also that of the privileged moment.

But this atmosphere appears only intermittently in *Against Sainte-Beuve* and is not sufficient to unify the work. As we saw, the scenes involving Proust's mother are particularly refractory to assimilation. It can be understood that Proust's attachment to his mother made it practically impossible for him to include her in the world of 'time lost'. There are, however, already indications of a solution to this problem. The most important of them are not to be found in *Against Sainte-Beuve*, but in the article 'Filial Sentiments of a Parricade', written in 1907. This article, the product of a sudden inspiration,[52] brought to an end a prolonged period of sterility which had followed his mother's death.

The immediate occasion of the article was a topical event – one of Proust's acquaintances had murdered his mother. Proust, however, takes this event as symbolic of his own selfish behaviour towards his mother, which he now sees as having contributed towards her death. He is therefore emotionally involved in the article with the deepest part of his being, and this is reflected in the poignancy and urgency of his style. But by removing his subject from his own direct experience to an indirect, symbolic level, he makes it possible to preserve a detached tone and to avoid the intrusion of the 'personal' self which marred the unity of tone in *Against Sainte-Beuve*. This gives the narrative 'I' of the article a compass and an impersonality which enable him to appear as both participant and commentator, and to introduce into the narrative general reflections – on memory, effects of the weather, reading a newspaper – without disrupting the unity of the passage.

The tendency to transpose subjects which move him deeply in order to treat them objectively appears therefore to be Proust's solution to the problem mentioned earlier. In another article, this time on the death of a friend's grandmother, Proust seems to be following the same course, though, as Painter notes, with less satisfactory results. The shortcomings of this article may have been due to the fact that the subject was too close to his own experience for truly symbolic treatment.

The substitution of the grandmother for the mother in this article is, however, significant. In *Against Sainte-Beuve*, Proust's grandmother appears, and although she plays a less prominent part than his mother, it is the grandmother, treated more objectively, who leaves behind a clearer impression, as in the scene when, admiring the architecture of Chartres cathedral, 'she smiled with gentleness at the old, worn stones'.[53] This figure is far remoter to Proust and, however touching, far closer to the world of 'time lost', than the diffuse presence of his mother whom he addresses dutifully, even in the middle of abstract discussions of Saint-Beuve, as *tu*.

'Filial Sentiments of a Parricide' is also significant from the point of view of myth. Proust takes the anecdote as a symbol of the general truth that, in a sense, all men murder their mothers. This general idea is dramatised by the incident; but the incident only receives it full significance from the idea dramatised. We have here an example of the situation qualified earlier as 'myth'. Moreover, in this article Proust accentuates the mythical element by introducing numerous references to parallel scenes in world literature and mythology, in particular to the myths of Ajax, Oedipus and Orestes, and to the death of Lear. The whole article is permeated by this symbolic element, which includes literary references and partly concealed quotations.[54]

In the light of this article it is necessary to define another aspect of myth in Proust's world. We have already seen that he employs two kinds of mythical vision, one charged with emotion, the other devoid of it. Both kinds of vision are applied to realities which formerly filled him with emotion but to which he is now indifferent. The first kind of vision presents realities as he experienced them at the time when they still filled him with feeling, the second kind presents them as they are seen later without it. But there has now appeared a third kind of mythical vision, which is applied to realities with which Proust is still emotionally involved as he writes about them. By presenting them in the symbolic form of myth he is able both to preserve an objective distance from his subjects and to express the emotion inherent in them.

A further example of this third use of mythical vision is to be found in another article of 1907, 'Days of Driving'. Here the chauffeur Agostinelli who, as is well known, caused Proust emotions of an intense, though here incipient, kind, is the occasion of some of Proust's happiest mythical allusions:

> my mechanic had put on a vast rubber cloak and a sort of hood which, enclosing the fullness of his beardless young face, made him resemble, as we plunged ever more quickly into the night, some pilgrim or rather some nun of speed. From time to time – a Saint Cecilia improvising on a still more immaterial instrument – he would touch the keyboard and pull out one of the stops of those organs concealed in the car. [55]

Here we can see too how Proust's mythical vision is bound up with a rich source of humour.

In a third important article of 1907 Proust again shows his mythologising power at a high pitch of development. It is confusingly entitled 'Days of Reading', and must of course be distinguished from the earlier passage with the same title. The whole of the first part of the article is devoted to an imaginative discourse on telephone conversations in which the operators are playfully, and with great virtuosity, transformed into mythical powers – 'the vigilant Virgins', 'those Danaides of the Invisible', 'the jealous Furies who, while we murmur a confidence to a girl-friend, ironically call: "I'm listening" '. Despite its playful tone, however, the article has for Proust a serious theme. The telephone conversation was for him above all a means of communication with his mother when he was separated from her. The emotional seriousness of this theme is partly revealed when he speaks of the separation of those who talk on the telephone as an 'anticipation of an eternal parting', and when he refers to 'words which I would have liked to be able to kiss as they passed on lips forever turned to dust'.[56] The operators who can cut him off from his mother are therefore genuinely a source of fear, and it is this which leads to their exaggerated, stylised presentation here.

A further important aspect of the use of myth is also clearly displayed in this article. Having developed his extended image of the 'vigilant virgins', Proust has provided himself with a stock of references which can be re-introduced later in the article to give it a kind of self-contained framework, a unity. So he finishes by saying that if in his next article he is diverted from his subject by a digression like the present one on telephones, he will firmly repel the intrusive idea: ' "We are talking, don't cut the line, mademoiselle!"' In a similar way in 'Filial Sentiments of a Parricide' he draws the mythical references together in the last sentence to give the work a kind of thematic unity.[57]

We can see here one of the chief advantages of mythical metamorphosis over the realistic description of reality. The former allows the writer far greater freedom; he is not bound by the laws of time, space and probability. His material can be manipulated and organised according to aesthetic principles; by the use of cross-references, repetition, etc., the elements of a book can be related together in the manner of musical themes. In this way the mythical world contains the possibility of a kind of structure which, as *Jean Santeuil* showed, is denied to the writer transcribing experience directly.

These articles are, however, of small scope, and the difficulty of giving them unity is not great. In *Against Sainte-Beuve* the problem is far more serious, and has not been solved by Proust. The mythical element is not sufficiently strong to impose its own structure and unity. Indeed, one of the essential characteristics of myth is still lacking in *Against Sainte-Beuve*. It is, as B. G. Rogers observes, essentially a static work;[58] action, and a plot-structure built around action, are virtually absent. This is in strong contrast to the mythical world described by Cassirer: 'The world of myth is a dramatic world – a world of actions, of forces, of conflicting powers'; 'its vital principle ... is a dynamic not a static one; it is describable only in terms of action'.[59]

Proust, then, has not yet discovered how to use narrative as a structural element. He has, however, realised the importance of thematic organisation as a basis for a unified structure. Several years before writing *Against Sainte-Beuve* he described how Ruskin gave unity to one of his works by bringing together in the last sentence all the principal themes. These had been introduced in the course of the book in what seemed a haphazard way; but underlying their apparent disorder there was, Proust says, a 'superior logic': 'it turns out that he has obeyed a sort of secret plan which, revealed at the end, retrospectively imposes a kind of order on the whole and shows it to us rising magnificently to this final apotheosis'.[60] It is worth noting that this was written at about the time of the first 'Days of Reading', in which a simple form of thematic structure was seen to be present.

At about the same time too, Proust was arriving at his conception of unity of atmosphere as the 'primordial quality' of a work of art. It might seem that the creation of atmosphere is a matter of style rather than of structure. For Proust, however, this was not the case, as is shown by his interpretation of Balzac. We have already seen that he thought the latter's style entirely lacking in unity; in spite of this he found in Balzac's works a pervasive, unifying atmosphere. It was conferred on them by Balzac's device of introducing the same characters in different novels; Proust saw this as a retrospective unity which Balzac created after the work was written, rather in the manner of Ruskin in the last quotation. That Proust's view of Balzac was in fact mistaken is irrelevant here, since we are concerned with what he saw in Balzac rather than what was actually there. For him, the reappearance of the same character in different books acted as a structural link between them; he compared it to a ray of light which, 'falling at the same time on different parts of his creation which had been inert up to then, has united them, made them live, lit them up'. But in linking the parts of the book together, this device creates not only a structure but a pervasive and characteristic atmosphere: the ray of light Proust refers to can be, for example, 'a troubled and melancholy glow'.[61] In Balzac's work, therefore, Proust sees how structure can be used to create atmosphere, and how characters can be used to create structure: in reappearing in different parts of the work they have a function analogous to that of musical phrases in a thematic composition.

It is not by accident, therefore, that music begins to play an important part in Proust's conception of literary creation in this period. In the conclusion to *Against Sainte-Beuve* he compares the writer's vague sense of his future work to a melody which is only indistinctly remembered.[62] This conception of artistic creation as a process of bringing to daylight musical structures buried within the self is at a far remove from the outward-turned, predominantly descriptive process of the middle period. The artist's task, Proust says in 'Sainte-Beuve's Method', is that of re-creating a 'self' which is 'deep within us',[63] and which he calls the 'deep self'[64] or the 'true self'.[65] There is of course a resemblance between this and his attempt to re-create a timeless self in *Jean Santeuil*. But whereas this attempt gave rise in the earlier work primarily to descriptive passages, it now involves not a visual effort, but what Proust calls an 'effort of the heart'.[66] That the new creative process is closer to music than to visual art is further indicated when he speaks of the artist's task as 'to produce the true sound of our heart'.[67]

The 'deep self' is again associated with music in the conclusion of *Against Sainte-Beuve*. It is this deep part of himself, says Proust, which enables him to grasp the 'music' of a writer's style, and thus to write his pastiches, 'for with a writer, once one has caught his melody the words soon come'.[68] Proust's task now is to 'catch the melody' of his own style; in 'Days of Reading' (1905) and in the early parts of *Against Sainte-Beuve*, when he achieved the distinctive narrative 'voice' discussed earlier, he had clearly begun to do so.

The 'deep self' has further significance; it is, says Proust, the part of us which experiences privileged moments. This self, for whom 'to exist and to be happy are the same things',[69] only comes into being

when he can discover 'a deep link between two ideas, two sensations'.[70]
And Proust says of this self; 'It is only he who ought to write my
books'[71] – in other words, his book should be made up only of the
substance of privileged moments. Later in the conclusion this idea is
stated explicitly:

> our sentences themselves, and the episodes too ought to be made of the
> transparent substance of our best moments, when we are outside reality
> and the present.

Proust goes on to express an idea which has far-reaching implications:
'It is of these fragments of light cemented together that the style and
the plot of a book are made.'[72] The privileged moment must be embodied not only in the style of a book but in its narrative element. We
have seen that so far Proust has been able to achieve such a result with
regard to style; but regarding narrative, while glimpsing the possibility in the work of Balzac, he has been unable to realise it in his own.

The task of embodying the privileged moment in a novel appears to
have two aspects which are not clearly distinguished by Proust here.
The first implies that the substance of the book should in some way
exhibit the heightened, unified quality of reality as perceived during
a privileged moment; Proust had already achieved this in his style. The
second aspect, indicated particularly when he refers to 'these fragments of light cemented together', implies that the privileged moment
should appear as an actual experience in the narrative. In *Jean Santeuil* Proust had tried all-too-assiduously to introduce privileged
moments into his narrative, but had neglected to bind them together.

In the preface to *Against Sainte-Beuve* he appears to recognise his
earlier mistake. Having described a number of privileged moments, he
says they are not in themselves sufficient material for a book: 'A writer
is not only a poet. Even the greatest of our century ... have connected
the jewels of feeling by an intellectual framework in which they appear
only here and there.'[73] Proust recognises here that the privileged
moment can only be incorporated into the narrative if it is made part
of a deliberately constructed framework. Thus the intelligence is given
a necessary if subordinate part in Proust's conception of the novel.

In the early sections of *Against Sainte-Beuve*, however, as in Proust's
other successful creative works after *Jean Santeuil*, there are no
descriptions of the privileged moment as an actual experience. These
are relegated to sections where style and atmosphere are not important
– to the preface and the essay on Nerval. Proust has only been able to
create the atmosphere of the privileged moment in his work at the cost
of excluding it as a narrative element. The reason for this may be that
he still valued the privileged moment too much for its own sake to be
able to subordinate it to the demands of a wider scheme. The eager-

ness with which he describes a whole series of privileged moments in the preface suggests that he was still concerned with the experience primarily as a source of existential pleasure. As long as he is attached to it in this way, he cannot see it, as his novel demands, as a part of the world of 'time lost'.

According to Painter, the privileged moment involving the dipping of toast into tea which is described in the preface to *Against Sainte-Beuve*, was experienced by Proust early in 1909. It was this experience which confirmed his belief in the superiority of intuition over intelligence; and the sense of disorientation it produced, which Proust likened to that of a man waking from sleep, gave him, says Painter,[74] the theme of the opening scenes of the book, in which the sensations of waking are explored. Proust now became increasingly absorbed in the writing of *Against Sainte-Beuve* until a point about the middle of 1909 when the process of creation became strong enough to shake off the theoretical ballast of that work, and Proust began to write the opening sections of a new version of his novel.

This version must be, or closely resemble, the preliminary sketch for a part of 'Swann's Way' which was published in *La Table Ronde* in April 1945. This sketch, according to Germaine Brée, is admirably written, as if in a single spate of inspiration.[75] The importance of the sketch, which need not be studied in detail here since it is virtually already *In Search of Time Lost*, lies in the fact that it has a structure leading to a spiritual revelation. A similar structure involving lessons taught by the two 'ways' was already present, as we saw, in Proust's 'agenda' for the 1908 version of the novel; but he has made a decisive addition: the truth is now revealed by an experience of involuntary memory, stimulated by a fork striking a plate.

In this way Proust has made the privileged moment, in the form of involuntary memory, the basis for a new kind of structure. The moment of recollection unites the narrator and the protagonist and thereby fuses together the two previously uncoordinated principles of structure existing in his work: the chronological structure of the 'narrative line', and the structure in depth created by the distance between the two 'I's, narrator and protagonist. Involuntary memory introduces the narrator into the narrative, he is now connected to the protagonist by a narrative thread which henceforth moves in three dimensions instead of two. In this way Proust opens to his novel a whole new dimension in which his people and episodes can proliferate on different levels which are all connected by a narrative structure developing around the progression in time of the 'I' who is remembered to the 'I' who remembers.

Involuntary memory, in bridging the distance between the two 'I's, makes perceptible the inner space of the novel. But this is a space made up of time seen in depth; once more, as with Rilke, we have arrived at a problematic dimension in which time is equated with space. This dimension need not be further explored here; it is sufficient to note that Proust was himself aware of its existence and that he symbolised it in a late episode of *Against Sainte-Beuve*. This is the passage describing the church at Guermantes, of which he writes: 'there time has taken the form of space, but it can easily be recognised'. Proust also makes explicit the link between this spatial sense of time and the act of remembering: 'One has the distinct feeling of passing through time, as when a memory from long ago comes back into one's mind.'[76]

Involuntary memory therefore provides Proust with the principle for the structure of his novel; at the same time it gives him the central theme of the book: the protagonist's progression towards the revelation of his artistic vocation and of the true nature of reality. The narrative structure thereby becomes a symbolic structure. At one stroke Proust has discovered both the form and the meaning of his novel. This has been made possible because he is no longer concerned with describing the privileged moment for its own sake, but sees it too as a part of the world of 'time lost'. He has solved the last and most fundamental problem posed by his future novel.

# CHAPTER FIFTEEN

## The Creative Process in the Late Period

### II. RILKE: 1910–1922

RILKE'S technique of visual contemplation, for the reasons discussed in Chapter Thirteen, became increasingly ineffective. By the winter of 1912–13, when he made a journey to Spain, the situation had reached the proportions of a crisis. 'I sit there and look and look until my eyes hurt,' he wrote, returning from a fruitless confrontation with the Spanish landscape, 'I show it and recite it to myself as if I had to learn it by heart and still I have not got hold of it.' At this point he realised the fundamental mistake of his earlier technique. He had overstrained his visual faculty, doing violence to his impressions by, as he put it, pressing them into his face; 'instead of penetrating me, impressions pierce me'.[1]

The technique of contemplation had been developed in order to achieve voluntarily the identification of subject and object characteristic of the privileged moment; Rilke had now lost this ability. Nevertheless the oneness with the outer world which it had made possible still remained his goal, as is made clear by a poem of this time, 'The Spanish Trilogy'. It begins with an explicit plea for identification with the landscape: 'Out of this cloud ... (and me)' – he goes on to list numerous features of the scene before him, interspersing them with the same parenthesis – 'Lord, to make a single thing.' The tone of the poem rises quickly to an almost frantic urgency: 'only out of me and what I do not know,/ Lord Lord Lord, to make the thing, the thing.'[2]

It is clear at once that Rilke here has departed completely from the manner of *New Poems*. Whereas he had been concerned there to achieve identification with the object contemplated by the suppression of self-consciousness, in 'The Spanish Trilogy' the 'I' remains prominent. In this respect, as in the invocation: 'Lord' and in the treatment of night rather than of daylight, Rilke seems closer here to *The Book of Hours* than to New Poems.

But there is an important difference between this poem and those of the early period. There Rilke used a stream of resonant language and imagery to obliterate the sense of a particular place and time. The separation between subject and object was overcome by the suppression of the objective world. But here the sense of a particular place at a particular time is clearly conveyed through details such as 'this cloud', 'this mountain', 'this river', while the 'I' too is preserved as a distinct entity, so that the identification of subject and object achieved earlier is impossible. Rilke seems to acknowledge this by his use of parentheses to separate the words 'and me' from the rest of the scene. This part of the 'Spanish Trilogy' is therefore illuminating in showing Rilke's intentions, but it does not show how they might be realised. He appears to wish to retain the clarity of description acquired during the middle period while reintroducing the 'I' which had been absent in that phase.

In the second part of the poem Rilke adopts a new approach to the problem of expressing the privileged moment. Now he no longer speaks of himself, but of a shepherd on a hillside at night, who is described as taking 'all the stars/ into his face'. Here Rilke is using an entirely different way of expressing the intimate contact between the man and the night than that attempted in part I of the poem. In order to see the full implications of these lines, we must first examine the particular meaning of the terms 'face' (*Gesicht*) and 'stars' (*Sterne, Gestirn*), as Rilke uses them.

As early as *The Book of Images*, as we saw in Chapter Eight, the stars were a motif associated with the privileged moment. This association continued in the following years, though mainly in poems not included in *New Poems*, such as 'Sunset (Capri)' (1907), and 'Night Walk' (1908). The connection between the privileged moment and the stars can be explained as follows: the stars forming a constellation have for Rilke the same kind of intense interrelatedness as the parts of a scene contemplated during a privileged moment. This is seen clearly in 'The Night of the Spring Equinox' (1907):

> doch drüber stehen, stark und diamanten,
> in tiefen feierlichen Zwischenräumen,
> die großen Sterne einer Frühlingsnacht[3]

but above them, strong, like diamonds, at deep majestic intervals, the great stars of a spring night stand.

The term 'face' is also connected to the privileged moment. From the time of *New Poems* it denotes the organ through which, by means of contemplation, man experiences a heightened visual awareness of reality. Examples of this are to be found in 'The Recluse' in *The Book of Images*, and in the poem with the same title in *New Poems*.

In this way the two terms symbolise complementary aspects of the privileged moment: that which is experienced and that which experiences. In bringing them together, as in the second part of the 'Spanish Trilogy', Rilke has therefore symbolically, if not actually, enacted the privileged moment. Yet this would be an artificial procedure which could hardly have satisfied him were there not, between these two symbolic terms, some deeper congruence which made their coming together not merely a juxtaposition but a true identification. Such a congruence does exist, however, because *Gesicht* (or the alternative terms *Antlitz* and *Angesicht*) can have an important second meaning in Rilke's poetry. It can itself express the sense of interrelatedness of the privileged moment:

> Nur manchmal, während wir so schmerzhaft reifen,
> daß wir an diesem beinah sterben, dann:
> formt sich aus allem, was wir nicht begreifen,
> ein Angesicht und sieht uns strahlend an.[4]

Only sometimes, while we so painfully mature that it almost brings our death, then: from everything we do not understand a face is formed, and radiantly beholds us.

The congruence between *Gestirn* and *Gesicht*, though latent in Rilke's poetry before 1910, gained new prominence through an experience during his North African journey of 1910–11. The Sphinx, contemplated at night, made an impression on Rilke which he described as follows: 'everything which is the world and existence took place on a higher stage where a star and a god silently faced each other'. Rilke is here presented concretely, in what is clearly a privileged moment, with the equivalence between the stars and the human face; it is to this aspect of the experience above all that he draws attention: 'it was unbelievable that this thing bore human features ... and that they were equal to its sublime situation'.

It is important to notice that the value of this privileged moment for Rilke does not lie primarily in the aesthetic pleasure it affords, as was the case in the middle period. The experience is now valued almost as a religious revelation. The equivalence Rilke sees between the human face and the stars seems to give him an insight into ultimate truth regarding man's place in the cosmos. He feels 'the conviction of connections and agreements ... beyond our comprehension'.

To express the relationship between the Sphinx's face and the stars, Rilke makes use of a concept which was central to *New Poems*: that of the mirror: 'This face had taken on the habits of the universe, ... the rising and sinking of skies had mirrored on to him enduring feelings.'[5] In the same letter, describing another Egyptian sculpture of a human head, Rilke introduces a further, related concept from *New Poems*: that of balance. The sculpture is able, he says, 'through the heightened ordering of a number of features, to create an equilibrium with the whole phenomenal world'.[6] In *New Poems*, these concepts had been applied primarily to the individual's experience of visible reality, although in some poems they had been used more widely to suggest man's relation to the cosmos. Now the cosmic implications take precedence and become a central concern of Rilke's poetry.

In the light of this discussion the importance of the shepherd in the 'Spanish Trilogy' can be more clearly seen. For Rilke the shepherd, exposed to the night sky like the Egyptian sculptures, occupies a privileged relationship to the cosmos. Like the sculptures, he takes on the qualities of the sky to which he is exposed: 'Have you not ordered shepherds' faces/ with more greatness',[7] the poet asks in one poem addressed to the night.

We saw in part I of the 'Spanish Trilogy' that it was Rilke's aspiration to achieve the same oneness with the night as that enjoyed by the shepherd. This aspiration, and an attempt at its realisation, appear in the poem last quoted; the poet, 'holding himself out' to the night, asks it: 'Work. Pass over as far as you can.' This is one of the 'Poems to the Night', written in the year following Rilke's return from Spain. In these poems it can be seen that he is exploiting a new way of achieving identification with the night, which goes beyond the unsuccessful attempt in part I of the 'Spanish Trilogy'. He now makes conscious use of the terms 'face', 'stars', etc., and the congruence established between them, in order to relate his own being to the night. In one poem, for example, he describes himself taking the sublimity of the night into his 'fleeting face';[8] towards the end of the poem, the aim of self-identification with the stars becomes fully explicit: 'Let there be only *one*/ single fearless Nature: this life and, yonder,/ that shaped constellation.'[9] In numerous other poems, the identification is attempted by more indirect means.

All these attempts at identification through exploiting the symbolic value of 'face', 'stars', 'night', etc., are, however, still directed towards realising the privileged moment as a direct experience. Although the use of language is symbolic, suggesting an indirect mode of experience, the prominent use of 'I', which is not symbolised, shows that Rilke is primarily concerned with the existential level of experience. For this reason the 'Poems to the Night' do not represent a significant advance beyond part I of the 'Spanish Trilogy', and it is noteworthy that many of them remain fragments.

The real significance of Rilke's adoption of symbolic terms in a central rôle is not seen in those poems in which 'face' is related closely to 'I'. The fundamental departure from previous practice lies in the fact that in 'face' and 'star' Rilke has now found two terms which can express objectively, that is, without reference to the 'I', the two poles – subject and object – of the privileged moment. Rilke's 'I' now is not necessarily involved when he introduces this experience.

A further point should be noted here: these two symbolic terms are really separate entities, despite the congruence between them. Their relationship to one another cannot be one of identification, such as was attempted by Rilke in some of the 'Poems to the Night'. It is more exact to see their relationship as that between an object and its mirror-image, or between a weight and its counterweight: the two terms are interrelated but apart, each reflecting and balancing the other. 'Face' and 'star' cannot be thought of without the space between them, and in several of the 'Poems to the Night' this space is represented. It is the medium in which the relation between 'face' and 'star' exists: 'How shall I hold out this face, that its feeling/ may permeate glacial alien spaces.'[10] The polarity of 'face' and 'star' creates a space, and the intense relationship between the two poles fills this space with tension. This tension-filled space is called by Rilke in a parallel context in a later poem 'heightened space'.[11]

As was seen in the previous quotation, the poet's feeling permeates this space as he seeks contact with the stars. We are now able to see emerging the fundamental structure generated by the symbolic expression of the privileged moment. The night and the stars are essentially distant and absent, and between them and man there is spread what in another poem is called a 'field of feeling'.[12] *Gefühl* ('feeling'), used to express an intensely-felt relatedness to the stars, is therefore a central concept in this poetry, and is in turn connected to Rilke's frequent symbolic use of 'heart'; for example: 'but so I exert my heart, flow out, and still/ the space has not enough'.[13] *Strömen* ('streaming') and *Fluten* ('flooding') are further important terms symbolising the flow of feeling between 'heart' and 'night'. The interplay between these two poles is symbolised by a flow which moves in both directions:

> Wer unterbricht,
> wenn du dort hin drängst,
> die Strömung? Keiner. Es sei denn,
> daß du plötzlich ringst mit der gewaltigen Richtung
> jener Gestirne nach dir.[14]

Who, when you strain to be yonder, interrupts the flow? No one. Unless it be that you suddenly wrestle with those stars' mighty direction towards you.

'Breathing', another important term, is a way of experiencing the flow of feeling: 'Did I not breathe from midnights/ ... such flooding',[15] and 'weeping' expresses, rather than grief in the normal sense, the nostalgic outflow of feeling from the 'face'.[16]

In the poetry written during these years, therefore, a number of terms are being absorbed into a common symbolic context, a 'poetic universe', a structure made up by a special use of language. This structure, as we have seen, has grown up around the experience of the privileged moment.

Into this symbolic structure the important figure of the angel is fitted. It has been seen that the structure contains a dimension of distance and absence separating man from the stars. It is this sense of distance above all which is symbolised by the angel, which exists as a powerful light on the extreme boundary of our awareness, in the vicinity of the pure configurations of the stars:

> Starker, stiller, an den Rand gestellter
> Leuchter: oben wird die Nacht genau

Man is related to the angel, and defined by this relation, as that which the angel transcends: 'We exhaust ourselves in unillumined/ hesitations at your base.'[17] Angels are beings permanently able to enjoy an intensity which is denied to man except at rare moments – 'Our white heat would be their coolness' – and they are at home in the heightened space which exists between 'face' and 'stars': 'See the angels feel through space/ with their never-ending feelings/ ... see, the angels blaze through space.'[18]

In Rilke's 'poetic universe', therefore, the privileged moment is represented not by one, but by a number of symbols, each of which expresses a certain aspect of the experience. The constellation of stars symbolises the totally interrelated order experienced during the privileged moment; the angel symbolises the intensity of this reality, and its superiority over normal human life, as well as its rare appearance, while 'space' symbolises the heightened awareness of space experienced in a privileged moment. *Bezug* ('relation') is a further important term; it expresses the heightened relationships existing in 'space', which are distinct from any relationship to a merely terrestrial object; in the night sky there is 'everywhere joy in relation and nowhere lust for possession'.[19]

In a similar way man, too, is represented by more than one symbol: 'heart' represents his capacity for feeling, and 'face' his faculty for experiencing external reality, particularly the visual faculty. In this way Rilke abstracts what are for him the fundamental terms of human existence, and omits those others which have no relation to the privileged moment.

It can be seen that in creating this symbolic universe Rilke is no longer trying to satisfy a need for the privileged moment as a direct experience on the existential level. Rather he is setting out the basic terms of an interpretation of existence in which the privileged moment is seen and presented symbolically as the most fundamental experience of life. This symbolic universe can be contemplated but it obviously excludes the direct participation of the existential 'I'.

Moreover, the structure of the universe itself symbolises the renunciation of the privileged moment as a direct experience. For, as we have seen, the axis of the structure is the distance separating the 'face' and the 'stars', that is, the distance separating man from the higher reality of the privileged moment. Though it is still the dominating experience, the privileged moment now dominates by its absence, it is experienced not as a possession but as distance – *Ferne*.

Rilke's poetic universe therefore embodies what he calls 'the spirit of most distant joys',[20] and *Ferne* becomes a positive concept in this poetry; 'I shall strip off my wishes and all other holds,/ and let my heart grow used to its most distant things'.[21] In this universe, in which the highest fulfilment of life is experienced only as absence and loss, man is defined as 'he who loses boundlessly'.[22] Similarly, angels do not exist to be actually experienced, but to be awaited in their absence.[23]

Paradoxically, it is this sense of absence which gives man his only link with the higher world. For his intense nostalgic feeling, flowing out as 'weeping' into space, creates a 'relation' which takes its place among those existing between the stars. So, in one poem, Rilke speaks of 'the curves of my longing through the universe', and calls them 'almost astral'.[24]

It can therefore be seen that the total structure which is now emerging in Rilke's poetry embodies the quality of interrelatedness which is characteristic of the constellation, of the mirror situation, and of the privileged moment in general. Rilke has renounced the privileged moment as a direct experience, but in so doing, on a symbolic level, he has made possible a more enduring possession of it. In the symbolic structure towards which his poetry is moving, man takes his place in a total order in which all is united by 'relations': the order of the privileged moment.

Having begun to create the basic structure of his universe, in which symbolised elements of the privileged moment are related together to form a kind of inner space, Rilke is able to place in this space other figures symbolising other dominant experiences of his life. In *New Poems* we saw that these cardinal experiences were represented by themes – those of love, childhood, death, the hero and the animal. In the poems now under discussion these themes are turned into symbols and incorporated in the symbolic universe.

Love is symbolised by 'the lovers'; as in Rilke's earlier work, the experience has two facets, positive and negative. The beginning of love is positive, because it brings a heightening of the sense of existence; as such it can be assimilated into the order of the stars: the fate of those soon to be lovers surrounds them 'like a constellation'.[25] But as soon as love becomes experience, its negative aspect appears. The lovers are no longer 'weightless on heavenly paths',[26] but are aware only of 'this helpless human heaviness'.[27] Similarly, in another poem, the lover is 'beside my centre, inexact,/ withdrawn from my relation to the world'.[28]

It should be noted in passing that in these poems 'centre' (*Mitte*) is a positive term denoting the centre of a system of 'relations' and connected to the idea of balance and weightlessness. As we have just seen, 'weightlessness' (*Schweben*) is another of the attributes of the privileged moment which have been taken over from *New Poems* and included in the symbolic structure. By associating love with these motifs Rilke incorporates the experience in his poetic universe. A further connection is through the motif 'heart' which, as the organ of feeling, is also involved in love. Love is seen as that which, as it becomes a human experience, distracts the heart from its relation to the angels.[29]

In this way love is assimilated organically into the symbolic universe. The hero is likewise related to the symbolic motifs: 'There he stands, visible afar, displacing/ destinies about another centre.' Because he is the centre of a system of 'relations', the hero has access to the order of the stars: 'At last/ his flourish flings him to the starry figures.'[30] The same process is applied to childhood. It is through childhood that we are raised above the level of trivial existence and are 'a place where heart and star are mingled'.[31] The dead child, too, remains a part of this symbolic world, subject to the law of weightlessness:[32] Rilke's poetic universe therefore includes the world of the dead. This is expressed also in connection with the hero: 'Together with the hero is: the circle:/ *One* plunging stream through birth and bloody death.'[33] To unite the two realms of life and death, the circle which, as we saw, was a fundamental motif in *New Poems*, is now taken over and used as a constitutive element in the symbolic universe.

A further important concept of *New Poems* which is included in the symbolic world is the 'smile'. This is used to express the positive experience of love,[34] and also the sense of contact with the stars.[35] Indeed, the 'smile', in its highest degree, is found not in the human face but in the starry sky. One of the 'Poems to the Night' begins:

> Ist dort nicht Lächeln? Siehe, steht dort nicht
> in Feldern, die von Fülle übergingen,
> was wir zu einem kleinen Aufblühn bringen,
> wenn wirs bemühn in unser Angesicht?[36]

Is not smile there? See, is not spread there, in fields that overflowed with fullness, what we bring to a little bloom when we constrain it into our faces?

We can now define the major advance which Rilke has achieved since the middle period. *New Poems*, as was seen in Chapter Ten, lacked overall unity because Rilke was unable to embody the dominant themes and motifs of the poems in a common formal framework. But now, in creating the symbolic structure of his poetic universe, he has provided such a framework. As a result, the themes which were previously linked only on the level of conceptual thought can now become an autonomous artistic structure.

Rilke is able to create this structure because he is no longer tied, as in the middle period, to the direct description of visible reality in a particular moment of time. Nevertheless, the visible world is not entirely excluded from his new structure. Rilke's world has its own landscape, in which elements from the landscape of the external world appear. But these elements are assimilated into the overriding symbolism. Landscape is not present as background, it is an integral part of the symbolic presentation of experience. This can be seen in the compound terms which occur frequently in the poems, such as: 'mountains of the heart', 'his feeling's peaks', 'mountains of the no-more', 'tree of rejoicing', 'towers of joy',[37] etc.

As these examples suggest, the dominating element in Rilke's landscape is the mountain and mountain-range. The mountain peak is both remote and, by its nature, related to the sky and the stars, and therefore has a natural place in Rilke's world. It is a symbol of distance, inaccessibility and difficulty of progress; it represents the hard terrain of human life, often called *Schicksal* – 'fate' – by Rilke, which is interposed between man and the distant radiance of the stars and the angel.

It is the existence of this distant light on the bounds of Rilke's universe which accentuates the unevenness of man's path through life and creates the relief of light and darkness which is now a primary feature of his landscape. This is made explicit in 'To the Angel':

> Unser ist: den Ausgang nicht zu wissen
> aus dem drinnen irrlichen Bezirk,
> du erscheinst auf unsern Hindernissen
> und beglühst sie wie ein Hochgebirg.[38]

Ours is: not to know the issue from the confines of our erring; you appear above our obstacles and light them up like mountain ranges.

Rilke's mountainous and starry landscape therefore has not only a symbolic, but even a religious significance, in its function of situating man's life in relation to the universe; and the distant splendour of his world gives it a quality reminiscent of the Transcendence of the Old Testament.

This remote, biblical landscape is strikingly removed from that of *New Poems* – the world of parks, trees and flowers, of brightly-lit objects seen at close quarters. The new landscape first appeared in Rilke's work at the end of *Malte Laurids Brigge* in the evocation of the crags of Les Baux in the symbolic episode of the Prodigal Son. Rilke's trip to Provence in 1909, which inspired that passage, undoubtedly played a large part in the creation of the new landscape. The assimilation of mountains into his poetic vision was carried further during his trip to North Africa in 1911– he wrote later: 'the Atlas Mountains in North Africa are among my sublimest memories',[39] – and likewise by the Spanish journey of 1912/13. On both these latter journeys Rilke was impressed by the symbolic, religious quality conveyed by the landscape. 'It is as if the Prophet was yesterday',[40] he wrote in North Africa, and he summed up his impression of the landscape around Toledo with the words: 'World, Creation, mountain and chasm, Genesis'.[41]

As may be seen in the case of the mountain, the elements of Rilke's landscape do not have a fixed symbolic meaning; rather they suggest a broad general context. It is not necessary here to study in detail that of other such terms – 'tree', 'tower', etc. – we need only note that the majority of the remaining symbols suggest less remote and more positive contexts, – 'tree of rejoicing', 'tower of joy', 'the valley of his arms'.[42]

The existence of this landscape enables Rilke to introduce into his symbolic world a further important motif from his previous work: the animal. As previously, the animal's spontaneity and lack of self-consciousness give it an enviable advantage over man. This is symbolised by the freedom with which it moves in the difficult terrain of the 'heart's mountains'; the mountain animals are 'secure', their consciousness 'intact'.[43] The common symbolic landscape now gives man the possibility of a more direct contact with the animal world: 'That the ibex [Capricorn] might, from the Zodiac,/ light with one bound on my heart's mountains.'[44]

At this point a further important characteristic of Rilke's symbolic world may be noted. In the discussion of mythical perception in the previous chapter, it was seen that in the world of 'mythical man' external objects are perceived not as neutral sense-data, but in terms of feeling. Rilke's symbolic landscape offers a clear parallel to this, and in such formulations as *Herzgebirg* (heart-mountains) *Jubel-Baum* (tree of rejoicing) the tendency to experience the world directly as emotion is taken to its extreme. Rilke's use of 'face' to describe intense configurations of reality might also be related to the 'physiognomic' quality of mythical reality referred to by Cassirer. Moreover, the introduction here of the idea of myth is in accordance with Rilke's own preoccupations during this period. Commenting on a book by Rudolf Kassner in 1911, he wrote: 'The passages about "mythical" man are magnificent', and added that their interest lay for him in their 'remarkable congruence' with his impressions in Egypt.[45]

In addition to the perception of the world in terms of emotion, Rilke's poems have other qualities of myth. The tendency to symbolise fundamental human aspirations and experiences by figures such as Rilke's angels, lovers, and children, etc., is a tendency inherent in religious mythologies as in all myth-making. Rilke not only creates his own mythical figures, but makes use of existing mythologies, classical and Christian, to present his themes, though the poems in which he takes this latter course, particularly when using Christian themes, are on the whole of a lesser quality and interest. He frequently introduces the figure of 'the god', partly his own creation, partly influenced by classical and literary connotations. This god appears in varying contexts, but generally symbolises the achievement of more-than-human perfection and full reality in contexts where the angel is inappropriate, such as war, as in 'Five Hymns', and above all, love, which 'is always wholly in him'.[46]

Finally, with regard to mythological parallels, Rilke's world, like that of primitive man as described by Cassirer, and like that of Proust, tends, as we have already seen in connection with the dead child and the hero, to override and deny the fact of death.

At this point, however, it should be noted that if Rilke's poetry at this time contains a consistent symbolic or mythical world, this world has not yet received systematic and unified expression. The picture of it drawn here has been inferred and reconstructed from references scattered throughout the poems and sketches written during these years. Rilke has not yet been able to embody his vision in a single work. What has been seen so far is that the possibility of expressing his vision now exists; its terms have been created, whereas they had not been created at the time of *New Poems*.

The attempt to give his world unified expression was begun in January and February 1912, when Rilke wrote the first two *Duino Elegies* and fragments of others. In the First Elegy he introduces in close succession many of the principal themes and motifs that have been discussed so far. The angel, the heart, the animals, 'a tree on the slope', 'the night, when the wind, full of celestial space,/ draws at our faces', the lovers, 'the spaces we breathe' – are referred to in the opening section of 25 lines. In the following sections the theme of love is further developed, and the hero-figure is introduced, as are the themes of death and the young dead.

The angel, existing 'behind the stars', reappears at the start of the Second Elegy, and is now presented more fully in relation to the symbolic landscape as 'chains of hills, dawn-reddened ridges/ of all creation'. In further images the angel is shown to subsume the attributes of higher reality: 'closed' movement, mirror-reflection, etc., which appeared in *New Poems* and, in a different way, in the poems written after 1910:

Räume aus Wesen, Schilde aus Wonne,[47] Tumulte
stürmisch entzückten Gefühls und plötzlich, einzeln,
*Spiegel*: die die entströmte eigene Schönheit
wiederschöpfen zurück in das eigene Antlitz.[48]

spaces made of essence, shields of bliss,[47] tumults of impetuous, rapturous
feeling and suddenly, singly, *mirrors*: drawing their own outflowed beauty
back into their own faces.

Man, in contrast, is shown as lacking the angel's ability to recuperate
its own being: 'For we, where we feel, evaporate away ... like dew
from the early grass/ our being lifts from us.'

It can be seen that man is here interpreted in terms of the angel:
without the angel, Rilke's vision of man could not be defined. To
attempt to live permanently in the state of intense consciousness enjoyed by the angel is beyond human endurance, as the writing and
aftermath of *Malte Laurids Brigge* had made clear. This is symbolised
by the words which appear twice in these *Elegies*: 'every angel is
terrible'.

To amplify his vision of man's limited nature, Rilke goes on in the
Second Elegy to elaborate further on the limitations of love. In the
Third Elegy, begun at Duino in 1912 and finished in the autumn of
1913, love is treated at length, and its position in Rilke's symbolic
universe established. The poet asks whether the lover's delight in his
beloved's face has not its source in the stars. Her features for him have
the quality of 'the pure constellation'.[49] It is noteworthy, however, that
this linking of love to the stars takes the form of a question.

After indicating some of the themes of the *Elegies*, we must look
briefly at their structure. The cycle begins with the words: 'Who, if I
cried out, would hear me from the angelic/ orders?' Rilke, at the
outset, expresses the renunciation of the attempt to summon the angel.
In so doing, he creates the space in which his work can exist – the
heightened space separating man from the stars which we have
studied. It is important to notice how, as the first act of creating the
work, Rilke establishes this central axis, the sense of distance, and at
the same stroke creates the atmosphere of intense nostalgic feeling
which fills this space: 'And so I hold back and swallow the call-note/
of dark sobbing.'[50] In this way a tension is built into the structure of
the *Elegies*. The angel is held at a distance but continues to exert a
dominating influence. Early in the Second Elegy the poet says: 'And
yet, woe to me, my song invokes you.'[51] The verb used here – *ansingen*
– expresses not an attempt to summon the angel, but the need to preserve the distant relationship to the angel which is essential to the
description of man's inadequacy which then follows.

A second feature of the structure of the *Elegies* which should be noted is Rilke's use, from the first line onwards, of the first person, which had been virtually absent from his poetry in the middle period. The 'I' of the *Elegies* suffers from none of the shortcomings of that of the 'Spanish Trilogy' discussed earlier. Whereas the 'I' of that poem was located and limited by a particular context in time and place, there are no such limitations in the *Elegies* which, because of their symbolic nature, transcend time and space.

The 'I' of the *Elegies* is the voice of the poet which comprehends and permeates the whole world of the poems. It is a generalised, impersonal voice, and it moves naturally to 'we' in contexts where the poem deals with the common human predicament: 'Who, alas,/ can we make use of?'[52] Later in the First Elegy, after showing the hopelessness of love, the voice addresses a 'you' (*du*) and the second-person is preserved as the poet evokes more particular memories than have appeared so far – impressions of spring, of the stars, a violin at an open window. The *du* addressed here is a part of the poet, the part which experienced these remembered scenes in his life. We recall a similar splitting of the poet into both 'I' and 'you' in *New Poems*. There, the split enabled the poet partly to cross over into the higher reality of the mirror and the privileged moment; the 'I' remained in 'this' world, while the 'you' moved in the poetic sphere. In the *Elegies*, this situation is reversed. The 'I' is the voice of the comprehending poet, the inspired voice. The 'you' is a former self still erring in the world of experience, unable to reach the higher plane which beckons him with signs on all sides:

> Das alles war Auftrag.
> Aber bewältigtest du's? Warst du nicht immer
> noch von Erwartung zerstreut, als kündigte alles
> eine Geliebte dir an?[53]

All that was a task laid on you. But did you perform it? Were you not still distracted by expectation as if all this were announcing a woman to love?

In this way Rilke delegates to the 'you' those elements which might limit and particularise the 'voice' of the poems. The 'I' remains above the level of experience, a pervasive medium of total consciousness in which the world of the *Elegies* exists. Rilke thus begins to solve the problem he had failed to solve in *Malte Laurids Brigge* where, as we saw, the confusion between the 'two Maltes', the Malte of experience and the more generalised, comprehensive Malte, destroyed the unity of the novel. The need to represent his life in an integrated whole had been one of the motives which caused Rilke to turn from *New Poems* to *Malte Laurids Brigge*. The novel did not satisfy this need; but now, in the *Elegies*, Rilke has found the means of doing so.

A third feature of the structure of the *Elegies* which must be noted here is the new rhythm used in the poems. The truly 'static' element of *New Poems* was their rhythm, which imposed a perpetual 'ritardando' so that each image, and almost each word, could be contemplated separately by the reader much as the poet would contemplate a 'Thing'. In the *Elegies* the opposite is the case. The rhythm is the dominating element giving the poems unity and movement. There is a 'taking hold and letting go of things' such as Rilke had admired in Dauthendey's work not long before (cf. p. 187). This mobility is accompanied too by what Rilke saw in Dauthendey's work: a sense of space created in the reader, an inner dimension of the work.

The *Elegies* and fragments written at Duino were the product of a sudden inspiration which marks a sharp break from the manner of composition of the middle period, the controlled creation produced by contemplation and work. The inspiration broke off after these poems – part of a larger totality – were written. Only isolated fragments were produced during the years which followed.

To explain why Rilke was unable to finish the work at this stage, it is not necessary to attribute the break merely to a caprice of inspiration. A more specific reason becomes apparent if the fragments already written are examined. In the *Elegies* Rilke had begun to work out a coherent mythology, a symbolic image of man's life. We have seen that in this period he had a quasi-religious sense of his task. He was not just writing poems, but fixing man's place in the universe. In the *Elegies* discussed so far, man was shown negatively in relation to the angel. But this is not sufficient to constitute a religious message; man's rôle in the space created by the renunciation of the angel, that is, in the world symbolised in the *Elegies*, has yet to be made clear.

In a fragment of an Elegy written in March 1912 at Duino, the question of the purpose of man's life is asked: 'why, then, have to be human'.[54] In another fragment, written between the First and Second Elegies, Rilke attempts to give an answer. Here the poet asks if his function is that of praising the world, in particular the cities, 'the great constellations of the earth'. It is noticeable, however, that this is put in the form of a question. Rilke tries to affirm that he loves the present (line 6), but he is forced to doubt whether the present has need of his song of praise, when a more passive participation would suffice – he need only 'vibrate in unison'. He realises that his song has no place in the 'metal action' of the modern age, and now falls back on the more modest function of praising the vanishing past, 'not accusing, but/ once more admiring'.[55] But this is now a very limited and clearly inadequate message for a work of religious scope, and the fragment is soon broken off.

H

This unsatisfactory solution betrays a fundamental confusion in Rilke's intentions at this stage. In appealing to the present, or the past, for his justification, Rilke is trying to base the meaning of the *Elegies* on what is normally accepted as reality – 'the interpreted world' – which, however, had been rejected early in the First Elegy. In the *Elegies*, and in the poetic universe which they express, the world is reinterpreted by Rilke in an autonomous system which implicitly denies reality to the world of normal experience. But in the fragment just discussed he has tried to cross from one order of reality to the other as if the separation between them did not exist. He has not fully realised, therefore, the implications of his symbolic manner of writing: that it involves the creation of a world, which, for him, supplants the world of external reality. The created world is an inner world, in a sense which will be discussed more fully later. The technique of contemplation of the middle period created an adherence to the outer world which Rilke has not yet broken. As we have seen, as late as the 'Poems to the Night' he still tries to make use of the symbols of his created world to achieve an experience in the outer world.

In a poem entitled 'Turning-Point', of June 1914, this confusion in Rilke's attitude is explicitly recognised. This poem, and that immediately preceding it, express a crisis of his artistic conscience, a radical questioning of the implications of contemplation. The poet asks what happens to the impressions which this technique of vision violently appropriates in the external world. They are, he now finds, oppressed and neglected within him. The world finds no love within this depersonalised recipient and finally refuses to be assimilated. The neglect of the inner world therefore leads to a loss of contact with the outer world also. Contemplation, Rilke now realises, is ultimately a self-limiting experience and progress lies in a new direction:

> Denn des Anschauns, siehe, ist eine Grenze.
> Und die geschautere Welt
> will in der Liebe gedeihn.[56]

For, see, there is a limit to looking, and the better-seen world wants love to flourish in.

In a letter to Lou in connection with 'Turning-Point' Rilke throws further light on this problem. He writes that he is 'wretchedly turned outwards' and that this over-exposure has driven his life into an 'innermost place' where it exists in a state of siege. Only rarely, he says, does this inner life make its existence felt by producing fragments of Elegies.

It is the aftermath of the middle period, therefore, which is blocking the completion of the *Elegies*. Rilke's creative faculties, which he here

divides into 'face' and 'soul', have become estranged; this estrangement he now recognises as the cause of his sterility.[57] 'Turning-Point'
expresses his decision to abandon the outward-looking activity of the
'face' in favour of the inner faculty:

> Werk des Gesichts ist getan,
> tue nun Herz-Werk
> an den Bildern in dir, jenen gefangenen.[58]

The work of the face is done, do now heart-work on the images imprisoned
within you.

'Face' is the faculty concerned with the outer visible world, whereas
'heart' as J. Steiner notes, is 'the organ of the inner self'.[59] Rilke's
realisation that his creation is no longer part of the outer visible world
is reflected in poems written soon after 'Turning-Point': 'For over the
inner landscape/ unsayable skies are spread,/ invisible.'

The term 'invisible' now becomes a central concept in his work. It is
the essential attribute of his inner world, which is opposed to the world
of experience, of *Schicksal*, for which Rilke reserves the term 'visible':
'One thing is Fate. There men grow/ more visible.'[60] The change of
emphasis from 'visible' to 'invisible' does not mean that Rilke has now
lost all interest in the visible world. But it means the end of the indis-
criminate assimilation of impressions as an end in itself. Impressions
taken in now must be related to those already assimilated, must be
'mastered, peacefully and tidily lodged in me'.[61] This is what is implied
by 'heart-work'.

This development does not therefore involve a turning away from
the outer world altogether, but the end of the technique of contemplation and an exclusively visual approach to reality. As might be expected, Rilke's attitude to the other arts is affected by this change. In
the middle period the visual arts had been the source of his inspiration,
while music was rejected; now his attitude to music is reversed. Music
is the art which has direct access to the 'heart' and intensifies the sense
of the inner life: 'My heart: *there*:/ see your splendour', says the poet
in one place, pointing to the music 'raised up before the heart'.[62] But
the value of music does not lie only in its power to intensify the inner
life. After the exhaustion of visual contemplation, it seems to Rilke to
provide a new means of assimilating the external world. This is made
clear in a letter referring to his Spanish experience: 'there I sat and was
at the end of my eyes, as if one would have to become blind around
the images one has taken in, or ... in future receive the world through
an entirely different sense: music, music: that would have been it'.[63]

This statement might seem to indicate, contrary to what has just
been argued, that Rilke still has not broken his contact with the outer

world: he has merely exchanged one way of experiencing it for another. There is justification for this view; but there is also a real change in his standpoint. The visual technique had led to a breach between inner and outer worlds; music provides a bridge between them. In music the world is experienced in a 'more dissolved' form which is already adjusted to the needs of the inner life and can be absorbed with 'an almost effortless joy'.[64] Rilke's attitude to the visible world can therefore now be more clearly defined. He is still interested in visual impressions, but only in so far as they conform to the demands of his inner world.

We have arrived at a paradoxical, indeed seemingly self-contradictory, concept: music as a means of absorbing, not sounds, but visual impressions. A major part of our task in the remainder of this chapter will be to clarify this concept. In a letter to Benvenuta, to whom we shall return in a moment, Rilke describes the experience which made him aware of the power of music to influence visual perception. In contemplating the Sphinx in Egypt Rilke had found his visual faculty unable to grasp the full reality of the face, particularly a certain curve of the cheek. Suddenly, however, the secret was totally revealed: the flight of an owl brushing the line of the cheek had translated the visual impression into one of sound, and this had been assimilated by the poet: 'now the contour of that cheek was inscribed as if by a miracle on my hearing which the hours of nocturnal stillness had made quite limpid'. Rilke concludes this description by remarking: 'With a few exceptions, my music up to now has always been like that.'[65] But he hopes from his future acquaintance with the significantly-named 'Benvenuta' – a professional pianist – a further initiation into the world of music; he expressed the belief that her music would be as helpful to his development as Rodin's sculptures had once been.[66]

But in his new attitude to music Rilke had not turned away from the visual arts as if they had taught him nothing. In a letter of 1916 he explained that without the more disciplined receptivity they had taught him he would have been unable to make use of music, which previously had merely submerged him in oblivion (*Vergessen*). Now with the firm sense of reality acquired during the middle period, he sees a possibility of controlling the previously dangerous power of music and using it to lift him to a higher level of existence, at which a new way of seeing, 'with fresh and rested eyes', would begin.[67]

A description of the 'musicalised' visual awareness with which Rilke is concerned here is given in the important prose passage entitled 'Experience I', written during his stay in Spain. Using the third person, Rilke describes an experience he had had at Duino about a year previously, shortly before writing the first two Elegies. Walking in the garden he leaned against the forked branch of a tree, in which restful position he sank into 'an almost unconscious contemplation'. This relaxed state is clearly different from the highly deliberate and strenuous visual technique he had practised earlier. In the next sentence he refers to 'a feeling he had never known before' which is at the root of the experience: 'it was as if barely perceptible vibrations were passing into him from inside the tree'. This mode of contact with the world gives him a finer receptivity than he had ever experienced. His body, as he expresses it, was 'being treated like a soul':[68] the estrangement referred to earlier between 'soul' and 'face' is here abolished. A subtle intimation is passing from the outside world direct to his inner being, through a sense which he cannot at first specify; though it includes the visual sense, the latter has been transformed, affected by a sense of 'oblivion' (*Vergessen*) such as he attributed to music in the letter just quoted. The scene immediately confronting him seems like a world long forgotten:

> Slowly looking about him ... he recognised everything, remembered it, smiled to it with, as it were, remote benevolence, left it alone like something in which he had been involved long ago, under circumstances which had ceased to concern him.

This 'forgotten' world has about it a quality which we have met before – that of Proust's 'time lost' as described in the last chapter. Both writers see the world as detached from their personal existence, but whereas Proust saw 'time lost' only in memory, Rilke here experiences it in the present. Like Proust's remembered world, the reality which Rilke perceives has a heightened intensity; he sees the world in the way described in the letter just quoted, 'with fresh and rested eyes':

> He looked after a bird, a shadow engaged his attention, even the path, as it went on its way out of sight ahead of him, filled him with a thoughtful comprehension.[69]

As was the case with 'time lost', interest is no longer restricted to those aspects of the scene which are relevant to an immediate practical purpose. Every detail takes on a radiance and importance of its own; a flower, for example, that he had often passed by, now 'affected him with such inexhaustible significance, as if nothing more were to be concealed'.

This heightening of visual impressions and of the meaning they convey is of course an essential feature of the privileged moment. The other primary quality of the privileged moment, unity, is also prominent in Rilke's experience. This unity, however, is not perceived in visual terms, but as a rhythm in time, communicated by the vibrations passing 'at strangely intense intervals' from the tree to his body. Because of this rhythm, the sense of time as succession is not banished from the experience, as is normally the case during a privileged moment; its continued presence is indicated by such phrases as 'telling himself from time to time that this could not last'.[70] This, however, is not the sense of time characteristic of normal life; the difference between them must now be explained.

It was seen in Chapter One that the unity of awareness experienced during a privileged moment could be of a primarily spatial or of a primarily temporal order. In the privileged moments described by Rilke previously, particularly those of the middle period, the spatial aspect was predominant. The two privileged moments in *Malte Laurids Brigge*, for example, were characterised by a spatial inter-relatedness of all parts of the scene. In deriving the concept of the 'Thing' from the privileged moment in the middle period, Rilke concentrated on the spatial aspect of the experience. The *Gesetzmäßigkeit* of the 'Thing' – its conformity to inner laws – was seen in terms of 'space' and 'eternity', while time, as the succession of moments, was expelled and virtually equated with chance. The expulsion of time as succession was effected, as we saw, by the notion of the 'closed movement'.

'Experience I' shows, however, that 'chance' can be eliminated from awareness without eliminating time as succession. The dominating element in this experience is rhythm: succession is not eliminated but ordered, and, by being ordered, accentuated. Awareness of passing time is not excluded, but is given a sense of necessity absent from normal experience. This conception of rhythm does not, however, mark a complete break with the concept of the closed movement. For rhythm, too, presupposes a closed and completed structure within which it exists, as can be seen in 'Experience I'. As in music, the end of the state of awareness is implicit in all its parts, but because of its necessity, this end can be contemplated with equanimity: 'all the same, he did not fear the end of the extraordinary state, as if one could expect from it, as from music, only an infinitely ordered [*gesetzmäßig*] closing'.[71]

The experience of rhythm in 'Experience I' helps us to understand the new importance of music for Rilke. He saw now that the essence of music was order in time; because of this, music's power over him could now be turned to creative advantage: the 'unique seduction' of music can be permitted as long as it 'seduces to order, to law itself'.[72] This conclusion was reached at about the time 'Experience I' was written.

The *Gesetzmäßigkeit* of music has a further important aspect for Rilke: because of it, music shares the essential quality of the 'constellation'. The equivalence between music and the stars in this respect is made explicit in the ode to the composer Bellman: 'Bellman, set your notes/ like stars assembled in the Plough'.[73] Similarly in one of the 'Poems to the Night', the sky is called a 'nocturnal music-sheet no player ever mastered'.[74]

The parallel between Rilke's ideas and those of Proust re-appears at this point. 'Swann's Way' was published in November 1913, and Rilke was one of the first to express admiration for the 'Combray' section of the novel. But he had less sympathy for 'Swann in Love', finding it 'often no more than a "novel"'. There was, however, one section in it which he singled out for praise: 'the passages towards the end about the phrase in the Sonata and about music as something which had been touched only here and there, at unconnected intervals, on the numberless keys of the universe'.[75]

Because of its affinities with the stars, music becomes involved in the preoccupation with ultimate, cosmic truth, which, as we have seen, was becoming prominent in Rilke's work. Behind the 'wall of sounds' formed by music, 'the universe draws near, on one side are we, on the other ... trembles the inclination of the stars'. Rilke is not here concerned with the sound-effects of music as such, or the pleasure they give, but with the 'other side' of music, its formal dimension which he calls 'the silent part of music ... its mathematical reverse side'.[76]

This notion of the 'other side' of music is in turn bound up with Rilke's notion of death. In one poem a ghost is seen as having access to the 'other side' of a bird-call, the side which is 'turned away from us'.[77] In this way music becomes a means of contact with the dead; it 'breaks the silence' between the living and the dead.[78] There is a similar situation in 'Experience I', where Rilke sums up his changed relation to reality by saying that he had 'got to the other side of nature'.[79] It is this which gives his vision its detached quality; he feels like a ghost returning from elsewhere and remarks that it would have caused him no surprise in this state to meet people long dead.

Rilke's notion of death as the 'other side' of life, which became prominent in his work during this period, is one of his most 'metaphysical' and inaccessible conceptions. But in a letter of 1915 he shows how it can be related to more familiar ideas. He argues that from earliest times men have projected the most terrible aspects of their experience on to gods, in order to achieve a more manageable relationship to them. In this way an intense part of man's experience has been renounced from the outset in order to facilitate an 'existence adapted to use and efficiency'. In particular, this process of repression through externalisation has been applied to the idea of death, which has become 'something external, held at a distance from day to day, lurking somewhere in emptiness'. In this way the full experience of life has been, as it were, short-circuited, giving rise to what Rilke calls 'the smaller cycle of the merely this-worldly ... so-called Progress'. In a world falsified in this way, he says, life in the full sense, far from being simplified, has been made impossible. For example, love, if it is to be fully experienced, transcends this one-sided world: it 'pays no attention to our divisions, but tears us, trembling as we are, into an infinite awareness of the whole'.[80] Life, experienced fully, therefore has a quality of wholeness, for which Rilke frequently uses the term *Vollzähligkeit*.

Rilke's notion of a total sphere in which death is a part of life therefore expresses symbolically the psychological truth that in an intense vision of reality, nothing can be repressed. He saw Tolstoy as having achieved such a vision of reality, permeated by 'the most finely-divided death'. This element of death gives his awareness a heightened intensity, it is 'a distinctive spice in the strong flavour of life'.[81]

During the years under discussion, Rilke saw it increasingly as his task to recapture the sense of the wholeness of life which had been destroyed by the externalisation of the idea of death. He had begun to express it in the first Elegies, particularly in the passage where he writes that the living make too sharp distinctions and that angels are often unaware whether they are among the living or the dead: 'The eternal stream/ forever bears all ages through both realms/ upon its flood and drowns their sound in both.'[82] But this vision of wholeness had been soon broken off. In 1913 Rilke wrote to Benvenuta of 'That life in the mind that I have been struggling for in all these indescribable years (in the mind, do you understand, which is so immensely mind that it can draw everything into itself and exclude nothing.'[83] The task of achieving and expressing this vision was bound up with the quasi-religious aspiration now prominent in his work. In 1915 he wrote that he was seeking to find and show 'the Old-Testamentary point where the terrible coincides with what is greatest'.[84] But the total sphere also included another dimension, that of his own past. In another letter of about the same time he wrote that the consciousness he was striving towards must include his whole childhood, 'everything that he was', so that he might have in himself 'the place which is also a cosmic place'.[85] It can be seen here that Rilke's purpose of discovering an ultimate religious and cosmic truth was, for him, identical with the search for completeness in his own inner life. In this he might seem to attribute undue significance to his individual existence. On the other hand, no reality can be perceived except through mental forms and concepts corresponding to it; during this period Rilke was working to produce such concepts.

A concrete example of what is meant by this is provided by his experience in Spain in 1912. It was here that he first had glimpses of the total sphere he had been striving towards in the preceding years: 'now it is to be the whole, shall I be able to bear it?'[86] To describe this reality Rilke cannot make use of terms derived from normal experience; he uses those taken from the vocabulary of his own inner world. Thus Toledo is 'full of law', it has 'starry presence'.[87] To sum up his impression of Toledo as a whole Rilke says the town is 'there in the same measure for the eyes of the dead, the living and the angels'. Rilke's experience can only be grasped through the terms he has elaborated in the preceding years. He himself gives an indication of this when he says: 'I am still astonished how much I was prepared for every detail of it.'[88]

Rilke's impressions in Spain therefore contained as an integral part the means by which they might be expressed; a letter of 1915, recalling the Spanish experience, makes this explicit:

> the outward thing itself: tower, mountain, bridge, already possessed the incomparable intensity of the inner equivalents through which one would have wished to represent it.[89]

It became a law of Rilke's sensibility that he could only experience reality intensely if he possessed such 'inner equivalents', which in a letter of 1919, he called: 'the felt inner parallel to it, through which alone the impression is made an experience'.[90]

The intensity of the experience in Spain resulted from an identity between inner and outer worlds, between object and vision: 'outward appearance and vision everywhere came together, as it were, in the object'. Because of its identity with the inner world, the object perceived in this way no longer appears simply as a part of the external world, and in the letter of 1915 quoted above, Rilke went on, in a somewhat esoteric formulation, to try to convey the new dimension in which it exists: 'in each object a whole inner world was exposed, as if an angel who encompasses space were blind and were looking within himself'. Rilke here is aware that he is moving towards a new conception of his vocation – and we must remember that it was the lack of such a conception which interrupted the *Elegies*: 'This world, contemplated no longer from the human standpoint but within the angel, is perhaps my true task, at any rate all my earlier endeavours would come together in it.'[91]

The feeling of correspondence between the inner and outer worlds discussed above is expressed in the important poem of 1914 which begins: 'From all things, almost, is a call to feeling' (*Es winkt zu Fühlung fast aus allen Dingen*). But in this poem, the correspondence is not one between the outer world and mental equivalents as in the Spanish experience, but between the present and the past. The unifying act is one of remembering the past: 'from every turning it is borne to us: Remember!' A past day, that we 'passed as strangers', is now

restored to us through a coincidence with the present, and the coincidence creates a sense of unity extending through time: 'Who separates/
us from the old, the vanished years?/ What have we discovered from
the first/ but that one thing is recognised in others?' In such moments
of recognition and unity the external world suddenly takes on the
intense configuration denoted by the second meaning of the term 'face'
and becomes an immediate, intimate experience:

> O Haus, o Wiesenhang, o Abendlicht,
> auf einmal bringst du's beinah zum Gesicht
> und stehst an uns, umarmend und umarmt.[92]

O house, O meadow slope, O evening light, suddenly your features
almost form a face and you stand tight against us embracing and
embraced.

This poem, in which 'what was indifferent is rekindled', is therefore
concerned with a privileged moment produced by involuntary memory. We have seen that involuntary memory played a part in Rilke's
earlier poetry, but in this important poem it achieves a new prominence. It is probable that in this development Rilke was directly influenced by Proust, though the term 'influence' implies here, as always, a
pre-existing affinity between the authors concerned. 'Swann's Way', as
already mentioned, was published late in 1913 and Rilke was one of its
first admirers. His early response is recorded in a letter of January
1914, in which he draws attention to the experience of involuntary
memory: 'it is very beautiful, too, how the "madeleine" dipped in tea
makes the whole of the past accessible to the grown man, gives it back
to him: all of time lost'.[93] In the poem just quoted Rilke uses the same
term – 'a gift' – to describe the past remembered in this way. His letters
to Benvenuta in early 1914 contain frequent references to Proust's
novel, and also a new preoccupation with the remembrance of his own
childhood.[94]

Towards the end of the poem *Es winkt zu Fühlung* Rilke reaches a
conclusion which introduces a new concept central to his late work, the
term which designates the unity between inner and outer worlds experienced in this poem through involuntary memory:

> Durch alle Wesen reicht der *eine* Raum:
> Weltinnenraum.

Through all beings spreads a single space: world-inner-space.

The relation of 'world-inner-space' to the creative process in this
period must now be explored. We have seen that this term refers to a
coincidence of inner and outer worlds to form a single space. The same

is true, however, of normal perception; any awareness of external reality involves a complex and indissoluble interchange between external objects and internal mental concepts. The difference between normal perception and that described by Rilke lies in the intensity with which reality is experienced. Whereas the external world is normally experienced as a neutral background, in 'world-inner-space' it has the highest possible intensity, to describe which Rilke has evolved special terms. As we saw earlier, 'space' and 'feeling', used in this poem, have intensely positive meanings; elsewhere he uses the expression: 'the world contemplated in the angel', to describe the experience.

It must be discovered why, in 'world-inner-space', the process of perception has this special intensity. Rilke's answer would be that in this experience he perceives a different and more intense reality than ours – the full reality of *Vollzähligkeit*. But it could be objected that a symbolic reality of this kind cannot be an object of perception since it is not real in the empirical sense. The question of the ultimate reality of Rilke's world need not, however, arise here. For the same question applies to all reality. Since Kant we have known that the external world has no absolute being but is determined by the *a priori* mental forms through which we perceive it. Rilke himself was aware of this truth: 'For the body too is body only in the mind.'[95]

The only aspect of reality which is open to empirical analysis is, therefore, these *a priori* mental forms. In examining them we shall discover the difference between Rilke's experience and our own. It is necessary, therefore, to analyse the forms, that is, the structure and composition, of the 'inner world' through which Rilke experiences reality. Firstly, what do we mean by this 'inner world'? We have seen that Rilke's inner life has two aspects in this period. On one hand, there is the 'life in the mind', which should ultimately encompass all being, including his past, of which he writes to Benvenuta. On the other hand, there is the symbolic universe analysed at the beginning of this chapter, which Rilke is building up in his poetry during this period. As we saw, this universe is an attempt to give unified expression to the meaning of his life. At the same time, both this and the 'life in the mind' are seen as a means of gaining access to the ultimate truth of the universe.

It is clear that all these are inseparable aspects of the single thing which may be called Rilke's inner life, and that the poetic universe is the expression of this inner life. As was seen in the Spanish experience, terms elaborated in the poetic universe are used to express the experience of 'world-inner-space'. The inner life can therefore be equated with the world of language which Rilke is creating. In discussing the properties of the poetic universe we are discussing the properties of the inner life.

Previously we were concerned with the content of this universe; now we must turn to its structure, since it is through this structure that Rilke perceives reality in 'world-inner-space'. It was seen earlier that the poetic universe was built up on the axis between man and the angel, that it incorporated a principle of polarity. This polarity also took other forms, such as that between 'face' and 'stars', and there was not only a distance separating the poles, but a resemblance between them, a tendency to come together. It was this that gave the universe its tension.

The relation between the poles is analogous, as we saw, to that between an object and its mirror-image: these, too, belong together yet cannot be united. In some poems the mirror-relationship is explicit;[96] implicitly, however, it has a far wider application. It is a fundamental law of the poetic universe that each thing should be reflected by others: 'Where is one thing that knows not of the other?'. The mirror-relationship, in which 'part and counterpart delicately surmise each other',[97] underlies Rilke's frequent use of compounds of 'counter' – gegen – in these poems, particularly in relation to love[98] and the 'life in the mind'.[99]

The mirror-theme is predominant in these poems as in New Poems; but it is present now not only as a theme but as a law of composition. As in New Poems the motif is accompanied by those of 'balance',[100] and 'weightlessness', which are now also embodied in the structure. The quality of total interrelatedness inherent in the constellation and in the whole of this universe is called 'the weightless relation' – der schwebende Bezug.[101] A further motif related to the idea of balance is 'centre', with its frequent attribute 'exact'.[102] Balance is expressed by all these motifs and is a fundamental structural law of the poetic universe. But there is a further important aspect to the structure: the balanced relationships between things in it are not static but dynamic.

Movement is the second fundamental characteristic of this universe. As was seen earlier, the central axis embodies a flowing movement: Strömung. Movement is also expressed by the motif Schwung, which might be approximately translated by 'swing', 'flourish', 'élan'; Schwung is an attribute of the highest categories of existence, and is applied to the stars[103] and to the angels.[104] The movement embodied in Rilke's universe is not a single, isolated movement. It conforms to the law of balance, each movement having a complementary opposite movement. We have already seen that the central axis consists not only of the 'streaming' of man's feeling towards the angel, but also of the 'direction' of the angel opposing it. Such complementary movements frequently form a circle: in a previous quotation the circle-motif was related to the hero – a single stream flowing through birth and death. Here, as in the lines of the First Elegy quoted on p. 232, we see that the closed movement is essential to Rilke's conception of the total sphere of life and death: the circle is another of the motifs of *New Poems* which have now become structural elements of the poetic universe. What we have seen, therefore, is that Rilke's inner world now embodies the qualities of the 'Thing' of the middle period. And as a result his inner world now has the same superiority over the outer world as the 'Thing' had over the reality surrounding it:

> Draußen Welten, Welt –, wieviel, wie vieles –;
> aber wer beschreibt
> Glück und Übermaß des Gegenspieles,
> das in uns Gesicht und Wesen treibt.

> Draußen Lüfte, Grüße, Wünsche, Flüge,
> Übertroffenheit, Betrug –,
> aber innen blühende Genüge
> und der unbeschreibliche Bezug.[105]

Out there worlds, the world –, how many, how diverse –; but who can describe the joy and the excess of the interplay that has its face and being in us.

Out there breezes, greetings, wishes, flights, being bettered and betrayed –, but within a blossoming abundance and the indescribable relation.

Like the 'Thing', the inner life is now characterised by *'Gesetzmäßigkeit'*: a total interrelatedness produced by the laws of balance and closed movement. Like the 'Thing' too, by virtue of these qualities, the inner life is cut off from the world around it. Being related only to itself, it is, for the outside world, non-existent. This situation is symbolised in one of the 'Narcissus' poems:

> Er liebte, was ihm ausging, wieder ein
> und war nicht mehr im offnen Wind enthalten
> und schloß entzückt den Umkreis der Gestalten
> und hob sich auf und konnte nicht mehr sein.[106]

He loved what went out from him back into himself and was contained no longer in the open wind and in delight he closed the ring of forms and cancelled himself out and could no longer be.

Being totally self-contained, Narcissus cancels himself out of existence. In the same way Rilke himself does not now exist in the outer world: 'Just as, truly, *I* am not./ For I live, you know it, within,/ where nothing can be grasped.'[107] Rilke's only existence now is in the world of language, in the poems expressing his inner life: 'See, I am not, and yet if I were/ I should be the centre of the poem.'[108]

The parallel traced here between the structures of the 'Thing' and the 'inner world' shows a fundamental continuity between the middle and late periods. The development which has taken place can be expressed as follows: Rilke has abstracted from the 'Thing' its chief attributes and used them as the structural principles of his inner world. He has made this possible by translating his experience and themes into symbolic terms which can be interrelated independently of the laws and conditions of the external world – gravity, chance, etc. – as an artist can arrange his material to form a 'Thing'.

Moreover, this interpretation of Rilke's development is not only a hypothesis; it corresponds to a consciously formulated decision of his own. In 1909, contemplating a fountain, which, as was seen in the chapter on *New Poems*, is for Rilke, like the thrown ball, a perfect manifestation of the ideal 'closed' movement, he wrote the following lines:

> Daß aus Aufsteigendem und Wiederfall
> auch ganz in mir so Seiendes entstände:
> O Heben und Empfangen ohne Hände,
> geistiges Weilen: Ballspiel ohne Ball.[109]

That from a rising up and falling back such being might appear in me: O lifting and receiving without hands, the mind's abiding, ball-play without a ball.

The fountain and similar structures became a kind of model for Rilke. In contemplating them he found it less difficult than at other times to recognise parallel movements in himself. A poem of April 1910 describes such an experience; 'so faltering and endlessly/ expressionless is what makes up our inner being', the poet writes, that we are suddenly helped by the sight of a fountain, with the relation of its bowls and its jet which 'coolly, involuntarily, and from above,/ forever sets a centre in the stillness'.[110] In a similar way in another poem, he looks for an equivalence between the movements in the night sky and those of his inner life. Contemplating the 'rising and descent' of the stars he asks: 'Do ebb and flow succeed each other/ in my blood according to this order?'[111] A later poem, of 1914, reveals that Rilke has begun to make progress in the direction indicated by these quotations. The stars now act as a kind of regulative pattern governing the movements of his inner life; as he raises his eyes from his book to the starry sky he describes this reaction: 'Oh, how the congested feelings range themselves, conforming to the stars.'[112]

We can now see more clearly the form taken by Rilke's efforts to achieve what he called 'That life in the mind that I have been struggling for in all these indescribable years'. The interpretation we have arrived at is reinforced by numerous formulations in the letters of this period.[113] The attainment of such a deliberately re-constructed inner life was a slow and uncertain process. But the goal towards which Rilke was striving, if it was only infrequently glimpsed at first, was clearly conceived, as can be seen in this passage from a letter of 1913 to Lou:

> If only, instead of all the confusing externals of time, I could keep my gaze fixed on this serene interior world of the crystals, which are unshaken by anything accidental and in which only the pure wheeling courses (*Umschwung*) of the stars are internalised to become an intimate, enclosed activity.[114]

More and more, Rilke experienced his own lived existence from the standpoint of this passage, in terms of the symbols and structures of his inner world. Thus he saw himself as forming with Benvenuta the ideal couple of 'the lovers', communicating to each other like stars[115] and related together like perfect movements: 'You great you greater circle around the infinite circle of my heart.'[116] This can be more easily understood if it is remembered that their relationship was established from a distance through letters. We can understand, too, his fear of actually meeting Benvenuta, of being, as he put it, 'born into the visible'.[117] When they did meet, the relationship soon came to a distressing end. Rilke's wife and daughter, from whom he lived separately, were for him a world which had no part in the patterns of his inner life: 'it does not really belong in the constellation of my heart, which rises and sets in solitude'.[118] That his mother, too, was a refractory element, can be seen from the poem: 'Oh woe, my mother is destroying me.'[119]

It is apparent from this that the inner forms and structures through which Rilke, more and more, now experienced reality, exerted a selective influence, tending to exclude from his life those elements which could not be assimilated. This was true not only of persons but also of places, even of certain parts of Paris associated with Rodin and a discarded past, which he could not see 'without everything in me, decomposed by sharp memories, taking on a new structure, coming to a standstill, growing rigid, and, if at all, re-composing itself only slowly and in different forms'.

Places which do not conform to the structures of his inner world are for Rilke a 'distraction into the external'[120] and he avoids them. This explains the restlessness of his existence, in which he moved from place to place in search of a spiritual homeland – *Heimat* – conforming to his inner needs: 'So it inevitably happened that I acquired homelands of adoption according to the degree of correspondence, that is, I could not resist inventing a heredity for myself wherever the visible possessed the quality of images which somehow matched more exactly my instinct's expressive needs.'[121] Toledo and Ronda briefly afforded such a *Heimat*, but Rilke's most stable home during the pre-war years was Paris, which corresponded most completely to his inner structures. In 1912 he described what was for him the essence of Paris as follows:

> its totality and multiplicity in which everything seems reciprocally to cancel itself out, to such an extent that only a weightless vibration of it, resonating together, remains in the air, like a temptation to something which in that moment has already ceased to exist[122]

If this vision of Paris is compared with what a 'realistic' or empirical description might be, we can see how far Rilke has progressed in his ability to see outward reality in terms of the structures of his inner world, and how far his vision of reality differs from our own. But from the fact that this vision was confined largely to Paris, and to parts of Paris, we can see that, at this time at least, Rilke still needs a measure of help from reality, a prior correspondence between elements in the outer and in the inner scene. These elements are isolated from the scene and then 'fed back' in intensified form to produce the vision.

This process seems to have taken place in Rilke's experience of the Spanish landscape. Although, as we saw, this experience would not have been possible if he had not already possessed inner equivalents which he projected on to the scene, nevertheless the outward landscape did to a certain extent determine or at least reinforce the nature of his inner landscape. This is stated in a letter of 1919:

> Spain was the last 'impression'. Since then my nature has been driven from within (repoussé work), so strongly and constantly that it can no longer be 'impressed'.[123]

Rilke's comparison of his perception of reality to 'repoussé work' – metal-work beaten into relief from the reverse side – makes it possible to take further the analysis of 'world-inner-space'. We should note that the existence of an inner 'poetic universe' is not in itself sufficient to constitute 'world-inner-space'. The latter only comes into being when the inner world fuses with the outer world in a moment of experience. This fusion, as we saw, can take two forms: a coincidence either between past and present impressions, or between external reality and an inner equivalent created by the mind. This latter form of the experience might be called the creative form.

But, as has already been noted, all experience is creative in this sense. Outward sense data do not present reality 'ready-made' to a passively recipient mind: the mind has to create order and meaning from them by isolating elements corresponding to the concepts and forms which it holds in readiness, and by discarding, excluding from awareness, those which do not correspond. The difference between this and Rilke's experience lies in the forms and concepts which his mind has at its disposal. Those of normal experience are of a predominantly practical order: in general, concepts define the uses of objects, structures embody the functional relations between them. But Rilke, by cultivating his inner life in the way studied, has replaced the concepts of normal experience by his symbols and motifs, and the relations of normal experience by his special balanced movements. Therefore, his mind isolates, and discards, different elements in reality than does the normal mind.

The special structures which his mind can isolate may be designated by his terms *Schwung* and 'curve'. But the term which is most appropriate and comprehensive, as Beda Allemann has shown in his detailed study, is *Figur*. The heightened formal order which Rilke's 'figures' impose on reality gives the experience of 'world-inner-space' its special intensity. The need to discard what is irrelevant to this formal order is what gives 'world-inner-space' its distinctive 'inward', isolated quality. The forms perceived are so complete and self-contained that to perceive them the rest of the external world, normally present as the background of consciousness, must be excluded completely. This throws light on Rilke's words in Spain: 'one would have to become blind around the images one has taken in', and on the otherwise mystifying language he used to describe the things he experienced there: 'a whole inner world was exposed in each object, as if an angel who encompassed space were blind and were looking inwards'.

The experience of 'world-inner-space' therefore involves the projection of 'figures' on to the external world. It is now possible to approach more directly the nature of the creative process in this period. 'Figures', as we saw, have as an essential attribute movement, and therefore time. To constitute 'world-inner-space' they must involve the dimension of time in the external world. Time is therefore fundamental to the creative form of 'world-inner-space' as to the form involving involuntary memory.[124]

Time as flux and transience, represented chiefly by the terms *Vergehen* (passing away, vanishing) and *Abschied* (departure), achieves a new prominence in Rilke's poetry of this period, and a new positive meaning. It is no longer opposed negatively to eternity and space in the simple manner of the middle period. Although space and its attributes remain positive and central concepts their relation to time as succession has become far more complex.

Transience is now for Rilke an inescapable condition of our existence, without which we could not experience reality at all: 'only what can pass away belongs to you./ Incomparable fate, to be in vanishing.'[125] Rilke's creative task is that of projecting 'figures' on to the element of transience. This reveals a further aspect of his renewed interest in music. By the balanced interplay it creates in time, music achieves in sound the structures corresponding to the 'ball-play without a ball' of the inner world. Thus it forms a bridge between the latter and the outer world of sensation. In this way it makes the inner world perceptible to the senses and creates a form of 'world-inner-space'.

Music achieves its effect not by destroying but by exploiting the sense of passing time, chiefly through rhythm. Rilke expresses the same idea in the ode to Bellman when, using a play on words, he suggests that music 'celebrates' the transience which is inherent in existence but which also makes possible the positive aspect of 'parting':

> Zwar ist uns nur Vergehn,
> doch im Vergehn ist Abschied uns geboten.
> Abschiede feiern: Bellman, stell die Noten
> wie Sterne ...[126]

Because of its internal order or *Gesetzmäßigkeit* music is able, as we saw earlier, to create self-contained structures in time – we might now call them 'figures' –, and thus to interrupt the continuity of time as normally experienced. By cultivating transience to the utmost, music therefore provides a liberation from it. This is expressed in the poem 'To Music', of 1918: 'You time,/ standing vertical upon the paths of hearts that pass away.'

This 'vertical' time presents a clear parallel to the 'total' time created by a closed movement. The opening lines of the poem reinforce this parallel: 'Music: breathing of statues. Perhaps:/ the stillness of pictures.' Rilke seems here to be referring intentionally to the opening poem of *New Poems*, 'Early Apollo', where the breathing of the statue provides the necessary circular movement of the poem (cf. p. 118). Nevertheless, there has been an important development in the notion of 'higher time' since the middle period. There, the 'total' time of the 'Thing' was essentially cut off from the onlooker's existence: to experience it he had to annihilate all self-consciousness by the technique of contemplation; he was entirely 'turned outwards'. But now that Rilke has brought the structure of his inner life into conformity with the laws of the 'Thing', it is able to participate, through the 'higher time' of music, in the outer world. It is indeed through music that the inner world becomes perceptible, as we have just seen. By linking it with the world of the senses, music externalises the inner world, and surrounds us, in 'world-inner-space' with a part of ourselves normally inaccessible to experience:

> Du uns entwachsener
> Herzraum. Innigstes unser,
> das, uns übersteigend, hinausdrängt, –
> heiliger Abschied:

da uns das Innre umsteht
als geübteste Ferne, als andre
Seite der Luft:
rein,
riesig,
nicht mehr bewohnbar.[127]

Your heart-space grown away from us, most intimate of ours which, transcending us, breaks out, – holy departure: when what is inward surrounds us as most accomplished distance, as the other side of the air: pure, immense, no longer inhabitable.

Here, 'departure' – *Abschied* – is positive because it represents a crossing-over to a higher order of existence, the 'other side' of nature. It is a death into the true life. *Abschied* has the same positive value in 'Experience I', where the world took on 'a bold sweet tang, as if all had been spiced with a trace of the bloom of departure'.[128] In this way *Abschied* is related to Rilke's notion of death as an element permeating and intensifying the perception of reality: 'a spice in the strong taste of life'.[129]

'Parting' therefore, in Rilke's sense, is concerned with the quality of perception. Music too, as 'holy departure', affects the perception of the world, rather than merely arousing disembodied emotion. In music, feeling and the world are one; this is expressed in the remaining lines of the poem 'To Music', which therefore have decisive importance for the question raised earlier in this chapter concerning the rôle of music as an agent in perception: 'Feelings for whom? O you who are feelings/ transformed into what? Into audible landscape.' Rilke's expression 'audible landscape' shows how far by now the orders of music and vision, time and space, have been fused by the concept of the 'figure' and how far, in this period, the creative process must involve both together.

To pursue the inquiry into this creative process further, it should be noted that for Rilke music is not the only means of experiencing the 'vertical' order of reality. In a letter of 1920 he wrote that 'all our deepest delights' are 'independent of duration and succession', and that they 'stand vertically on the directions of life as death too stands vertically on them'.[130] In this letter Rilke is concerned particularly with love as such a 'vertical' experience. The following poem throws further light on the nature of these 'deepest delights':

Du nur, einzig du *bist*.
Wir aber gehn hin, bis einmal
unsres Vergehens so viel ist,
daß du entstehst: Augenblick,

schöner, plötzlicher,
in der Liebe entstehst oder,
entzückt, in des Werkes Verkürzung.[131]

You only, you uniquely *are*. But we pass away, until there is so much of our passing that you arise, sudden, beautiful moment, arise in love or, delighted, in the work's foreshortening.

As might be expected with Rilke, these sudden moments of 'deepest delight' can here be recognised as privileged moments. Like music, the privileged moment now involves not a suspension of time but an accentuation of it: 'until there is so much of our passing'. But privileged moments of this kind depend on certain conditions; their occurrence is limited to love and 'the work'.

The relevance of love here may be briefly explained. Love remains for Rilke a 'privileged' experience because it begins with a heightening of the sense of existence. But it is by its nature impermanent: *Abschied* is implicit in it from the start. Love must therefore be accepted as both a rising and a falling experience; this is the hard lesson of these years, which causes Rilke to write to Benvenuta: 'to speak of love is to speak of hardness'.[132] But because of its inseparable upward and downward movements, love can be seen as a 'figure' and, as such, belongs to the highest order of experience. This ideal vision of love is expressed in a poem of 1921:

Kurve der Liebe, laß sie uns zeichnen. Ihr Steigen
soll uns unendlich rühmlich sein.
Aber auch später, wenn sie sich neigt –: wie eigen.
Wie deine feine Braue so rein.[133]

The curve of love, let us trace it. Its rising shall be to our endless glory. But later too, when it falls –: how fitting. As pure as your fine eyebrow's line.

But in the present context it is with the second kind of 'delight', arising in 'the work's foreshortening', that we are primarily concerned. We noted earlier in connection with the Spanish experience that Rilke was only able to experience reality intensely through a creative act involving an 'inner equivalent'. The nature of this act is now becoming clearer. The next section of the poem just quoted, in which the privileged moment is addressed, is as follows:

Dein bin ich, dein; wieviel mir die Zeit auch
anhat. Von dir zu dir
bin ich befohlen. Dazwischen
hängt die Guirlande im Zufall, daß aber du sie
auf- und auf- und aufnimmst:
siehe: die Feste![134]

Yours I am, yours; whatever the hold time has on me. From you to you I am commanded. Between, the garland hangs in time, but that you lift it up, and up, and up: behold: the feasts!

Rilke's expression here is necessarily figurative. Nevertheless, in the context now established, certain meanings can be clearly inferred. The creative privileged moment is the dominating goal of Rilke's life. It is seen as a series of points where the 'garland' of life, normally hanging in the realm of time and chance, is 'taken up'. These points are 'feasts', a word used from early on by Rilke to denote the creative privileged moment.

Above all, the idea of 'lifting up' – *Aufnehmen* – is stressed in this stanza. In interpreting its meaning, we should remember that it is characteristic of Rilke to exploit the multiple meanings of compound words and expressions; *Abschied feiern* – to 'celebrate departure' – was a recent example. Here *aufnehmen* means 'to lift up' but it can also mean 'to take up', as a movement is taken up by a matching movement. In the 'feast' the flux of time is 'taken up' by 'the work's foreshortening'. In the abbreviated compass of the poem – for with Rilke 'work' can have no other meaning – experience in time is ordered and foreshortened: ordered by the formal devices of poetry, particularly rhythm, and foreshortened in that the significant elements in an experience, that is, those corresponding to a 'figure', are taken up, and the rest is excluded.

The poem is therefore a means of projecting a 'figure' on to existence; and through the poem, as through music, the poet has contact with the 'other side' of experience, as is suggested by Rilke's statement: 'The poem enters language from within, on a side which is forever turned away from us.'[135] Poetry, through its sounds and images, provides a bridge between the inner and outer worlds. Thus, like music, it externalises the inner life and makes it perceptible. In the moment of creation the poet's inner world is identified with the outer world: 'When you hear your own voice soar,/ then the world sings, then your stars are sounding.'[136] But the identification is mediated through a 'figure' involving free and perfect movement. This demands a spontaneous and effortless process of creation far removed from the patient labour of the middle period. The poem is now a brief and sudden outpouring, like bird-song. The poet can only wait for the moment which will surround him with his inner world: 'Bird, how you reach out/ for your heart. Who may/ hope that inner things/ might so spring forth from him.'[137] Such an experience can only take place within the word-structure of the poem. It is only within his world of language that the poet, in moments of inspiration, escapes the destructive force of time as chance, into 'vertical' time and total being:

Wie doch im Wort die Flamme herrlich bleibt.
Die Zeit geht hin und kann sie nicht verwehen.
Nur daß ihr Gang auch uns, wenn wir geschehen,
ins Innre dieser Wort-Gestalten treibt.[138]

How in the word the flame stays splendid. Time goes past and cannot put
it out. Only that its going drives us too, when our moment comes, into the
interior of these word-formations.

Conceived in this way the poem does not offer the poet a permanent
escape from transience. The existence of the poem implies an 'ordered
closing', like that of 'Experience I', after which the poet is again in the
world of common time, the 'garland' again hangs in the realm of
chance and must be lifted by a new 'figure'.

This conception of poetry is reflected clearly in Rilke's ode to
Hölderlin, written in 1914. Hölderlin was an important influence on
Rilke in these years, both in the formation of the inner symbolic world
– Rilke's use of 'the god' and 'holy', for example is clearly prefigured in
Hölderlin – and in the return to a strongly rhythmical verse. Hölderlin
was for Rilke in this period what other 'influences' – Jacobsen, Rodin,
to a lesser extent Dauthendey – had been at different times: idealised
embodiments of an achievement towards which Rilke was groping. His
vision of them reveals his own unrealised aspirations, to him as to us.
It is this aspect of the earlier poet which is valuable for this study, and
appears with extreme clarity in 'To Hölderlin'.

The first section expresses the necessary mobility of the poet who
must move from 'figure' to 'figure' in a world of transience:

Verweilung, auch am Vertrautesten nicht,
ist uns gegeben; aus den erfüllten
Bildern stürzt der Geist zu plötzlich zu füllenden; Seen
sind erst im Ewigen.

To linger, even at the most familiar, is not granted us; from the filled
images the spirit is flung to others suddenly to be filled: lakes are only in
eternity.

The second section shows Hölderlin as expressing the whole of life,
which includes death; for him 'a whole/ life was the urgent image, ...
a death was/ even in the gentlest line'. In the third section this universal vision achieved through mobility in time is contrasted to the
limited existence of poets who take refuge in the false eternity of the
particular poem: 'O you roaming, you most roaming spirit! How they
all/ already live in the poem's homely warmth, dwelling/ at length in
the narrow comparison. Taking part.' Rilke seems clearly in these lines
to be repudiating his own *New Poems* where, as we saw, metaphor –
now 'the narrow comparison' – was a principal means by which the

poet achieved identification with the particular 'Thing'. Rilke exploits
the double meaning of *teilnehmend* – 'taking part' – to contrast such
poetry with his ideal of 'wholeness'. Unlike these limited poets, Hölderlin, in perpetually passing on, achieves the experience of what is later
to be called 'audible landscape', made possible by the positive implications of 'holy departure': 'You alone/ wander like the moon. And
below grows bright and dark/ in holy fright your nightly landscape,/
which you feel in departures.' Hölderlin appears to have realised the
ideal of the poet in a world of transience: Rilke even sees Hölderlin's
final madness as enabling him to experience the world permanently as
'world-inner-space'. For him, the inner world is constantly externalised:

> So auch
> spieltest du heilig durch nicht mehr gerechnete Jahre
> mit dem unendlichen Glück, als wär es nicht innen, läge
> keinem gehörend im sanften
> Rasen der Erde umher, von göttlichen Kindern verlassen.

So also you spent years, no longer counted, in holy play with the unlimited
joy, as if it were not within but lay all around, belonging to no one, in the
gentle grass of the earth, abandoned by divine children.

The closing lines of the poem show explicitly that this is the state towards which Rilke too aspires: 'Why do we, when such an eternal one
was,/ still mistrust the earthly.'[139]

In a letter to Benvenuta the same aspiration is expressed; what he
wanted, he wrote, was 'to pass everywhere from looking and joy into
the law – for there one's tread is light, and there is no weariness'.[140] As
the word 'looking' implies, Rilke is still concerned with the visual world
in his poetry. But this is no longer the painful and deliberate visual
preoccupation of the middle period. The poems he writes towards the
end of the phase now under discussion, both in their rhythm and in
their visual quality, have a lightness and movement which are new in
Rilke's poetry:

> Schmetterling, das meine und das ihre,
> der Natur und meins, wie du's verbrückst:
> *unser* Glück, wenn du an dem Spaliere
> leicht, wie in Entwürfen, weiterrückst.

Butterfly, what is mine and hers, Nature's and mine, how you bridge it:
*our* happiness, making your way along the espalier with movements lightly
drawn, like sketches.

Here, the flight of the butterfly provides a 'figure' bridging the outer
and inner worlds: 'now you have drawn by glance's thread/ into the
weft of April'.[141]

It is now clear that Rilke's development in this period is leading him towards two distinct kinds of poetry. The first is the *Elegies*, the completion of which remains the chief purpose of his life.[142] The second is the short, essentially effortless poem involving the projection of a 'figure', which in 1919 Rilke referred to as 'a flourish [*Schwung*] under the open sky of life'. The spontaneous nature of such poetry, as well as its relation to 'figure', is indicated when Rilke adds: 'And that it would like to inscribe a trace in the space it has crossed is a sudden fancy of this flourish, no more.'

In the same letter, written to a young poetess, Rilke connects this kind of creativity to the presence of 'an inner spaciousness' and 'a sound from the centre of your inner space'.[143] A similar sense of an inward music at the origin of creation is expressed in Rilke's poetry by such phrases as 'There, the heart is giving sound.'[144] Here a parallel to Proust's development in the corresponding period can be clearly seen; for Proust, as we saw, creation became the pursuit of an inward melody, and the artist's task was to 'produce the true sound of his heart'. (Cf. p. 208.)

Fundamental and indispensable to both these kinds of poetry, however, is the achievement of the unified inner world discussed earlier. The *Elegies* are the attempt to give systematic expression to the symbolic inner world. The *Schwung*-poems unite this inner world with the world of the senses. For Rilke, who spent long periods in these years without writing anything, the actual production of poems was ultimately secondary to the attainment of the inner state he desires:

> Creation too, even the most productive, only serves the establishing of a certain inner constant, and art is perhaps only so much because a few examples of its purest formations testify to the attainment of a more reliable inner adjustment.[145]

Elsewhere, he writes of the work of art as a means to the end of achieving 'a sounder condition at the centre of one's own being'.[146]

Rilke's progress towards such an inner state, begun about 1910, was interrupted by the war, which obliged him to leave Paris for the less congenial Munich. He tried at first to assimilate the war into his symbolic inner world by seeing it as a god revealing to men a new, higher level of reality and pain. But events soon proved him mistaken and thereafter 'not understanding',[147] as he put it, was his only occupation during the war years.

The break with Paris and the world he knew dislocated the movements and unity of his inner life. In 1919 he was still unable to feel the slightest trace of inner movement: 'the point of intersection of my forces has lost its stellar quality, it has fallen out of the great constellations which used to give it shelter and support in mental space'.[148]

The Fourth Elegy, written in 1915, symbolises Rilke's inner state during these years. He is unable to detect in himself the desired configurations of feeling – 'We know not the contour/ of feeling' –, but resolves to contemplate the empty stage of his inner life in the hope that the absent quality might finally appear. He visualises as the ideal performer on his inner stage a combination of the puppet, which, lacking the hindrances of normal self-consciousness, is free to perform pure, balanced movements, and the angel, a consciousness capable of giving these movements the widest possible significance. Embodied in such a being, the inner life would encompass the total sphere: 'Only then is formed/ out of our seasons the circle of the whole performance.'[149]

The end of this period of stagnation was reached in October 1920, when a visit to Paris restored Rilke's sense of inner continuity. 'My consciousness has given up its restrictions,' he wrote with elation, 'the standing about on the same spot has finished, I am circling again in my consciousness.'[150] Soon after this, further good fortune made it possible for him to spend long periods in a new landscape congenial to him, first at Schloß Berg am Irchel and then at Schloß Muzot in the Swiss Valais, where he lived from July 1921 to the end of his life.

His description of the landscape around Muzot makes it clear that Rilke had found at last the 'homeland' conducive to his inner development. The following passage from a letter of September 1921 is representative of many others; the landscape derives its special character from the effect of the light:

> the light ... participates indescribably, creating an event in every interval and filling the distance from one thing to another with such particular tensions that they (trees, houses, crosses, chapels and towers) seem to be held together in the same pure relatedness which unites the single stars for our gaze in a constellation.

This tension-filled distribution of things seems, Rilke goes on, to 'generate space'.[151] In other letters he calls the landscape 'biblical' and speaks of the appearance of the mountains as 'imaginary ... like reflected images of mountains'.[152]

In this landscape, therefore, the special qualities we have been concerned with in this chapter are resumed. Rilke has found the perfect outward equivalent of his inner vision. Under its influence he is able to approach again the 'life in the mind' in which past and present, living and dying, form a unity. 'And even life and death! How open are the ways from one to the other for us,' he writes in a letter of November 1921, and he goes on, as if with bated breath, 'how close, how close to almost-knowing it, how almost word already is this this, in which they rush together in an (as yet nameless) unity.'[153] As he writes these words Rilke is on the verge of creation, he is again on the threshold of the world to which he had brief access at Duino in 1912: the world of 'wholeness' which is also a world of language.

# CHAPTER SIXTEEN

## *The Final Works*

THE *Duino Elegies* and *In Search of Time Lost*, despite their obvious differences of form, have one essential feature in common. They are both concerned with the fundamental question: What is life? and they both attempt to answer it by the same means: by the creation of a symbolic structure.

In *Time Lost\** an important element in the symbolic structure is provided by the series of social reunions running from the beginning of the novel to the end and occupying a particularly prominent place in the two central sections, 'The Guermantes Way' and 'Cities of the Plain'. These social scenes not only give Proust an opportunity for social satire or for recording the historical process by which the bourgeoisie invaded the upper regions of society; on a more general level the *monde* of high society is symbolic of the world itself, as is shown explicitly by such phrases as: 'that gallery of symbolic figures which is the "*monde*"'.[1] For Proust, the study of people's behaviour in society reveals laws applicable to human behaviour in general. Society life in its pure form is only 'a simpler problem initiating us into difficulties which are more complex but of the same order'.[2]

The driving force in social life as depicted by Proust is the desire of individuals to achieve a higher position in the social hierarchy, a desire which is frustrated by the exclusiveness of the social circles above them. The inaccessibility of these circles heightens their attraction; the individual becomes obsessed by the need to penetrate the *salons* closed to him. He can attempt this either on his own or as part of a social group, exemplified by the Verdurins' 'little clan' which raises itself up in society by assimilating elements from above it and repulsing those below.

The principle that whatever is inaccessible must be desirable is seen to operate on all levels of society. For example, Françoise automatically considers Tante Léonie superior to the visitors she refuses to receive. But it is in high society that this principle is seen in its purest form, for here social life consists solely of a complex etiquette of visits and invitations. The only values existing in this world are those conferred by the status of the people whom one admits to one's *salon*.

The hostesses' concern for the composition of their *salons*, their horror of admitting anyone who might 'make a blot'[3], appears as the pursuit of an almost aesthetic ideal, a cult of perfection. But Proust

* This abbreviation of the title will be used throughout the chapter.

makes it clear that this is a misapplied perfectionism with egoism at its root. This fundamental criticism of society is built into the structure of the novel. Each of the social reunions in 'The Guermantes Way', for example, is prefaced by a section which undermines social values in advance. Mme de Villeparisis' matinée is introduced by a summary of her own social decline brought about by her too-acute intelligence. The Guermantes' dinner is preceded by a description of Elstir's paintings which proclaim the nullity of outward appearances, on which social values depend. But most damning of all to the values of society are the scenes which immediately precede and follow the soirée given by the Princesse de Guermantes. As they leave for the soirée, the Duc and Duchesse de Guermantes show themselves more concerned with the colour of Oriane's shoes than with the news that their old friend Swann is dying. After the soirée, in order to be able to go on to a fancy-dress party, the Duc dismisses the news of the death of a relation as 'exaggeration'.[4] The same word is used later in an almost identical context by M. Verdurin,[5] the repetition underlining its symbolic value.

M. de Guermantes, with his heartless complacency and his fatuous speech, and Mme de Guermantes, whose dazzling wit reveals not intellectual depth but an insatiable need for egoistic gratification, symbolise the moral and intellectual nullity of the highest aristocracy. Their only interest, in the absence of further social heights to conquer, is the pursuit of pleasure. But because of 'the impossibility of finding pleasure when one is content to seek it',[6] Mme de Guermantes derives only disgust and irritation from her social brilliance. Nevertheless, lacking all other resources, she becomes addicted to society – hence her sterile effusions to momentary confidants and her horror of facing the end of a soirée.

Those lower down in society, who are still impelled by the illusory attraction of anything beyond their reach, are presented by Proust as puppets driven on mechanically by an inhuman force. The essential nature of the snob, who, as we noted, has symbolic implications regarding human nature in general, is revealed in a scene early in the novel where Legrandin is shown in the act of achieving a brief success:

> Rapt in a kind of dream, he was smiling, then he came hurrying back towards the lady and, as he was walking more quickly then he was used to, his shoulders oscillated ridiculously from side to side, and, given up to it so entirely, without a care for anything else, he seemed the inert and mechanical plaything of pleasure.[7]

Rilke, in the Fifth Elegy, also gives a symbolic representation of human life. The acrobats he describes, like Proust's snobs, are driven on by a relentless force – the will to achieve perfection in their chosen activity. But, as in the case of the snob, there is in this perfection, when

it is achieved, a sterility which leads to ennui and shows their goal to
have been an illusion. Their act is compared to a flower fertilising
itself without pleasure:

Um diesen
Stampfer, den Stempel, den von dem eignen
blühenden Staub getroffnen, zur Scheinfrucht
wieder der Unlust befruchteten, ihrer
niemals bewußten, – glänzend mit dünnster
Oberfläche leicht scheinlächelnden Unlust.[8]

Around this pounding pestle, the pistil, touched by its own dust's pollen,
fertilised again to the false fruit of disgust, disgust never recognised
beneath the thin shining surface of its faint, false smile.

Their perfection is 'that empty too-much':[9] virtuosity achieved in a
meaningless activity. Towards the end of the Elegy the image of the
acrobats is extended to include 'the restless paths of the earth'; the
whole of human activity is seen as analogous to that of the acrobats.

In this way both Proust and Rilke place in a dominant position at the
centre of their works a generalised image of human life. In both
images man's existence is seen to be governed by an implacable will to
realise a certain notion of perfection. In both cases, when the goal is
reached no sense of fulfilment results, but only a feeling of emptiness
and ennui. And in both, this result springs from the same causes. For
the kind of activity involved in each case is one directed towards an
outward goal, involving active participation in the world of men. The
snob's sense of his own value depends on the consensus of opinion of
the social world. The acrobat depends both on his fellow acrobats and
on the 'rose of onlooking'[10] for the success of his performance.

What Proust and Rilke symbolise is therefore the futility of attempting to satisfy human aspirations in the pursuit of any external goal.
This message is underlined by Rilke in the next Elegy, the Sixth, in
which he introduces the figure of the hero who attains the ultimate
that can be achieved in terms of action. But although the hero's existence does gain an enviable intensity from his ability to live constantly
in the face of danger, it is clear that the ideal he represents is in practical terms unrealisable; it can only be an object of longing, the dream
of a boy: 'O were I,/ were I a boy and might still become it.'[11] In
Proust's novel the same message is underlined in a different way by the
repeated disappointment of travel – another attempt to gain satisfaction by reaching an outward goal.

But in presenting these images of society and of the acrobats, Proust
and Rilke also show the existence of another possible way to fulfilment,

an inward way. Towards the end of 'The Guermantes Way', Proust writes: 'We can at our choice give ourselves up to one or the other of two forces, one arises from ourselves ... the other comes to us from outside.' It is only the latter force, the current which 'tries to introduce into us the movement agitating people outside us', that is involved in social ambition and its ennui. It is devoid of pleasure; but, Proust goes on, we can supplement it in social life by 'an intoxication so artificial that it quickly turns to boredom, to sorrow; whence the doleful faces of so many men of the world'.[12]

Rilke, in the Fifth Elegy as in the Fourth, shows likewise that the theatre of outward action is paralleled by an inward theatre. It must be remembered that the *Elegies* form a continuous sequence, a development reflecting Rilke's own long development discussed in the last chapter. The Fourth Elegy, as we saw, symbolised a point in this progression when the poet's inner life lacked the sense of balance and movement which he saw as his goal. The Fifth Elegy expresses a similar situation: the state of the poet's inner life corresponds to the acrobats' first unsuccessful attempts to master their act:

> Wo, o *wo* ist der Ort – ich trag ihn im Herzen –,
> wo sie noch lange nicht *konnten*, noch von einander
> abfieln, wie sich bespringende, nicht recht
> paarige Tiere; –
> wo die Gewichte noch schwer sind[33]

**Where, o where is the place – I bear it in my heart –, where they were still far from virtuosity, still fell off each other's backs like animals ill-made for mating; – where weights are still heavy.**

Inwardly, the poet is still in this 'laborious nowhere'.[14] But because it is an inner state, it contains the possibility of a real fulfilment unlike the sterile virtuosity of the acrobats. The Elegy ends with a vision of lovers, who, perhaps, realise inwardly what the acrobats achieve outwardly – 'their bold/ high figures of the heart's swings [*des Herzschwungs*]'. But it must be stressed that this is only a glimpsed possibility, presented in the conditional and as a question. It is not a final statement, but an intuition pointing towards the definitive interpretation of love in the Seventh Elegy and beyond that to the message of the Ninth and Tenth Elegies.

Rilke therefore, after exhausting the possibilities of fulfilment offered by external action, turns to love as an experience which is more inward and perhaps more capable of giving fulfilment. The same development is present in Proust's novel. Marcel,* after discovering the illusory nature of the social world, begins to find behind the façade

---

* For convenience it will be assumed that this is the name of the protagonist.

of society a new dimension of reality – the hidden world of love and, more particularly, of vice.

In this world too, as in society, men are seen as propelled by an insatiable desire for gratification and pleasure. Nevertheless, for Proust, love is a far more valuable area of experience than that symbolised by society, just as Charlus, who now begins to dominate the book, is a figure of far greater stature than the Duc or the Duchesse de Guermantes. Proust's conception of the relative values of society and love, and of the similarity of the laws operating in both, is revealed clearly in the following observation: 'It seems that in society life, an insignificant reflection of what happens in love, the best way of being sought after is to refuse yourself.'[15]

Love, for Proust, is an inward experience in that the lover does not fall in love with a real person but with an image in his mind which has arbitrarily attached itself to a person. The lover believes, however, that he can gain fulfilment by possessing that person, he seeks in outward reality what exists only in his mind, and thereby condemns himself to the pursuit of an illusion. This conception of the subjective and illusory nature of love is accentuated in the novel by the prominent place given to homosexuality, which is for Proust only a more extreme form of the aberration from reality inherent in any form of love. It is a part of this view of love that the possession of the loved person can only bring disappointment and ennui. The only thing which can restore desire, and indeed intensify it to the point of an obsession, is jealousy. In this way the psychology of love parallels that of society, where possessive jealousy is also seen as a dominating motive, exemplified in Mme Verdurin's attitude to her 'little clan'.

The only value which Proust sees in love is its power to stimulate the imagination and to intensify the inner life. Swann's growing sensitivity to music and 'the fullness of impressions that he had been having for some time',[16] are a part of his growing love for Odette.

Rilke's lovers, too, experience a heightened awareness of existence – the knowledge that 'Being here is glorious'.[17] But because they are turned outwards towards another person, and towards the outside world in general, their moments of happiness escape them:

Nur, wir vergessen so leicht, was der lachende Nachbar
uns nicht bestätigt oder beneidet. Sichtbar
wollen wirs heben, wo doch das sichtbarste Glück uns
erst zu erkennen sich giebt, wenn wir es innen verwandeln.

Only, we so easily forget what the laughing neighbour does not confirm or envy. We want to display it visibly, when the most visible happiness will only show itself to us if we transform it inwardly.

At this point, in the Seventh Elegy, the limitations of love as Rilke conceived it are finally shown, and at the same time he points to the only real way to fulfilment: 'nowhere, beloved, will there be world but within'.[18] The ultimate hopelessness of love is expressed in the Eighth Elegy: 'Something, as if by oversight, is left unclosed/ behind the other ... But past him/ no one can advance'.[19] A similar inescapable dependence on the other is symbolised by Proust in the lovers' attempts to imprison their partners.

Love is therefore presented by both writers as a supreme attempt to achieve happiness outside oneself. It fails, not only because it involves a relationship to the outside world, but because it is a pursuit of happiness for its own sake. In the Ninth Elegy, Rilke finally renounces happiness as a goal, dismissing it as 'this premature precursor of a coming loss'.[20] Coupled to this is an affirmation of suffering as a positive value. Whereas happiness is sterile, in that its pursuit binds us to illusions, suffering can be fertile in freeing us from them. In the First Elegy Rilke asks: 'Shall not these oldest sufferings at last/ become more fruitful? Is it not time that we, in loving,/ freed ourselves from the beloved.'[21] In the last Elegy this question receives a positive answer; the sufferings inseparable from a fulfilled existence are called: 'a place, a settlement, a camp, a ground, a dwelling-place'.[22]

A similar view of suffering is expressed in *Time Lost*, not only in the long abstract argument in 'Time Regained', but as a central element in the symbolic structure of the novel. At the heart of 'The Guermantes Way' and of 'Cities of the Plain' – the sections where the pursuit of happiness is all-pervading – Proust places symmetrically two episodes which annihilate the values of society and of sexual love. 'The Guermantes Way' is interrupted by the description of the death of Marcel's grandmother after a horrible illness. In 'Cities of the Plain' Proust inserts the episode of 'the intermittences of the heart' in which, by an association of memories, Marcel is suddenly overwhelmed by grief for his dead grandmother.

A similar juxtaposition of contrasting elements, for a similar purpose, is used by Rilke in the Tenth Elegy, where the description of the symbolic fairground of illusory pleasures is immediately followed by that of the landscape of the Laments. Moreover, there is a further important parallel between the two authors in their symbolic treatment of suffering. The sombre episodes which they introduce do not end on a note of unmitigated pessimism. In each case the final images are not of death and ugliness, but of youth, beauty and renewal. Proust's description of the grandmother's body after her death, which ends the episode, closes with the following words:

A smile seemed to be settled on my grandmother's lips. On this funeral bed, death, like the medieval sculptor, had laid her to rest under the appearance of a girl.[23]

The episode of 'the intermittences of the heart' ends with Marcel going for a walk and thinking of past walks with his grandmother. He comes upon an apple orchard in blossom. The description of the orchard brings this section to an end; these are the closing lines:

> Then the sun's rays gave way suddenly to those of the rain; they striped the whole horizon, drawing the row of apple-trees into their grey net. But the trees went on holding up their beauty, flowering and pink, in the now icy wind under the downpour: it was a day in spring.[24]

Rilke, in closing the description of the landscape of suffering and death in the Tenth Elegy, uses the same image as Proust in the passage above:

> Aber erweckten sie uns, die unendlich Toten, ein Gleichnis,
> siehe, sie zeigten vielleicht auf die Kätzchen der leeren
> Hasel, die hängenden, oder
> meinten den Regen, der fällt auf dunkles Erdreich im Frühjahr.[25]

> But if they aroused in us, those dead without end, a similitude, see, they would point, perhaps, to the empty hazel's catkins, downward-hanging, or they would think of the rain that falls on dark earth in spring.

By this use of image and structure, Proust and Rilke suggest that happiness is not to be found where it is normally sought, that it is inseparably bound up with suffering. Suffering is indeed the source of happiness, as Rilke makes explicit in the First Elegy: 'we ... for whom so often from mourning/ blessed progress springs'.[26]

Proust and Rilke are in agreement, therefore, in rejecting large areas of human existence as sterile. They do so because neither love, nor outwardly directed activities symbolised by society and the acrobats, are able to satisfy what they see as the fundamental desire of human nature. Throughout the *Elegies* and *Time Lost* there is an underlying lament for an unrealised possibility, an absent splendour – a sense that what is experienced from moment to moment is not reality at all. 'The flowers which I am shown for the first time today do not seem like real flowers',[27] Proust writes early in the novel, and this motif is repeated towards the end in the narrator's mournful contemplation of trees and flowers by the railway which fail to arouse in him the slightest pleasure. Rilke, in the Eighth Elegy, writes in similar terms:

> *Wir* haben nie, nicht einen einzigen Tag,
> den reinen Raum vor uns, in den die Blumen
> unendlich aufgehn ...
> das Reine,

Unüberwachte, das man atmet und
unendlich *weiß* und nicht begehrt.[28]

*We* never have, not for a single day, pure space before us, into which
flowers open endlessly ... the pure, unsupervised realm that one breathes
and endlessly *knows* and does not covet.

This is echoed in the *Sonnets to Orpheus*, written during the period
of inspiration in which Rilke finished the *Elegies*: 'But *when*, in which
of all our lives,/ are we at last spread open and receive?'[29]

This sense of an absent splendour at the heart of life is strengthened
by the recollection of childhood. Both writers see childhood as a lost
paradise, a state of bliss unequalled in adult life. Significantly, the
child's capacity for bliss is coupled to a defencelessness against suffering and fear, particularly the fear of darkness. Proust and Rilke both
use the same image – the figure of the mother bending over the child
at night to dispel the fear of the unknown (in 'Combray' and in the
Third Elegy) – to show this feature of the child's existence.

As Marcel grows into adolescence, certain impressions he receives on
country walks – a scent or an effect of sunlight – fill him momentarily
with an inexplicable joy. He feels it is his duty to attach himself to the
impressions to discover what they contain, but the effort demanded is
too great and the duty is neglected. Frequently, the exaltation of these
moments finds an easier outlet. It becomes absorbed by another
emotion, the vague hope that a peasant girl might appear, in possessing
whom he would also possess the essence of the landscape concealed in
his impression. But the peasant girl never appears and Marcel returns
home, not enriched by his experience, but persuaded that such impressions must be illusory.

So begins Marcel's alienation from reality and from nature, which
lose all their charm and meaning and are soon no more than the 'conventional framework'[30] of his life. So also begins the series of erotic
experiences and disappointments which, through Gilberte and then
Swann, remain associated with this country walk 'the Méséglise way'.
All these experiences follow the same pattern: Marcel attempts to
realise through a human relationship an impression which stirred his
imagination. Possessing Albertine, for example, seems to him a way of
possessing the essence of Balbec. Love is therefore for Proust a confusion between two separate impulses – those of sensuality and of
imagination. This confusion, which he sees as an integral part of
human experience, is symbolised in the novel by 'the Méséglise way'.

In the First Elegy, the poet recalls certain impressions which
had seemed to contain a special meaning and to impose a duty on
him:

Ja, die Frühlinge brauchten dich wohl. Es muteten manche
Sterne dir zu, daß du sie spürtest. Es hob
sich eine Woge heran im Vegangenen, oder
da du vorüberkamst am geöffneten Fenster,
gab eine Geige sich hin. Das alles war Auftrag.

Yes, the springs had need of you. Many a star demanded your awareness.
In the past a wave built up, or at an open window as you passed a violin
gave itself. All that was a task laid on you.

But, as with Proust, the task imposed by these impressions becomes
confused with that of satisfying erotic desire, which dissipates the
energy the former would have needed: 'But were you equal to it?
Were you not always/ distracted by expectation, as if all this/ were
announcing a woman to love?'[31] This fundamental confusion is
pointed to also in the *Sonnets* where it is seen as inherent in man's
nature: 'His sense is division. At the crossing of two/ heart's ways no
temple for Apollo stands.'[32]

In *Time Lost* there is another 'heart's way' (*Herzweg*) – or 'inner
direction'[33] to use Proust's term – which adds further confusion to
Marcel's life. This has its origin in his other childhood walks, 'the
Guermantes way'. On these walks he also experiences the moments of
exaltation described earlier. But now they become absorbed by the
imagined figure of the Duchesse de Guermantes, who in Marcel's mind
is still associated with the magic-lantern images of his childhood and
with the supernatural atmosphere of the Merovingian past. The landscape of the walk reminds him of that described in a book which has
captured his imagination. All these elements are now translated into a
vision of external happiness as the friend of Mme de Guermantes: he
would go trout-fishing, he would go for boat-trips on the river and,
'avid for happiness,' he would ask for 'nothing other of life than that
it should be made up always of a succession of happy afternoons'.[34]
When Marcel encounters Mme de Guermantes in reality, she progressively loses this imaginative charm, which is only restored when he
finds himself excluded from her *salon*. Now again she becomes an
object of desire. In this way Marcel is drawn into the world of social
ambition, symbolised by 'the Guermantes way'.

Society and love are the two wrong turnings in Marcel's life. In both,
a desire of the imagination has become attached to an inappropriate
external object. But both have at their origin an idea which, says
Proust, was the prime mover even of his most material desires: 'the
idea of perfection'.[35]

In his early life there is only one occasion when this idea of perfection achieves fulfilment. Obeying for once the duty imposed by one
of his impressions, Marcel writes a page of poetic prose, and is

rewarded by complete happiness. In later life he experiences a series of intense recollections of the past, during which he is momentarily freed from his habitual dissatisfaction: 'I had stopped feeling mediocre, contingent, mortal.'[36] His past life, as now revealed to him, has an intensity and radiance which were previously concealed. He resolves to embody this transfigured world in a novel; only in so doing can he fully live his life and fulfil at last the aspirations of his adolescence.

In the Ninth Elegy the poet's message is finally revealed: the purpose of life is an act of 'saying', by which the things of the world are given an intensity they otherwise lack:

> Sind wir vielleicht *hier*, um zu sagen: Haus,
> Brücke, Brunnen, Tor, Krug, Obstbaum, Fenster, –
> höchstens: Säule, Turm.... aber zu *sagen*, verstehs,
> oh zu sagen *so*, wie selber die Dinge niemals
> innig meinten zu sein.[37]

Are we perhaps *here* to say: house, bridge, well, gate, jug, fruit-tree window, – at the most: column, tower.... but to *say*, you understand, oh to say in such a way as the things themselves never fervently believed to be.

The act of 'saying' symbolises the activity of the artist who, by his creation, is able to bring the objects of the outer world into an invisible, inward realm. This process now becomes the justification and final purpose not only of human existence but of the world itself: 'Earth, is not this your wish: to arise in us/ *invisible*?' At the height of this revelation the poet experiences a state of exaltation which, like that of Proust in the moments of recollection, is the fulfilment of the aspiration for full existence which has been present throughout the work:

> Siehe, ich lebe. Woraus? Weder Kindheit noch Zukunft
> werden weniger.... Überzähliges Dasein
> entspringt mir im Herzen.[38]

See, I am living. From what? Neither childhood nor future is growing less.... Superabundant existence springs up in my heart.

In this way, Marcel and the poet of the *Elegies* experience in the discovery of their artistic vocation what had been denied to them by life. Whereas all other experiences lead outwards into the world, art leads into the inner world of the self. Whereas other experiences have happiness as their goal, art, as the Tenth Elegy and 'Time Regained' make clear, involves the renunciation of this goal and the acceptance of suffering.

According to the interpretation of life offered by Proust and Rilke in these works, there is in man a fundamental driving force more profound than egoism and sensuality with which, in seeking an object, it may become confused. It is the 'never contented will' of the acrobats, Marcel's 'idea of perfection', which ultimately can only be satisfied by artistic creation. In this way the question: What is life? receives, in the case of both writers, substantially the same answer – Rilke: 'Song is existence' – Proust: 'The true life ... is literature.'[39]

Through the symbolic structures their final works, therefore, Proust and Rilke offer a systematic and comprehensive interpretation of human life. It is an interpretation which – in *Time Lost* as much as in the *Elegies* – lays claim to universal truth. In 'Time Regained' Proust makes it clear that only Marcel is 'saved'; all the other characters have lived in vain. On its own terms, such a message invites the question concerning its truth: is life really as these works depict it? Before considering this question, however, it is worth noting that the form of salvation offered by both writers can be realised only by creative artists. Their general picture of life corresponds exactly to their own particular experience: in symbolising mankind they symbolise themselves. And on the basis of our study in previous chapters we can see how they have come to do so.

In the middle period both writers were prevented from achieving unified large-scale works by their adherence to the direct description of experience. They have now overcome this problem by translating their experience entirely into symbolic terms. We saw in the last chapter how this process gave rise to Rilke's personal mythology, embodied in the *Elegies*, in which particular cardinal experiences are represented by symbolic figures.

In *Time Lost*, in the different medium of the novel, Proust has followed a similar course. We noted in Chapter Fourteen that his experience of reality, even on the level of sense-perception, was charged with emotion, and in this sense 'mythical'. But in *Contre Sainte-Beuve* the process of myth-making was not complete. Proust had not found a means of dramatising the emotional forces in his life, of presenting them in terms of action. In *Time Lost* the process is completed. Proust personifies emotional forces as characters in his narrative, in a way analogous to the tendency of primitive peoples to create gods representing the forces beyond their control which are their main sources of emotion and suffering. The analogy between these processes is made clear by Proust himself in 'Time Regained':

> The whole art of living is to use those who make us suffer only as steps giving access to their divine form and thus joyously to people our lives with divinities.[40]

We know that in Proust's life there were four main areas of emotional stress through which he was particularly exposed to suffering. These were his homosexuality and sexual love in general, his relationship to his mother, his social ambition, and his desire to be a writer. These forces within him brought him into conflict not only with others but with himself; out of these conflicts the divinities of his work are born.

Proust's homosexuality is projected primarily into Charlus, his social personality mainly into Swann. But, as Germaine Brée has observed,[41] in the novel a given character trait is not confined to one individual, it is present to a lesser degree in a number of others and thus becomes more pervasive. Homosexuality is found or suspected in Odette, Albertine, Saint-Loup and, by the end of the novel, in a host of other characters; snobbery is present in Legrandin, Bloch and many others.

In this way the driving forces in Proust's personality are projected outwards into vivid fictional creations. By a similar process those people surrounding him who, because of his emotional needs, are in a position to cause him pain, are also made into divinities. The social world in which he had once sought favour crystallises into the Guermantes and the Verdurins and their respective circles. The erotic partners on whom he depended are precipitated, above all, in Albertine, Odette and Morel.

In giving outward form to these characters Proust does not copy directly from life; he concentrates impressions absorbed over a long period: 'there is not one name of an invented character under which [the writer] could not put sixty names of people he has seen'.[42] For Proust it is not people who really exist and can be expressed, but the 'ideas' underlying them.[43] The character who most nearly resembles a person in Proust's life is the narrator's mother, who, as Germaine Brée points out, is not so much a character as a presence[44] and is doubled by the far more vividly-portrayed grandmother who is her symbolic projection.

Other characters symbolise other dominant aspects of Proust's emotional life. Into Tante Léonie he has put his hypochondria, into Swann and Bloch separate aspects of his Jewishness, one fastidious, the other vulgar. In Saint-Loup he has embodied his young aristocratic male friends and the 'idea' of friendship.

Even minor characters are still bound to Proust's own life by an emotional link. For instance, Cottard, who with other figures exemplifies the co-existence of medical competence with intellectual nullity, enables Proust to give expression to feelings from an intimate part of his life: the sense of reproach constantly offered to him by the 'positive mind' and worldly success of his father and brother, both medical men, in contrast to whom his own existence seemed painfully frivolous and unproductive. Similarly Brichot and Norpois, though brilliant comic creations in their own right, personify a materialist attitude to literature against which Proust had constantly to defend his own conception of art, and to justify his long infertility.

In the 'pantheon of gods'[45] peopling his novel Proust has therefore externalised the emotions of his life, not only those, like social ambition, which had already run their course when he began writing the novel, but those, like love, to which he was still susceptible. In Chapter Fourteen, we saw how, by transferring emotions to a symbolic figure, Proust could detach them from his personal life. In 'Time Regained' he describes the liberation from immediate emotions which this process brings; while we work, he writes, the person we love is 'dissolved in a vaster reality' so completely that we are able to forget him, and the suffering of love, in which he no longer has any part, is felt now as nothing more than a purely physical condition, 'a kind of illness of the heart'.[46]

But emotions transposed in this way are not themselves diminished. Their intensity is transferred from the life of the author to his creation, and it is their presence which gives Proust's novel its singular vitality. Indeed, it was because he saw that transposed emotions were essential to his work that Proust attached positive value to suffering:

> let our body crumble, since each new fragment which breaks from it comes, now luminous and legible, – completing it at the price of sufferings of which others more gifted have no need, making it more solid as emotions eat away our life, – to be added to our work.[47]

It can be seen here how an important aspect of Proust's general interpretation of life was bound up with his particular experience as an artist.

The statements quoted above are made by the narrator when he is already in possession of his artistic vocation. But during the novel, when Marcel is still only a struggling dilettante, the artistic experiences which were a central part of Proust's life are symbolised by other figures: Bergotte, Elstir and Vinteuil and by the works attributed to them. In this way Proust's creative emotions, also, are partly externalised.

At this point a further parallel with Rilke may be drawn. In writing the *Sonnets* Rilke added to the symbolic figures discussed in the last chapter a further divinity: Orpheus. Orpheus symbolises the perfect creative consciousness towards which Rilke had been developing. In the opening lines of the first Sonnet the complex creative process, analysed in the last chapter, in which visual awareness is permeated by a kind of music, is symbolically enacted:

> Da stieg ein Baum. O reine Übersteigung!
> O Orpheus singt! O hoher Baum im Ohr!

There rose a tree. O pure transcending! O Orpheus sings! O tall tree in the ear!

But the process of externalisation is not applied by either writer to the whole of the creator's experience. Rilke, as we saw, uses a generalised first person in the *Elegies*, and this is preserved in the *Sonnets*. In *Time Lost* Proust also uses a first-person voice having a similar generalised quality. If the 'I' who appears in Proust's narrative is examined, he is found to be only a pale reflection of the qualities embodied so vividly in the characters around him. He is a snob, he has erotic experiences, he is ill, but none of this gives him the intensity of existence or the stature of Swann, Charlus or Tante Léonie. Moreover, although we can feel Proust's emotions animating the other characters, it is clear that he is totally detached from his hero. In this respect Marcel is the opposite of Jean Santeuil. For Marcel, Proust has none of the sentimental indulgence which made Jean an inadequate fictional creation. On the contrary, he sees Marcel with an unclouded gaze which lays bare his most unattractive traits, in particular his 'total egoism'.[48]

Marcel is not so much a character having an emotional link with the author, as a medium through which the world of the novel can be revealed. He has, in fact, the quality which apropos of Bergotte Proust describes as genius. Though mediocre in himself, he has the power to become a mirror reflecting the lives of those around him. To this function Marcel's character, or lack of it, is ideally suited. His egoism impels him to explore the world of experience and its wrong turnings, makes him a vehicle of discovery; but he is without those aggressive emotions – pride, material ambition and hatred[49] – which would give him a one-sided view of the world he discovers. He is susceptible to suffering, but only in so far as this emotion heightens his interest in reality. In 'The Fugitive' the narrator writes: 'This was the greatest misfortune of my life. And yet the suffering it caused me was perhaps still surpassed by my curiosity to know the causes of my misfortune.'[50]

But the Marcel who is involved in the action is only a fraction of the 'I' of the novel. Between the protagonist and the narrator who finally writes the novel from his distant standpoint after 'Time Regained', there are a number of intermediate 'voices' representing different points of view. A critic has distinguished nine such separate facets of the 'I'.[51] These intermediate voices, however, are not characters or aspects of a character involved in the story, but modalities of Proust's technique of analysis and narration. Proust does not project his emotions into them, but uses them as a vehicle for his intelligence and memory.

The 'I' of the novel has, however, one voice which is charged with emotion and which participates intensely in the world evoked. This is the voice farthest removed from the action and from the fortunes of the hero, and closest to the standpoint of the reader. This voice is indeed so close to the reader that it seems almost internal, almost, to use Proust's own word, 'visceral'. It is the voice of the aged novelist who has ceased to participate in the particular interests of his former self and feels in their place an intense, generalised nostalgia for the world in which he lived. This is the voice which we saw developing in Chapter Fourteen, for which the past in its entirety is irrecoverable 'time lost'.

After having, as it were, delegated all other emotions to external figures, Proust has reserved for the character who says 'I' the nostalgic emotion which can give the voice of the novelist the broadest and strongest possible emotional connection to the world of the novel. For this voice, the world of the past has itself taken on a mythical quality. Fragments of remembered landscape enter his mind 'like a Delos full of flowers',[52] and to live once again in the village of his childhood would be 'to have a more marvellously supernatural contact with the Beyond than if I made the acquaintance of Golo or spoke to Genevieve of Brabant'[53] – figures in the legends of his magic lantern.

The intervention of this emotionally-charged voice in the neutral tone of the narrative is marked by a heightening of the style which is at once perceptible. Proust was himself aware of this feature of his novel and symbolised it in Bergotte's works, in which there were 'certain moments when a hidden flood of harmony, an interior prelude, lifted up his style'. This 'song of harps'[54] is heard in Proust's novel when the vision of the past is most poignant, above all in 'Combray'. It appears when the gulf separating present and past is felt most directly, in the passages evoking the kitchen smell at Combray 'which still at moments rises up in me as intermittent and as hot';[55] or the belfry in an unfamiliar town which he contemplates for hours, reminded of Combray and forgotten streets: 'I seek my way, I turn a corner... but... it is in my heart...';[56] or the vanished splendour of the Bois de Boulogne: 'the houses, the roads, the avenues, are fleeting, alas! like the years'.[57]

This urgent and harmonious voice, the 'song' of Proust's prose, which is intermittent elsewhere in the novel, is heard unbroken in the last pages of 'Combray', rising to its climax in the final sentence of the sustained evocation of the past:

> Quand par les soirs d'été le ciel harmonieux gronde comme une bête fauve et que chacun boude l'orage, c'est au côté de Méséglise que je dois de rester seul en extase à respirer, à travers le bruit de la pluie qui tombe, l'odeur d'invisibles et persistants lilas. [58]

> When on summer evenings the harmonious sky growls like a wild beast and everyone huddles away from the storm, it is the Méséglise way that makes me stay alone in rapture, breathing through the noise of the falling rain the scent of unseen and lasting lilacs.

The sonority of this sentence is echoed in the closing words of 'Combray' one page later: 'this pale sign traced above the curtains by the raised finger of the day'. It is no doubt to these sentences, which together bring to an end the 'overture' of the novel, that Proust refers later when he writes of Bergotte: 'There are in his book certain sentence-endings where the accumulation of sonorities is prolonged, as in the closing chords of the overture of an opera.'[59]

The nostalgia expressed by this voice is the emotion which impelled Proust to re-create the world of his past. In 'Time Regained' he writes of the 'desire, [the] regret for certain non-existent things, which is the precondition for working'.[60] In this way he has isolated and given symbolic expression in his novel to the most profound feeling of his life, the creative emotion. Appropriately, this is the emotion which is reserved for the narrator.

Proust and Rilke have therefore distributed among a gallery of symbolic figures their fundamental emotions and experiences. We saw in the case of Proust that this applies even to minor figures, and the same is true of Rilke; as E. C. Mason notes, even the child and the animals of the *Elegies* have borrowed their fate from that of their creator.[61] Moreover, this symbolic transposition of their lives does not apply only to people and emotions, but also to places. Combray symbolises Proust's childhood at Illiers and Auteuil, Balbec his seaside holidays at various resorts. The landscape of the Tenth Elegy symbolises the essence of Rilke's experience of Egypt: 'a reflection of the Nile-land in the desert-clear consciousness of the dead'.[62]

Finally, the process of symbolisation is applied to the experience which, for the two writers, underlies all others: the privileged moment. In the *Elegies*, as we have seen, this experience is symbolised primarily by the angel. Proust, in the context of a novel, cannot, of course, use a symbol so far removed from experience; his treatment of the privileged moment is symbolic in a different way. He no longer, as in *Jean Santeuil*, transcribes examples of the experience directly, but abstracts the essential elements from a number of different moments and re-composes from them an experience having generalised, symbolic value.

This is most easily seen in the case of the first of the privileged moments described in the novel, an impression received by Marcel on one of his walks 'the Méséglise way':

> After an hour of rain and wind which I had battled against joyfully, as I came to the edge of the Montjouvain pond, in front of a little tile-roofed hut where M. Vinteuil's gardener kept his tools, the sun had just come out again and its gold, washed by the shower, gleamed anew in the sky, on the trees, on the wall of the hut and on its tiled roof, still wet, with a hen strutting along its ridge. Playful grasses growing on the face of the

wall, and the hen's downy feathers, were tugged horizontal by the wind, letting its gusts stretch them out full-length at will, one like the other, with the abandon of things light and inert. The tiled roof made in the pond, which shone again like a mirror in the sunlight, a pink marbled effect which I had never paid attention to before. As I saw, on the water and on the face of the wall, a pale smile answering the smile of the sky, I cried out in my enthusiasm, brandishing my closed umbrella: 'Damn, damn, damn, damn.' But at the same time I knew that my duty required that I should not stop short at these opaque words but try to gain a clearer understanding of my delight.[63]

In this description we recognise features of the privileged moment which have become familiar. Sensations are given a heightened vigour by the sudden appearance of sunshine and by the animation imparted by the wind. They also take on an abnormal interest for their own sake: 'a pink marbled effect which I had never paid attention to before'. In addition, the various sensations composing the scene are unified, firstly by the wind giving a common movement to the grass and to the hen's feathers, secondly by the sunlight reflected in different parts of the scene, and by the reflection of one part in another. It is in perceiving this unifying reflection that Marcel utters his spontaneous cry of enthusiasm. But Proust also indicates that this uncontrolled shout is not an adequate realisation of the experience.

To create this symbolic privileged moment Proust has used the same method as in creating characters. He has abstracted and concentrated elements spread more diffusely in his own experience. In so doing he departs widely from his actual experience in some external respects, while adhering to it entirely with regard to its essential meaning. For example, this privileged moment is not drawn from the period of Proust's life corresponding to its position in the novel, but from a more recent time, his stay with Reynaldo Hahn at Réveillon in 1894. In the section of *Jean Santeuil* in which this stay is described in a barely-disguised form, we find many specific elements which are incorporated in the experience quoted above. The following extract will make this clear:

And, standing on the roof of the keeper's house, letting its blue throat shine in the sun beside its green tail, two-coloured like the sea in this radiant, boisterous weather, a peacock, quite still, had some small feathers on its side that trembled in the wind as if it had become an inert thing, without other movements than those imparted to it by the wind, and without the strength to resist them.[64]

This scene in *Jean Santeuil* is not presented as a privileged moment as such, but, as we saw in Chapter Seven, the whole Réveillon section is filled with the radiant atmosphere of the privileged moment. It is this atmosphere which Proust has symbolised in his later reconstruction.

Numerous other details from this section of *Jean Santeuil*, apart from those in the quotation, recur in the passage of *Time Lost* under discussion. The scene in *Jean Santeuil* is followed by the imaginative stimulation produced by reading which precedes it in *Time Lost*. The passer-by who fails to share Marcel's enthusiasm, and the lesson drawn from this, appear in the same passage of *Jean Santeuil*. In the reconstruction of the original experience Proust has changed the peacock to a hen, but the peacock, and the image comparing its colours to the sea, remain associated with the privileged moment and reappear in another reconstructed privileged moment in 'Time Regained': the napkin which summons up a vision of Balbec 'unfurled, arrayed among its surfaces and folds, the plumage of an ocean green and blue like a peacock's tail'.[65]

The same process of symbolisation is applied to all the other privileged moments in *Time Lost*. The original of the 'three steeples' incident was a car journey near Caen in 1907, the incident of the three trees near Hudimesnil is an amalgam including 'Artistic Contemplation' and an incident in the preface of *Against Sainte-Beuve*. If the privileged moment involving the 'madeleine' dipped in tea, and the similar experiences in 'Time Regained', are compared with those in the preface of *Against Sainte-Beuve*, it will be seen that all have been changed in their external details. Because Proust has now departed from the direct transcription of experience, it will not be necessary to study the privileged moments in *Time Lost* in detail for their own sake, but only from the point of view of the part they play in the novel.

One of the most important results of Proust's new treatment of the privileged moment is the reduction in the space devoted to them in *Time Lost* as compared to *Jean Santeuil*. The advantages of this from the novelist's point of view are clear. The accumulation of descriptions of privileged moments in the earlier novel had made a connected narrative impossible and had contributed to the failure of the work. The reduction in the descriptions of privileged moments in *Time Lost* does not mean, however, that the importance of the experience in the novel is also reduced. Its importance is expressed no longer primarily through description, but through the symbolic narrative structure.

The decisive part played by privileged moments in Marcel's literary vocation is shown by incidents in the narrative which are more dramatic for being discreetly prepared and long awaited. As already mentioned, he experiences early in the novel a number of privileged moments involving direct impressions of nature. The incident involving the Martinville steeples, already discussed in Chapter Five, shows how these moments can lead to literary creation. But Marcel fails to take advantage of them, and it is not until the end of the novel that a series of privileged moments of involuntary memory reveals his vocation to him and at the same time provides him with the material for his novel.

It is noticeable that in symbolising his vocation in this way, Proust has given most weight to involuntary memory; experiences involving the direct perception of reality play a relatively minor rôle. The reasons for this are evident: moments of direct perception can provide only a limited amount of material, more useful to a poet than to a novelist, whereas involuntary memory can provide, symbolically at least, whole stretches of past experience, including narrative. The Martinville steeples give rise to only one page of descriptive prose, whereas the 'madeleine' dipped in tea provides the whole evocation of Combray.

But there is in Proust's representation of his vocation a possible inconsistency. The vocation is first revealed by moments of direct perception, but is only realised through involuntary memory. Proust's task is to show that there is a continuity between the two kinds of experience, that the reality revealed by the steeples is the same as that disclosed by the 'madeleine', the napkin, etc. In 'Time Regained' he argues that the two experiences are the same because they both demand a creative effort:

> In short, in one case as in the other ... it was necessary to attempt to interpret the sensations as the signs of as many laws and ideas, by trying to think, that is, to draw out of the half-light what I had felt, to convert it into a spiritual equivalent.[66]

But this link between the two experiences exists only on the level of theoretical argument; Proust's task is also to embody it concretely in his narrative structure. He does this in the incident of the three trees near Hudimesnil. Here Marcel experiences the characteristic pleasure of the privileged moment coupled to the feeling that he must go beyond his impression to discover what it conceals. But, even writing from his standpoint after 'Time Regained', he never discovers whether the reality concealed in his impression was a memory or a new idea like those produced by the steeples. In this way the identical nature of the sensations involved in privileged moments of direct perception and those of involuntary memory, is concretely shown. For this reason, as well as through its position in the narrative, this incident acts as a bridge between the early privileged moments and those in 'Time Regained'.

Proust's use of the privileged moment now therefore corresponds to that of Rilke as discussed in the last chapter. Instead of evoking the experience as a source of direct enjoyment, he uses it as a structural element in his work. And, just as Rilke, in his structure, uses a technique of juxtaposition in which the symbolised privileged moment throws light on other experiences, so too does Proust in *Time Lost*. For this purpose the privileged moment is symbolised not only by the reconstructed experiences already discussed, which are used only in direct relation to Marcel's vocation, but by a number of images symbolising more generally the higher reality which the privileged moment reveals. By this means Proust's symbolic use of the privileged moment is given greater flexibility. The images which symbolise the privileged moment in this way are of two kinds: things of exceptional natural beauty – particularly flowers and blossoming trees – and works of art.

The symbolic value of these images is shown by their position in the narrative in relation to other experiences. In 'Combray', Marcel contemplates the hawthorns just before seeing Gilberte for the first time. In 'Within a Budding Grove' the hawthorns, now without flowers, reappear on a walk near Balbec when Marcel is talking to Andrée about Albertine. In 'The Guermantes Way', Marcel sees the flowering cherry- and pear-trees while walking with Saint-Loup and Rachel. In all these episodes the lover is mistakenly pursuing in the woman's face the reflection of the reality symbolised by the flowers. In 'Cities of the Plain', as already mentioned, a flowering orchard is introduced in relation to 'the intermittences of the heart'. Its symbolic meaning is given a further aspect by the brief and disappointing visit of Albertine immediately preceding the description of the trees.

Experiences connected with art provide a parallel stream of images, or scenes having the value of images, running through the novel. Like the images from nature, those from art symbolise the central theme of the book: the aberration from Marcel's vocation represented by experiences such as society and love. The name of Bergotte is from an early stage associated by Marcel with Gilberte; Mlle Vinteuil introduces the theme of homosexuality. Marcel's first visit to Elstir's studio is interrupted by a visit by Albertine, to whom Marcel hopes Elstir will introduce him. Swann's love for Odette is associated from beginning to end with the 'little phrase' of Vinteuil's sonata, the meaning of which Swann misinterprets in falling in love. Marcel looks at Elstir's paintings just before the dinner with the Guermantes and his disappointment with their world. While listening to Vinteuil's septet he realises that there is a world more real than that in which he loves Albertine, and the performance is followed by the tragic denouement of Charlus' affair with Morel. The revelation of human mortality in 'Time Regained' follows the playing of a piece of music.

The symbolic implications of these images from nature and art are further heightened by a specific use of terminology. In describing the experience of listening to Vinteuil's septet, Proust repeatedly refers to

angels and the world of angels; Bergotte's books beside his death-bed
are also compared to angels. The angel is traditionally a messenger
from a higher world, and it is precisely this function which the image
has in Proust's novel. This is made explicit in the description of the
flowering trees in 'The Guermantes Way':

> Guardians of the memories of the golden age, witnesses to the promise
> that reality is not what it is believed to be, that the splendour of poetry,
> the marvellous light of innocence can shine there and can be the reward
> which we strive to deserve, the tall white creatures bending resplendently
> over the shade propitious to siestas, to fishing and reading, were they not
> rather angels?[67]

It is scarcely necessary to point out the proximity of Proust's symbolism here to that of Rilke, who defined the angel of the *Elegies* as
'that being who bears witness to the possibility of finding in the invisible a higher degree of reality'.[68] For Rilke as for Proust the angel
symbolises and guarantees the existence of an order of reality which is
outside normal human experience, but without which human experience cannot be understood. As we saw in the last chapter, the attempt
to summon the angel is renounced at the outset of the *Elegies*. Rilke
goes on to give a symbolic representation of the human world, but the
angel remains as a presiding figure, invoked whenever the possibility
of a more real existence is glimpsed: in 'Angel and puppet' in the
Fourth Elegy; in the smile of the young acrobat in the Fifth – the one
redeeming moment in the sterile performance, which is at once offered
to the angel: 'Angel! O take it';[69] in the vision of another realm at the
end of the same Elegy: 'Angel!: there might be a place';[70] in the re-
affirmation of earthly existence, insofar as it is experienced inwardly,
in the Seventh Elegy 'O marvel, angel, for *we* are this';[71] and in the
final message of the Ninth Elegy: 'Praise the world to the angel.'[72]

In this way both writers symbolically preserve the possibility of a
higher dimension of existence without which, for them, life is incomplete and even incomprehensible. In their symbolic presentation of
this higher existence, particularly in their use of the angel-motif but
also in their other terminology – Rilke's 'the Open', 'the invisible', and
Proust's 'other world' and 'lost homeland'[73] – both writers give the
impression of a metaphysical realm cut off from the world of empirical
experience.

We saw in the last chapter, however, that it is possible to look at the
poet's 'higher reality' in another way: as a modification in the awareness of reality brought about by a modification in mental processes.
This second possibility of interpretation is also contained in Proust's
novel, where the metaphysical aspect is supplemented by extensive
psychological analysis. In the discussions of art throughout the novel

Proust develops a comprehensivee psychology of aesthetics. These ideas need not be examined in detail here, however, since they coincide largely with those already discussed in previous chapters, particularly in connection with *Jean Santeuil* and the middle period. Here a brief summary of Proust's argument will be sufficient.

Every moment of experience, Proust believes, contains at a certain level a rich tissue of sensations and impressions provided by perception and memory. This most intense and immediate level of our experience of reality is, however, prevented from reaching consciousness by the intellectualising activity of the mind. Impressions are interpreted and frequently distorted to fit ready-made concepts in conformity with the dictates of what Proust calls 'the interested, active, practical, mechanical, lazy, centrifugal disposition ... of our minds'.[74] Reality for Proust is not to be found at the level of the dessicated intellectualised experience which normally reaches consciousness, but at the immediate level where our experience is intense, unified and individual. As we grow older this unique reality recedes farther and farther from us behind a wall formed of the concepts which we substitute for what we really experience.[75] Of the true nature of reality, which he calls 'the true life', we retain only a dim intuition, the sense of a 'lost homeland'. In this way Proust's 'other world' can be understood no longer in metaphysical but in psychological terms.

But the lost reality can occasionally be glimpsed, says Proust, under exceptional circumstances. It can be revealed when the rational mind relaxes on the verge of falling asleep,[76] or in moments of contemplation of nature when our abstract notions of reality are briefly put aside.[77] But above all it is experienced through involuntary memory, when reality is seen 'rid of what is imperfect in external perception, pure and disincarnate'.[78]

The importance of art for Proust is that it too can reveal this normally hidden level of our experience. It does so by by-passing or reversing the process of intellectualisation which normally accompanies experience. Elstir re-creates the world by 'taking away the names' of things, by breaking down 'that aggregate of reasonings which we call vision'. In this way his art is a 'sincere return to the very root of the impression'.[79] Music, communicating by sounds devoid of conceptual meaning, is the art-form which is able to give us the most immediate contact with reality – its sounds 'seem to take on the inflection of being, to reproduce that innermost point of sensations'.[80] Literature can produce a similar effect by replacing the false conventional relations between things by metaphors corresponding to the writer's original impressions.

A primary function of art for Proust is therefore to restore to our vision a pristine intensity which it normally lacks. But art has a second, equally important function: it shows us in reality a unity which is absent from normal experience. Art achieves its effect not only by abolishing the intellectual categories and constructions which normally govern our experience, since this by itself could only lead to a chaos of unconnected and undifferentiated sensation: it imposes on the sensation liberated from the rational mind a structure and unity of its own. Elstir's paintings are characterised by a 'manifold and powerful unity'[81] brought about by the systematic cultivation of a visual metaphor. In music, although the first impression given by a musical phrase is purely qualitative – 'sine materia',[82] this impression is followed by the perception of structures which finally become 'dazzling architectures'.[83] In literature, too, although Marcel is first charmed by individual passages of Bergotte, this pleasure is multiplied when he is able to relate such passages together to create 'a sort of thickness, of volume, by which my mind seemed enlarged'.[84]

The unity of art, therefore, is not 'given' by reality and passively recorded by the artist, although Proust's terms sometimes suggest this. It is created by the artist, as Proust makes most clear in the case of Elstir, who seeks constantly to detect in reality, or to project on to it, a basic formal pattern already existing in his mind:

> I understood that to a certain ideal type resumed by certain lines, by certain arabesques which recurred endlessly in his work, to a certain canon, he had indeed attributed an almost divine character, since his whole time, the whole mental effort of which he was capable, in a word his whole life, he had consecrated to the task of better distinguishing these lines, of more faithfully reproducing them.[85]

There is clearly a parallel between this activity of revealing the intensity latent in experience by imposing on reality certain preconceived 'ideal' structures, and Rilke's creative process discussed in the last chapter. We saw there that Rilke could only experience the 'total' reality of 'world-inner-space' by projecting 'figures' on to experience.

If this theoretical parallel between the two writers is to hold good, however, it must be supported by a recognisable similarity in the quality of vision embodied in their works. In order to undertake a comparison from this point of view we must decide first which passages in their works are most representative of the vision in question. In *Time Lost* we saw that Marcel's 'true life' is revealed to the primarily through involuntary memory. His 'lost homeland' is his own past life, and it is in the passages where he invokes this lost world directly, passages corresponding to the 'prayers' in Vinteuil's music, that his style rises to the 'song' identified earlier: 'What I want to see again is the Guermantes way I knew ...'[86] This lost world is symbolically restored to Marcel by the 'madeleine' incident, and its particular atmosphere, embodying the quality of vision with which we are concerned, is conveyed by Proust's style in the section of 'Combray' following that incident. Rilke, in writing the remaining *Elegies* and *Sonnets*, fulfilled both the aspirations of his long period of development discussed in the last chapter. In the *Elegies* he completed the unified expression of his poetic universe; in the *Sonnets* he produced a series of spontaneous, effortless poems involving the projection of 'figures'. This aspect of the *Sonnets* is made explicit in certain lines: 'For in truth we live in figures';[87] 'that projecting spirit, master of the earthly,/ loves nothing in the figure's swing [*Schwung*] more than the turning-point'.[88] The first part of the *Sonnets* was written immediately before the *Elegies* in a period of continuous creativity lasting several days. It was this experience of creativity, so long awaited, which enabled Rilke to complete the message of the *Elegies*. For he had now himself carried out the redeeming task which the *Elegies* proclaim; as he wrote later, the *Sonnets* show 'details' of the activity of translating the earth into the realm of the invisible.[89] It is to the joy and intensity of this creative experience that Rilke refers in the concluding lines of the Ninth Elegy: 'Superabundant existence/ springs up in my heart.'*

The analogy between the creative processes of Proust and Rilke should therefore be reflected by a likeness between the quality of vision embodied in 'Combray' and that in the *Sonnets*. These two works will now be briefly compared. It would be artificial to pursue the analogy too far in two so dissimilar writings. It should be noted, however, that their dissimilarity of form can be accounted for within the terms of the present analysis if it is remembered that this dissimilarity corresponds to the difference between two alternative forms of the creative process, that involving direct perception and that involving involuntary memory. As we have seen, both writers became aware of both possibilities, but Proust as a novelist cultivated primarily the latter, Rilke as a poet the former. In comparing their works we shall therefore concentrate on the quality of vision in both, leaving aside the element particular to narrative fiction in 'Combray' and to poetry in the *Sonnets*.

Early in the section of 'Combray' under discussion Proust evokes the scents and the atmosphere in Tante Léonie's rooms, the immediate scene recalled by the 'madeleine'. In half a page he accumulates the following phrases involving combinations of adjectives:

> a whole secret, invisible, superabundant and moral life suspended in the atmosphere ... stay-at-home, human and enclosed [scents], an exquisite, industrious and limpid jelly of all the fruits of the year ... seasonal, but

---

* This is no less true for the fact that these lines were written during the earlier inspiration of 1912. It was only the inspiration of 1922 that enabled Rilke to give them their place at the apex of his work.

smelling of furniture and domesticity ... leisurely and punctual like a village clock, sauntering and steady, careless and provident, redolent of washed linen, early-rising, pious, blithe ... a silence so nourishing, so succulent ... [90]

It can be seen that in rendering the quality of a scent Proust uses groups of adjectives drawn from other orders of sensation or experience as an analogy for it. He creates in fact an extensive and composite metaphor for the reality he is concerned to express. The meanings of the different and often contrasting adjectives 'converge'[91] to form a specific, individual meaning corresponding to the unique nature of the sensation. In this way Proust has expressed an aspect of reality which could not be conveyed by a single adjective or by any ready-made formula.

In the *Sonnets* Rilke shows a similar concern for registering the precise quality of a sensation normally all-but-inexpressible, such as the taste of an apple. He too uses an accumulation of adjectives to give a composite yet particular effect:

> Wagt zu sagen, was ihr Apfel nennt.
> Diese Süße, die sich erst verdichtet,
> um, im Schmecken leise aufgerichtet,
>
> klar zu werden, wach und transparent,
> doppeldeutig, sonnig, erdig, hiesig –:
> O Erfahrung, Fühlung, Freude –, riesig![92]

Dare to say what you call apple. This sweetness which first concentrates in order, in the tasting softly held erect, to grow clear, awake, transparent, of two meanings, sunny, earthly, this-worldly –: O discovery, feeling, joy –, immense!

Like Proust, Rilke draws his analogies from a number of different orders of experience. In this way both writers make concentrated use of metaphor to bring to consciousness a level of experience which normally cannot be accounted for in words.

But in addition the metaphors are used to relate the impressions described here to others in other parts of the works. Proust's evocation of Tante Léonie's rooms contains numerous elements associated more widely with Combray. A number of adjectives refer to moral qualities, in particular to religious devotion. These connect the scene to the 'strange and pious sadness'[93] particular to Combray, an astringently religious atmosphere in which the 'blackish stones'[94] of the houses, the biting wind at Easter, and above all the church, are all involved. Other adjectives dealing with qualities of domesticity suggest the protected well-being of Marcel's family, indefatigibly maintained by Françoise. Others evoke the sensations of the palate which figure largely in his impressions. Other adjectives – 'leisurely', 'sauntering' – suggest the atmosphere of summer days spent reading, their stillness punctuated by chimes from the church.

In this way the atmosphere of the whole period evoked in 'Combray' is present in one of its parts. The technique which we saw at an early stage of development in 'Days of Reading' (1905) in Chapter Fourteen, has now been perfected. Combray itself is a complete world of intense, interrelated sensations organised round the church, which, flooded with multi-coloured light from its stained-glass windows, provides a luminous centre-piece. Through the flowers on the altar in the 'month of Mary', the fuchsias on its walls, and the proximity of the 'patisserie', the church is linked to the flowers, the young girls, and the joys of eating which, in an indissoluble unity, are the images constantly pre-occupying Marcel's naïve sensuality.

It is beyond the scope of this study to show in detail how these images are interwoven by Proust to form the complex and unified fabric of 'Combray'. A few examples will, however, illustrate his technique, while showing in a more general way his ability to use metaphor to convey an abundance of interrelated sensations: 'the steeple, golden and baked itself like a larger blessed "brioche", with flakes and sticky oozings of sun, pricked its sharp point into the blue sky';[95] 'these flowers had chosen just one of those tints found in edible things or in a delicate adornment to a dress';[96] 'so, in her fresh pink dress, the catholic, delicious bush shone smilingly'.[97] By this use of specific and interrelated imagery Proust gives to Combray the pervasive and unified atmosphere which characterises this part of the book.

Rilke too, in the *Sonnets*, uses a number of dominant images which give the work a unified atmosphere. Words such as 'clear', *gelöst* (loosened, dissolved), 'awake', 'gleam', appear frequently, and images of running water, sunlight, flowers, fruit and girls, often related together, contribute an atmosphere which not only has a particular freshness and radiance, but also recalls that of Combray, perhaps because the *Sonnets*, through the figure of Wera, the dead girl to whom the poems are dedicated, are like Combray associated with the world of childhood.

There are further analogies between the two works. In order to embrace a multiplicity of impressions, Proust's sentences character-istically progress by a kind of dilation; syntactical completeness is delayed so that a maximum of elements can be introduced to express a composite and unique reality:

Combray, de loin, à dix lieues à la ronde, vu du chemin de fer quand nous y arrivions la dernière semaine avant Pâques, ce n'était qu'une église résumant la ville, la représentant, parlant d'elle et pour elle aux lointains, et, quand on approchait, tenant serrés autour de sa haute mante sombre, en plein champ, contre le vent, comme une pastoure ses brebis, les dos laineux et gris des maisons rassemblées qu'un reste de remparts du moyen âge cernait çà et là d'un trait aussi parfaitement circulaire qu'une petite ville dans un tableau de primitif.[98]

Combray, from far off, from ten miles around, seen from the railway when we arrived the last week before Easter, was nothing but a church resuming the town, representing it, speaking of it and for it to the distances, and, as you drew nearer, clasping around her tall dark cloak, in the open fields, against the wind, like a shepherdess her flock, the woolly grey backs of the clustering houses which a remnant of the medieval ramparts ringed here and there with a line as perfectly circular as a little town in a primitive's painting.

Of this and similar sentences it could well be said, as Holthusen says of the syntax of Rilke's sonnets:

There are no main clauses, but a kind of prime or pivotal noun, from which issue the sequences of associations. And while the normal sentence advances as it were dynamically from subject to predicate, what we find here is a static identity of the subject. The sentence, then, unfolds itself in space.[99]

Holthusen gives as an example of this tendency in Rilke the sonnet beginning:

Blumen, ihr schließlich den ordnenden Händen verwandte,
(Händen der Mädchen von einst und jetzt),
die auf dem Gartentisch oft von Kante zu Kante
lagen, ermattet und sanft verletzt[100]

Flowers, akin at last to the hands that arrange you, (hands of girls of once and now), which often on the garden table lay from edge to edge, listless and gently harmed

Many other examples could be given. This use of syntax supplements that of adjectives discussed earlier, in linking in a single structure a wealth of descriptive material. The assimilation of this material is facilitated by a carefully-organised and unfaltering rhythm which in Proust's prose as in Rilke's sonnets is a fundamental unifying agent.

These stylistic devices help to give the vision of reality in both works its specific, individual quality. This sense of uniqueness is further enhanced by the self-contained, 'inward' quality of the two worlds. Combray is cut off from the outer world by its symbolic emergence from a cup of tea, and by the narrator's sense of it rising up inside himself. Likewise the world of the *Sonnets* is presented, in an image impossible to paraphrase, as the sleep of an 'inner maiden' (cf. 'Turning-Point'), who may also now be connected to Wera, contained in the poet: 'And slept in me. And all things were her sleep ... she slept the world.'[101]

These closed worlds are unified from within not only by the use of imagery already discussed, but by a structural backbone provided in Proust's novel by the Combray church, which appears in the first sentence and reappears throughout, and by the figure of Orpheus who has a similar presiding rôle in the *Sonnets*.

In the inward dimension of these worlds, past and present coexist. In the *Sonnets*, girls' hands are 'of once and now', and the horse seen long ago is as intensely present as the immediate landscape.[102] In 'Combray' the chronological sequence is indistinct and eclipsed by a particular kind of timelessness. Time is still seen passing in the gestures and actions evoked, but these impressions do not pass away to be replaced at once by those following them; they are, as it were, transfixed, eternalised by Proust's use of the imperfect tense, to become, in the phrase he applied to Flaubert, 'something indefinite which is prolonged'.[103] This quality, present also in the *Sonnets*, can scarcely be defined; it is conveyed more easily by examples:

> nous apercevions dans l'ombre, sous les tuyaux d'un bonnet éblouissant, raide et fragile comme s'il avait été de sucre filé, les remous concentriques d'un sourire de reconnaissance anticipé. C'était Françoise ... [104]

> we discerned in the shadow, under the flutings of a bonnet that was dazzling, stiff and fragile as if made from wafered sugar, the concentric eddies of a smile of anticipated gratitude. It was Françoise ...

> *Was* war wirklich im All?
> Nichts. Nur die Bälle. Ihre herrlichen Bogen.
> Auch nicht die Kinder... Aber manchmal trat eines,
> ach ein vergehendes, unter den fallenden Ball.[105]

> *What* was real in the universe? Nothing. Only the balls. Their wonderful flights. Not the children either... But sometimes one, oh, a vanishing one, stepped under the falling ball.

In this way the worlds of both works lack the clear distinctions of time and space, resulting from the subordination of sense-impressions to the needs of action, characteristic of normal life. They are worlds in which sensation has become self-sufficient, so rich and manifold as to submerge and dissolve the categories and distinctions which normally govern the awareness of reality. Conventional attributes are replaced by a unity far more pervasive, and by a quality both more intense and more precise, than those of normal experience. To borrow the words of the writers themselves, the world as expressed in their works is no longer 'muffled and enveloped by our purposes',[106] but 'rid of what is imperfect in external perception, pure and disincarnate'.[107] The analogy between the quality of vision of the two writers, established earlier in theory, has therefore been found now to exist concretely in their works.

'Combray', however, is only a part of *In Search of Time Lost*. It is one of the numerous 'worlds' – Balbec, Venice, Doncières, etc. – making up the complex universe of the novel. These worlds are not always large-scale episodes like Combray and Balbec; they may be much more limited in extent like Rivebelle or the box at the Opéra. There may also be separate individual worlds within a larger one, like the two 'ways' in 'Combray'.

What all these worlds have in common is the possession of a distinctive individual atmosphere, frequently denoted by a group of adjectives; the atmosphere of Balbec is: 'pure, azure, saline',[108] that of Rivebelle: 'translucent, compact, fresh and sonorous'.[109] This atmosphere is usually established by a descriptive 'set-piece' of highly imaginative prose, or a number of such scenes taken together, for example, the description of the church and later of the hawthorns in 'Combray', or that of the promenade at Balbec against the background of the sea. It is frequently Proust's practice to precede such set-pieces by one or more shorter descriptions which establish the tone for the full-scale passage. In 'Combray' the full description of the church is anticipated by the view from a distance; the description of the hawthorns personified as girls is prepared by a briefer passage on the lilacs personified as 'young houris'.[110] The dominating image of Balbec, the brilliant expanse of sunlit sea and sky, frequently framed in the window of the restaurant or of Marcel's room or reflected in the glass bookcases, first appears briefly at the beginning of 'Place-Names: the Name', far in advance of the extended description. The set-piece comparing the box at the Opéra to a mythological 'marine grotto' is prepared by a brief glimpse about two pages earlier.[111] Georges Piroué has noted the widespread use of this technique of 'double exposition' in the novel: 'The majority of the main episodes in his novel go by twos',[112] and compares it to the exposition and repetition of a theme in music. As in music, the sensibility is prepared by the prior introduction of the theme, and when the full development takes place, the response to it is enriched by memory. To use Proust's terms, the experience of the theme introduced a second time is no longer 'thin and linear' like those in normal life; it is given by memory 'the base, the consistency of a rich orchestration'.[113]

In the case of the worlds of the novel, this interrelatedness of the descriptive elements helps to give each world a self-contained quality, cut off from the rest. It is Proust's purpose to show each of these worlds as 'isolated, enclosed, immobile, arrested and lost'.[114] They are all hermetically closed like the two 'ways' at Combray, 'the sealed vases, without communication between them, of different afternoons'.[115] The only access which Marcel has to these worlds is through involuntary memory. Voluntary memory replaces the uniqueness of a particular experience by elements common to all experience and so dissipates the individual atmosphere of the past. The series of moments of involuntary memory in 'Time Regained' gives Marcel a sense of the volume of his own past in which these 'sealed vases' are distributed, 'disposed on all the height of our years ... situated at very different altitudes'.[116]

But the existence of these isolated worlds confronts Proust with a fundamental artistic problem: that of unity. 'Combray', as we saw, is unified by its atmosphere, but how, out of the accumulation of totally distinct atmospheres making up his past, is Proust to create a work which is unified as a whole? In the novel he gives several hints at the solution to this problem. It is his practice to introduce scenes which, read symbolically, illuminate the structure of the novel or the vision underlying it. One such scene is the dinner at Rivebelle when Marcel, his vision heightened by alcohol, sees the tables surrounded by bustling waiters as forming a complex but harmonious planetary system. The factor which unifies the separate 'worlds' of this system is the human element: the curiosity of the people composing them and the activity of the waiters moving between them:

> Moreover, an irresistible force of attraction was exerted between these different stars and at each table the diners had eyes only for the tables at which they were not ... The harmony of these astral tables did not prevent the incessant revolution of the numberless servants, ... their perpetual courses finally disclosed the law of their vertiginous and ordered circulation.[117]

The full symbolic implications of this passage will become clear in the course of an analysis of the structure of *Time Lost*. It can be seen at once, however, that the presence of people in the novel provides the possibility of a unity and harmony composed by its disparate worlds analogous to that in the restaurant. Proust gives a further hint of this when he includes in the novel his idea, which we have already encountered in *Against Sainte-Beuve*, that Balzac gave his work a 'retrospective unity' by using the same characters in different novels.

The various worlds of *Time Lost* are united by Marcel's presence in all of them and his constant curiosity to penetrate other worlds, and by his meeting other characters from different worlds in new surroundings. Moreover, the presence of the same character in more than one world does not constitute merely an abstract link between them: it unites their atmosphere, their essence. This happens because each character is associated by Marcel with the landscape or 'world' in which he first saw them, or with which his imagination surrounds their name. A person for him is also an image: Saint-Loup and Albertine are always framed by the sea at Balbec, Gilberte is seen against the hawthorn hedges, Mme de Guermantes' name has attached to it not only the Merovingian past but the landscape of the 'Guermantes Way', Mme de Stermaria is silhouetted against a fragment of Brittany. Each person, moving through the novel, evokes the image of a past world in the manner of a *leit-motiv* in Wagner, as Georges Poulet has observed.[118] As a result, Mme de Guermantes, for example, brings into a *salon* in Paris a part of the countryside near Combray:

> Her name, being accompanied by her title, added to her physical person her duchy which projected about her the Guermantes woods, diffusing their shaded and golden freshness in the middle of the *salon*, around the stool where she was seated.[119]

This method of organisation, in which one world gives way to another and is then found projected on to it by the reappearance of a character, is symbolised during Marcel's first train journey to Balbec. He sees out of his window in the early morning a band of red sky, then at a turning in the line finds it replaced by a section of starry sky, against which he then discovers a fragment of red sky reflected in a window.

But during the course of the novel Marcel is largely unaware of this unifying factor, and experiences his life as discontinuity. In each person he sees only the aspect which they present at the moment. At the final matinée, however, which is separated from the rest of the novel by a long period in sanatoria, and is preceded by the moments of involuntary memory which restore to him a sense of the different 'worlds' of his past, Marcel is able to see and compare in retrospect the different images which have become attached at different periods to the same person:

> Gilberte's shadow lay not only in front of a church in the Ile-de-France where I had imagined her, but on a walk in a park the Méséglise way, Mme de Guermantes' on a wet path where clusters of violet and deep-red flowers climbed, or on the early-morning gold of a Parisian pavement.[120]

By the end of the novel, therefore, each character has attached to him not one, but a multiplicity of disparate images. Moreover, a similar substitution of different images has taken place in their physical appearance. Marcel's old acquaintances are so much changed that at first he fails to recognise them. In order to identify them he must reconcile two or more totally dissimilar impressions: 'I had to read at the same time on several planes which were situated behind them and gave them depth'. People recognised in this way reveal concretely the depth of the past, they become 'puppets immersed in the immaterial colours of the years, puppets externalising time'. Normally invisible, time needs bodies in order to reveal itself, and where it finds them, 'takes possession of them to show on them its magic lantern'.[121] Proust's comparison to the effect of the magic lantern, showing the symbolic significance of the Combray episode, conveys the sense of translucence, of 'diaphanous depth'[122] which now replaces the normal opacity of the present. Marcel's vision of his life now embodies a new dimension, the dimension of time, which was symbolised early in the novel by the Combray church, and, as we saw, by the Guermantes church in *Against Sainte-Beuve*. Each period of Marcel's life, each 'world' is seen no longer in isolation, but as a layer in a series of superimposed layers extending back to his childhood. The act of recognition makes possible 'an optical view of the years'.[123]

The structural value of recognition for the novel can now be seen. Involuntary memory had been able to reveal the essence of the past, but it did so by obliterating all other periods, including the present. It created a void around the world resurrected. Recognition now fills this void with a continuous medium through which each world is joined to the others.

Roger Shattuck, whose study of Proust's 'binocular vision' makes clear the importance of recognition in the novel, assumes that this implies the relegation of involuntary memory to a secondary rôle. He sees involuntary memory as tending to 'encourage the substitution of pleasure for effort',[124] a tendency which is brought to an end by the final assertion of recognition, a 'larger, more responsible, more mature act' involving the renunciation of 'lesser pleasures and illusions'.[125] But it is hoped that the present study has shown that Proust was by now beyond the stage of exploiting the privileged moment for pleasure, and that he saw it, as 'Time Regained' makes explicit, only as a source of 'as many laws and ideas'.[126]

We saw that the principal of these laws, as applied to literature, was that of metaphor, which alone, for Proust, is capable of showing the true unity of experience. In the first place Proust applied the discovery of this law to style. In the passage in which Proust defines metaphor as the only source of truth – 'truth will only begin when the writer takes two different objects, poses their connection ... and encloses them in the necessary rings of a beautiful style'[127] – he is concerned with descriptive style and not yet with narrative structure. Proust is here defining the style which he used in conveying the individual quality of Combray, Balbec, etc., and without which his kind of novel would be impossible. But style alone is not sufficient to make a novel; it must be complemented by a structure. It is here that recognition becomes important. In recognition the law of metaphor – that is, 'similarity with a difference'[128] – is applied no longer on the stylistic but on the structural level. In this way the advent of recognition, far from cancelling the message of involuntary memory, completes its application by extending the law of metaphor to all levels of the novel, as Shattuck himself observes: 'The action which dominates all of [*Time Lost*] ... is the action of metaphor: the reconciliation of a duality or, in more complex cases, of a multiplicity.'[129]

Proust applies the law of 'similarity with a difference' to the narrative structure by contriving the reappearance at different points in his life of 'the same beings, but in different forms and for varied ends'. By this process his life is given a quality of balance and symmetry: 'my life was already long enough for me to find, for more than one being that it presented to me, in my memories of opposed regions, another being to complete it'.[130]

The symmetrical structure produced in this way by recognition is extended and completed by Proust's device of organising the characters of the novel into two groups, associated with the 'ways': the world of Guermantes and society, and that of Swann – the world of love and vice. At the end of the novel the two worlds are symbolically united in Mlle de Saint-Loup, the daughter of Gilberte and Saint-Loup. In 'recognising' her Marcel becomes aware of the full extent of the structure unifying his own past:

> was she not like the 'stars' of forest cross-ways where paths from the most different points, for our lives too, converge? ... And above all there came together in her the two great 'ways' where I had had so many walks and dreams ... Already, between these two, transverse paths were being established[131]

Marcel's past life now appears to him as a complex fabric, a totally interrelated system in which everything is connected to everything else: 'between the smallest point of our past and all the others a rich network of memories leaves only the choice of communications'.[132]

But recognition in the novel does not unite only places and 'worlds'. The changes in people do not only concern the different image attaching to them or their altered physical appearance; they also include psychological changes brought about through time. Recognition involves the perception of unity underlying these changes also, which in Proust's novel are often singularly drastic, involving the substitution for one personality or 'self' of an entirely different one several times in a lifetime. The most dramatic example of this phenomenon is Saint-Loup, but it is universal in the novel and is particularly visible at the final matinée.

The recognition of unity underlying changes of this kind not only means applying the same name to the different successive 'selves' of the same person; it also involves the recognition of common characteristics appearing in different people. For Proust, moral qualities are not inherent in individual characters; they are almost external to the individual – 'pre-existent, general, inevitable'[133] – attaching themselves to him only temporarily. The real psychological unit for Proust is not the person but these 'moral cells'[134] more lasting than the individual, which manifest themselves in individuals according to certain laws, such as that of heredity.

A large part of *Time Lost* consists of psychological analysis devoted to revealing these laws. This is the 'less pure matter, but still imbued with spirit',[135] with which Proust supplements the material provided by involuntary memory – the poetic evocation of the past. It is often considered that there is total discontinuity between the psychological and the 'poetic' sections of *Time Lost*.[136] But we have seen that the fundamental law of the novel is the law of metaphor, the creating of unity out of multiplicity. It will now be argued that the psychological section of the novel involves not an exception to this law but a further extension of it.

A critic has remarked that Proust's 'laws' appear to be the product of intuition rather than of observation and induction.[137] Proust is highly selective in the laws he embodies in his novel. He includes only those which serve to give a unified explanation of his created world, that is, laws demonstrating the discontinuity of the moral personality and above all the mental nature of reality and the impossibility of self-realisation through external action. In taking over existing scientific laws, Proust particularly favours those which embody most clearly the principle of metaphor – sameness in difference – such as the law of heredity which determines that 'if things repeat themselves, it is with great variations'.[138]

Proust's laws explain not only the behaviour of the individual personality but that of society. It is because a *salon*, in its changing composition, manifests certain laws, that it takes on a meaning it would otherwise lack: 'the interest of these transformations in the *salons* was that they too were an effect of time lost and a phenomenon of memory'.[139] Proust justifies the inclusion of social scenes in his novel on the grounds that they too contribute a structural element, 'important truths worthy of cementing a part of my work'.[140]

Proust's psychological laws enable him to perceive an underlying unity in the manifold spectacle of human life, not only on the level of social manners but on that of fundamental impulses and passions:

> Just as, listening to Cottard, Brichot and so many others talking, I had felt that, through culture and fashion, a single undulation propagates throughout the length and breadth of space the same ways of speaking and thinking, so throughout the whole duration of time a mighty ground-swell lifts from the depths of the ages the same angers, the same

sorrows, the same acts of bravery, the same manias through the overlaid generations, each section made several times in the same series showing the repetition, like shadows on successive screens, of an ... identical picture.[141]

It can be seen here how for Proust the discovery of laws contributes to the same vision of repetition in depth on different levels as is produced by recognition. Proust's impulse in searching for laws of human behaviour is not primarily scientific or sociological, still less is it humane: it is an aesthetic impulse.

Marcel himself recognises this in connection with his attitude to Saint-Loup. The pleasure he gains from Saint-Loup as a friend is insignificant beside the aesthetic satisfaction of seeing him as a mani-festation of the law of heredity:

> Sometimes I reproached myself for thus taking pleasure in considering my friend as a work of art, that is, in seeing the play of all the parts of his being as harmoniously regulated by a general idea from which they were suspended.[142]

At the end of the book Marcel derives the same aesthetic pleasure from the whole spectacle of his past life, which he is able to see as 'this whole immensity regulated by laws'.[143]

Proust's 'psychology in space'[144] is therefore an integral part of the structure constituted by his novel. The depth of this structure, as we have seen, is contributed by the dimension of time. Time becomes visible in the novel because one moment is not annihilated by the next but continues to exist, visible through the translucence of succeeding moments. Successive time is replaced by what Shattuck calls 'simul-taneous time',[145] and Poulet 'the simultaneity of the successive'.[146]

Time implies movement, and movement is an essential element of *Time Lost*. The movements in the novel are however, like time, pre-served in the structure, a structure composed of movements all parts of which are simultaneously visible. The principal movement is Marcel's progression from childhood to maturity, which gives a clear temporal axis to the structure. This movement is not a straight line, but a circle, or, as Shattuck says, a spiral,[147] for Marcel at the end ex-periences the revelation giving him back his past and enabling him, now as a novelist, to start his life again at the beginning. The novel is therefore closed on itself. By creating this circular movement in the narrative 'line' Proust has solved the problem which Rilke failed to solve, as we saw, in *Malte Laurids Brigge*.

Within this all-embracing movement secondary movements are con-tained. Marcel's path through the novel follows a winding course like the railway-line on the journey already mentioned, and like all journeys in vehicles in the novel. It is a property of such sinuous journeys in Proust, as Poulet notes, that they communicate their movement to the surrounding landscape, making, for example, 'a *château*, a hill, a church and the sea' cross back and forth and change places as in a dance or a children's game.[148] In a similar way, the changes in position of the characters in the novel, together with the real changes in them, appear in the dimension of 'simultaneous time' as a complex system of interlocking movements:

> So each individual – and I was myself one of these individuals – measured the passage of time for me by the revolution which he had accomplished not only around himself, but around the others, and notably by the positions which he had occupied successively in relation to me.[149]

Similar movements are presented by the spectacle of society seen in time; individuals and coteries are constantly rising and falling and changing places on the social scale. The principal movements in this plane are those of the Guermantes and the Verdurins, in which the descent of the former is matched by the rise of the latter, until both are united at the end when Mme Verdurin becomes the Princesse de Guermantes. In this way the movements of social groups show a quality of harmony and balance which enables Proust to compare them to heavenly bodies: 'the conglomerations of coteries broke up and recomposed themselves according to the attraction of new stars which, moreover, were to move away in their turn, then to reappear'.[150] In the moral plane, similar balanced movements are present; for example, the decline of Saint-Loup is matched by the rise of Morel, and vice versa.

In this way Marcel's past life in his final vision is animated by a universal movement in which all things circulate in interrelated patterns: 'Just as a bucket rising on a windlass touches the rope at various intervals and on opposite sides, there was not a person and hardly even a thing in my life which had not, by turns, played different rôles in it.'[151] The full symbolic implications of the description of the restaurant at Rivebelle quoted earlier can now be seen. In the novel the human elements – characters, 'moral cells' and *salons* – circulate constantly between the fixed worlds revealed by involuntary memory like the waiters of whom Proust wrote: 'their perpetual courses between the round tables finally disclosed the law of their vertiginous and ordered circulation'.[152]

The 'universe' of Proust's novel, with its interrelated movements and its laws of balance and symmetry, clearly bears a striking resemblance to the 'poetic universe' of Rilke's late period, analysed in the last chapter. It was to the quality of interrelatedness in the novel that

Rilke drew particular attention in a letter of 1922, occasioned by the news of Proust's death:

> any other would have been able to risk such connecting-lines from event to event only as auxiliary lines in a diagram, but with Proust they immediately take on an ornamental beauty as well and so have, as a pictorial element too, validity and permanence.

When this was written, 'The Prisoner', 'The Fugitive' and 'Time Regained' had not yet been published. But Rilke already saw Proust as possessing a command of the whole spectacle of life as an ordered structure: 'this strange sooth-sayer must have seen life constantly open before him, like a gigantic hand whose lines were so ingrained in the essential that they could no longer have any surprises for him'.[153]

In Chapter Fifteen it was seen that the basic axis of Rilke's 'poetic universe' is provided by the distance between man and the angel, and that the depth of the structure, produced by this sense of distance, symbolises the renunciation of the direct experience of the privileged moment (cf. p. 217). A similar situation is present in Proust's novel. The depth is provided by the distance between the narrator and the world of 'time lost' which, as we have seen, is that of the privileged moment. Moreover Proust, like Rilke, introduces this basic structural axis in the first sentence of his work: 'For a long time I went to bed early': 'Who, if I cried out, would hear me from the angelic/ orders?' In both cases the two extreme poles of the structure – the 'I' and the distant world of the privileged moment – are present at the outset. The distant reality is not possessed, but is held in a relationship to the 'I' by an intense nostalgic feeling, intermittently expressed openly by the 'song' of Proust's voice, which corresponds to the 'dark sobbing' of the First Elegy. Rilke summed up this standpoint, fundamental to both works, in a letter of 1923: 'instead of possession one learns relation [*Bezug*]'.[154]

The 'relation' introduced in the first line of both works opens up the inner space – 'that transposed, deep and intrinsic space',[155] in Rilke's words – in which the work of art exists. Into this space both writers project the dominant experiences of their lives, externalised as symbols or as characters having symbolic value, which are in turn related not only to the symbolised higher reality but also to each other. In this way the symbolic structure is produced in which the privileged moment, though not directly possessed, is related to the whole of the writer's life.

The totality of experience embodied in this structure is reflected in the consciousness of the 'I' which permeates the work. The *Ich* of the *Elegies*, as we saw, transcends Rilke's personal self. In a similar way, the *je* of *Time Lost* includes and transcends all its modalities, both the protagonist and the later Marcel whose 'song' permeates the poetic sections of the novel. As Gaëtan Picon observes:

> the self which this work presents and which fills it, indeed, as water fills a basin, is by no means ... the narrow track of a life, and the echoes which a personal consciousness recovers from it, but a mirror of the world as clear and vast as possible, a mirror whose frame is no doubt that of a personal consciousness, but of a consciousness directed on the world, working to distend itself until it equals the world.[156]

Towards the end of *Time Lost* Marcel has a glimpse of the structure of his future work and momentarily experiences an expansion of his awareness which fills him with joy: 'the happiness I felt ... came ... from an enlarging of my mind in which this past was being reconstituted and actualised, giving me, momentarily, alas! a value of eternity'.[157] For Rilke too the creation of his work meant embracing in his mind the totality of his life: 'we must attempt to achieve the largest consciousness of our existence'.[158] Moreover, this expansion of awareness involved also, as he writes in the same letter, a joyful affirmation of life and death.

The final works therefore embody an expanded consciousness in which the whole of the writer's life is reflected. The world thus reflected is characterised by qualities of harmony, unity and necessity, and communicates a sense of joy. In these works the writers have therefore realised, in the highest possible degree, the conditions of the privileged moment. The world is totally reflected in and identified with the self – though admittedly this is no longer the biographical self of the writer. The identification is made complete by the fact that not only the consciousness reflecting the world, but the passions and emotions animating the figures in this world, are embodiments of the writer's self.

But in what sense is the term 'self' used here? An analogy with music may help to establish its meaning. It can be argued that a composer cannot write one part of a rigorously-structured work without in some way being aware of the other parts. In the same way the consciousness of the Proust – no longer the biographical Proust – who writes 'I' in the opening sentence of *Time Lost* might, because the work is totally interrelated, be equated with the totality of the experience embodied in the book. The same would apply to the 'I' of the *Elegies*. It may be said that a piece of music exists 'ideally', because of the existence of fixed relationships between its notes, whether or not it is being played. In the same sense we might speak of the 'ideal' existence of Proust's novel and of the self embodied in it, and similarly with Rilke.[159] We have arrived, therefore, at the conception of an 'ideal self' present in the work and totally severed from the writer's actual biographical existence. In a letter of 1923, Rilke expressed a similar conception of the way in which Proust existed in his completed work: 'how he was one with all that, scarcely detained here any longer, now that it lay finished before him'.[160] Of this ideal self it may be said that he continues to exist in the relationships built into the works, whether or not the author is alive.

In a sense, therefore, the writers have indeed escaped from time. Henceforth, in a 'monumental circular subjectivity',[161] their experience is totally and permanently reflected in their consciousness. They have achieved the only complete and lasting realisation of the privileged moment. Whereas in the early period the identification between subject and object was effected only by suppressing the objective world, and in the middle period only by suppressing the subject's self-consciousness, here the 'I' and the world are both equally and totally present in a true identification. Admittedly, this has been achieved only at the price of renouncing the direct enjoyment of the privileged moment and substituting the 'ideal' for the existential self.

So far, in discussing the unified world of *Time Lost*, we have been concerned with the vision underlying the book. Proust's task as a novelist was to convey this vision using the resources of literature. Out of a succession of words and sentences he must create the inner space and the 'simultaneous time' of his novel.

We have seen that there is an analogy between the structure of the novel and that of a work of music. Proust himself specifically compares the 'volume' of his past life to that of a piece of music,[162] and it is well known that he adopted certain principles of musical composition in constructing his novel. It is beyond the scope of this study to discuss this question in detail; mention should be made, however, of a recent contribution, J. M. Cocking's demonstration of a close parallel between the structure of *Time Lost* and that of Franck's Quartet of 1889.[163]

Fundamental to the analogy with music is Proust's use of thematic composition. His 'double exposition' of themes has already been discussed with regard to individual scenes; this technique is extended to provide the structure of the novel as a whole. At the start, Proust evokes his world from darkness by introducing a narrator without identity on the threshold of sleep, in whose mind there appears a rapid succession of fragmentary impressions and memories. These impressions are at once spread out and spatialised by the image of 'a sleeping man holding in a circle around him the succession of hours, the order of years and worlds'.

The themes of the novel – people and places and times as well as emotions and ideas, are thus briefly indicated in the opening pages,

K

and by the end of 'Combray' a part of Proust's world is solidly established and the foundations of the rest have been laid. When the major
developments of the themes take place, they have already been prepared by the 'overture' or 'exposition' at the start. In this way,
throughout the novel, nothing occurs in isolation, everything is related
forwards and backwards in time; as Piroué observes: 'Every sentence
he writes will be at once a premonition and a reminder.'[164] At the end
of the novel all the themes are drawn together and the final revelation
gives meaning to Marcel's life and to the work as a whole.

The analogy with Franck's Quartet, in which, as Cocking says,
'every part is bound to every other part, and the last movement explains the rest', can therefore be clearly seen. But if, as Cocking suggests
Franck influenced Proust, it was in the manner of the influences previously discussed. He did not provide Proust with his vision, but helped
him to discover the technical means of realising it. That the thematic
form was already latent in the vision can be shown by reference to
Rilke's Elegies. In expressing a vision which we have seen to be
analogous to Proust's, Rilke arrived at a markedly similar form. The
thematic manner of composition necessitates the 'taking hold and
letting go of things' which Rilke had admired earlier in Dauthendey
and which he also admired in Proust; he wrote of the 'tact of his exposition, which nowhere becomes fixed but playfully lets go of what it
had just seemed to be holding'.[165] In writing the Elegies Rilke showed
a similar ability to manipulate simultaneously a number of themes,
and produced, in a much simpler form, a thematic structure resembling that of Time Lost. As E. Buddeberg shows, the Elegies are 'a
logically self-contained whole of the strictest architectonic completeness'.[166] Themes are first introduced briefly in an expositive section,
then elaborated in individual Elegies: 'By the close of the Second
Elegy all the themes have been sounded. Each subsequent Elegy takes
up one or several closely-related themes again.'[167] In the Ninth and
Tenth Elegies, as at the end of Time Lost, the themes are brought
together and the general significance of the work is revealed.

At this point, however, a fundamental difference between music and
literature must be taken into consideration. Whereas music deals with
themes and motifs consisting of conceptually meaningless sounds,
literature operates with concepts and on a larger scale with values and
whole areas of experience. The themes of Proust's and Rilke's works
are fundamental human experiences: love, friendship, solitude, society,
suffering, death, art. In reconciling all these themes in a conclusion
revealing the general meaning of the work, Proust and Rilke are
not only completing a formal structure, but giving a total meaning to
life.

For this reason the 'message' of their final works has much in common with a religious teaching. Like a religion these works establish an all-embracing framework within which each particular experience can be given meaning. The influence of this religious aspect of their work on critical interpretations is notorious and need not be discussed here. It is perhaps more important to note that it gave to their own lives a kind of religious framework which, once created, was not changed. Each new experience was interpreted through it and accommodated within it. For example, Proust assimilated the long experience with Agostinelli into his novel without violating its plan or its philosophy. It has been said that Rilke's last poems mark a new departure. But in poems such as 'Music', 'Gong', 'Shawl', 'The Heart's Swing', etc., Rilke is still working within the 'word-field'[168] built up in the period which gave rise to the *Elegies*. In another group of poems Rilke follows the other direction traced in Chapter Fifteen, writing spontaneous descriptive poems evoking the landscape around Muzot and involving the projection of 'figures'. This group includes the poems written in French. It would be mistaken to compare these later poems in importance with the *Elegies* and *Sonnets*, which Rilke continued to speak of as the high point of his creative life,[169] whereas he referred to the poems in French, for example, in much more modest terms.[170]

The general interpretations of life contained in the late works of both writers are frequently criticised on the grounds that they fail to do justice to whole areas of human experience, and in particular, that they give an inadequate account of human relationships such as friendship and love. But we have seen that at the centre of their works there is a myth, which in the case of both writers is essentially the same. It is a myth according to which there is a state of being incomparably superior to everyday life; only in this higher state of being can fulfilment be experienced, yet a man who lives a normal human life, devoted to outward action, will be led farther and farther away from this fulfilment. He will have only rare glimpses of the higher world and will misinterpret them as incitements to further action and further frustration. So he will condemn himself to live his life in a treadmill of false hopes and perpetual dissatisfaction. Such a picture of life, with its single conception of human fulfilment, brings with it a scale of values and a morality which are essentially simple. Those experiences which lead man away from fulfilment – and these include all experiences which involve a commitment in the outer world, through action or personal relationships – are bad; those which lead towards fulfilment – solitude, inwardness and, above all, artistic creation – are good. Both writers adhere to this morality throughout their final works, with only two minor exceptions. Marcel's relationship to his grandmother, and in general Proust's attitude to the 'Combray virtues', introduce a scale of moral values incompatible with those central to his work. Rilke's Third Elegy, written in close proximity to his interest in psycho-analysis, contains implications which conflict with the monistic conception of human fulfilment put forward in the *Elegies* as a whole. But neither writer allows these inconsistent elements to develop far enough to threaten the impression of unity conveyed by his work.

In this way the interpretations of life offered by Proust and Rilke, although they may conflict on many points with general human experience, do not contradict themselves. It is this above all which gives them their power to convince, to carry the reader with them despite his misgivings over their account of particular experiences. The value of such interpretations of life does not lie primarily in the truth to empirical reality of each of their parts, but in the relation of the parts to one another. Proust and Rilke do not offer a philosophy in the strict sense, but an image of life, in which all the important human experiences are seen to form a pattern. Such an image of life seeks finally to be judged, like a work of art, according to its qualities of internal coherence, harmony, and wholeness. The appeal of a total explanation of life, whether in literature, religion or philosophy, is an aesthetic appeal. As Thomas Mann has written apropos of Schopenhauer – another great system-builder, whose work, incidentally, Proust, at least, read and admired:

> The pleasure we take in a metaphysical system, the satisfaction afforded us by the intellectual organisation of the world into a logically complete, harmoniously self-contained structure of ideas, is always predominantly of an aesthetic kind; it is of the same origin as the delight, the high and ultimately always serene gratification, which the ordering, shaping activity of art, making the confusion of life transparent and comprehensible, bestows on us.[171]

In such a system, 'beauty is truth'. For the writer producing it, the impulse towards truth is inseparable from his sense of beauty. This interdependence of truth and beauty is found throughout Proust's novel. In 'Combray' he writes of them as the goals of a single impulse: 'the secret of truth and beauty, half fore-known, half incomprehensible, the discovery of which was the vague but permanent goal of my thought'.[172] His definition of truth in 'Time Regained' is one in which beauty plays an essential part: 'truth will only begin when the writer takes two different objects, poses their connection ... and encloses them in the necessary rings of a beautiful style'.[173] For Rilke, rhyme, the most basic of the means by which the poet gives aesthetic order to experience, is a manifestation of a profound truth bound up with the nature of language and reality; he calls it 'the divinity of very secret and very ancient coincidences ... The true rhyme is not a poetic device, it is an infinitely affirmative "Yes" which the gods deign to set against our most innocent emotions'.[174]

We can now return to the question raised earlier in this chapter, concerning the truth of the two writers' answers to the question: What is life? The truth of the symbolic structure embodied in their works is clearly not the same as that of a logical proposition, or of a scientific proof, or, at the other extreme, of a metaphysical revelation. It is the truth of art; it satisfies the desire, not for detailed factual information, but for completeness, for total consistency, for a unified vision of the whole of life. Which of these two distinct impulses is the desire for truth? If we are finally unable to assess their answer to the question: What is life? it is because this answer raises the further question: What is truth?

But the nature of the desire satisfied by their final works, whether or not it is the desire for truth, has now been established. It is the desire to survey the whole of life in a single act of contemplation. But to contemplate life in this way is to experience it as reality is experienced during a privileged moment. We have seen that the impulse to realise the privileged moment in their works was fundamental to the development of the two writers; the attempt, through writing, to give the intensity and unity of the privileged moment to their awareness of particular moments of experience led to the attempt to give these qualities to their awareness of the whole of their lives. But, as we saw, they were unable to do this as long as they wrote directly about themselves; to achieve a unified presentation they were obliged to symbolise their experience, to present it as that of all mankind. In this way their attempt to produce a general interpretation of life can be seen to be the result of a specific process. Not only their answer to the question: What is life? but the question itself is a manifestation, far removed from its source but still issuing directly from it, of the impulse to realise the privileged moment.

# Conclusion

THE phenomenon of expanded consciousness, we have now seen, played a decisive rôle in the work of Proust and Rilke. The writers' preoccupation with the privileged moment determined not only the nature of the creative process throughout their development, but also their interpretation of particular experiences and of life in general. Their fundamental creative impulse might be summed up as the attempt to transfer the whole of their experience from the sphere of everyday life to that of the privileged moment.

In the case of these two writers the dominance of the privileged moment is so complete that it might seem reasonable to suppose that any writer who has direct knowledge of the experience will be dominated by it in a similar way. This supposition, however, meets with immediate objections. The five writers introduced in Chapter One, for example, all of whom experienced privileged moments of the highest intensity, did not develop in the same way as Proust and Rilke. The diversity of their development would seem to invalidate any generalisation based on the experience.

These writers do conform to a pattern, however, even if it is not that set by Proust and Rilke. This pattern can be only briefly indicated here, but it is sufficiently definite to make brevity permissible. All the five writers, in the early part of their development, were concerned with the pursuit of a metaphysical absolute clearly connected to their experience of the privileged moment. But in all cases this was followed at a relatively early stage by a sharp reaction. The reaction is least distinct in the case of Baudelaire, but it has been defined by L. J. Austin as the reversion from *symbolique*, where symbols give access to a metaphysical realm, to *symbolisme*, where they are confined to the personal sphere.[1] In Flaubert, the reaction is more obvious – the abandonment of the mystical effusions of *The Temptation of Saint Anthony* for the realism of *Madame Bovary*. Hofmannsthal's 'Letter of Lord Chandos' reflects the crisis attending his transition from 'pre-existence' to 'existence', Valéry's 'Genoa night' marks the rejection of a 'spiritual' mysticism in favour of one of 'pure intellect', in O. Nadal's terms.[2] Sartre's early quest for metaphysical truth – 'For a long time I sought the Absolute: up to the time of *Nausea*'[3] – gives way to political commitment.

In all cases, therefore, the pursuit of the privileged moment is abandoned as a primary goal. To explain this, a further way in which these five writers differ from Proust and Rilke must be noted. The last two, as we have seen throughout this study, never experienced privileged moments as intense and clear-cut as those described in Chapter One. It is indeed at first sight puzzling why two writers whose experience of the privileged moment was comparatively marginal should be so persistently concerned with it. The explanation is, however, perhaps the following: in experiencing the privileged moment at its full intensity, the five writers in Chapter One were presented with its full implications. They saw that in its extreme form the privileged moment is incompatible with rational thought and practical action: 'that way madness lies', or, if not madness, the inarticulateness and inaction of the mystic. They were presented with the 'choice' between the world as experienced during the privileged moment and the world of normal life, and all five, with a greater or lesser degree of conviction, 'chose' the latter.

But Proust and Rilke were not presented with this choice. For them the full intensity of the privileged moment was never more than a tantalising possibility, something 'contained and concealed', to use Proust's phrase, in their impressions. But because they were denied direct access to it, the privileged moment took on for them an entirely new significance: it became an impulse to create. We have seen in this study that the creative process in all its phases was directed towards the realisation of the privileged moment. By using words in a particular way, the writers could, as it were, manoeuvre their consciousness closer to the maximum intensity of the privileged moment. The discovery of certain words was accompanied by a heightening of awareness and an increase in pleasure, which led to the discovery of further words and a further increase.

It is unnecessary now, in considering the final significance of this process, to recall particular instances in detail. Its essential nature is symbolised in a passage of *In Search of Time Lost*, describing the composer Vinteuil in the act of creating, which will serve as a recapitulation:

This Vinteuil whom I had known so timid and sad, had, when it was a question of choosing a timbre, of joining it to another, an audacity and, in the full sense of the word, a felicity of which a hearing of one of his works left no doubt. The joy which certain sonorities had caused him, the added strength it had given him to find others, led the listener too from discovery to discovery, or rather it was the creator himself who led him, drawing from the colours he had just found a wild joy which gave him the power to discover, to fling himself on those they seemed to call, entranced, quivering as if from an electric shock when the sublime sprang of itself from the meeting of brass with brass, breathless, drunk, distracted, dizzy, as he painted his great musical fresco like Michelangelo tied to his ladder, head down, hurling tumultuous brush-strokes against the ceiling of the Sistine Chapel.[4]

The similarity between artistic creation as presented here, and the other realm of human activity governed by the 'pleasure principle' – that of sexuality – need scarcely be pointed out. Both experiences involve a state of intoxication brought about by a progressive heightening of sensation which finally obliterates self-consciousness. It is easy to understand why art is frequently seen as a sublimation of the erotic impulse.

The proximity between the creative and erotic impulses makes it possible, however, to see an essential difference between them. Unlike sexuality, art, and its goal the privileged moment, involve an intensification of sensation received through the senses employed in normal perception – particularly vision and hearing. On the physiological level, the difference between the two impulses is that between the different nerve-centres which are involved in each case. On the level of experience, it is that between the two different sets of actions – one set involving human relationships, the other, as we saw, tending to exclude them – by which the impulse can be satisfied.

The first conclusion to be drawn from this study is therefore that the human drive for happiness, the 'pleasure principle', has not one goal, or source, but two (leaving aside the question of a pleasure-governed drive for destruction). The impulse towards the privileged moment is seen as a psychological mechanism operating alongside the erotic impulse according to similar principles. The two impulses are so alike that they are frequently amalgamated. In particular, the goal of the erotic impulse, being far more easily accessible, is frequently substituted for the other. As we have seen, this substitution is a central theme of the works of Proust and Rilke. But their works also show clearly that a confusion of the two impulses is a fundamental misunderstanding of human nature.

This conception of the privileged moment as a source of the 'pleasure principle' throws light on general human actions, of which Freud has taught us to see a whole range of human actions, of which neurotic symptoms are among the most obvious, as manifestations of the erotic impulse, the implications of the privileged moment, too, can be seen to permeate the whole field of human behaviour. They are present in the general human tendency to create patterns and ornamentation, to prefer symmetry, order and harmony to the absence of these qualities. They are seen not only in works of art but also, in however dilute a form, in any suburban window-display, advertisement hoarding or flower-bed.

It will be objected that this hypothesis, even if true, is unnecessary.

The human tendency to create order and art is self-evident; the idea of an impulse towards the privileged moment adds nothing to what is already known. According to this argument, the privileged moment is to be seen as a concomitant, an extreme manifestation, even a by-product, of well-known tendencies. This argument is, however, no more justifiable, and no less absurd, than the argument that the climax of erotic pleasure is a by-product of, for example, the well-known human tendency towards courtship. The value of this theory of the privileged moment is the power it gives to relate a whole range of human phenomena, of which mysticism, drug-taking and artistic creation are only the most obvious, to a specific principle.

A second objection to this theory is that it reduces literature to a means – and a particularly circuitous and cumbersome means – of achieving what could be had far more simply by other means such as taking drugs. Aldous Huxley's *The Doors of Perception*, for example, shows beyond doubt that states of consciousness identical to the privileged moment can be induced by mescaline. The answer to this objection has two parts. In the first place, the present theory does not attempt to account for all the impulses which produce a work of literature, but only for one among others. The impulse it explains is that which directly determines only the formal aspects of a work, although indirectly, as in the case of Proust and Rilke, it can extensively influence the subject-matter – the interpretation of experience – also. But even this particular impulse operates in a way essentially different from the action of drugs. It is in defining this difference – the second part of the answer to the objection above – that the value of literature, as conceived here, can be seen.

It has been observed throughout this study, and particularly in Chapter One, that the process of conceptualisation limits both the intensity of consciousness and the degree of significance and value experienced in reality. Only a small part of the potential intensity and value of experience is normally permitted to enter consciousness. The potential intensity of experience may be represented for convenience by a vertical scale; the actual intensity of consciousness is able to rise on this scale only as far as a point determined by the concepts which the mind has at its disposal. The coarser and cruder these concepts, the less experience will be admitted and the lower will be the intensity of consciousness.

The effect of drugs such as mescaline is to incapacitate the conceptualising faculty of the mind and thereby to remove the upper limit to the intensity of consciousness, which rises, as in the privileged moment, to cover the entire scale. But the rational concepts which are sacrificed in the process are the only means man has of controlling his external environment – they are the hard-won fruits of what Freud

K*

calls the 'reality principle'. To argue that man would be better without these concepts would be literally madness, just as it would be literally madness to recommend the general distribution of drugs like mescaline and other 'psychedelic' requisites as a way of enhancing the well-being of mankind.

The creative process, however, produces its effect in an entirely different way. It does not abolish the upper limit of intensity, but raises it by developing and refining the concepts at the disposal of the mind. In this way it produces an intensification of consciousness without forfeiting control over the rational faculties. Admittedly, in so doing it does not use concepts in the exclusively practical way characteristic of normal life.

It can be seen from this that the degree of value experienced in reality does not depend only on a fixed, intrinsic value present in the outside world. It depends also on the concepts through which the world is experienced. Progress therefore – if progress is taken to be an increase in the value experienced in reality – is not brought about solely by changes made in the external world, although this assumption underlies the word as commonly used. Progress is produced also, and to a large extent, by the modification of language.

In the course of this study we have seen how this modification takes place in the work of a creative writer. In order to realise the experience of a privileged moment, the writer must refine and extend his language to cover a new area of experience. When the experience has passed, the refinement and extension in his language remain behind as a permanent acquisition. Repeated experiences of this kind serve to raise the general level of the writer's power of conceptualisation; the intensity of his experience of reality is permanently raised on the scale referred to just now. This is the process by which such a writer acquires and improves his 'style', and it explains Proust's statement that style is ultimately a question not of technique but of vision.

But this acquisition is not confined to the writer; it is embodied in the increased resources of the language he uses and is at the disposal of all who use this language. In this way the progress of an individual is passed on to the culture in which he lives. The contribution made by Rilke and Proust in this way has been summed up by H. E. Holthusen:

> Rilke's new discoveries and inventions in the world of words amount to an unparalleled extension alike of sensibility and of the capacity for expression. To a degree inconceivable before him, the German language seems to have been softened, made more intimate, inward and spiritual, more limpid – and yet at the same time more precise, intellectual, and factual. Rilke has done for German lyrical poetry what Proust did for French prose: both have opened up an entirely new microcosmic con-

sciousness, both have discovered a kind of microphysics of the heart. And this discovery they have accomplished by the same means: the remembrance of things past, a heightened state of inwardness, and the subtle play of intellectual distinctions. [5]

Admittedly, in the present cultural situation, the contribution of such writers is far outweighed by the constant debasement of language through politics and the mass media.

Proust and Rilke make available to the reader of their works an optical instrument, to use Proust's expression, through which the reader can recognise in his own experience a degree of meaning and value which would otherwise remain invisible. For this reason writers like them who devote a lifetime to perfecting a literary style should not be seen, in the way we may be inclined to see them, as fanatics of an esoteric cult, but in their true light: as bearers of progress. In expanding their own consciousness they have expanded ours. Through their eyes, as Proust said of Ruskin, future generations will see the world.

## Conversion Table for Translated Titles

This table is intended to mitigate some of the shortcomings inherent in the study of literature in translation. It has two main purposes: first, to facilitate reference to the original texts by readers fluent in the foreign languages; and second, to enable those who do not read the foreign languages to refer in translation to the full contexts of passages quoted in part. The table therefore gives the original versions of translated titles, together with sources of English translations of texts referred to, where they exist.

The table includes titles of poems, essays and major works. In the case of poems without titles, first lines are given. Titles where the translation is identical with or an obvious literal translation of the original are generally not included.

The following abbreviations are used in the table:

SelW I—Rilke, *Selected Works*, I, Prose.
SelW II—Rilke, *Selected Works*, II, Poetry.
P 06–26—Rilke, *Poems* 1906–1926.

Details of editions used are given in the bibliography.

| TRANSLATED TITLE | ORIGINAL TITLE | ENGLISH TRANSLATION |
|---|---|---|
| Adventurer, The | Der Abenteuerer | |
| *Against Sainte-Beuve* | *Contre Sainte-Beuve* | Proust, *By Way of Sainte-Beuve* |
| Alchemist, The | Der Alchimist | |
| Angel, To the | An den Engel | SelW II, 290 |
| Anticipation | Vorgefühl | SelW II, 117 |
| Apple-Orchard, The | Der Apfelgarten | SelW II, 183 |
| Archaic Torso of Apollo | Archaische Torso Apollos | SelW II, 143 |
| Artistic Contemplation | La contemplation artistique | Proust, *By Way of Sainte-Beuve*, 229 |
| Artist's Confiteor, The | Le 'Confiteor' de l'artiste | Baudelaire, *Paris Spleen*, 5 |
| At the Night's Edge | Am Rande der Nacht | |
| Bachelor, The | Der Junggeselle | |
| Before the Summer Rain | Vor dem Sommerregen | SelW II, 165 |
| Bellman, Ode to | Ode an Bellman | P 06–26, 211 |
| Birth of Venus | Geburt der Venus | SelW II, 193 |
| Black Cat | Schwarze Katze | SelW II, 177 |
| Blind Man's Song, The | Das Lied des Blinden | SelW II, 131 |
| Blind Woman, The | Die Blinde | SelW II, 137 |
| Blue Hydrangea | Blaue Hortensie | |
| *Book of Hours, The* | *Das Stunden-Buch* | SelW II |
| *Book of Images, The* | *Das Buch der Bilder* | |
| Bowl of Roses, the | Die Rosenschale | SelW II, 195 |
| Boy, The | Der Knabe | SelW II, 111 |
| Buddha | Buddha | SelW II, 171 |
| Buddha in Glory | Buddha in der Glorie | SelW II, 186 |

| TRANSLATED TITLE | ORIGINAL TITLE | ENGLISH TRANSLATION |
|---|---|---|
| Capital, The | Das Kapitäl | |
| Cathedral, The | Die Kathedrale | SelW II, 160 |
| *Celebration for Myself* | *Mir zur Feier* | |
| *Celebration for You* | *Dir zur Feier* | |
| Child, The | Das Kind | SelW II, 186 |
| Childhood | Kindheit | SelW II, 110 |
| Coat of Arms, The | Das Wappen | |
| Corpse-Washing | Leichenwäsche | |
| | | |
| David Sings before Saul | David singt vor Saul | SelW II, 149 |
| Days of Driving | Journées en automobile | Proust, *A Selection from his Miscellaneous Writings*, 11 |
| Days of Reading | Journées de lecture | Ibid. 107 and 146 |
| Death Encountered | Todes-Erfahrung | SelW II, 165 |
| Decline of Inspiration, The | Le déclin de l'inspiration | Proust, *By Way of Sainte-Beuve*, 227 |
| Donor, The | Der Stifter | SelW II, 159 |
| *Duino Elegies, The* | *Die Duineser Elegien* | See Bibliography |
| | | |
| Eliah's Consolation | Tröstung des Elia | |
| Elopement, The | Die Entführung | SelW II, 175 |
| Esther | Esther | SelW II, 152 |
| Evening in Skåne | Abend in Skåne | SelW II, 117 |
| Experience I | Erlebnis I | SelW I, 34 |
| | | |
| Falconry | Falken-Beize | |
| Filial Sentiments of a Parricide | Sentiments filiaux d'un parricide | Proust, *A Selection from his Miscellaneous Writings*, 177 |
| Five Hymns | Fünf Gesänge | P 06–26, 187 |
| Flamingoes, The | Die Flamingos | SelW II, 177 |
| From a Stormy Night | Aus einer Sturmnacht | |
| From all things, almost, is a call to feeling | Es winkt zu Fühlung fast aus allen Dingen | P 06–26, 193 |
| | | |
| Gazelle, The | Die Gazelle | |
| Girl's Lament | Mädchen-Klage | |
| Guardian Angel, The | Der Schutzengel | |
| | | |
| Heart's Swing, The | Schaukel des Herzens | P 06–26, 281 |
| Hölderlin, To | An Hölderlin | P 06–26, 194 |
| | | |
| *In Search of Time Lost* | *A la recherche du temps perdu* | *Remembrance of Things Past*, see Bibliography |
| Is not smile there | Ist dort nicht Lächeln | P 06–26, 161 |
| Island, The | Die Insel | SelW II, 182 |
| | | |
| Jeremiah | Jeremia | SelW II, 151 |
| | | |
| Lace-Work | Die Spitze | SelW II, 167 |
| Lady at the Looking-Glass | Dame von dem Spiegel | |
| L'Ange du Méridien | L'Ange du Méridien | SelW II, 159 |

| TRANSLATED TITLE | ORIGINAL TITLE | ENGLISH TRANSLATION |
|---|---|---|
| Snake-Charming | Schlangen-Beschwörung | |
| *Sonnets to Orpheus, The* | *Die Sonnette an Orpheus* | see Bibliography |
| Spanish Trilogy, The | Die Spanische Trilogie | P 06–26, 134 |
| Stranger, The | Der Fremde | SelW II, 184 |
| Sun-Dial, The | Die Sonnenuhr | |
| Sunset | Sonnen-Untergang | P 06–26, 93 |
| Turning-Point | Wendung | P 06–26, 183 |
| Unicorn, The | Das Einhorn | SelW II, 163 |
| Within the Rose | Das Rosen-Innere | |
| Woman Going Blind | Die Erblindende | SelW II, 168 |
| Woman in Love | Die Liebende | SelW II, 170 |

# REFERENCES

References are to sources in the original languages. Where a number of consecutive quotations in the text are taken from a single source, the reference is given after the last quotation in the group.

The following abbreviations are used:

| | |
|---|---|
| AR | *A la recherche du temps perdu.* |
| B 02–06 ... 21–26 | *Briefe aus den Jahren 1902–06 ... 1921–26.* |
| B I, II | *Beiefe 1897–1914, 1914–26.* |
| BB | *Briefwechsel mit Benvenuta.* |
| BC | *Briefe über Cézanne.* |
| BLAS | *R. M. Rilke und Lou Andreas-Salomé, Briefwechsel.* |
| BT I, II | *R. M. Rilke und Marie von Thurn und Taxis, Briefwechsel* |
| BTF | *Briefe und Tagebücher aus der Frühzeit, 1899–1902.* |
| C | *Correspondance générale.* |
| CSB | *Contre Sainte-Beuve.* |
| JS | *Jean Santeuil.* |
| P I, II | G. Painter, *Marcel Proust* (2 vols). |
| PJ | *Les plaisirs et les jours.* |
| PM | *Pastiches et mélanges.* |
| SW I–VI | *Sämtliche Werke.* |

Details of editions used are given in the Bibliography.

## *Introduction*

1 K. Clarke, *Moments of Vision*, 4.   2 PM, 109.

## *Chapter 1*

1 *Oeuvres Complètes*, 347–8.   2 *Correspondance*, II, 395.   3 *Gesammelte Werke, Prosa II*, 14.   4 Ibid. 16.   5 *Oeuvres*, I, 1364.   6 Ibid. 1321.   7 *La Nausée*, 81.   8 Ibid. 82.   9 *La Tentation de Saint Antoine*, 417.   10 Op. cit. II, 512–13   11 Op. cit. 81.   12 Op. cit. 14.   13 Op. cit. 1257.   14 Op. cit. II, 514.   15 Op. cit. I, 1170.   16 Ibid.   17 Op. cit. 234.   18 Ibid. 237.   19 *Par les champs et par les grèves*, 129.   20 Op. cit. I, 1170.   21 Op. cit. 974.   22 Op. cit. 81.   23 Op. cit. I, 1363.   24 Op. cit. 232.   25 Ibid. 234.   26 Op. cit. *Gedichte und lyrische Dramen*, 81.   27 H. Laitenberger, *Der Begriff der 'Absence' bei P. Valéry*, 4.   28 Cf. *Nouvelles Histoires Extraordinaires*, p. XV; *Oeuvres Complètes*, 1037.   29 Op. cit. 81–2.   30 Ibid. 84.   31 *Etudes sur le temps humain*, 322.   32 Op. cit. II, 322.   33 Op. cit. 234.   34 *Par les champs et par les grèves*, 131.   35 Op. cit. 377.   36 Op. cit. I, 1322–3.   37 Op. cit. 1296.   38 Ibid. 1256.   39 Op. cit. II, 322.   40 Op. cit. 234.   41 Op. cit. 81–2.   42. Op. cit. 338.   43 Op. cit. 322.   44 Op. cit. 82.   45 Op. cit. 15.   46 Ibid. 16.   47 Op. cit. *Gedichte und lyrische Dramen*, 82.   48 Op. cit. 233.   49 Ibid. 1061.   50 Ibid. 1256.   51 Op. cit. 15.   52 Op. cit. 418.   53 Op. cit. 233–4.   54 Op. cit. 15.   55 *Par les champs et par les grèves*, 130.   56 Op. cit. II, 514.   57 Op. cit. 338.   58 *Par les champs et par les grèves*, 131.

59 Op. cit. II, 514.   60 Op. cit. 83.   61 Op. cit. 417–18.   62. Ibid. 422.
63 Op. cit. 83.

## Chapter 2

1 A. Ferré, *Les années de collège de Marcel Proust*, 139.   2 Ibid. 120.   3 SW IV,
540.   4 Ibid. 563–4.   5 R. Dreyfus, *Souvenirs sur Marcel Proust*, 57.   6 Ibid.
58–9.   7 Cf. P. Demetz, *René Rilkes Prager Jahre*, 113.   8 SW IV, 482–4.
9 SW I, 10.   10 Ibid. 107.   11 Ibid. 145.   12 BLAS, 18–19.   13 Ibid. 27,
31.   14 SW III, 194.   15 BLAS, 20.   16 Ibid. 32.   17 *Tagebücher aus der
Frühzeit*, 80–1.

## Chapter 3

1 H. March, *The Two Worlds of Marcel Proust*, 56.   2 Cf. P I, 175–6.   3 PJ,
241.   4 Ibid. 206.   5 Ibid. 145.   6 Ibid. 52–3.   7 Ibid. 74.   8 Ibid. 58.
9 Ibid. 11.   10 Ibid. 220.   11 Ibid. 11.   12 Ibid. 52.   13 Ibid. 163.
14 Cf. R. Dreyfus, op. cit. 37–40.   15 Op. cit. 228–9.   16 Ibid. 11.
17 Cf. P I, 118.   18 Op. cit. 188–9.   19 Ibid. 218–19.   20 Ibid. 170.
21 Ibid. 223.   22 C IV, 17.   23 Op. cit. 226.   24 Cf. P I, 138–9.   25 Op.
cit. 214.   26 Ibid. 146.   27 Ibid. 120.   28 Ibid. 225.   29 Ibid. 9.   30 Ibid.
181.   31 Ibid. 48.

## Chapter 4

1 B I, 304.   2 SW I, 319.   3 Ibid. 316.   4 Ibid. 264.   5 Ibid. 254–5.
6 Ibid. 254.   7 Ibid. 286.   8 Ibid. 258.   9 Ibid. 259.   10 Ibid. 255.
11 Ibid. 287.   12 Ibid. 281.   13 Ibid. 279.   14 Ibid. 289.   15 Ibid. 287.
16 Ibid. 327.   17 Ibid. 310.   18 Ibid. 330.   19 Ibid. 298.   20 Ibid. 262.
21 Ibid. 268.   22 Ibid. 269.   23 Ibid. 262.   24 Ibid. 339.   25 Ibid. 263.
26 Ibid.   27 Ibid. 291.   28 B I, 303.   29 SW I, 288.   30 Ibid.   31 Ibid.
253.   32 Ibid. 263.   33 Ibid. 256.   34 Ibid.   35 Ibid. 313.   36 Ibid. 253.
37  Ibid. 263.   38 Ibid. 284.   39 Ibid. 260.   40 Ibid. 274.   41 Ibid. 276.
42 Ibid. 297.   43 Ibid. 283.   44 Ibid.   45 Ibid. 254.   46 Ibid. 253.
47 Ibid.   48 Ibid. 264.   49 Ibid. 291.   50 Ibid. 284.   51 Ibid. 308.
52 Ibid. 295.   53 Ibid. 339.   54 Ibid.   55 Ibid. 330.   56 Ibid. 278.
57 Ibid. 268.   58 Ibid. 307.   59 Ibid. 288.   60 Ibid. 308.   61 Ibid. 294.
62 Ibid. 317.   63 Ibid. 291.   64 Ibid. 283.   65 Ibid. 319.   66 Ibid.
67 Ibid. 260.   68 Ibid. 321.   69 Ibid. 267.   70 Ibid. 277.   71 Ibid. 278.
72 Ibid. 315.   73 Op. cit. 11.   74 Cf. SW III, 837–8.   75 BLAS, 21.
76 Ibid. 364.   77 Ibid. 365.   78 *Briefe an einen jungen Dichter*, 17–18.
79 SW I, 366.   80 Ibid. 350.   81 Ibid. 314.   82 Ibid. 365.   83 Ibid. 339.
84 Ibid. 280.

## Chapter 5

1 SW I, 300.   2 Ibid. 305–6.   3 Ibid. 308.   4 Ibid. 301.   5 Ibid. 286.
6 Ibid. 276.   7 Ibid.   8 Ibid. 259.   9 Ibid. 306.   10 Ibid. 344.   11 Ibid.
351.   12 Ibid. 257.   13 Ibid. 297.   14 Ibid. 279.   15 Ibid. 255.   16 Ibid.
327.   17 SW III, 323.   18 Ibid. 319.   19 B I, 303.   20 BTF, 244.
21 CSB, 346–7.   22 C IV, 38.   23 JS III, 303.   24 AR I, 155.   25 Ibid.
180–1.   26 SW I, 333.   27 Ibid. 281.   28 PJ, 226.   29 Ibid. 189.   30 SW
I, 268.   31 Ibid. 315.   32 Ibid. 358.   33 Ibid. 276–7.   34 PJ, 214.

35 B I, 303.  36 SW I, 284.  37 BTF, 298.  38 Ibid. 375.  39 PJ, 189.
40 Ibid. 214.  41 SW I, 352.  42 Ibid. 353.  43 PJ, 214.

## Chapter 6

1 B I, 59.  2 BTF, 295–6; 275–6.  3 *Hommage à Marcel Proust*, 33–4.  4 CSB
348–9.  5 BTF, 231.  6 Ibid. 246.  7 CSB, 346–7.  8 B 02–06, 41.
9 BTF, 258–62.  10 Ibid. 268.  11 Ibid. 342.  12 JS I, 147–8.  13 BTF,
267–8.  14 B I, 198–9.  15 K. Kippenberg, *R. M. Rilke, ein Beitrag*, 104.
16 B II, 517.  17 A. Maurois, *A la recherche de Marcel Proust*, 86.  18 BTF,
359.  19 Ibid. 251.  20 Ibid 295.  21 Ibid. 339.  22 Ibid. 373.  23 SW I,
365.  24 BTF, 341.  25 Ibid. 301.

## Chapter 7

1 Henry James, *The House of Fiction*, 34.  2 B. G. Rogers, *Proust's Narrative
Techniques*, 46.  3 JS I, 70.  4 Ibid. 85–6.  5 Ibid. 86.  6 Ibid. 53, 178.
7 Cf Maurois, op. cit. 29.  8 JS III, 284.  9 Ibid. II, 336, cf. also Ibid. I,
164, 251–2; II, 56, 219, 225, 254, 302, 308; III, 135.  10 Ibid. III, 284.
11 Ibid. II, 253.  12 Ibid. 29.  13 Ibid. 338.  14 Ibid. I, 289.  15 Ibid. II,
12.  16 Ibid. 307.  17 Ibid. 233.  18 Ibid. 305.  19 Ibid. III, 299.
20 Ibid. I, 137–8.  21 Ibid. II, 44–6.  22 Ibid. 51.  23 Ibid. III, 161.
24 Ibid. II, 231.  25 Ibid. 253.  26 Ibid. 233.  27 Ibid. 340.  28 Ibid. I,
194.  29 Ibid. II, 46.  30 Ibid. III, 159.  31 Ibid. I, 185.  32 *Lettres à une
amie*, 5.  33 JS III, 127.  34 Cf. Ibid. 226.  35 Ibid. II, 140.  36 Ibid.
133.  37 Ibid. 81.  38 Ibid. 114.  39 J. M. Cocking, *Proust*, 17.

## Chapter 8

1 SW I, 472.  2 Ibid. 405.  3 Ibid. 397.  4 Ibid. 402.  5 Ibid. 472.
6 Ibid. 379.  7 Ibid. 381.  8 Ibid. 382.  9 Ibid. 422–3.  10 Ibid. 386.
11 Ibid. 403.  12 Ibid. 460.  13 JS II, 333.  14 SW I, 458.  15 Ibid. 399.
16 Ibid. 465–9.  17 Ibid. 471–6.  18 Ibid. 456–7.  19 Ibid. 371.
20 Ibid. 401.  21 Ibid. 465–9.  22 Ibid. 382.  23 Ibid. 380.  24 Ibid.
376–7.  25 Ibid. 379–80.  26 Ibid. 449.  27 Ibid. 387–8.  28 Ibid. 404.

## Chapter 9

1 B I, 59.  2 Ibid. 58–9.  3 BLAS, 98.  4 SW V, 146.  5 PM, 154–5.
6 SW V, 181.  7 PM, 147; SW V, 224.  8 PM, 155.  9 Cf. P I, 282.
Painter draws attention to the passage discussed here.  10 Ruskin, *Praeterita*
283, 285.  11 SW V, 210–11.  12 Ibid. 211.  13 Ibid. 262.  14 Ibid. 265.
15 Ibid. 211.  16 CSB, 392.  17 Ibid. 390.  18 Quoted by Maurois, 108.
19 BLAS, 95.  20 SW V, 226.  21 BLAS, 97.  22 SW V, 208.  23 Ibid.
211.  24 Ibid. 258.  25 B I, 55.  26 SW V, 219–20.  27 Ibid. 157.
28. Ibid. 160.  29 BC, 26.  30 Ibid. 33.  31 Ibid. 23.  32 Ibid. 43.
33 Ibid. 44.  34 CSB, 373.  35 BC, 20.  36 CSB, 375.  37 SW V, 143.
38. Ibid. 158.  39 Ibid. 159; BC, 46.  40 SW V, 149 (cf. also ibid. 217;
B I, 55.)  41 SW V, 166.  42 B I, 57.  43 SW V, 176.  44 PM, 157, 191.

45 SW V, 178. 46 PM, 156. 47 Ibid. SW V, 180. 48 B I, 55. 49 Ibid. 56. 50 SW V, 215. 51 CSB, 374. 52 Ibid. 392. 53 B I, 57, 58. 54 Ibid. 54. 55 SW V, 222. 56 Ibid. 159. 57 Ibid. 220. 58 BC, 33. 59 SW V, 174. 60 Ibid. 220. 61 B I, 40. 62 *Lettres à Rodin*, 108. 63 SW V, 142. 64 PM, 175–6, 146. 65 Ibid. 195–6.

## Chapter 10

1 E.g. H. E. Holthusen, *Rilke*, 86; H. Singer, *Rilke und Hölderlin*. 87; E. C. Mason, *R. M. Rilke*, 65. 2 SW I, 529. 3 Ibid. 499–500. 4 Ibid. 501. 5 Ibid. 502. 6 E. v. Schmidt-Pauli, *R. M. Rilke, Ein Gedenkbuch*, 20. 7 SW I, 552–3. 8 Ibid. 500. 9 Ibid. V, 258. 10 Ibid. I, 497. 11 Ibid. 640. 12 Ibid. 507. 13 Ibid. 496, 528, 642. 14 Ibid. 641. 15 Ibid. 515. 16 Ibid. 507. 17 Ibid. V, 194. 18 Ibid. I, 634. 19 Ibid. 539. 20 Ibid. 534. 21 Ibid. 633. 22 Ibid. 510. 23 Ibid. 513. 24 Ibid. 531. 25 Ibid. 527. 26 Ibid. 507. 27 Ibid. 559. 28 Ibid. 605. 29 Ibid. 481. 30 Ibid. 629–30. 31 Op. cit. 61. 32 SW I, 519. 33 Ibid. 506. 34 Ibid. 536. 35 Ibid. 520. 36 Ibid. 631. 37 Cf. Ibid. 518–19. 38 Ibid. 491. 39 Ibid. 483. 40 Ibid. 589. 41 Ibid. 593. 42 Ibid. 594. 43 Ibid. 641. 44 Ibid. 516. 45 Ibid. 636. 46 Ibid. 627. 47 Ibid. 580. 48 Ibid. 587. 49 Mason, op. cit. 68. 50 SW I, 530–1. 51 Cf. Ibid. 485, 521, 542. 52 Ibid. 482. 53 Ibid. 622. 54 Ibid. 483. 55 Ibid. 482. 56 Ibid. 617. 57 Ibid. 612–4. 58 Ibid. 526. 59 Ibid. 508–9. 60 Ibid. 641. 61 Ibid. 585, 586. 62 Ibid. 565, 567. 63 Ibid. 577. 64 Ibid. 563. 65 Ibid. 494. 66 Ibid. 508. 67 Ibid. 568. 68 Ibid. 511. 69 Ibid. 639. 70 B I ,57.

## Chapter 11

1 B I, 59. 2 BLAS, 159. 3 BB, 94. 4 Quoted by G. Buchheit, *R. M. Rilke*, 123. 5 B 06–07, 214. 6 B I, 141. 7 SW I, 518. 8 BC, 36. 9 Ibid. 10 Ibid. 43. 11 Ibid. 29. 12 SW I, 637. 13 Ibid. 14 BTF, 268. 15 JS II, 230. 16 Ibid. 10. 17 Ibid. 50. 18 Ibid. III, 299. 19 Ibid. 300. 20 CSB, 351–2. 21 Ibid. 349. 22 BLAS, 95. 23 Ibid. 24 B 06–07, 305. 25 SW I, 498. 26 Ibid. 508. 27 BTF, 295. 28 CSB, 349. 29 Ibid. 352. 30 Cf. B I, 95. 31 Eg. PM, 194–5, 263. 32 JS I, 194. 33 JS II, 45. 34 SW I, 553. 35 JS I, 24 (preface). 36 Ibid. 150–1. 37 SW VI, 895. 38 E. Gasser, *Grundzüge der Lebensanschauung R. M. Rilkes*, 131. 39 Jacobsen, *Niels Lyhne*, 354. 40 B 02–06, 156. 41 Gasser, op. cit. 124. 42 B 14–21, 113. 43 Kohlschmidt, *Rilke-Interpretationen*, 10. 44 B 14–21, 99. 45 SW I, 619–20. 46 JS I, 149–50. 47 SW I, 550–1.

## Chapter 12

1 SW VI, 710. 2 Ibid. 712. 3 Ibid. 755. 4 Ibid. 5 Ibid. 784–5. 6 B 7–14, 95. 7 B II, 453. 8 SW VI, 735. 9 Ibid. 733. 10 Ibid. 734. 11 Ibid. 848. 12 Ibid. 850. 13 Ibid. 721. 14 Ibid. 15 Ibid. 726–7. 16 Ibid. 856. 17 Ibid. 801. 18 Ibid. 797. 19 Ibid. 20 Ibid. 804. 21 Ibid. 808. 22 Ibid. 817. 23 Ibid. 765. 24 Ibid. 766–7. 25 Ibid. 766. 26 Ibid. 777. 27 Ibid. 767. 28 Ibid. 751. 29 Ibid. 755–6. 30 Ibid. 756. 31 Ibid. 755. 32 Ibid. 775. 33 Ibid. 743–4. 34 Ibid. 775. 35 Ibid. 732.

36 Ibid. 825. 37 Ibid. 897. 38 B 21–26, 319. 39 Ibid. 320. 40 SW VI, 884. 41 Ibid. 912. 42 Ibid. 870. 43 B 21–26, 319. 44 Op. cit. 71. 45 BTF, 356–8. 46 SW VI, 774, 842. 47 BLAS, 54. 48 Baudelaire, *Oeuvres complètes*, 231, 237. 49 Op. cit. 71. 50 SW V, 657–8. 51 Ibid. 52 BC, 30. 53 SW V, 661. 54 B 21–26, 330. 55 Ibid. 325. 56 SW VI, 826. 57 Ibid. 829. 58 Ibid. 910–11. 59 Ibid. 750–1. 60 Ibid. 723. 61 F. Angelloz, op. cit., 216–17. 62 E. Buddeberg, *R. M. Rilke, eine Biographie*, 543. 63 B 07–14, 100. 64 Ibid. 95. 65 SW V, 658. 66 A. H. Wright, *Jane Austen's Novels*, 90. 67 BC, 29. 68 Cf. p. 156. 69 SW VI, 769. 70 D. Daiches, *The Novel and the Modern World*, Ch. 6. 71 B I, 208. 72 B 07–14, 196. 73 Cf. W. Gunther, *Weltinnenraum*, 96. 74 B 07–14, 148. 75 H. F. Peters, *R. M. Rilke: Masks and the Man*, 91. 76 SW VI, 826. 77 B 07–14, 63. 78 E. Buddeberg, op. cit. 172. 79 SW VI, 826. 80 Ibid. 818. 81 Ibid. 733. 82 Ibid. 926.

## Chapter 13

1 B 07–14, 147. 2 Ibid. 150. 3 BLAS, 45–6. 4 Ibid. 121. 5 Ibid. 120. 6 Ibid. 96–7. 7 Ibid. 70. 8 Ibid. 9 Ibid. 54–5. 10 Ibid. 58. 11 Ibid. 64. 12 Ibid. 99. 13 Ibid. 115. 14 Ibid. 87. 15 Ibid. 88. 16 Ibid. 120. 17 Ibid. 121. 18 Ibid. 159. 19 B I, 180. 20 Ibid. 181. 21 Ibid. 207. 22 Ibid. 208. 23 B 07–14, 54. 24 Ibid. 48. 25 Ibid. 128. 26 Ibid. 74. 27 Ibid. 147. 28 Ibid. 54. 29 B I, 172. 30 B 07–14, 49. 31 Ibid. 58–9. 32 B I, 209. 33 B 07–14, 147. 34 Ibid. 130. 35 Ibid. 157. 36 Ibid. 127. 37 Ibid. 149. 38 Ibid. 147. 39 Ibid. 111. 40 B 07–14, 128–9. 41 Ibid. 197. 42 Ibid. 185. 43 Ibid. 231. 44 Ibid. 185. 45 Ibid. 111. 46 Ibid. 166. 47 JS III, 303. 48 Ibid. 298. 49 B 07–14, 95. 50 Cf. Barker, 111. 51 B 07–14, 113. 52 Ibid. 156–7. 53 Ibid. 130. 54 Ibid. 116. 55 Ibid. 117. 56 Ibid. 121. 57 Ibid. 176. 58 SW VI, 942. 59 Cf. Mason, 75. 60 B 07–14, 125. 61 Ibid. 154. 62 Ibid. 168. 63 Ibid. 128. 64 Ibid. 184.

## Chapter 14

1 C II, 86–7. 2 Ibid. 85. 3 Ibid. 86. 4 CSB, 207. 5 Ibid. 209. 6 Ibid. 160–8. 7 P II, 34. 8 E.g. PM, 226–7. 9 Ibid. 231–4. 10 Ibid. 226. 11 Ibid. 235. 12 CSB, 22. 13 Ibid. 61. 14 Ibid. 78–9. 15 Ibid. 77. 16 Ibid. 61. 17 Cf. P II, 43, 45. 18 Cf. Ibid. 106–7. 19 CSB, 14. 20 Op. cit. II, 118. 21 CSB, 137. 22 Ibid. 143, 155. 23 Op. cit. II, 124. 24 Ibid. II, 108. 25 Quoted by E. R. Jackson, *L'évolution de la mémoire involontaire dans l'oeuvre de Marcel Proust*, 153. 26 R. Wellek and A. Warren, *Theory of Literature*, 190. 27 CSB, 113. 28 E. Cassirer, *An Essay on Man*, 76–7. 29 CSB, 122. 30 Ibid. 111. 31 Ibid. 124. 32 Op. cit. 82. 33 Ibid. 83, 84. 34 CSB, 114. 35 Op. cit. 81. 36 CSB, 87. 37 Ibid. 90, 92, 91. 38 Ibid. 251. 39 Ibid. 115. 40 Ibid. 116. 41 Ibid. 88. 42 Cf. ibid. 91. 43 Ibid. 276. 44 Ibid. 248. 45 Ibid. 269. 46 Ibid. 267. 47 Ibid. 270. 48 Ibid. 271. 49 Ibid. 270. 50 Ibid. 273. 51 Ibid. 246. 52 Cf. P II, 68. 53 CSB, 289. 54 Cf. PM, 217. 55 Ibid. 96. 56 *Chroniques*, 84–6. 57 Cf. H. Bonnet, *Marcel Proust de 1907–1914*, 20–1. 58 Op.

cit. 75. 59 Op. cit. 76, 79. 60 *Sésame et les lys*, 61. 61 CSB, 220, 219.
62 Ibid. 312. 63 Ibid. 137. 64 Ibid. 141. 65 Ibid. 143. 66 Ibid. 137.
67 Ibid. 140. 68 Ibid. 301. 69 Ibid. 303. 70 Ibid. 301. 71 Ibid. 303
72 Ibid. 309. 73 Ibid. 59. 74 P II, 130–1. 75 G. Brée, *Du temps perdu au temps retrouvé*, 17. 76 CSB, 285.

## Chapter 15

1 BLAS, 284–5. 2 SW II, 43–4. 3 Ibid. 26. 4 Ibid. 10. 5 BB, 24.
6 Ibid. 22. 7 SW II, 75. 8 Ibid. 66. 9 Ibid. 67. 10 Ibid. 408. 11 Ibid.
459. 12 Ibid. 73. 13 Ibid. 392. 14 Ibid. 54. 15 Ibid. 70. 16 Ibid. 54.
17 Ibid. 48. 18 Ibid. 69. 19 Ibid. 78. 20 Ibid. 401. 21 Ibid. 53.
22 Ibid. 412. 23 Ibid. 390. 24 Ibid. 387. 25 Ibid. 61–2. 26 Ibid. 62.
27 Ibid. 416. 28 Ibid. 426. 29 Ibid. 43. 30 Ibid. 213–14. 31 Ibid. 449.
32 Ibid. 439. 33 Ibid. 214. 34 Ibid. 61–2. 35 E.g. ibid., 75. 36 Ibid.
405. 37 Ibid. 94, 85, 397, 84, 98. 38 Ibid. 48. 39 B 14–21, 252. 40 B
07–14, 119. 41 BT I 227. 42 SW II, 85. 43 Ibid. 95. 44 Ibid. 98.
45 B 07–14, 134. 46 SW II, 413. 47 Cf. 'The Coat of Arms', SW I, 634.
48 Ibid. 689. 49 Ibid. 693. 50 Ibid. 685. 51 Ibid. 689. 52 Ibid. 685.
53 Ibid. 686. 54 Ibid. 717. 55 SW II, 386. 56 Ibid. 83. 57 BLAS, 350,
353. 58 SW II, 83–4. 59 J. Steiner, *Rilkes Duineser Elegien*, 15. 60 SW II,
221. 61 BB, 19. 62 SW II, 60–1. 63 BB, 18. 64 Ibid. 65 Ibid. 25. 66 BT,
I, 369. 67 B 14–21, 114. 68 SW VI, 1037. 69 Ibid. 1038. 70 Ibid.
1039. 71 Ibid. 72 BT I, 235–6. 73 SW II, 101. 74 Ibid. 405. 75 BB,
82. 76 BT I, 263, 265. 77 SW II, 41. 78 Ibid. 99, 79. Ibid. VI, 1038.
80 B 14–21 88–91. 81 Ibid. 92–3. 82 SW I, 688. 83 BB, 75. 84 B
14–21, 67 85 Ibid. 73. 86 BT I, 219. 87 Ibid. 218. 88 Ibid. 226–7.
89 B 14–21, 80. 90 Ibid. 252. 91 Ibid. 80. 92 SW II, 92. 93 BT I, 349.
94 E.g. BB, 42, 60–1. 95 SW II, 238. 96 E.g. Ibid. 70. 97 Ibid. 214.
98 Ibid. 435, 436, 233. 99 Ibid. 456, 230. 100 E.g. Ibid. 99, 384. 101 Ibid.
96. 102 E.g. Ibid. 224, 426. 103 Ibid. 98. 104 Ibid. 399. 105 Ibid. 230.
106 Ibid. 56. 107 Ibid. 234. 108 Ibid. 224. 109 Ibid. 366. 110 Ibid.
376. 111 Ibid. 53. 112 Ibid. 77. 113 E.g. B, 14–21, 197–8, 53, 76, 108.
114 BLAS, 299. 115 BB, 116. 116 Ibid. 91. 117 Ibid. 128. 118 Ibid.
81. 119 SW II, 101 2. 120 B 07–14, 333. 121 Ibid. 14–21, 399. 122 Ibid.
07–14, 198. 123 Ibid. 14–21, 264. 124 Cf. B. Allemann, *Zeit und Figur beim späten Rilke*, 13–25. 125 SW II, 402. 126 Ibid. 101. 127 Ibid. 111.
128 SW VI, 1039. 129 Cf p. 232. 130 *Briefe an eine junge Frau*, 21.
131 SW II, 431. 132 BB, 97. 133 SW II, 128. 134 Ibid. 431. 135 BB,
66. 136 SW II, 242. 137 Ibid. 387. 138 Ibid. 242. 139 Ibid. 93–4.
140 BB, 83. 141 SW II, 124. 142 Cf. B 21–26, 15. 143 Ibid. 14–21, 241.
144 SW II, 231. 145 B 14–21, 386. 146 B 21–26, 48. 147 Ibid. 14–21,
292. 148 Ibid. 219. 149 SW I, 697, 9. 150 B 14–21, 323. 151 BLAS,
451–2. 152 B 21–26, 94; ibid. 14–21, 321. 153 Ibid. 21–26, 47.

## Chapter 16

1 AR II, 197. 2 Ibid. III, 964. 3 Ibid. II, 206. 4 Ibid. 725. 5 Ibid.
III, 228. 6 Ibid. II, 472. 7 Ibid. I, 125. 8 SW I, 701–2. 9 Ibid. 704.

10 Ibid. 701. 11 Ibid. 707. 12 AR II, 547–8. 13 SW I, 704. 14 Ibid. 15 AR III, 369. 16 Ibid. I, 223. 17 SW I, 710. 18 Ibid. 711. 19 Ibid. 714–15. 20 Ibid. 717. 21 Ibid. 687. 22 Ibid. 721. 23 AR II, 345. 24 Ibid. 781. 25 SW I, 726. 26 Ibid. 688. 27 AR I, 184. 28 SW I, 714. 29 Ibid. 754. 30 AR I, 159. 31 SW I, 686. 32 Ibid. 732. 33 AR I, 718. 34 Ibid. 182. 35 Ibid. II, 46. 36 Ibid. I, 45. 37 SW I, 718. 38 Ibid. 720. 39 SW I, 732, AR III, 895. 40 AR III, 899. 41 G. Brée, *Marcel Proust and Deliverance from Time*, 242–3. 42 AR III, 900. 43 Ibid. 908. 44 G. Brée, *The World of Marcel Proust*, 184. 45 Howard Moss, *The Magic Lantern of Marcel Proust*, 13. 46 AR III, 904. 47 Ibid. 906. 48 AR I, 852. 49 Cf. ibid. III, 77. 50 Ibid. 427. 51 M. Muller, *Les voix narratives dans la recherche du temps perdu*, 8. 52 AR I, 184. 53 Ibid. 49. 54 Ibid. 94. 55 Ibid. 48–9. 56 Ibid. 67. 57 Ibid. 427. 58 Ibid. 186. 59 Ibid. 554. 60. Ibid. III, 914. 61 E. C. Mason, *Lebenshaltung und Symbolik bei R. M. Rilke*, 204. 62 B II, 484. 63 AR I, 155. 64 JS II, 49. 65 AR III, 869. 66 Ibid. 878–9. 67 Ibid. II, 160–1. 68 B II, 484. 69 SW I, 703. 70 Ibid. 705. 71 Ibid. 712. 72 Ibid. 719. 73 AR I, 349; ibid. III, 257. 74 Ibid. I, 658. 75 Cf. ibid. III, 895. 76 E.g. ibid. III, 374, 875. 77 Ibid. I, 156. 78. Ibid. III, 869. 79 Ibid. II, 419. 80 Ibid. III, 374. 81 Ibid. I, 836. 82 Ibid. 209. 83 Ibid. III, 373. 84 Ibid. I, 94. 85 Ibid. I, 850. 86 Ibid. I, 185. 87 SW I, 738. 88 Ibid. 758. 89 B II, 485. 90 AR I, 49. 91 Cf. Y. Louria's comprehensive study of this device in *La convergence stylistique chez Proust*. 92 SW I, 739. 93 AR I, 172. 94 AR I, 48. 95 Ibid. I. 65. 96 Ibid. 139. 97 Ibid. 140. 98 Ibid. 48. 99 H. E. Holthusen, *Rilke*, 41. 100 SW I, 755. 101 Ibid. 731–2. 102 Ibid. 743–4. 103 *Chroniques*, 199. 104 AR I, 53. 105 SW I, 756. 106 SW II, 267. 107 AR III, 869. 108 Ibid. I, 383. 109 Ibid. II, 398. 110 Ibid. I, 135, 139–40. 111 Ibid. II, 38, 39–41. 112 G. Piroué, *Proust et la musique du devenir*, 209. 113 AR II, 396. 114 Ibid. 397. 115 Ibid. I, 135. 116 Ibid. III, 870. 117 Ibid. I, 810–11. 118 G. Poulet, *L'espace proustien*, 35. 119 AR II, 204. 120 Ibid. III, 989–90. 121 Ibid. 924. 122 Ibid. 69. 123 Ibid. 925. 124 R. Shattuck, *Proust's Binoculars*, 37. 125 Ibid. 30. 126 AR III, 079. 127 Ibid. 889. 128 Cf. R. Shattuck, op. cit. 58. 129 Ibid. 126. 130 AR III, 972. 131 Ibid. 1029. 132 Ibid. 1030. 133 Ibid. 970. 134 Ibid. 943. 135 Ibid. 898. 136 A. Feuillerat (*Comment Marcel Proust a composé son roman*) expresses this view in its most extreme form. 137 Cf. Shattuck, op. cit. 89. 138 AR III, 78. 139 Ibid. 993. 140 Ibid. 967. 141 Ibid. 944. 142 Ibid. I, 737. 143 Ibid. III, 897. 144 Ibid. 1031. 145 R. Shattuck, op. cit. 55. 146 G. Poulet, op. cit., 117. 147 R. Shattuck, op. cit. 132. 148 AR II, 1006. 149 Ibid. III, 1031. 150 Ibid. III, 992. 151 Ibid. 973. 152 Ibid. I, 810–1. 153 B II, 372–3. 154 Ibid. 395. 155 Ibid. 489. 156 G. Picon, *Lecture de Proust*, 29–30. 157 AR III, 1036. 158 B II, 480. 159 Cf. J. Steiner, *Rilkes Duineser Elegien*, 9–10. 160 B II, 392. 161 R. Shattuck, op. cit. 82. 162 AR III, 372. 163 References are to a broadcast talk: 'Proust and Music', printed in enlarged form in *Essays in French Literature*. 164 G. Piroué, Op. cit. 207. 165 B II, 373. 166 E. Buddeberg, *Die Duineser Elegien R. M. Rilkes*, XLI. 167 E. Buddeberg, *R. M, Rilke*, 543. 168 Cf. H. Mörchen, *Rilkes Sonette an Orpheus*, 28. 169 B II.

403. 170 E.g. Ibid. 519. 171 T. Mann, *Leiden und Größe der Meister*, 161. 172 AR I, 84. 173 Ibid. III, 889. 174 *R. M. Rilke et Merline: Correspondance 1920–26*, 272.

### Conclusion

1 L. J. Austin, *L'univers poétique de Baudeliare*, 20. 2 Introduction to Valéry-Fourment, *Correspondance*. 3 Quoted by F. Jeanson, *Sartre par lui-même*, 175. 4 AR III, 254. 5 H. E. Holthusen, *Rilke*, 10–11.

# Selected Bibliography

## PROUST

### I. Works

*A la recherche du temps perdu*, 3 vols, Paris, 1954.
*Jean Santeuil*, 3 vols, Paris, 1952.
*Les Plaisirs et les Jours*, Paris, 1924.
*Chroniques*, Paris, 1927.
*Pastiches et Mélanges*, Paris, 1919.
*Contre Sainte-Beuve, suivi de Nouveaux Mélanges*, Paris, 1954.
Ruskin, J. *Sésame et les Lys*, Traduction, notes et préface par Marcel Proust, Paris, 1906.
Ruskin, J. *La Bible d'Amiens*, Paris, no date.

### II. Works in English Translation

*By Way of Sainte-Beuve*, translated by S. Townsend Warner, London, 1958.
*Jean Santeuil*, translated by G. Hopkins, New York, 1956.
*Marcel Proust: A Selection from His Miscellaneous Writings*, translated by G. Hopkins, London, 1948.
*Pleasures and Regrets*, translated by L. Varèse, London, 1950.
*Remembrance of Things Past*, translated by C. K. Scott-Moncrieff and S. Hudson, 12 vols, London, 1957.

### III. Correspondence

*Correspondance générale*, 6 vols, Paris, 1930–36.
*Choix de lettres* (ed. Philip Kolb), Paris, 1965.
*Correspondance avec sa mère*, Paris, 1953.
*Correspondance de Marcel Proust avec Jacques Rivière*, Paris, 1956.
*Lettres à Reynaldo Hahn*, Paris, 1956.
*Lettres à André Gide*, Neuchâtel/Paris, 1949.
*Lettres à la NRF*, Paris, 1932.
*A un ami*, Paris, 1948.
*Lettres à une amie*, Manchester, 1942.

### IV. Critical Studies

Autret, J. *L'influence de Ruskin sur la vie, les idées et les oeuvres de Marcel Proust*, Geneva, 1955.
Barker, R. H. *Marcel Proust, a Biography*, London, 1958.
Beckett, S. *Proust*, Chatto & Windus, London, 1931.
Bell, W. S. *Proust's Nocturnal Muse*, New York, 1962.
Bonnet, H. *Marcel Proust de 1907 à 1914*, Paris, 1959.
Brée, G. *Marcel Proust and Deliverance from Time*, Chatto & Windus, London, 1956.
Brée, G. *The World of Marcel Proust*, Chatto & Windus, London, 1967.

Butor, M. 'Les "Moments" de Marcel Proust' in *Essais sur les modernes,* Paris, 1964.

Cocking, J. M. 'Proust and Music', *Essays in French Literature,* University of Western Australia, 1967, No. 4, pp. 13–29.

Cocking, J. M. *Proust,* London, 1956.

Dreyfus, R. *Souvenirs sur Marcel Proust,* Paris, 1926.

Ferré, A. *Les années de collège de Marcel Proust,* Paris, 1959.

Feuillerat, A. *Comment Marcel Proust a composé son roman,* New Haven, 1934.

Jackson, E. R. *L'évolution de la mémoire involuntaire dans l'oeuvre de Marcel Proust,* Paris, 1966.

Jauss, H-R. 'Proust auf der Suche nach seiner Konzeption des Romans', *Romanische Forschungen,* Vol. 66, Frankfurt/M., 1955, pp. 255–304.

Kolb, P. 'The Genesis of Jean Santeuil' *Adam International Review,* No. 260, 1957, pp. 112–19.

Kolb, P. 'Proust et Ruskin: nouvelles perspectives', *Cahiers de l'Association Internationale des études françaises,* XII, 1960, pp. 260–78.

Louria, Y. *La convergence stylistique chez Proust,* Geneva, 1957.

March, H. *The Two Worlds of Marcel Proust,* Philadelphia, 1948.

Maurois, A. *A la recherche de Marcel Proust,* Paris, 1949.

Monnin-Hornung, J. *Proust et la peinture,* Geneva, 1951.

Moss, H. *The Magic Lantern of Marcel Proust,* London, 1963.

Painter, G. D. *Marcel Proust. A Biography,* 2 vols, London, 1959, 1965.

Picon, G. *Lecture de Proust,* Paris, 1963.

Piroué, G. *Proust et la musique du devenir,* Paris, 1960.

Rogers, B. G. *Proust's narrative techniques,* Geneva, 1965.

Shattuck, R. *Proust's Binoculars,* Chatto & Windus, London, 1964.

Vigneron, R. 'Structure de Swann: Balzac, Wagner et Proust', *French Review,* XIX, 1946, pp. 370–84.

*Hommage à Marcel Proust. Les Cahiers Marcel Proust,* Vol. I, Paris, 1927.

# RILKE

## I. Works

*Sämtliche Werke,* 6 vols, Wiesbaden, 1955–66.

*Bücher, Theater, Kunst* (Ed. R. von Mises), Vienna, 1934.

*Tagebücher aus der Frühzeit,* Leipzig, 1942.

## II. Works in English Translation

*Duino Elegies,* German text with English translation by J. B. Leishman and Stephen Spender, London, 1963.

*The Notebook of Malte Laurids Brigge,* translated by J. Linton, London, 1930.

*Poems 1906 to 1926,* translated by J. B. Leishman, London, 1960.

*Selected Works; Vol. I; Prose,* translated by G. Craig Houston, London, 1954.

*Selected Works; Vol. II: Poetry* translated by J. B. Leishman, London, 1960.

*Sonnets to Orpheus,* German text with English translation by J. B. Leishman, London, 1936.

## III. Correspondence

*Briefe und Tagebücher aus der Frühzeit,* 1899–1902, Leipzig, 1931.

*Briefe aus den Jahren 1902–06, 06–07, 07–14, 14–21, 21–26,* 5 vols, Leipzig, 1929–35.
*Briefe 1897–1914, 1914–1926,* 2 vols, Wiesbaden, 1950.
*Briefe an seinen Verleger,* 2 vols, Wiesbaden, 1949.
R. M. *Rilke und Marie von Thurn und Taxis, Briefwechsel,* 2 vols, Zürich/ Wiesbaden, 1951.
R. M. *Rilke und Lou Andreas-Salomé, Briefwechsel,* Zürich/Wiesbaden, 1952.
*Briefwechsel mit Benvenuta,* Esslingen, 1954.
*Briefe an eine junge Frau,* Leipzig, 1946.
*Briefe an einen jungen Dichter,* Frankfurt/M., 1963.
*Die Briefe an Gräfin Sizzo,* Wiesbaden, 1950.
R. M. *Rilke et Merline, Correspondance 1920–26,* Zürich, 1954.
*Lettres à Rodin,* Paris, 1928.
*Briefe über Cézanne,* Frankfurt/M., 1962.

## IV. CRITICAL STUDIES

Allemann, B. *Zeit und Figur beim späten Rilke,* Pfullingen, 1961.
Angelloz, J.-F. *Rilke,* Paris, 1952.
Buchheit, G. *R. M. Rilke,* Zürich, 1928.
Buddeberg, E. *R. M. Rilke. Eine innere Biographie,* Stuttgart, 1955.
Demetz, P. *René Rilkes Prager Jahre,* Düsseldorf, 1953.
Emde, U. *Rilke und Rodin,* Marburg/Lahn, 1949.
Fülleborn, U. *Das Strukturproblem der späten Lyrik Rilkes,* Heidelberg, 1960.
Gasser, E. *Grundzüge der Lebensanschauung R. M. Rilkes,* Diss., Bern, 1925.
Guardini, R. *R. M. Rilkes Deutung des Daseins,* Munich, 1953.
Günther, W. *Weltinnenraum,* Berlin, 1952.
Holthusen, H. E. *Rilke,* Cambridge, 1952.
Holthusen, H. E. *Rilke in Selbstzeugnissen und Bilddokumenten,* Hamburg, 1958.
Kippenberg, K. *R. M. Rilke. Ein Beitrag,* Leipzig, 1935.
Kohlschmidt, W. *Rilke-Interpretationen,* Lahr, 1948.
Magr, C. *R. M. Rilke und die Musik,* Vienna, 1960.
Mason, E. C. *Lebenshaltung und Symbolik bei R. M. Rilke,* Oxford, 1964.
Mason, E. C. *R. M. Rilke. Sein Leben und sein Werk,* Göttingen, 1964.
Mörchen, H. *Rilkes Sonette an Orpheus,* Stuttgart, 1958.
Peters, H. F. *R. M. Rilke: Masks and the Man,* New York, 1963.
Salis, J. R. von. *R. M. Rilke: The Years in Switzerland,* London, 1964.
Schmidt-Pauli, E. v. *R. M. Rilke, Ein Gedenkbuch,* Stuttgart, 1946.
Singer, H. *Rilke und Hölderlin,* Köln, 1957.
Steiner, J. *Rilkes Duineser Elegien,* Bern, 1962.

## GENERAL

Austin, L. J. *L'univers poétique de Baudelaire,* Paris, 1956.
Baudelaire. *Oeuvres Complètes,* Paris, 1961.
*Nouvelles Histoires Extraordinaires,* Paris, 1933.
*Paris Spleen,* translated by L. Varèse, London, 1951.
Cassirer, E. *An Essay on Man,* New Haven, 1962.
Clark, K. *Moments of Vision* (The Romanes Lecture, 1954), Oxford, 1954.
Daiches, D. *The Novel and the Modern World,* Chicago/London, 1960.

Flaubert, G. *Correspondance*, Vol. II, Paris, 1926.

*La Tentation de Saint Antoine*, Paris, 1924.

*Par les champs et par les grèves*, Paris 1927.

Hofmannsthal, *Gesammelte Werke*, Fischer Verlag, Gedichte und lyrische Dramen, 1952, Prosa II, 1959.

Hofmannsthal, *Selected Prose*, translated by M. Hottinger and T. and J. Stern, New York, 1952.

Huxley, A. *The Doors of Perception and Heaven and Hell*, Penguin Books, 1961.

Jacobsen, J. P. *Sämtliche Werke*, Leipzig, no date.

James, H. *The House of Fiction*, London, 1957.

Jeanson, F. *Sartre par lui-même*, Paris, 1963.

Laitenberger, H. *Der Begriff der 'Absence' bei P. Valéry*, Wiesbaden, 1960.

Mann, Th. *Leiden und Größe der Meister*, Frankfurt/M., 1959.

Maire, G. *Les Instants Privilégiés*, Paris, 1962.

Nadal, O. Introduction to Valéry-Fourment correspondence, see Valéry.

Poulet, G. *Etudes sur le temps humain*, Edinburgh, 1949.

Ruskin, J. *Praeterita*, London, 1949.

Sartre, J.-P. *La Nausée*, Paris, 1962.

Underhill, E. *Mysticism*, London, 1960.

Valéry, P. *Oeuvres*, 2 vols, Paris, 1957, 1960.

Valéry, P. and Fourment, G. *Correspondance*, 1887–1933, Introduction by O. Nadal, Paris, 1957.

Wellek, R. and Warren, A. *Theory of Literature*, Penguin Books, 1963

Wright, A. H. *Jane Austen's Novels*, Penguin Books, 1964.